The Aeroplane and the Making
of Modern India

The Aeroplane
and the Making
of Modern India

AASHIQUE AHMED IQBAL

OXFORD
UNIVERSITY PRESS

Great Clarendon Street, Oxford, ox2 6dp,
United Kingdom

Oxford University Press is a department of the University of Oxford.
It furthers the University's objective of excellence in research, scholarship,
and education by publishing worldwide. Oxford is a registered trade mark of
Oxford University Press in the UK and in certain other countries

Published in the United States of America by Oxford University Press
198 Madison Avenue, New York, NY 10016, United States of America

British Library Cataloguing in Publication Data

Data available

Library of Congress Control Number: 2022943059

ISBN 978-0-19-286420-8

DOI: 10.1093/oso/9780192864208.001.0001

For my mother
Sajidabanu Iqbal

Acknowledgements

Reading acknowledgements to gain insights into the human being behind an otherwise impersonal piece of academic writing has always been one of my favourite guilty pleasures. Writing acknowledgements of my own I am certain will be an even greater pleasure. My deepest thanks are due to Dr Yasmin Khan, who took a leap of faith in agreeing to supervise the doctoral thesis from which this book has emerged. Her ability to provide insightful feedback for very long pieces of writing in very short periods of time has always surprised me and her words of encouragement have proven to be one of my greatest sources of strength. Special thanks are also due to Dr Radhika Singha, my MPhil supervisor, who first suggested that I work on Indian aviation. Without her unstinting support and her emphasis on academic rigour this text might never have come into existence. I would also like to express my sincere gratitude to Dr Robert Johnson, who co-supervised my doctoral work, for bearing with my many demands on his time. David Arnold and Rosalind O'Hanlon acted as DPhil examiners and provided useful advice on improving the text.

A number of professors have contributed to my development as a scholar including Dr Janaki Nair, Dr Faisal Devji, Dr Aditya Mukherjee, Dr Rudra Chaudhury, and Dr Bernard D'Sami. Dr Mahesh Rangarajan encouraged me to begin working on publication. As MPhil examiner, Dr Srinath Raghavan predicted from a very early point that my research would one day take the form of a book. His support over the years has been invaluable. I remain especially deeply indebted intellectually to Dr M.S.S. Pandian, whose passing I continue to mourn.

The writing of this book has been made possible by the kindness of absolute strangers, the donors behind the Felix Scholarship, which funded my doctoral studies. I was also exceedingly fortunate to receive a Royal Historical Society doctoral fellowship which I held at the Institute of Historical Research. Extra funding was received from the Frere Exhibition for India studies and the St Edmund Hall writing up grant. A Ministry of Minority Affairs Fellowship from the Government of India helped fund my MPhil research, which forms the foundation for the present work. Krea University allowed me the time and provided me funding necessary to prepare my research for publication.

This book has depended on the services of archivists in both India and the United Kingdom, to all of whom I am deeply grateful. I wish to thank Sq. Ldr. Rana Chhina, perhaps the foremost expert on the history of the Indian Air Force, for advice, encouragement, and most of the photographs in this book. Special thanks are due also to Dr Narendra Yadav from the Interservices History Division archives of the Indian Ministry of Defence. Though relations with archivists in some of the larger archives have necessarily been less personal, because of their size, I must express my thanks to the staff of the British Library, the Royal Air Force Museum, the Tata Central Archives, and the National Archives. The staff at the Bodleian Education Library especially have my grateful appreciation for cheerfully putting up with me for the three years when I lived thirty metres from the library.

Thanks, are also due to Mr J.R. Nanda who in addition to providing me with access to the Harjinder Singh papers also provided several images for this thesis free of cost from his private collection. I would also like to extend my gratitude to Mrs Anuradha Reddy, whose generous advice and extensive collection have served to fill many gaps in my own understanding of Indian aviation. Jagan Pillarisetti too has materially helped this work by providing some extremely rare images for this book at very short notice. Krishna Shekhawat gathered archival material from the Mehrangarh Museum Archives. Nandini Ganguli and the team at OUP provided timely support and the two anonymous reviewers they chose provided me with excellent feedback. They have done their best to save me from any errors, and any mistakes that remain are my own.

C.J. Kuncheria has aided my work for several years now in too many ways to recount both as scholar and as friend. Vipul Dutta, Zahra Shah, Ankita Pandey, and Rafael Pereira helped with earlier drafts of this work. John Mathew, Mahmood Kooria, and Aparajith Ramnath advised me on the intricacies of book publication. Shyama Rajendran and Ramachandra Guha provided important feedback while the manuscript was under revision. Antony Julian, Sonia Kurup, Akshi Singh, Radha Kapuria, Gayatri Nair, Rashmi Singh, Joachem Mowinckel, Amal Sasikumar, Naveen Richard, and David Clarence opened their homes to me while

I was visiting archives. Priyasha Mukhopadhyay's advice on writing and funding has been crucial. The generous friendship of Lipika, Priya, Claudia, Kalpita, Soumyajit, Gayatri, Bethany, Debak, Dirk, Kapil, Abdul, Parigya, Akash, Niyati, Harsha, and Abhilasha, has sustained me through the often gruelling process of writing. Uttam Kandregula has my ever-lasting gratitude for acting as my mentor for the past decade and teaching me to have faith in myself.

I would also like to thank my extended Tamil-Marathi-Parsee-Turk family for their love and support, even if I have not always explained what it is I do very clearly to them. I would also like to extend my sincere thanks to Theophilus Joachim, whose family provided me with a home away from home in Boston, England. Nazifa Ahmed, my wife, has filled my life with love and laughter. Her help with map making and formatting constitutes only a small fraction of her contributions to this book.

Tom Varkey's generous support put me through college and pro-pelled me from Ooty to Oxford. Words do not convey my deep thanks to Thomas and Sunita Varkey.

Everything I am and everything I will ever be I owe to my mother, Sajidabanu Iqbal, a single mother and a school teacher. Her courage and optimism in the face of even life's greatest difficulties is both a lesson and an inspiration. It is to her that I dedicate this book with pride.

Contents

Illustrations and Tables

Illustrations

Tables

Abbreviations

AAC	Army Airlift Committee
AFRC	Armed Forces Reconstitution Committee
AHQ (I)	Air Headquarters (India)
AIRC	Aeronautical and Industrial Corporation
AII	Air India International
APSA	Andhra Pradesh State Archives, Hyderabad.
ATIC	Air Transport Inquiry Committee
ATLB	Air Transport Licensing Board
BCA	Balliol College Archives, Oxford
BL	British Library, London, United Kingdom
BOAC	British Overseas Airways Corporation
CoP	Chamber of Princes
CPWD	Central Public Works Department
CRO	Commonwealth Relations Office
DCA	Director of Civil Aviation
DGCA	Director General of Civil Aviation
EFTS	Elementary Flying Training School
EIC	East India Company
FEU	Forward Equipment Unit
GoP	Government of Pakistan
HAL	Hindustan Aircraft Limited
HMG	His Majesty's Government
IAF	Indian Air Force
IAFVR	Indian Air Force Volunteer Reserve
IATC	Indian Air Training Corps
IEAL	Indian Eastern Airways Limited
INA	Indian National Airways
IOA	Indian Overseas Airways
IWAL	Indian Western Airways Limited
JNU	Jawaharlal Nehru University
KSA	Karnataka State Archives.
MMA	Mehrangarh Museum Archive
MEO	Military Evacuation Organisation
MoD (I)	Interservices History Division, Ministry of Defence, New Delhi, India

NAI	National Archives of India, New Delhi.
NFAI	National Film Archive of India, Pune.
NMML	Nehru Memorial Museum and Library, New Delhi.
NSR	Nizams State Railway
NWFP	North West Frontier Province
ORB	Operations Record Book
PC (AR)	Anuradha Reddy Private Collection
PC (JRN)	J.R. Nanda Private Collection
PJDC	Provisional Joint Defence Council
RAF	Royal Air Force
RIAF	Royal Indian Air Force
RAFM	Royal Air Force Museum, London, United Kingdom
RPAF	Royal Pakistan Air Force
RIN	Royal Indian Navy
TAS	Tata Aviation Services
TAL	Tata Air Lines
TNA	The National Archives, London, United Kingdom
ToI	Times of India
USAAF	United States Army Air Force
USI	United Services Institute, India
UKHC	United Kingdom High Commissioner
UNICIP	United Nations International Committee for India and Pakistan

A Note on Terminology and Spelling

This book uses the term 'Government of India' and 'Indian government' to refer to the central government of India both during the colonial period and in the period after independence. The Government of India is the official title of the colonial administration which was then adopted by independent India. While the use of the term 'Indian government' instead of 'British government' to describe the colonial government might seem confusing to readers, it is used advisedly. Historians commonly use the term 'Indian government' to denote the colonial government, with its capital in New Delhi, which was subordinate to but also separate from the 'British government', in London, that directly administered Britain. Referring to the colonial government as the 'British government' also runs the risk of ignoring the hybrid nature of the colonial state which was made up of a relatively small number of British officials, usually at the top, and a very large number of Indians.

The term 'India' and 'Indians' refers to the subcontinent and its inhabitants, respectively, before 1947. After independence subjects of the British Empire in India were divided on the basis of nationality between the two new dominions of India and Pakistan. 'India' after 1947 therefore refers to the country of the same name. South Asia commonly includes India, Pakistan, Bangladesh, Sri Lanka, Bhutan, Nepal, and also occasionally Afghanistan.

Contemporary spellings for proper nouns have been used consistently for reasons of clarity. So for instance Madras is used instead of Chennai and Cawnpore is used instead of Kanpur.

Introduction: Aviation and the Indian State 1939–1953

After all our country is going to be free and I think that will be soon. Where after independence shall we get persons who can fly aeroplanes? It is obvious even to the most superficial observer that this victory over the air in Europe and America will bring far reaching results to the world, foremost being the effect on the methods of warfare. It is now established that the old-fashioned armies and ships cannot stand up to aeroplanes and gas. Aeroplanes can annihilate a big army and can ruin several cities with a bomb. The work of the ordinary army will gradually become what the police are doing today and guns and canons will be reduced to the level of *lathis* (batons). Our leaders, who are striving to secure for Indians also commission in the army, should consider this a little. Otherwise our officers and army will be mere glittering dummies on parade and be worth nothing else.[1]

—Jawaharlal Nehru,
Aaj, 28 September 1927

Jawaharlal Nehru's quote above, from an essay titled 'Victory over the Air', succinctly sums up Indian hopes and fears about aviation. Indians during the years leading up to the Second World War were certain that aviation represented an exponential technological leap with especially critical military consequences. Bombing would make other forms of warfare obsolete and enable countries that possessed aircraft to prosecute

---

[1] Jawaharlal Nehru, 'Victory over the Air' (Original in Hindi), in Sarvepalli Gopal and Uma Iyengar eds, *Essential Writings of Jawaharlal Nehru* (New Delhi: OUP, 2003), p. 635.

The Aeroplane and the Making of Modern India. Aashique Ahmed Iqbal, Oxford University Press.

genocidal warfare against countries that did not. Indian opinion was hardly unique in believing what was a near universal axiom at the time. Conventional wisdom, the world over, regarded air bombing in much the same apocalyptic terms as nuclear warfare is regarded today. Apocalyptic visions of the aeroplane as a tool of warfare and genocide in European science fiction had preceded the invention of the aeroplane.[2] Following the First World War, during which aircraft had demonstrated the ability to bring death to civilians hundreds of miles away from the frontline, fears about the devastating potential of bombing in future conflicts had become commonplace throughout the world.[3]

What differentiated Indian concerns about bombing from those of Western states, such as Britain, was the sense of helplessness springing from India's status as a colony of the British Empire. Many Indians were alarmed at the prospect of a conflict in which India might find itself defenceless because it did not have its own air force. They assumed, correctly as future events would prove, that the Royal Air Force would prioritize the defence of the British Isles over that of India in case of the outbreak of a general conflict. Aviation was recognized as a prerequisite for true independence since in the absence of sufficient air defences, a formally independent India would find itself at the mercy of enemy states possessing aircraft. Conversely if India came to possess aviation of its own it would achieve the substance of sovereignty even if the colony was not granted formal independence. The question of who would fly aeroplanes in India came increasingly to be tied with the question of who would rule India.

This book is the first major academic history of aviation in India. It is a study of the Indian state and its engagement with aviation during the period of its transformation from British colony to independent republic. Through the prism of aviation, both civil and military, I chart the long process of decolonization from the Second World War to the emergence of India as a sovereign centralized state. Drawing on fifteen archives and untapped personal collections, I point to the critical role the aeroplane played in the shaping of modern South Asia. In the process, I raise several questions. What can the engagement between the Indian state(s) and

---

[2] Sven Lindqvist and Linda Haverty, *A History of Bombing* (London: Granta, 2002), p. 73.
[3] Uri Bialer, *The Shadow of the Bomber* (London: Royal Historical Society, 1980), Chapter II.

Indian aviation reveal about the process of decolonization? What, if any, legitimation did aircraft provide South Asian regimes, real and putative, colonial and postcolonial? How do we evaluate the ruptures and continuities in the relationship between technology and politics before and after Indian independence?

The aeroplane would play a small but critical role in state formation in South Asia. Though very few Indians would ever see, let alone set foot in a plane, the impact of aviation would touch the lives of millions of Indians. Aircraft would play a crucial role in defending the Indian state through the crises that followed independence. Civil and military aircraft would help the Indian state evacuate important government officials and restore order in the face of mass violence accompanying partition. Without aeroplanes it is doubtful whether India might have been able to intervene in the 1947 Kashmir conflict, given the difficulty of the mountainous terrain there. Aircraft were also an important part of the story of the integration of the princely states. In addition to enforcing state power, the aeroplane also played a crucial ideological role. As the pre-eminent marker of modernity of its time, the aeroplane also served to legitimate the authority of the state. This was not lost on Indian nationalists who spent the interwar period contesting the British monopoly on aviation. The importance of aeroplanes as paraphernalia of modern statehood was also not lost on other claimants to sovereignty in South Asia such as the princely states and Pakistan.

A study of the aeroplane in India is informative of the wider ways in which poor decolonizing states like India engage with advanced technologies like aviation. The Indian government had to carefully prioritize the use of very limited aviation resources and an examination of how these were deployed illustrates the key goals of its leadership. Though aviation doubtless remained an elite preserve it also, precisely for this reason, arguably offers greater insights into the preoccupations, priorities, and self-conceptions of political leaderships in South Asia than any other contemporary technology. The sheer scarcity of aviation resources also meant that the lines between civil and military aviation remained blurry at best. Given the scarce aviation resources at its disposal, the Government of India had little regard for whether aircraft belonged to the civil or the 'service' category when confronted with an emergency. Civil aircraft were constantly pressed into military service while the

Indian Air Force (IAF) was a central part of the government response to civil emergencies such as refugee evacuation. Indian airline companies undertook what was often dangerous work in the Second World War, the Kashmir war, and the 1950 Bengal crisis. The IAF meanwhile served in a humanitarian role during Partition and the Assam floods of 1950. The line between civil and military aviation in India could be blurred in less obvious ways. The Director of Civil Aviation for instance was responsible for the maintenance of the IAF aircraft for much of the Second World War. Whether aircraft served as civil or military technology was far more a function of the use to which they were put rather than the designation they might have had. I contend that the boundaries between civil and military aviation, in a poor colony facing multiple emergencies, were often far from fixed. Pushing this point further, I take seriously the idea that the aeroplane from its inception conceived of primarily as a weapon.[4] While many in India, as elsewhere, were enamoured with the speed, the commercial value, and even the promise of universal brotherhood held out by aircraft, the predominant sentiment surrounding the aeroplane during the period under discussion was one of anxiety around controlling a devastating weapon. 'Airmindedness' the dominant discourse on aviation imported from the metropole to India emphasized the military uses of aircraft. Indeed, many seemingly pacifist Indian civil aviation initiatives, like the establishment of flying clubs, glider societies, and airlines had a definite military undercurrent.

The broad sweep of the story that *Sovereign Skies* will tell is as follows. Though the aeroplane made its debut in India as early as 1910, Indians were largely excluded from flying and servicing aircraft. To remedy this, Indian politicians pushed for policies similar to 'Indianization', the steady replacement of British personnel with Indians, in the field of military aviation.[5] Indianization would serve to reduce expenditure on high British salaries. The Indianization of military aviation, like the Indianization of the railways, army, and civil service, would also ultimately place India on the road to self-rule by making Indians more responsible for the running

---

[4] David Edgerton, *England and the Aeroplane: Militarism, Modernity and Machines* (London: Penguin, 2013), p. 3.

[5] David C. Potter, 'Manpower Shortage and the End of Colonialism: The Case of the Indian Civil Service', *Modern Asian Studies*, vol. 7, no. 1 (1973), 47–73. A longer discussion of Indianization of the military will follow in the next chapter.

of their country. Despite the establishment of Indian airline companies and the raising of the IAF in the interwar years, Indian participation in the aviation sector remained negligible. The outlook for the development of Indian aviation on the eve of the Second World War could be best described as bleak. This is perhaps best demonstrated by the aeroplane with which the IAF was still flying in 1939; the Westland Wapiti. Dubbed the 'What-a-pity' by British pilots, the two-seater biplane was constructed out of wood and metal tubing. The Wapiti was built largely to serve not as a fighter but as an army co-operation aircraft. A cheap and ageing aeroplane, it was allocated to the IAF, largely to serve in 'air-control' duties on the frontier.[6] As the official history of the IAF would later note, the force was 'swaddled in the castaway garments of the Royal Air Force'.[7]

By 1950, IAF fighter pilots were flying state of the art De Havilland Vampire jets. The IAF's rapid transition from biplanes to the jet age in a little over a decade is impossible to explain without taking into consideration the political processes that fundamentally reshaped India. In 1939, India was a colony of the British Empire whereas by 1950, the country had emerged as an independent republic. The rapid transformation of aviation and the Indian state, I argue, was rooted in the Second World War. The war effort would necessitate the expansion of the IAF, fulfilling the long-cherished goal of Indian nationalists, like Jawaharlal Nehru above, who had contended that Indian control of military aviation was a necessary pre-requisite for Indian independence. Indian airline companies would benefit immensely from the pool of trained pilots, aircraft, and airfields left behind by the war. The gains of the war would be seriously endangered by the partition of colonial India which saw the division of air forces, airlines, airports, and air routes between India and Pakistan. The crises of partition, war in Kashmir and the integration of the princely states, faced by the Government of India in the immediate aftermath of independence helped confirm the central role of aircraft in projecting the state. In the five years after independence the Indian government would move to strengthen the links that bound the aviation sector to the state, culminating in the nationalization of airline companies in 1953.

---

[6] K.S. Nair, *The Forgotten Few: The Indian Air Force in World War II* (New Delhi: Harper Collins, 2019), p. 28.

[7] Prasad, *History of the Indian Air Force 1933–45* (New Delhi: Orient Longman, 1956), p. xix.

The nationalization of civil aviation and the Indianization of military aviation, completed the next year, would inaugurate a new era in which Indian aviation would become a near-monopoly of the Indian state for four decades.

This book makes two revisions to received histories of decolonization. First, though the independent Indian government inherited several colonial institutions and legitimated itself with claims of continuity, a study of aviation is revealing of the ruptures that marked the passing of the British Raj. Independent India conceptualized new notions of sovereignty, and embarked on a programme of unprecedented centralization. Unlike the colonial state which had recognized a number of subordinate sovereignties, such as those of the princely states, independent India projected what I term as 'deep sovereignty'. The new state sought to project unmediated sovereignty within its territorial bounds and pursued policies that favoured centralization of state power, such as the nationalization of airlines in 1953. Understanding the new state's approach to sovereignty is essential to making sense of India's seemingly contradictory stances on Pakistan and the princes, which entailed managing escalation with the former and aggressive coercion with the latter. To be sure India's ruling party, the Congress, was predisposed to centralization. However, experiences of the chaos surrounding partition, war, and integration would serve to push the independent government towards centralization.

Indian conceptions of sovereignty would also be affected by the emergence of a new international order which privileged the nation state over older ways of organizing sovereignty. The new international order heavily privileged the nation state as the sole legitimate repository of national authority and did little to accommodate alternative sovereignties such as that of the Indian princely states. There was, therefore, for instance, little concern in the United Nations following the Indian invasion of Hyderabad in contrast to the immense interest caused by the Kashmir war.[8] Like every other modern sovereign state, India would be both simultaneously unique in its territorial configurations and perfectly modular in its international agreements. The emergence of deep sovereignty,

---

[8] Witmer, *The 1947–48 India-Hyderabad Conflict* (unpublished thesis, Temple University, 1995), p. 316.

as revealed by the Indian state's use of aircraft, is indicative of its novel nature in the face of claims of continuity.

Second, the circumstances of decolonization were highly contingent on the control of technology. The Republic of India that emerged as a result of independence, partition, and the integration of the princely states is merely one version of many possible states that might have emerged from the process of decolonization. Teleological national histories notwithstanding, the contingent nature of the nation state is one that the history of the aeroplane emphasizes. Control of aviation was crucial for the survival of the Indian state in the face of the crises accompanying the transfer of power from British to Indian hands. Aircraft enabled New Delhi to project power across the burning villages of Punjab and the mountainous Kashmir valley. If the aeroplane was a crucial tool for projecting the colonial and postcolonial states then it was also an instrument in the toolbox of those who wished to resist deep sovereignty. The princely states would push hard for control of aviation as a means of resisting both pressure from the colonial state and integration by its independent successors. The aeroplane enabled Indian princely states to conceptualize sovereignties outside those on offer by the colonizer and the nationalists. This could take on diverse forms but almost always entailed mobilizing the aeroplane as a symbol of modernity. Locating aviation in the wider context of sovereignty helps explain the extensive and understudied contributions of the princely states to aviation.[9] A focus on the relationship between princely states, the aeroplane, and sovereignty also enriches our understanding of the collapse of the princely order by connecting this to the Cold War. Much has already been written about the contingent nature of the formation of Pakistan but that point bears being made again in the context of high technology.[10] Pakistani leaders understood the crucial importance of the aeroplane as both a strategic asset to connect the two wings of their country, which were separated by over a thousand kilometres of Indian territory, and an ideological prop that presented their new country as an independent state. Holding many of the same views as their Indian counterparts they would assiduously

---

[9] For a list of works on the Indian States see Chapter 4.
[10] See for instance: Ayesha Jalal, *The Sole Spokesman* (Cambridge: Cambridge University Press, 1985); Faisal Devji, *Muslim Zion: Pakistan as a Political Idea* (London: Hurst, 2013).

lobby for the rapid establishment of a Pakistani aviation sector soon after the principle of Pakistan was conceded. A history of the aeroplane, therefore, serves to highlight the contingent nature of state making in modern South Asia and the central role of technology in this process.

Despite its immense significance for the projection of state power by national elites, aviation has received little by way of attention in the academy. Aviation remains an important lacuna in the fields of science and technology history on the one hand and military history on the other. This is a consequence of a series of different factors. Technology history has, until recently, received little scholarly attention in India.[11] Though this trend is in the process of being reversed, historians focusing on the relationship between technology and the state have given aviation little attention, choosing to focus instead on larger statist projects such as dams, nuclear power, and the railways.[12] Writing on Indian military history has been dominated by the Indian army which is considerably older and several times larger than the other two services.[13] The Indian navy

---

[11] Some of the key works in the burgeoning field of Technology studies include: Roy Macleod and Deepak Kumar eds, *Technology and the Raj: Western Technology and Technical Transfers to India 1700–1947* (New Delhi: Sage, 1995); David Arnold, *Science, Science, Technology and Medicine in Colonial India* (Cambridge: 2000); Arun Mohan Sukumar, *Midnight's Machines: A Political History of Technology in India* (Gurgaon: Viking, 2019). David Arnold, *Everyday Technology: Machines and the Making of India's Modernity* (Chicago: University of Chicago Press, 2013); Aprajith Ramnath, *The Birth of an Indian Profession* (New Delhi: OUP, 2017). The history of science in India is not discussed here in the interests of brevity. For a detailed survey of Indian science history see: Deepak Kumar, *Science and the Raj: A Study of British India* (New Delhi: OUP, 2006), Gyan Prakash, *Another Reason: Science and the Imagination of Modern India* (New Delhi: OUP, 2000).

[12] Dan Haines, *Rivers Divided: Indus Basin Waters in the Making of India and Pakistan* (Gurgaon: Viking, 2017); Dan Haines, *Building the Empire, Building the Nation Development, Legitimacy and Hydro-politics in Sind, 1919–1969* (Karachi: OUP, 2003); Itty Abraham, *The Making of the Indian Atomic Bomb Science, Secrecy and the Postcolonial State* (New Delhi: Zed books, 1998); Jahnavi Phalkey, *Atomic State: Big Science in Twentieth-century India* (Ranikhet: Permanent Black, 2013); Ian Derbyshire, 'The Building of Railways, the Application of Western Technology in the Colonial P Periphery 1850–1920', in Macleod and Kumar (eds), *Technology and the Raj* (London: Sage, 1995), pp. 177–215

[13] Kaushik Roy, *Brown Warriors of the Raj: Recruitment and the Mechanics of Command in the Sepoy Army, 1859–1913* (New Delhi: Manohar Publishers, 2008); Kaushik Roy, *The Army in British India: From Colonial Warfare to Total War, 1857–1947* (London: Bloomsbury, 2013). Anirudh Deshpande and Parthasarathi Gupta, *The British Raj and Its Indian Armed Forces 1857–1939* (New Delhi: OUP, 2002); Anirudh Deshpande, *British Military Policy in India 1900–1945: Colonial Constraints and Declining Power* (New Delhi: Manohar, 2005); Gajendra Singh, *The Testimonies of Indian Soldiers and the Two World Wars: Between Self and Sepoy* (London: Bloomsbury Academic, 2014); David Omissi, *The Sepoy and the Raj: The Indian Army, 1860–1940* (Basingstoke: Macmillan, 1994); Daniel Marston and Chandar Sundaram eds, *A Military History of India and South Asia* (Westport: Indiana University Press, 2007); Daniel Marston, *The Indian Army and the End of the Raj* (Cambridge: CUP, 2016).

also has received some academic attention though this tends to be disproportionately skewed towards the Royal Indian Navy mutiny of 1946.[14] The history of Indian aviation, both civil and military, has also been marginal to more global histories of aviation.[15] This is not to say that India does not feature prominently in histories of aviation but rather to point to the relative absence of Indian aviation from aviation histories even when they deal with the region.[16] The neglect of Indian technology history, the focus on other military services, and the perceived marginality of India to global aviation have all combined to ensure that Indian aviation has not been the subject of historical inquiry.

The absence of academic work on the subject however does not mean that there is no literature on Indian aviation. On the contrary there exists a very large corpus of writing by non-academic authors on aviation, most of which focuses on the history of the IAF. IAF history has been the subject of a number of official, semi-official, and non-official histories as well as a number of biographies.[17] In the absence of attention from the

---

[14] For the Indian Navy see: Satyindra Singh, *Under Two Ensigns: The Indian Navy, 1945–1950* (New Delhi: IBH publishers, 1986); Daniel Owen Spence, *Colonial Naval Culture and British Imperialism 1922–67* (Manchester: Manchester University Press, 2016); Chris Madsen, 'The Long Goodbye: British Agency in the Creation of Navies for India and Pakistan', *The Journal of Commonwealth and Imperial History*, vol. 43, no. 3 (December 2014), 463–88. For the 1946 RIN Mutiny see: Anirudh Deshpande, *Hope and Despair: Mutiny, Rebellion and Death in India, 1946* (New Delhi: Primus books, 2016); Ronald Spector, 'The Royal Indian Navy Strike of 1946: A Study of Cohesion and Disintegration in Colonial Armed Forces', *Armed Forces and Society*, vol. 7, no. 2 (January 1981), 271–284; Chris Madsen, 'The Royal Indian Navy Mutiny, 1946', in Christopher M. Bell and Bruce A. Elleman (eds), *Naval Mutinies of the Twentieth Century* (London: Frank Cass, 2003), pp. 212–231; John M. Meyer, 'The Royal Indian Naval Mutiny of 1946: Nationalist Competition and Civil Military Relations in India', *The Journal of Commonwealth and Imperial History*, vol. 45, no. 1 (December 2016), 46–69; D.O. Spence, 'Beyond Talwar: A Cultural Reappraisal of the 1946 Royal Indian Navy Mutiny', *The Journal of Commonwealth and Imperial History*, vol. 43, no. 3 (2015), 489–508.

[15] See for instance: James J. Halley, *The Squadrons of the Royal Air Force and Commonwealth 1918–1988* (Tonbridge: Air-Britain Historians, 1988).

[16] See for instance: David Omissi, *Air Power and Colonial Control: The Royal Air Force, 1919–1939* (Manchester: Manchester University Press, 1990).

[17] For official histories see: Bisheshwar Prasad and S.C. Gupta, *History of the Indian Air Force, 1933–45* (New Delhi: Orient Longman, 1961); S.N. Prasad, *Operation Polo* (New Delhi: Manager of Publications, 1972); S.N. Prasad and Dharm Pal, *History of Operations in Jammu and Kashmir* (New Delhi: Controller of Publications, 1987); Shaukat Riza, *The Pakistan Army 1947–49* (New Delhi: Natraj, 1977); Bisweshwar Prasad ed, *Expansion of the Armed Forces and Defence Organisation 1939–45* (Calcutta: Combined Interservices Historical Section, 1956). For semi-official histories produced by the IAF Warrior Study Cell (henceforth IAFWSC) see: J.P. John and B.S.K. Kumar, *Wing Commander K.K. Majumdar DFC BAR* (Secunderabad: IAFWSC, 2003); T.S. Rana Chhina, *Air Marshal Subroto Mukherjee* (Secunderabad: IAFWSC, 2002); P.P. Khandekar ed, *Air Commodore Mehar Singh* (Secunderabad: IAFWSC, 2006); P.P. Khandekar ed, *Dragons Forever: History of No. 6 Squadron* (Secunderabad: IAFWSC, 2006). For an example

academe non-official histories have been penned by a variety of authors.[18] IAF veterans themselves have written a number of books, of which Rana Chhina's *The Eagle Strikes* is perhaps the finest example.[19] These books and the official histories cover IAF operations in painstaking detail, and serve as an important foundation upon which the present work is based. In addition to official and non-official histories, autobiographies and official biographies of IAF personnel serve as important sources.[20] While non-academic IAF histories often serve their stated goals as operational accounts and commemorative works well, they do not address the concerns of the academic historian, which is to locate events in the context of broader shifts, such as decolonization, that defined the period. Furthermore, a lot of the writing on aviation in India rigidly adheres to the civil-military divide which provides an incomplete picture of the state's engagement with aviation.[21] In comparison to the IAF, the history of Indian civil aviation has received almost no attention, both in and out of the academy. Writing on the history of Indian civil aviation is almost entirely limited to the province of political economy.[22] A small but significant genre of Indian aviation history is work by aviation enthusiasts on the princely states. Anuradha Reddy's *History of Aviation in the Hyderabad Dominions* and Peter Vacher's *History of the Jodhpur Flying Club* serve to alert us about the crucial contributions of the Indian

of an official history of the Pakistan Air Force see: Syed Shabir Hussain, *History of the Pakistan Air Force 1947–1982* (Masroor: Pakistan Air Force Press, 1982).

[18] Pushpindar Singh, *Himalayan Eagles* (New Delhi: Society for Aerospace studies, 2007); Jasjit Singh, *Defence from the Skies* (New Delhi: Knowledge World Publishers, 2007); Somnath Sapru, *Combat Lore* (New Delhi: Knowledge World Publishers, 2014); Nair, *The Forgotten Few*.

[19] T.S. Rana Chhina, *The Eagle Strikes: The Royal Indian Air Force 1932–50* (New Delhi: Ambi Knowledge Resources, 2006); Bharat Kumar, *An Incredible War Indian Air Force in Kashmir War* (New Delhi: Knowledge World Publishers, 2007).

[20] Om Prakash Mehra, *Memories Sweet and Sour* (New Delhi: Knowledge World Publishers, 2010); Pratap C. Lal, *My Years with the IAF* (New Delhi: Lancer, 1986); Jasjit Singh, *The Icon* (New Delhi: Knowledge World Publishers, 2009); Jack Loveday, *RAF and Raj* (Norwich: J. Loveday, 2002); Mike Edwards, *Spitfire Singh* (New Delhi: Bloomsbury Publishing, 2016), Raghu Karnad, *Farthest Field: An Indian History of the Second World War* (Noida: Harper Collins, 2015).

[21] For a work that tries, unsuccessfully, to straddle this boundary see: Pushpindar Singh, *History of Aviation in India: Spanning the Century of Flight* (New Delhi: Society for Aerospace Studies, 2003); Helen Doe, *Fighter Pilot* (Stroud, Gloucestershire: Amberley Publishing, 2015).

[22] D. Panduranga Rao and J.V. Rāmārāvu, *Indian Airlines: A Study of Its Performance* (New Delhi, Inter-India Publications, 1997); Baldev Raj Nayar, *The State and International Aviation in India: Performance and Policy on the Eve of Aviation Globalization* (New Delhi: Manohar Publishers & Distributors, 1994). A.W. Nawab, *Economic Development of Indian Air Transport* (Delhi: National Pub. House, 1967).

princes to the early history of Indian aviation.[23] This book will attempt to build on these works to locate the princes at the centre of the story of Indian aviation.

Aviation and Decolonization

Telling the story of India's decolonization through the lens of aviation means referencing a wider body of literature than works pertaining to Indian aviation. This text, therefore, has drawn from works on Imperial and postcolonial aviation on the one hand and histories of decolonization in India on the other.

Many writers have interrogated the relationship between aviation and the state. Aircraft have been used to legitimate regimes as varied and antithetical as Soviet Communism, American Democracy, and Italian Fascism.[24] British aviation was used to connect, enforce, and justify Imperial rule. While Imperial Airways connected London to Sydney and Cape Town, the Royal Air Force imposed empire on the cheap in India and Iraq.[25] David Edgerton has argued that the 'aeronautical England' was a 'warfare state' committed to using the aeroplane as a weapon of war.[26] Meanwhile Gordon Pirie has emphasized the extent to which Imperial Airways was an ideological project, aimed at boosting the prestige of the British Empire.[27] Whereas most histories of the aeroplane have tended to focus on aviation in rich, predominantly western states, a small but growing literature looks at aviation in the poor world. Alan Baumler's survey of Asian aviation has persuasively argues that aviation offered

---

[23] Peter Vacher, *History of the Jodhpur Flying Club* (Ontario: Griffin media, 2008); P. Anuradha Reddy, *Aviation in the Hyderabad Dominions* (Secunderabad: Avi-Oil, 2001).

[24] Gore Vidal, 'On Flying', in *Armageddon? Essays 1983–87* (London: Deutsch, 1987); Stephen Call, *Selling Air Power* (Williams-Ford: Texas A&M Press, 2009); J.J. Corn, *The Winged Gospel: America's Romance with Aviation* (London: Johns Hopkins University Press, 2002); K.E. Bailes, 'Technology and Legitimacy: Soviet Aviation and Stalinism in the 1930s', *Technology and Culture*, vol. 17, no. 1 (January 1976), 55–81.; Willard Bohn, 'The Poetics of Flight: Futurist "Aeropoesia"', *MLN*, vol. 121, no. 1 (2006), 207–24.

[25] Peter Ewer, 'A Gentlemen's Club in the Clouds: Re-assessing the Empire Air Mail Scheme 1933–1939', *Journal of Transport History*, vol. 28, no. 1 (March 2007), 75–92; Priya Satia, 'The Defense of Inhumanity: Air Control and the British Idea of Arabia', *The American Historical Review*, vol. 111, no. 1 (February 2006), 16–51.

[26] David Edgerton, *England and the Aeroplane* (London: Penguin Books, 2013).

[27] Gordon Pirie, *Air Empire: British Imperial Civil Aviation, 1919–39* (Manchester: Manchester University Press, 2009).

Asians a chance to narrow the technological lead that Europeans enjoyed in other fields.[28] Waqar Zaidi's work on Pakistan reinforces this book's assertion that the development of civil aviation in South Asia was closely linked with military concerns.[29] In Thailand, one of the few states in Asia to have the distinction of not being fully colonized, Edward Young has painted a vivid picture of the challenges faced by a poor state in fielding aircraft.[30] William Hiatt's well written *The Rarified Air of the Modern* strikes a distinctly ambivalent tone on the benefits of aviation for Peru in the early 20th century.[31]

While this book addresses the history of Indian aviation, it also tells the story of the political transition of the Indian state from colonial rule to independence, from the perspective of aviation. This transition, with its deep implications for understanding modern India, has been the subject of a great deal of academic interest. A number of studies have attempted to explain the ways in which the Indian state was transformed as a consequence of decolonization, utilizing a variety of perspectives. Faisal Devji has pointed to the importance of the history of political ideas in contributing to the eventual partition of the subcontinent.[32] Christopher Bayly and Tim Harper have illustrated the profound impact on the Second World War on South Asia.[33] Further, Yasmin Khan and Srinath Raghavan have argued for the need to place the war at the centre of the process of decolonization.[34] Raghavan has also conducted a pioneering study on Indian foreign policy to show that independent India led by Jawaharlal Nehru pursued a highly sophisticated foreign policy that juggled domestic, regional, and international priorities with more success than was previously assumed.[35] Daniel Marston has traced the end of colonial

[28] Alan Baumler, 'Aviation and Asian Modernity 1900–1950', in *Oxford Research Encyclopaedia of Asian History*, 28 June 2017. Accessed 5 May 2022. https://oxfordre.com/asianhistory/view/10.1093/acrefore/9780190277727.001.0001/acrefore-9780190277727-e-177.

[29] Waqar Zaidi, 'Pakistani Civil Aviation and US Aid to Pakistan, 1950 to 1961', *History of Global Arms Transfer*, vol. 8 (2019), 83–97.

[30] Edward Young, *Aerial Nationalism* (United States: Smithsonian, 1995)

[31] Willie Hiatt, *The Rarified Air of the Modern: Airplanes and Technological Modernity in the Andes* (New York: OUP, 2016).

[32] Devji, *Muslim Zion*.

[33] Christopher A. Bayly and Timothy N. Harper, *Forgotten Armies: Britain's Asian Empire and the War with Japan* (London: Penguin books, 2005).

[34] Srinath Raghavan, *India's War: The Making of Modern South Asia* (London: Allen Lane, 2016); Yasmin Khan, *The Raj at War: A People's History of the Second World War* (Gurgaon: Penguin, 2015).

[35] Srinath Raghavan, *War and Peace in Modern India* (Ranikhet: Permanent Black, 2010).

rule in India from the perspective of the Indian army, illustrating its centrality in ensuring a relatively successful transfer of power from British to Indian hands.[36] Pallavi Raghavan has challenged existing understandings of Indo-Pakistani relations immediately after independence by showing that the two countries may have co-operated more than was previously assumed.[37] Tracing the political transformation of the Indian state through its engagement with aviation, therefore, means referencing both a growing historiography on aviation in Imperial and postcolonial contexts and engaging closely with new interpretations of the decolonization of the subcontinent.

Scope, Sources, and Structure

This book consists of five chapters that are organized both thematically and chronologically. Each chapter is organized around an event, such as the Second World War, and a major theme, such as the expansion of aviation to meet wartime demands. Though a chronological framework is broadly adhered to, this work features a number of overlaps, particularly when events in one chapter had effects on events in another. As such the book is organized around five key themes that defined aviation: expansion, partition, escalation, integration, and nationalization.

Chapter 1, 'Indian Aviation in the Second World War', studies the transformation of the Indian aviation sector as a consequence of the Second World War. The outbreak of the Second World War forced the colonial government to embark on a large-scale expansion of the IAF that saw the single squadron force grow to ten squadrons by 1946. Waging technologized war in the colony placed unprecedented pressures on the Government of India. Finding the educated recruits, aircraft, and advanced infrastructure necessary to wage war in the air would prove difficult in the colony. Consequently, the Government of India would mobilize whatever aviation resources were at hand. Indian airline companies would be tapped for planes, pilots, and expertise during the war,

---

[36] Marston, *The Indian Army and the End of the Raj.*
[37] Pallavi Raghavan, *Animosity at Bay: An Alternative History of the India-Pakistan Relationship, 1947–1952* (Oxford: Oxford University Press, 2020).

blurring the lines between civil and military aviation. Air Headquarters (India) would also mobilize the Indian princes, many of whom had invested extensively in aviation in the interwar years. While the IAF would perform well in the war, earning the prefix 'Royal' from the King Emperor for its distinguished service in 1945, its rushed expansion would result in a wave of 'strikes' in 1946. The RIAF strikes would raise new questions among RIAF men over what it meant to serve in a colonial armed force. They would combine with other major mutinies that year to erode British military control in India, contributing to the end of colonial rule.

Chapter 2 entitled 'Ittehad Mein Shakti (Strength in Unity): Aviation and the Partition of India 1946–47' looks at both the impact of partition on the Indian aviation sector and the role played by aircraft in restoring order during the transfer of populations. The Second World War was followed by a boom for Indian air services as cheap planes and demobilized pilots became available. However, Partition would seriously destabilize post-war aviation planning and would result in the division of air routes, and air forces. A study of this division is revealing of the ruptures that would come to characterize the emergence of the independent dominions of India and Pakistan. It is also illustrative of the critical importance of high technology in re-asserting the state's monopoly on violence. Despite being freshly 'reconstituted' after Partition, the RIAF would play a key role in protecting and protecting the state through the mass violence of 1947. Civil aviation too would play a key role, though it would soon become clear that the task of evacuating key government officials and refugees was beyond their capacity. Consequently, both the governments of India and Pakistan would hire British companies to carry out important evacuations that would come to be known as 'Operation Pakistan' and 'Operation India'.

Chapter 3, 'War in Kashmir 1947–48', points to the central role played by aircraft in initiating, sustaining, and eventually escalating the conflict between India and Pakistan. Aircraft would allow independent India's leadership to intervene in Kashmir with a speed that shocked Pakistani planners, who had orchestrated a tribal invasion of the state. Subsequently aircraft would allow India to maintain an air bridge with garrisons of politically crucial towns like Punch and Leh without dangerously escalating the conflict into an all-out war that both India and Pakistan were keen to prevent. Politicians and military officers from both countries attempted to evolve a framework to manage escalation, in which the actions of the IAF were carefully regulated. As the conflict dragged on, however, aircraft would inadvertently play a dangerously escalatory role that has been misunderstood by both contemporaries and historians. Focusing on the Srinagar airlift, the siege of Punch and the bombing of Palak during the war, this chapter traces the evolving role of the aeroplane in the calculus of escalation. Further, I argue that for all its hostility to Pakistan, the conflict was revealing of the Indian leadership's recognition of Pakistani territorial sovereignty in stark contrast to its often aggressive approach to the princes.

Chapter 4, 'Of Princes and Planes: Aviation in the Indian States 1931–48', studies the role of aviation in the semi-autonomous princely states in the lead up to their integration with India in 1947–48 using the case studies of Jodhpur, Mysore, and Hyderabad. Assailed by both nationalists and the colonial government the Indian princes attempted to construct their own 'native modernity'.[38] To do this they turned, among other things to modern technologies like aviation. Jodhpur attempted to fashion a martial modernity centred around its Maharaja. Mysore sought to use an aircraft factory established in the state to kickstart industrial development. Hyderabad established its own airline, tried to form an air force, and would ultimately rely on airborne gun running to resist integration with India. While all three states broadly sought to legitimize themselves through the modernist aura of the aeroplane, the ways in which they did so could vary radically depending on their political and material circumstances. A study of the princely engagement with aviation alerts us to the contingent circumstances of decolonization and opens a window to a South Asia that might have been.

The fifth and final chapter of this book, 'Towards Sovereign Skies: Aviation in Independent India 1948–53', tells the story of Indian aviation in the first five years after independence through a focus on three key events: the establishment of Air India International (AII) in 1948, the 1950 Bengal crisis, and the nationalization of airline corporations in 1953. The successful establishment of India's flag carrier, AII was far from a foregone conclusion relying as it did on wider shifts in the international

---

[38] A longer discussion of 'native modernity' follows in Chapter 4. Bhagwan, Manu, *Sovereign Spheres* (New Delhi: OUP, 2003).

aviation scene. The emergence of the United States as a global super-power and the decline of the British Empire laid the foundation for the emergence of a new global order in which the nation state was the sole legitimate wielder of state sovereignty. In the aviation sector this took the shape of bilateral agreements which made flag carriers like AII necessary. Civil Aviation would also play a key role in the evacuation of refugees during the Bengal crisis when India and Pakistan were on the brink of war. While the crisis would eventually be resolved peacefully, it would confirm the increasing militarization of the Indian state. Moving to a dis-cussion on the nationalization of airlines I point to the popularity of an undefined policy of nationalization that would have highly uneven re-sults across the aviation sector. While much of the debate over the causes of nationalization has centred on the apparent financial failures of Indian airlines, this chapter argues that seen from the perspective of defence, Indian airline companies may well have been victims of their own suc-cess. The chapter, and the book with it, ends with the reordering of avia-tion as a near monopoly of the state.

This study limits itself to an analysis of Indian aviation. As such it is concerned primarily with the IAF and airline companies formed in India. Foreign airlines and air forces are not the objects of research here, with a few significant exceptions, despite the fact that their impact on India was significant. This deliberate choice is made for a number of reasons. Indian aviation has received little academic attention, as opposed to aviation in India, which was predominantly Western. Furthermore, as this book is an examination of the political transformation of the Indian state, Indian aviation is naturally of the most relevance. This may not be the narrow lens that it at first appears to be since, as we shall see, the story of Indian aviation is not only a story of Indians but of Australian smugglers, British air hostesses, Polish pilots, and French diplomats among others.

This work will also concentrate on those facets of aviation that fore-ground the political transformation of the subcontinent as a result of decolonization. This is a fine point to make given the statist nature of avi-ation. I have also not engaged with the social and cultural aspects of avia-tion, outside their direct impact on the state. The politics of aviation and the state that is the focus of this work preclude an examination of these themes but it is hoped that the present text might inspire further research. Further, Mahatma Gandhi makes very few appearances in the pages of this book, despite his importance to the national movement, as well as his thoughts on modern technology.[39] This is partially because he played no role, to the best of my knowledge, in setting aviation policy.

While the IAF is a subject of central interest it is important also to state that this is not meant to be a purely operational history. A number of highly detailed official and unofficial operational histories already cover nearly all the conflicts in this study. This book will instead seek to embrace a framework that is reflexive about the axioms of military history. The boundaries between war and peace, combatants and non-combatants, and above all social and military history will thus be treated as convenient social constructs rather than rigid discrete categories.[40] Detailed discussions of military operations undertaken in this study will therefore aim to illustrate the often profound impact of tactical actions on state formation in South Asia.

The research for this book has involved consultation of archives in the United Kingdom and India. It has made use of the papers of well-known personalities such as Lord Mountbatten, Vallabhbhai Patel, Mohammed Ali Jinnah, and Roy Bucher. It has also made use for the first time of the papers of Air Vice Marshal Thomas Elmhirst, the first commander of the IAF after independence and the papers of Air Vice Marshal Harjinder Singh who has the distinction of rising from the lowest rank in the IAF to its deputy commander. Further I draw on two previously untapped private collections belonging to Mr J.R. Nanda and Mrs Anuradha Reddy. I have also attempted to engage seriously with the wealth of visual material on aviation from the period available both online and offline.[41]

While focused on the aeroplane the present work is also an attempt to tell the story of the political transformation of the Indian state in the 1940s. It is a story that spans over a decade and features a vast cast of characters including Maharajas, refugees, tycoons, admirals, engineers,

---

[39] Interestingly Gandhi's assassin was captured by RIAF personnel. Further the Mahatma's funeral procession was photographed by the RIAF from the air. Chhina, *The Eagle Strikes*, p. 258.

[40] This is in keeping with calls by several leading scholars in the field for military historians to be more reflexive with their research. See: Jeremy Black, *Rethinking Military History* (London: Routledge, 2004), p. x; John Shy, 'The George C. Marshall Lecture in Military History; History and the History of War, 2008', *Journal of Military History*, vol. 72, no. 4 (2008), 1033–1046; Martin Van Creveld, 'Thoughts on Military History', *Military History*, vol. 18, no. 4 (October 1983), 549–566.

[41] Special note here needs to be made of *www.bharat.rakshak.com*.

sentries, labourers, and airmen. This book makes several interventions into historical debates about the nature of decolonization. It argues that independent India is, in significant ways a new state, and offers insights into such themes as development, modernity, sovereignty, aviation law, warfare, and commerce. Indeed, the interdisciplinary nature of much of this work means that it draws on and carries some relevance for subjects other than history, particularly cultural studies, international relations, and political science. By telling the story of India and the aeroplane, I hope to answer David Edgerton's call to regard technologies, even high technologies such as aviation, as 'things' since things are owned, used, and have a politics that is revealing of the roots of social power.[42] In doing so this book sheds new light on the complex relationship between high technology, decolonization, and state formation in 20th-century South Asia.

---

[42] Edgerton, *Shock of the Old*, p xvii.

1

Indian Aviation and the Second World War

The Second World War led to the end of British rule in India. The war reversed India's financial relationship with Britain, placing His Majesty's Government in debt to the Government of India for the first time. As the price for Indian support in prosecuting the war the British government was forced to accept constitutional negotiations, with the major Indian political parties, after the war.[1] The massive expansion of the colonial state, to meet the demands of the conflict, would also ensure that more Indians were recruited by the colonial government than ever before. This accelerated 'Indianization', the process of replacing British personnel with Indians with a view to setting India on the path to self-government.[2] Indianization would ensure that Indians could take control not only of the bureaucratic mechanisms necessary to govern India, but also the technological apparatus that had been the basis of colonial rule. Sectors like railways and engineering, which had been British preserves, were opened up to Indians during the war, thus removing one of the greatest sources of Indian dependence of Britain; technological know-how.[3] The wartime transfer of technology from British to Indian hands would presage the end of colonial rule.

One of the fields in which this was most apparent was in the field of aviation. The war fundamentally reshaped Indian aviation. It would necessitate the expansion of the tiny Indian Air Force (IAF), the construction of a vast network of infrastructure, and position Indian airline companies to benefit from the pool of planes and pilots that would become available once hostilities ended. In doing so the war would go some way towards

---

[1] Haines, *Rivers Divided*, p. 27.
[2] Marston, *The Indian Army and the End of the Raj*, p. 98.
[3] Ramnath, *Birth of an Indian Profession*, p. 180.

The Aeroplane and the Making of Modern India. Aashique Ahmed Iqbal, Oxford University Press.
© Oxford University Press 2023. DOI: 10.1093/oso/9780192864208.003.0002

fulfilling nationalist demands for the Indianization of aviation, which in turn would make Indian independence possible. However, this expansion would prove difficult to complete in an impoverished colony which was in the midst of a global war.

The purpose of this book is to study the transformation of the Indian state from British colony to independent republic through the prism of aviation. That process would begin in earnest with the Second World War, which laid the foundations of Indian aviation. The aims of this chapter are threefold. First, to argue that the transfer of technology from the colonial government to its Indian subjects, in order to prosecute the war, would undermine the technological and ideological logic of colonialism. The Second World War served to establish a substantial Indian aviation sector and this in turn contributed, albeit in complex ways, to the eventual decision to terminate colonial rule in India. Second, I use this chapter to provide the wider context in which Indian aviation operated at the beginning of what would prove to be the most turbulent decade of the 20th century, the 1940s. Just as the war served as the foundation for Indian aviation, this chapter is meant to serve as the foundation for arguments that will be made in subsequent chapters of the present work, by introducing the wider debates around the shape sovereignty should take in India. Third, I argue that the sudden and rapid reversal of policies of the Government of India that constrained Indian aviation caused immense difficulties for both civil and military aviation.

I begin this chapter with a brief discussion on the constraints on the growth of Indian aviation in the interwar years. The rest of the chapter is divided into two sections that examine the expansion of Indian aviation during the war and the difficulties that accompanied it. In the first section, I focus broadly on the expansion of Indian aviation in the Second World War. The IAF grew tenfold as a result of the war and granted Indians the wherewithal for an independent Air Force. The war also blurred the lines between civil, military, and princely aviation. Confronted with the need to defend India from the air, the Government of India turned to Indian airline companies and the semi-autonomous princely states for aid. This would lay the foundations for a post-war civil aviation boom and also help the Indian princes pursue crucial political goals. The second half of this chapter studies the difficulties that accompanied the expansion of the IAF during the Second World War. Though the IAF grew rapidly during the war, its expansion remained incomplete and it struggled to recruit educated Indians. These failures can be tied to the twin problems of substitution and wastage, which in turn were caused by older colonial structures. Finally, I turn to the 1946 'strikes' by RIAF personnel which caused divides within the force and contributed to the end of colonial rule in India.

Indian Aviation in the Interwar Years

Like many young people, Harjinder Singh was swept up in the patriotic wave convulsing India in 1930, the year of Gandhi's Salt March. The 21-year-old student leader had led a major strike at Maclaghan Engineering College protesting against British rule. After receiving favourable press coverage, letters of support from across the country and the enthusiastic backing of Congress leaders, Singh was convinced that 'independence was at hand' if only Indians would 'shout "Long Live Revolution", boycott British goods and non-cooperate with the civil administration.'[4] Singh would be disabused of this view at a meeting with the College's Principal, one Captain Whittaker (Late Royal Engineers). Whittaker argued that without the expertise and experience necessary to operate modern technology Indians were destined to remain a subject people of the British Empire. To Singh's claim that revolution would mean Indian control of the army, Whittaker responded 'the Indian Army is an out-of-date, outmoded weapon. We on the other had have the latest and most modern force—The Royal Air Force.'[5] Whittaker asked Singh to read the Hunter Commission Report of 1920 which had concluded that aircraft were extremely effective at putting down revolts in India, after RAF aircraft bombed rioting Indian mobs at Gujranwalla on 13 April 1919.[6] Deeply shaken by his meeting with the principal, Singh would conclude that a

---

[4] Saigal, *Birth of an Air Force*, p 8.
[5] Ibid., p. 9.
[6] Ibid., p. 9; *Disorder Inquiry Committee 1919–1920*, (Calcutta, Superintendent of Government Printing, India, 1920), pp. xxvii–xxviii. Recalling the bombing of Gujranwalla, which had coincided with the Jallianwalla Bagh massacre, the majority report would state 'that the dropping of bombs on the riotous crowds within Gujranwalla city was not only justified but, in their view, invaluable, and the fact that the disorders were ended long before troops arrived is attributable to this act'.

career in the air force was his foremost patriotic duty.[7] He called off the strike and upon completing his studies volunteered for the position of an airman or *Hawai Sepoy* (Flying Soldier) in the IAF instead of pursuing the vastly more lucrative career paths his educational qualifications afforded him.[8] As will be seen, Singh would go on to play an important role in the IAF.

Harjinder Singh was not alone in envisioning the aeroplane as a weapon Indians would have to master if they were ever to be free. Control of aviation would prove to be a key concern for Indian politicians in the interwar years. Though the aeroplane had made its debut in India as early as 10 December 1910, at the United Provinces Industrial and Agricultural fair, Indians were largely excluded from aviation in India.[9] This scared many Indians who held the view, especially popular in Britain at the time, that the aeroplane was the ultimate weapon of mass destruction. Indian fears about the aeroplane had deep roots. Sven Lindqvist has shown that the aeroplane was conceived of as a weapon of war, and even genocide, in the pages of Western science fiction, years before the first fixed-wing aircraft were flown.[10] The bombing of civilians from the air, hundreds of kilometres away from the front during the First World War, gave rise to a growing popular conviction that air forces would dominate future wars, with their ability to bomb ships, armies, and cities into oblivion.[11] The sense of dread inspired by air bombing in the interwar years was akin to the horror evoked by the prospect of nuclear war today. During a debate in the Central Legislative Assembly in 1940, for instance, Pandit Krishna Kant Malaviya claimed that the reason that Britain and Germany did not bomb each other was because devastating retaliation was all but certain.

---

[7] Singh was also driven to join the IAF by several other factors including widespread racist discourse on the inability of Indians to service aircraft. Saigal, *Birth of an Air Force*, pp. 10–12.

[8] Saigal, *Birth of an Air Force*, p. 14.

[9] India had the distinction of being the birthplace of air mail and Indian pilots had served in the Royal Flying Corps in the First World War. One of them, Indra Lal Roy would posthumously be awarded the Distinguished Flying Cross after becoming the first Indian fighter ace. Further the Maharaja of Patiala had become the first Indian to own aircraft when he bought two Farman biplanes and a Bleriot monoplane in 1911. Despite this as one observer noted, these developments had no 'organic connection' with the development of Indian aviation. Nayar, *The State and International Aviation in India*, p. 43.

[10] Stories such as *The Last War, or the Triumph of the English Tongue* penned by Samuel W. Odell in 1898 imagined a world in which flying machines were used by white nations to prosecute a war of extermination against 'the Chinese Empire and black Africa'. Lindqvist and Haverty, *A History of Bombing*, section 55.

[11] See: Bialer, *The Shadow of the Bomber*.

Malaviya restated the commonly held view that bombing would have apocalyptic consequences when he stated, 'Both the countries are vulnerable and the result (of bombing) will be that Industrial centres will be wiped out'.[12] The importance of the aeroplane was further confirmed in Indian minds when the Royal Air Force (RAF) was tasked with policing tribal groups in Iraq and India's Northwest Frontier Province as part of a campaign of 'air control'.[13]

In this context it is not surprising that aviation would take an important place in the debates around Indianization. Indian opinion in the interwar years was increasingly concerned about the inclusivity of the armed forces for which they footed the bill. The inclusion of Indians into the Indian army's officer corps, or the Indianization of the military, would work not only to reduce the steep costs of defence that India bore but also prove it was on the path to self-government within Empire.[14] Indian politicians also made the claim that Indianization would buttress the British claim that their government in India was premised on consent rather than force. Calls for the commissioning of Indian officers in the army were soon accompanied by demands for the greater association of Indians with military aviation. As early as 1923, B.S. Kamat would enquire, in the Central Legislative Assembly whether Indians could be allowed into the RAF.[15]

When their demands were met by indifference from the Government of India, legislators cast about for ways to promote 'air-mindedness' among Indians outside the legislature.[16] This would lead to the establishment of the Royal Aero Club of India and Burma (RACIB). It would serve as the umbrella organization under which flying clubs would be set up across India, including at New Delhi, Karachi, Allahabad, Calcutta, Bombay, Lahore, Jodhpur, and Hyderabad. Though the famed magnate, Sir Ellice Victor Sassoon, is credited with founding the RACIB, with the support of Lord Irwin, the Viceroy of India, Sassoon himself described the club as a 'child of the legislature'.[17] The Indian princes too were keen

---

[12] CS, *Legislative Assembly Debates* (New Delhi: Government Central Press, 1940), p. 206.

[13] Satia, 'The Defence of Inhumanity', pp. 16–51.

[14] CS, *Legislative Assembly Debates*, p. 2441.

[15] Ibid., p. 2424.

[16] For a brief discussion of airmindedness see: Jane Hu, 'Are you air minded? The slang of war'. Accessed August 28, 2020. *https://www.theawl.com/2011/06/are-you-airminded-the-slang-of-war/*

[17] 'Aero Club for India', *Times of India*, September 12, 1927. Proquest.

supporters of the flying clubs and Indian states like Jodhpur, Bhopal, and Hyderabad were quick to set up flying clubs in their territories. The Maharaja of Jodhpur was the first of many princes to earn a flying license. Where flying might have started out as a luxury activity, the princes were not slow to comprehend the importance of aviation for commerce and communication in their states.[18]

In 1926, the Skeen committee, which had been brought into existence to look into the possibilities of Indianizing the Indian army officer corps by establishing an 'Indian Sandhurst', somewhat exceeded its brief by recommending the admission of Indians into the RAF. This recommendation sprang from the committees' two most ardent advocates of Indianization, Mohammed Ali Jinnah and Motilal Nehru.[19] The RAF's response to the recommendation was immediate. Arguing that the RAF enjoyed the same status as the British Army in India, as opposed to the Indian Army, Air Vice Marshal Geoffrey Salmond stated that if Indians were given commissions in the RAF they would be required to serve all over the world. Salmond's unwillingness to permit Indians to serve in the RAF may also have sprung from concerns, similar to those often voiced by British officers with regard to Indianization, surrounding the possibility that providing Indians with commissions might upset racial hierarchies by placing Indian officers in command of British servicemen.[20] The Air Vice Marshal suggested that instead of allowing Indians to serve in the RAF, the Air Ministry should form a separate 'Indian Air Unit' in which Indians could be commissioned.[21] Initial plans to limit the unit to a single flight, totalling four aircraft, were abandoned only because it would be uneconomic to maintain a unit smaller than a squadron.[22] Though the new force was to be completely Indianized, it would continue to rely on the British RAF for commanding officers and technical tradesmen until Indians could achieve the training and experience needed to fill all roles

---

[18] I discuss the crucial role of the Indian princely states in promoting aviation in India in Chapter IV.

[19] BL, A. Skeen et al., *Report of the Indian Sandhurst Committee* (London: H.M.S.O., 1927).

[20] This was in some ways reminiscent of the Illbert bill controversy of the late 19th century which had upheld the right of the British defendants never to be tried by Indians magistrates. Chandra et al., *India's Struggle for Independence* (New Delhi: Random House, 1988), p. 73.

[21] Clive Richards, 'The Origins of Military Aviation in India and the Creation of the Indian Air Force 1910–1932: Part Two', *Air Power Review*, vol. 11, no. 1 (2008), p. 42.

[22] 'The IAF Statement of Case', 14 August 1930, Army Department in India to Secretary, Military Department, India Office London cited in R. Chhina, *The Eagle Strikes*, p. 307.

in the force. Significantly, recruitment to the force would not be confined to the so-called martial races, unlike the Indian army. Increasing Indian representation in the legislatures had made the idea of limiting military recruitment to the 'martial races' politically unacceptable and the need for educated personnel to fill in technical roles meant that the new air force would be free to draw from an all-India pool.[23]

The IAF was established on 8 October 1932 by an act of the Central Legislative Assembly.[24] Its first squadron, No. 1 Squadron, was raised the next year on 1 April 1933, the 15th anniversary of the establishment of the RAF.[25] More than half a decade later, at the outbreak of the war in 1939, the IAF consisted of no more than a single understrength squadron equipped with obsolete Wapiti aircraft (see Figure 1.1).[26] The establishment of a separate token air force for Indians was part of a wider script of colonial military control wherein the government made insubstantial concessions to Indian opinion, in the form of segregated military units, in order to maintain a pretence of Indianization while retaining military control.[27]

Civil aviation fared relatively better. India's first major airline companies Tata Air Services and Indian National Airways were set up around the same time as the IAF, in 1932 and 1933 respectively (see Figure 1.2). They had to contend with an absence of government investment in aviation infrastructure outside of the militarily important Northwest Frontier region and along the Imperial air routes that connected Britain to Australia. As TAS manager Neville Vintcent pointed out, 'government must accept the blame for the lack of any ground organisation apart from on the trans-India route.'[28] They also had to deal with the fact that the colonial government's airline subsidies were few and far between. In these circumstances, the All-Up Empire Air Mail Scheme conceived in 1934 came as a great boon to India's commercial airline companies. The scheme aimed at improving the declining

---

[23] CS, *Legislative Assembly Debates* (New Delhi, Central Government Press, 1923), p. 2642.
[24] Chinna, *The Eagle Strikes*, p. 3.
[25] Saigal, *Birth of an Air Force*, p. 34.
[26] Sapru, *Combat Lore*, p. 79.
[27] This closely resembled similar measures taken to limit Indianization such as the infamous '8 unit scheme' in which Indian officers were given commissions but subsequently limited to 8 units. Daniel Marston has described this as the 'platoonization' of the Indian officer corps since it limited Indian command to tiny platoon sized units. There is also evidence that British colonial authorities were practising similar policies aimed at limiting aviation in Egypt where a token air force was established. CS, *Legislative Assembly Debates*, p. 3364; D. Marston, *The Indian Army and the End of the Raj*, p. 31; Capua, 'Common Skies, Divided Horizons', p. 932.
[28] *Flight*, 22 March 1934. Accessed 16 April 2017. https://www.flightglobal.com/pdfarchive/

Figure 1.1 Officers, Hawai Sepoys (airmen) and Westland Wapitis of No. 1 Squadron, Indian Air Force on parade at Kohat in 1936. The IAF was kept small and equipped with outdated aircraft until the Second World War.
© USI of India

competitiveness of Imperial Airways and also preventing 'sectionalization', the setting up of independent international airlines in the Dominions. India's airline companies would act as feeders for the scheme and began receiving the substantial subsidies they required to operate profitably from 1938. Unfortunately for them the outbreak of the war brought the scheme to an end and with it their subsidies.[29]

Both civil and military aviation in India showed few signs of growing as a result of government policies. The Government of India showed little inclination to provide infrastructure and subsidies to Indian airline companies until imperial interests tied to the All-Up Empire Air Mail

---

[29] It is very likely the scheme would have needed to be discontinued, even if the war had not stopped it, in the future due to the enormous losses that it had incurred. See Ewer, 'A Gentlemen's Club', pp. 75–92.

Figure 1.2 J.R.D. Tata and Neville Vintcent at Juhu aerodrome, Bombay after the Tata Air Service's inaugural flight. A talented pilot and entrepreneur, Tata worked closely with Vintcent to set up the airline company that would eventually become India's flag carrier; Air India. Courtesy: Tata Central Archives.

Scheme, demanded it. It also did very little to expand the IAF.[30] When the Chatfield Committee of Enquiry on Indian Defence in 1939 recommended the setting up of a modest Indian Air Force Volunteer Reserve (IAFVR) to protect India's coasts the Indian government moved slowly to recruit necessary personnel. The committee's recommendation, that the IAF be expanded to two squadrons, was still in the process of being implemented in late 1940.[31] While it is true that the Government of India subsidized some of the new flying clubs and provided princely states with assistance in setting up aerodromes, this translated into a commitment to aviation that was limited at best. This meant that the foundational institutions upon which the government could base the air defences of India

---

[30] Prasad, *History of IAF*, p. xx.
[31] TNA, T 161/1079, India Office to Treasury, 29 January 1941. The committee also recommended that the total strength of air forces be brought up to ten squadrons in India.

were unpromising. The policies that had stunted the growth of flying in India would prove difficult for the government to reverse despite the imperatives of the Second World War.

The IAF in the Second World War

Though the mobilization of Indian aviation during the Second World War was not without its difficulties, as a subsequent section will show, it laid the foundations for Indian aviation. The IAF would grow enormously from a single squadron force of 16 officers and 269 airmen in 1939 to a nine-squadron force that in July 1945 included 1638 officers and 26,900 other ranks.[32] The dramatic reversal of interwar policies constraining the growth of the IAF would make an independent Indian state possible, and would eventually contribute to the British decision to depart from India.

Governor General Lord Linlithgow declared India to be at war with Germany on 3 September, without consulting India's political parties. Despite this little was done to speed up the expansion of Indian air defences. As late as 8 February 1940, government representatives in the Legislative Assembly continued to resist demands for the training of Indian youth for air warfare. Arguing against a modest resolution that the government set up an 'auxiliary air force' to be 'manned by Indians', Defence Secretary C.M.G. Oglivie claimed that 'anything in the way of a vast expansion ... , would be absolutely beyond our powers to attain'.[33] Not only was the Government of India, unwilling to send Indians to participate in the Empire Air Training scheme in Canada, which was turning out thousands of pilots and airmen, but it would also not consent to the establishment of any training centres in India. Responding to the Defence Secretary in the assembly, M.S. Aney, a moderate nationalist, presciently observed that, 'invasion during the present war will be possible when the British Air Force and other air forces which are in Europe will be so engaged that the British government will not be able to divert any of them for the defence of this country'. He went on to argue that the absence of

---

[32] Prasad, *Expansion of Armed Forces*, p. 153. This figure does not include the 13,727 enrolled and 24,469 non-enrolled Indian followers since they were shared between the RAF and IAF.
[33] CS, *Legislative Assembly Debates* (New Delhi, Central Government Press, 1940), p. 213.

a serious effort on the part of the government to tackle the issue showed that 'it is certainly not preparing the country for dominion status or any kind of autonomous condition at all'.[34] Less than a year later Governor General Lord Linlithgow was writing to the Secretary of State Leo Amery, enquiring about the possibility of expanding the IAF to 15 squadrons.

The volte-face of the Government of India was caused by fears of a Soviet attack. The USSR had concluded a non-aggression pact with Germany and many in the Indian establishment believed it was likely that the 'Russian menace' would turn its attention to India.[35] With the RAF tied up in Europe, the Red Air Force might well strike at the Indian Northwest Frontier. Given India's serious lack of air defences as well as the terror evoked by aircraft even light air raids on the frontier would likely have had a devastating impact on the Indian populace.[36] Consequently, the Government of India turned to the only air force it had, the IAF. The Governor General's extraordinary proposal, codenamed Plan A, would see the IAF expand to 15 squadrons over the next two and a half years. The plan would make use of whatever aircraft Britain could spare, even if these were obsolete, until better aircraft became available.[37] It would aim to make use of as many Indian recruits as it possibly could though these would for a time have to be commanded by British officers and backed by the RAF's technical organization. 'Plan A' however was doomed to fail due to severe shortages of equipment and personnel. Britain could not spare the shipping space required to send India planes, let alone the planes since she was going through a shortage of her own. Even the reduced estimates of personnel that New Delhi had requested from the Air Council for RAF training were not forthcoming.[38]

Despite this 'Plan A' is highly significant. It indicated the government's willingness to reverse its policy of treating the IAF as a token force meant to pacify Indian opinion. From 1940 onwards the colonial government indicated its willingness, if not its ability, at the highest levels to expand the IAF. Perhaps just as crucial, was the political decision to

---

[34] CS, *Legislative Assembly Debates*, p. 216.
[35] TNA, T 161/1079, Government of India Defence Department to Secretary of State, 18 May 1940.
[36] Raghavan, *India's War*, p. 43.
[37] TNA, AIR 19/159, Air Officer Commanding-in-Chief to Air Ministry 26 December 1940.
[38] BL, IOR/L/WS/1/496, Linlithgow to Amery, 22 December 1940.

align government policy with Indian political rhetoric. Both Amery and Linlithgow saw that expanding the IAF would be well received in India. As the Governor General noted, expansion of the IAF would be 'unmistakably and universally welcomed by Indian opinion.'[39] Expanding the IAF, as opposed to the RAF, would enable the Government of India to recruit Indians by appealing to their patriotism. This entailed an adoption of the political discourse of the interwar years, which held that control of aviation would provide Indians with the substance of sovereignty. As I have pointed out above, Indian nationalists had claimed, for at least two decades, that without control of military aviation, India could never be truly free. Conversely once military aviation was Indianized, Indian freedom would become inevitable. Plan A would mark the inauguration of a new script of colonial military control in which the Government of India held out the prospect of some form of independence after the war in return for Indian support in winning it. To be sure, colonial authorities had promised Indian nationalists' greater autonomy in return for their support during the First World War only to step up repression after the war.[40] Nevertheless the tacit agreement between the Raj and its IAF personnel would later prove consequential.

The expansion of the IAF would take on a new urgency after the outbreak of war with Japan in December 1941. IAF operations in the Second World War have been the subject of several detailed works.[41] As such I limit the present discussion to an abbreviated summary of IAF operations, followed by a brief discussion of its implications for the evolution of colonial military control.

Though it fought gallantly against the Imperial Japanese Army Air Force (IJAAF), No. 1 Squadron, the sole squadron of the IAF, was forced to retreat from Burma along with other allied air forces, by March 1942.[42] The force was expanded to six squadrons in 1943 and No. 2 Squadron's Hurricanes would provide crucial reconnaissance support to Orde Wingate's 'Chindits' far behind enemy lines.[43] Later that year four IAF squadrons, Nos. 4, 6, 8,

---

[39] BL, IOR/L/WS/1/496, Linlithgow to Amery, 22 December 1940.
[40] Aravind Ganachari. 'First World War: Purchasing Indian Loyalties: Imperial Policy of Recruitment and 'Rewards', *Economic and Political Weekly*, vol. 40, no. 8 (2005), 779–88.
[41] See: Prasad and Gupta, *History of the IAF*; Chhina, *The Eagle Strikes*; Sapru, *Combat Lore*; Nair, *The Forgotten Few*.
[42] TNA, AIR 23/2205, Air Forces in India, March 1942.
[43] Nair, *The Forgotten Few*, chapter 5 'Chasing the Chindits'.

and 9, participated in the Second Arakan campaign.[44] By 1944 the IAF had expanded to its wartime peak of nine squadrons and distinguished itself in the battles of Kohima and Imphal (see Table 1.1).[45] In the final year of the war the IAF would serve as a key part of the allied advance in the battles of Akyab, Kangaw, and eventually Rangoon itself. On 12 March 1945, the IAF received the prefix 'Royal' from His Majesty the King Emperor in recognition for its services. Two Spitfires from No. 8 Squadron would accompany Lt. Gen. Takazo Numata to the ceremony marking the surrender of Japan, held at Mingaladon just outside Rangoon on the 26 August 1945.[46] At the end of the war the Royal Indian Air Force (RIAF) could boast 1 Distinguished Service Order, 22 Distinguished Flying Crosses, 1 bar to Distinguished Flying Cross, 3 Air Force Crosses, 2 Orders of the British Empire, 7 Members of the British Empire, 5 British Empire Medals, 45 Mentions in Dispatches, and 285 *Jangi Inams* (War prizes).[47]

IAF squadrons were tasked primarily with photographic and tactical reconnaissance, as well as dive-bombing. The IAF distinguished itself for its ability to spot enemy positions. No.6 Squadron for instance flew over 1500 sorties during the Second Arakan campaign and took over 16,000 photographic prints in seven months.[48] It would earn the epithet 'The eyes of the 14th army'.[49] Tactical and photographic reconnaissance was unglamorous and dangerous work that required a very high level of skill to accomplish. The IAF also became proficient in dive-bombing using the Vultee Vengeance aeroplane (see Figure 1.3). The Vultee had been produced by the United States but never used by the country's air service branch the United States Army Air Force (USAAF), which considered it to be a substandard aircraft.[50] IAF Vultee squadrons would serve as flying artillery, bombing enemy strong points with precision. The IAF would also carry out a series of more specialized operations like dropping propaganda leaflets, supporting deep penetration raids and in one instance dropping the salaries of pro-British Burmese levies.[51] All this, while the IAF was given the sole responsibility of policing the turbulent border on India's Northwest Frontier.

---

[44] Chhina, *The Eagle Strikes*, p. 146.
[45] See for instance MoD (I), ORB No. 1 Squadron, 18 May 1944.
[46] Sapru, *Combat Lore*, p. 545.
[47] Chhina, *The Eagle Strikes*, p. 236.
[48] TNA, AIR 23/3426, History of the Royal Indian Air Force.
[49] Chhina, *The Eagle Strikes*, p. 121.
[50] Nair, *The Forgotten Few*, p. 186.
[51] For an instance of the last see: MoD (I), 601/9621/H, ORB No. 8 Squadron, 28 October 1945

Table 1.1 List of IAF Squadrons 1933–1946

Squadron Name	Date raised	Aircraft flown until 1946
No. 1 Squadron	1st April 1933	Westland Wapiti, Westland Lysander, Hawker Harts, Hawker Audax, Hawker Hurricane
No. 2 Squadron	1st April 1941	Westland Wapiti, Hawker Audax, Westland Lysander, Hawker Hurricane, Supermarine Spitfire
No. 3 Squadron	1st October 1941	Hawker Audax, Hawker Hurricane, Supermarine Spitfire
No. 4 Squadron	1st February 1942	Westland Lysander, Hawker Hurricane, Supermarine Spitfire
No. 6 Squadron	1st December 1942	Hawker Hurricanes, Supermarine Spitfires
No 7. Squadron	1st December 1942	Westland Wapiti, Hawker Audax, Vultee Vengeance, Hawker Hurricane, Supermarine Spitfire
No. 8 Squadron	1st December 1942	Vultee Vengeance, Supermarine Spitfire
No. 9 Squadron	3rd January 1944	Hawker Hurricane, Supermarine Spitfire
No. 10 Squadron	20th February 1944	Hawker Hurricanes, Supermarine Spitfires
No. 12 Squadron	1st December 1945	Supermarine Spitfire, Dakota C-47

Source: Prasad and Gupta, History of the IAF 1933-45, Chapter II; Bharat Rakshak, 'Indian Air Force Databases,' Accessed August 28, 2020. http://www.bharat-rakshak.com/IAF/Database/.

Expanding the IAF meant more than training and equipping new squadrons. Air Force operations required the mobilization of science for war in India like never before. A number of new technical departments had to be set up within the IAF. A balloon branch was formed to set up barrage balloons and officers and men were transferred to the IAF from the army.[52]

[52] RAFM, AC 71/13/82, Report on the Expansion of the Air Forces in India by ACM R.E.C. Peirse.

Figure 1.3 Sergeant Dasgupta and Aircraftsman Hussain load a No. 7 Squadron Vultee Vengeance for operations on the Assam front in May 1944. The IAF earned a reputation for dive bombing using the notoriously dangerous Vengeance. © USI of India

The Indian Observer Corps was expanded and its men were sent to Eastern India to observe Japanese aerial moves. An IAF Meteorological branch was established to help with weather predictions by borrowing personnel from the Indian Meteorological department.[53] As the IAF grew in size it became necessary to regulate it more carefully. The Inspectorate General of the IAF was formed in February 1943 to 'inspect the IAF units ... and advise on policy for the development and conditions of service of the Indian Air Force.'[54] It would suggest the creation of a maintenance organization for the IAF once the war ended so that the force would not have to rely on RAF technical tradesmen. It would recommend keeping a large number of RAF pilots and crews in the IAF in order to spare Indian personnel for more

[53] TNA, AIR 29/36, 5 Forecast Centre, IAF Jiwani, formed 10 July 1943.
[54] TNA AIR 23/5310, Report on work, 9 February 1943.

advanced training.[55] The expansion of the IAF necessitated the creation of a complex scientific and bureaucratic apparatus. This was in keeping with the broader trend of technologized warfare that characterized the Second World War. Both the Indian army and the Royal Indian Navy (RIN) would also become reliant on educated recruits possessing technical skills. This changed the composition of the Indian armed forces by bringing in larger numbers of educated recruits from the politically alert middle classes. This substantially modified India's status as the British Empire's leading source of military labour.

Despite its sophisticated technical apparatus, the IAF bore the hallmarks of a colonial military force. Even as the exigencies of the war raised the force from its status as a token arm, it continued to be limited to an auxiliary role. The force was consistently denied the most advanced aircraft and equipment. In a theatre of the war that has often been described as the 'Forgotten', it remained last in the queue to receive new equipment.[56] The IAF remained a junior partner in the air war in South Asia with only nine squadrons in 1945, compared to the substantially larger RAF and USAAF. IAF squadrons were also not tasked, for much of the war, with air superiority operations, and there is only one known case of IAF aircraft downing an enemy fighter.[57] IAF squadrons would only be equipped with Spitfire aircraft late in the war, with No. 8 Squadron being the first to receive the advanced fighter in July 1944 (see Figure 1.4).[58] The lack of air-to-air combat can also be explained as being a consequence of the changing nature of the war in the air. If the Burma front was 'forgotten' by the Allies it certainly does not seem to have been remembered by the Japanese for whom the war in the Pacific and China took precedence.[59] Consequently the Japanese dedicated limited military aircraft to the Burma theatre meaning that the emphasis for allied air forces, particularly in the aftermath of the battles of Imphal and Kohima in 1944, was on supporting the advance on the ground rather than focusing on air

---

[55] Ibid.

[56] The China-Burma-India front was one of the least important for the RAF which prioritized Europe and Africa. For the IJAAF also the front would come third in order of importance after the Pacific and China.

[57] Nair, *The Forgotten Few*, p. 221.

[58] MoD (I), 601/9621/H, ORB No. 8 Squadron, July 1944.

[59] R.C. Mikesh, *Broken Wings of the Samurai: The Destruction of the Japanese Air Force* (Livesey: Airlife 1993), p. 22.

Figure 1.4 A Spitfire VIII of No. 8 Squadron near Calcutta in May 1945.
The RIAF only received the famous Supermarine Spitfire in July 1944. © USI
of India

superiority. The IAF was also not trained or equipped with heavy bomber
aircraft since the USAAF had taken responsibility for heavy bombing on
the China-Burma-India front.[60] With the benefit of hindsight it is now
possible to argue that this did not prove to be a stumbling block for Indian
military aviation. The experience of tactical reconnaissance gained in
Burma would prove crucial for independent India's post-war conflicts.
As a subsequent chapter will show, in the 1947 Kashmir war, independent
India's mastery over terrain, rather than dogfighting and heavy bombing
skills, would prove decisive.

Despite being relegated to the third position in the defence of India,
the Indian Air Force had proven successfully that, given the resources,
Indians could fly and maintain military aircraft. Whatever the strategic
role played by the aeroplane, its ideological role, as a symbol of sovereignty must not be lost sight of. The war had undermined the British
claim that enlarging the IAF was simply not possible over a short period
of time and that India would require extended colonial rule, not least because it required RAF squadrons for its defence. While, as we will see, this

[60] Chhina, *The Eagle Strikes*, p. 116.

expansion had been difficult to undertake, its political consequences were important. India had the air force its political leaders had been calling for since the Great War. The Indian government's mobilization of technology to win the war in the air would have consequences far beyond the expansion of the IAF. It is to these that we now turn.

Blurring the Boundaries between Civil and Military Aviation

The Second World War was India's first air war. Fighting and winning a war in the air would confront the Government of India with novel challenges. Years of neglect of aviation in the colony, outside the Imperial air route and aerodromes on the Northwest Frontier, would have to be overcome in short order. This would necessitate the mobilization of scientific and technological resources on an unprecedented scale. Not only would the IAF have been expanded exponentially but aviation infrastructure in India would also need to be upgraded. To do this it would draw on India's meagre existing air resources including civilian airline corporations, flying clubs, and the Indian princes. This would transform the Indian aviation landscape beyond recognition. In this section I focus on the complex infrastructure that needed to be mobilized in order to enable the Indian state to wage war in the air. My objective here is to point to the technical challenges the air war posed for the Government of India and to assert that this would require not only the mobilization of military resources but also of civil aviation.

In the absence of a strong RAF or IAF Works Directorate, the Government of India leaned heavily on the Directorate of Civil Aviation (DCA) to manage the air war effort. The DCA served as the primary recruiting body for the IAF in the first years of the war until the IAF set up its own recruitment apparatus. It released planes to serve as light aircraft and trainers from its aircraft pool.[61] At the beginning of the war the DCA was responsible for the training of pilots for the Air Forces in India and was running training courses for the IAF as late as 1943 when it handed over training facilities at Guindy to Headquarters, South East Asia.

---

[61] TNA, AVIA 2/1490, Gurunath Bewoor to Under Secretary of State, 17 August 1942.

Similarly, it ran a civil Aviation Repair Establishment which was eventually transferred to the Department of Supply to rationalize the war effort.[62] Perhaps most significantly of all, the DCA would work with the Public Works Department and Army engineers to construct the vast network of airfields needed to host the Allied Air Forces.[63] This mammoth construction effort, the largest undertaken by the India Command during the war, would redraw the map of Indian air routes (see Figure 1.5). Where, as seen earlier, India had only featured a small number of aerodromes along the Imperial Karachi-Calcutta route and the strategically vital Northwest Frontier, over two hundred airfields would be constructed over the course of a mere three years, between 1942 and 1945.[64] More than eight decades later Indian aviation has still not grown large enough to exploit more than a fraction of the airfields constructed during the war. The DCA's centrality to the war effort is a testament to the extent which the requirements of the war blurred the lines between civil and military aviation.

The war was initially disastrous for Indian airline companies. Indian National Airways and Tata Airlines were effectively absorbed by the war effort and played a crucial role that has thus far received little attention. The war had brought an end to the lucrative All-Up Empire Air Mail Scheme, which had served as one of the sole sources of sustenance to a chronically unsupported civil aviation sector. The government commandeered Tata's Dragon Rapides and Express aircraft to act as spotters along India's vast coastline, whittling the airline down to its smaller Wacos and Stinsons.[65] Civil aircraft were pressed into the evacuation of thousands of refugees from Burma. Indian National Airways began evacuations on 23 December 1942, the day after the first bombing of Rangoon by Japanese aircraft. It would ferry refugees for over a month between Calcutta and Rangoon, from airfields that were under constant air attack. Tata Air Services too took part in the evacuation of Rangoon, as did a number of foreign airlines including the Dutch carrier KLM and the Chinese National Aviation Corporation. One INA Airspeed Envoy plane was lost in operations and one Tata Aviation Services Stinson was badly damaged.

---

[62] Ibid.

[63] TNA, AVIA 2/1490, Gurunath Bewoor to Undersecretary of State, 29 July 1943.

[64] Raghavan, *India's War*, p. 401.

[65] *Centenary of Civil Aviation in India* (New Delhi: Ministry of Civil Aviation, Government of India, 2011), p. 17.

Figure 1.5 Labourers extend the runway on Cochin aerodrome in March 1942. Millions of Indian men and women would be mobilized to build a vast network of aerodromes after the outbreak of the war with Japan. © USI of India

The retreat from Burma in 1942, hit INA particularly hard since it lost major sections of its air routes.[66] Both the airlines also haemorrhaged pilots and ground crews to the IAF.

Civil aircraft were deputed to a wide variety of military tasks. Tata airlines carried out survey work to find an air route to the United Kingdom through Oman and Saudi Arabia and its planes helped at the new school for camouflage at Pune.[67] Both major airlines also provided the DCA with personnel to undertake advanced repairs of RAF and IAF aircraft. As the war progressed INA and Tata airlines were tasked with delivering military freight and vital passengers to various parts of the country. Thus,

[66] TNA, AVIA 2/1490, Gurunath Bewoor to Under Secretary of State, 17 August 1942.
[67] Russi M. Lala, *Beyond the Last Blue Mountain: A Life of J.R.D. Tata* (New Delhi: 1992), p. 106.

INA for instance operated services on India's North West Frontier province from Lahore to Quetta and in the East from Calcutta to Dinjan.[68] When Iraqi nationalists led by Rashid Ali revolted against the British in 1941, Tata Air Lines participated in the evacuation of British nationals from Baghdad where it had been operating a non-scheduled service from Karachi to Baghdad via Jiwani and Sharjah to meet the needs of the war in the Middle East using a single Douglas DC-2 loaned to it by the RAF.[69] The problems with dedicating civil aircraft to military communications would however become apparent the next year when there were serious difficulties in moving supplies to flood-affected parts of India in 1942, a task normally carried out by civil aviation. Meanwhile India's flying clubs did their bit. The North India Flying Club, Karachi Aero Club, Bihar Flying Club, Bombay Flying Club, and Madras Flying Club conducted Army co-operation duties for war preparation. The Flying clubs of Hyderabad and Jodhpur, both princely states, were turned over to the RAF as Elementary Flying Training Schools.[70] Many flying club members were recruited into the IAFVR when it was established. Pratap Chandra Lal, who would go on to command the IAF as its Air Chief Marshal, for instance, was recruited into the IAFVR directly from his flying club after the outbreak of the war made it impossible for him to return to England to finish his law degree.[71]

The dangerous and vital work carried out by commercial operators would serve to underline the indispensability of civil aviation, as a strategic reserve, in the eyes of the Government of India. It had realized the need for civil aviation to help with the war effort as early as 1941 when it had planned the establishment of two Civil Air Transport Units (CATU). The CATUs were to help with the transport of mail, freight, and passengers in the country's hinterland to aid civil aviation.[72] Though the plan did not translate into action, resulting in severe shortages of air transport during the Japanese invasion of Burma, the Indian government did try to supplement its civil aviation resources through appeals to its British counterpart. When this failed, the Indian DCA asked for and received

---

[68] TNA, AVIA 2/2412, Aircraft for Civil Aviation purposes in India.
[69] *Centenary of Civil Aviation in India*, p. 18.
[70] AVIA 2/2412, Aircraft for Civil Aviation purposes in India.
[71] Lal, *My Years with the IAF*, p. 12.
[72] BL, IOR/L/WS/1/496, Government of India to Secretary of State, 29 March 1941.

aircraft from the RAF, which by now was keen that certain Indian routes such as those from New Delhi to Calcutta be operated daily by civil aviation aircraft to aid with the prosecution of the war.[73] As the war continued the availability of aircraft for airline companies grew along with the number of air routes that they were operating. Though the war was initially not beneficial for commercial airline companies, the vast schemes of airfield construction and the needs of the war led to an unprecedented increase in the density of air routes they could operate. New aerodromes at places like Jiwani and Jorhat allowed them to penetrate further into the subcontinent and older aerodromes such as the one at Trichinopoly were reactivated for civil use during the war. The regularity and number of services also grew thanks to the demands of the war. Indian National Airways alone ran four different routes at least twice a week by 1944.[74]

When the war ended, civil aviation had opportunities for growth that would have been difficult to conceive of before the war. A large number of aircraft, personnel, and aerodromes were suddenly available. In the words of an official history released by the Director General for Civil Aviation (India), 'a phenomenal increase in passenger freight and mail occurred during the six years of the war' developing civil aviation 'which might otherwise have taken another two decades'.[75] The story of the expansion of civil aviation at the end of the Second World War is the subject of a later chapter. Here it suffices to point out that the mobilization of technical resources necessitated by the need to wage total war, transformed civil aviation as much as it did the IAF. In a colony with limited aviation resources, like India, the war prompted the utilization of every aeroplane, pilot, and aerodrome, regardless of whether they were military or not.

---

[73] TNA, AVIA 2/2412, Aircraft for Civil Aviation purposes in India.
[74] TNA, AVIA 2/1490, M.D. Bhansali to Undersecretary of State, 7 August 1944.
[75] *Centenary of Civil Aviation in India*, p. 17.

Constraints on the Expansion and Indianization of the IAF

Building the IAF in a colony while a world war raged would not be easy. Plans for the expansion and Indianization of the force would remain incomplete despite the efforts of Air Headquarters (India) [AHQ (I)] largely as a consequence of personnel shortages. Personnel shortages were a result of many factors, which can be traced back to the structure of the colonial military labour market. These would be considerably worsened by the substitution of IAF personnel to the RAF as well as by the high levels of wastage. In an attempt to recruit more educated Indians, AHQ (I) would launch the largest propaganda campaign of the war. This would, among other things, adopt much of the discourse surrounding Indianization of the IAF, by making appeals to Indian patriotism.

Though as outlined above, the highest officials of the Government of India, had decided to put the entire weight of the state behind rapidly expanding the IAF in 1940, expansion proved difficult. Early plans for a 15-squadron force had to be pared down to ten squadrons and even this target was not achieved during the war. The tenth squadron of the IAF, No. 12 Squadron had only been formed after the war ended, on 1 December 1945.[76] In its attempt to mobilize all the aerial resources at its disposal, the expansion of the IAF had been carried out with little regard for the cause of Indianization. Thus, IAF squadrons in addition to having failed to expand to meet relatively modest goals had also failed to fully Indianize. A large portion of the force continued to be drawn from outside of India. IAF Squadron Nos. 4, 7, 8, 9, 10, and 12 drew personnel from other Commonwealth air forces.[77] In the instance of Squadron No. 8, for example, an entire flight was drawn from the RAF.[78] The problems that plagued the force, slow expansion and incomplete Indianization, can be traced back to one factor; a serious manpower shortage.

This was a new situation for the Government of India to find itself in. In previous conflicts India had exported military labour to other theatres. Indian sepoys had served in no less than eleven theatres during

---

[76] Halley, *The Squadrons of the RAF and Commonwealth*, p. 524.
[77] Doe, *Fighter Pilot*, p. 163.
[78] MoD (I), 601/9621/H, ORB No. 8 Squadron, 16 November 1944.

and immediately after the Great War. They had held British possessions in China and gone into action against the Soviet Union's new Bolshevik government.[79] The Second World War inverted this equation forcing the Indian military to rely on a tiny pool of educated recruits possessing the skills necessary to wage new forms of war. What differentiated the mobilization of the Second World War from the First was the high reliance of the state on sophisticated systems of high technology to wage war. The Government of India was called upon to manage complex technical systems for all three wings of its armed forces. The Indian army required skilled technicians for its signals, armoured, and engineering branches.[80] The RIN needed technicians for its growing fleet and for the network of coastal facilities that came to dot India's shores.[81] Needless to say the IAF depended on skilled personnel such as meteorologists, balloonists, and observers for its air and ground crews as well as for the battery of facilities necessary to enable air warfare. Manpower shortages led to severe difficulties in the expansion of the force and also had an adverse impact on Indianization. Recruitment remained a significant constraint on the IAF till the end of the war and beyond it.

Initially the IAF's growth was limited by a lack of equipment. As seen above the Indian government had proposed to increase the size of the IAF to 15 squadrons in 1940 under 'Plan A', even if this meant equipping the force with obsolescent equipment.[82] The British Empire however was at the time engaged in Europe and North Africa, meaning that no equipment could be spared for the expansion of the IAF. When the Indian government acquired a shipment of Tomahawk planes they were diverted to serve the RAF in Iran by the British government.[83] As relations with Japan grew more strained, India was not only denuded of aircraft which were then deployed further East, but the IAF was de-prioritized as the RAF in India moved to consolidate what assets it continued to have in the country.[84] Through 1942 as the Japanese advanced through Burma and new RAF squadrons arrived in India there was nearly no expansion. The

---

[79] Vedica Kant, 'If I Die Here, Who Will Remember Me?': India and the First World War (New Delhi: Roli books 2014).

[80] Roy, The Army in British India, p. 151.

[81] Singh, Under Two Ensigns, p. 27.

[82] TNA, AIR 19/159, Governor General to Secretary of State, 22 December 1940.

[83] Prasad, Expansion of the Armed Forces, p. 142.

[84] TNA, AIR 23/1973, Expansion.... IAF, p. 5.

situation however began to change in 1943 as IAF units were equipped with Hawker Hurricanes and Vultee Vengeances. Despite the fact that the IAF remained low on the list of priorities of Air Headquarters (India), as production of aircraft increased in the United States and Britain in 1944, even it began to be equipped with the latest aircraft, the Supermarine Spitfire.[85] Though equipment shortages, particularly of spare parts, continued to dog the IAF till the war's end, it is fair to say that equipment shortages gave way to personnel shortages as the key factor holding back an increase in the size of the IAF.

As early as 1940 shortages of manpower were holding back expansion.[86] The trouble with recruiting personnel in the right quantity and of the right quality only deepened as the war proceeded (see Figure 1.6). J.M. Spaight, a contemporary expert on aviation, wrote in *Aeronautics* magazine in June 1942 that 'There is little surplus of skilled labour in the country and competing demands of industry militate against the satisfaction of the needs of the IAF'.[87] Indeed the competing demands of the other services also militated against the needs of the IAF as the army and navy rushed to recruit whatever skilled labour that they could. Inter-service rivalries for skilled manpower were heavily weighted in favour of the army, which by virtue of being the largest force, fielded the majority of recruiters.[88] The IAF also found itself at a disadvantage on the questions of commissions and salaries. Educated recruits who could get commissions in the army were not likely to join the ranks in the IAF. Moreover, the pay rates of the IAF remained uncompetitive in the early years of the war when most of the best recruits were still available.[89]

If the IAF's manpower woes owed something to inter-service rivalries, then the force was also severely disadvantaged by the RAF effectively poaching its personnel through the 'substitution' scheme. Under this scheme, implemented in 1943, the RAF would recruit IAF personnel to a man 20 per cent of vacancies in non-operational units. Doing so, somewhat ironically, reversed the key argument for the formation of the IAF advanced by the RAF leadership that a separate IAF was necessary since

[85] V. Seth, *The Flying Machines* (New Delhi, Seth Communications, 2000), p. 30.

[86] Prasad, *Expansion of the Armed Forces*, p. 143.

[87] J.M. Spaight, 'The Indian Air Force', *Aeronautics*, vol. 6, no. 3 (June 1941).

[88] TNA, AIR 23/1973, Expansion ... IAF, p. 6.

[89] TNA, AIR 23/2205, National Defence Council, 1943.

Figure 1.6 New IAF recruits receiving their kit and uniforms at an Initial Training School in South India. The IAF would consistently suffer manpower shortages throughout the war. © USI of India

Indians could not hold posts in the RAF.[90] Five Indians were to be recruited for every four RAF vacancies 'to guard against loss of operational efficiency'.[91] Interestingly a similar 'substitution' policy had been undertaken in Britain itself to substitute women for male RAF personnel.[92] This reflected the racial and gendered hierarchies of the British empire which were being pressured by the exigencies of the war. Predictably this was a

[90] This position had already been significantly undermined by the induction of two dozen Indians into the RAF in Britain during the Battle of Britain. See for instance Graham Russell, *For King and Another Country: An Amazing Life Story of an Indian World War Two RAF Fighter Pilot: The Recollections of Squadron Leader Mahinder S. Pujji* (Ilfracombe: Arthur H. Stockwell, 2010).

[91] TNA, AIR 23/1973, Expansion ... IAF, p. 9.

[92] See: Julie Fountain, *Modern Jobs for Modern Women, Female Military Service in Britain 1945–62*, PhD Thesis, University of Illinois at Chicago, 2015.

recipe for demoralization and may go some way to explain some of the post-war disturbances that were to rock the RAF.

Recruitment was also affected by the fact that knowledge of English was a requirement for serving in the IAF. While the English-speaking middle classes had protested the most loudly about their exclusion from the higher echelons of the armed forces they were also highly conflicted about the war's political objectives. The shortage of skilled recruits proficient in English led the IAF to briefly consider the possibility of hiring semi-skilled labourers who did not know the language. The measure, however, was not eventually taken by the IAF since if nothing else the knowledge of English was necessary to work with the many RAF personnel who were posted in IAF squadrons with no language training.[93]

When recruits did volunteer for service, they did not always successfully complete their training. Wastage was a serious problem in the IAF as recruits were not always capable of mastering required skills.[94] When they were re-mustered or assigned to lower-level trades than they had volunteered for recruits naturally felt they had been wronged. At least one observer has held that the high levels of wastage were caused by the racism and incompetence of British instructors in Flying Training Schools.[95] While this possibility cannot be discounted it is also the case that the number of technically skilled personnel available to AHQ (I) was vanishingly small as a consequence of the economic and educational backwardness of the colony. Another equally worrying source of wastage was the loss of aircrew that the IAF suffered, as new planes replaced old ones. When Squadron No. 8 converted from Vengeances to Spitfires, for instance, it lost all the 'backseater' co-pilots who had earlier flown in the two-seater aircraft. As training with the Spitfires continued it was found that many pilots who had earlier been able to handle the slower Vultees would not be able to fly Spitfires.[96]

AHQ (I) vigorously tried to overcome the IAF's recruiting problems. An Indian Air Training Corps (IATC) was formed in 1942 to foster interest in the IAF in universities.[97] Aimed initially at training ground

[93] Prasad, *Expansion of the Armed Forces*, p. 181.
[94] TNA, AIR 29/616, No 2 EFTS Jodhpur, July 1943.
[95] Nair, *The Forgotten Few*, p. 211.
[96] MoD (I), 601/9621/H, ORB No. 8 Squadron, 9 October 1944.
[97] TNA, AIR 23/2205, National Defence Council.

crews the emphasis shifted to turning out cadets who could join the air-crews as it became clear that university students were not interested in entering the ranks. To attract cadets the IATC offered a uniform and a twenty-rupee stipend. By the end of the war over 24 universities and their affiliated colleges had IATCs.[98] New efforts were made to coordinate with the recruitment directorate in order to limit the army's control of the recruitment process.[99] Attempts were also made to improve pay and conditions of work though these were not always successful.

Serious personnel shortages in the IAF also led AHQ (I) to embark on the largest recruitment propaganda drive among the three Indian armed services.[100] Film, a medium which had long been associated with the aeroplane, was deployed to drum up enthusiasm for the IAF. Talented film-makers including Alexander Shaw and V. Shantaram working closely with the Film Advisory Board of the Government of India produced a series of short propaganda movies on the IAF which were screened before the main feature in Indian cinemas.[101] Films like *The Awakening* (1941), *Cavalry of the Clouds* (1942), and *Behind the Wings* (1943) emphasized the glamour and heroism of a career in the IAF.[102] Colonial propagandists were also keen to point out that serving in the IAF during the war could lead to a career in civil aviation. 'Today the IAF is India's first line of Defence' a recruiting leaflet urges 'Tomorrow Civil Aviation is bound to grow with the development of India after the war.'[103] An IAF exhibition unit was formed to drum up enthusiasm for the IAF. The unit travelled the country from one War services exhibition to another in a special train in which it carried aircraft parts to show off to university students. The exhibition usually featured flypast by planes from nearby air force stations and speeches by notable Indians from diverse religious and political backgrounds including the entrepreneur Cowasjee Jehangir, the Nawab of Bhopal Hamidullah Khan, and the scholar-administrator Bhimrao Ambedkar.[104]

---

[98] Chhina, *The Eagle Strikes*, p. 81.
[99] TNA, AIR 23/1973, Expansion … IAF, p. 18.
[100] For a detailed analysis of the propaganda campaign see: Deshpande, *Hope and Despair*.
[101] P. Woods, 'From Shaw to Shantaram: The Film Advisory Board and the Making of British propaganda films in India, 1940–43', *Historical Journal of Film, Radio and Television*, vol. 21, no. 3 (2001), 293–308.
[102] Films accessed at National Film Archive of India, Pune.
[103] TNA, AIR 23/2206 Defence Consultative Committee.
[104] TNA AIR 29/481, No. 1 IAF exhibition unit formed at New Delhi (India) in March 1942.

An official history of the Indian armed forces in the Second World War has lamented that the IAF failed to appeal to Indian patriotism in order to raise recruits for the war effort.[105] This was not necessarily the case since IAF propaganda did in fact appeal to Indian patriotism, albeit in somewhat ambiguous terms. Recruitment advertisements and posters prominently featured Indians operating aircraft or servicing aviation machinery. Care was taken to exclude images of British personnel in government propaganda so as to avoid the suggestion that Indians were being asked to serve in a subordinate capacity.[106] Several IAF posters urged Indians to join the IAF to 'Make India Strong'.[107] Another 1940 poster exhorts pilots to be 'Protectors Today-Pioneers tomorrow' (See Figure 1.7).[108] While such calls can be read as promises to develop rather than free India, placing them in the wider context of the pre-war Indianization debates indicates that IAF propaganda can be read in a variety of ways.[109] As previously seen, no less a staunch imperialist than Lord Linlithgow had conceded the need to appeal to Indian patriotism to mobilize educated Indians for the war, when he called for the rapid expansion of the IAF in 1940. With the outbreak of the war and the growing need for Indian recruits from the educated classes, the government had adopted much of the rhetoric of the pre-war Indianization debates, which held that Indianizing the armed forces, especially the air force, would lead eventually to Indian independence (see Figure 1.8). Slogans like 'Make India Strong' were a tacit appeal to this line of thinking. To be sure AHQ (I) deliberately kept patriotic appeals vague since this had the benefit of allowing them to be read in a variety of ways. Given the political instability of the decade however it is difficult to see what form a more explicit appeal to patriotism could have taken. During the war it was unclear what, if any, kind of independent state may emerge in India after the defeat of the Axis powers. With the Congress leadership jailed and the Muslim League demanding a homeland for South Asian Muslims, vague slogans that could that promised a 'strong' India were a far safer bet for AHQ (I). In any event, the appeal to patriotism would legitimize discourse around a post-colonial future for

[105] Prasad, *Expansion of the Armed Forces*, p. 184.
[106] P. Woods, 'Shaw to Shantaram', p. 299.
[107] 'Make India Strong' poster', Accessed July 17, 2015. http://www.bharat-rakshak.com/IAF/Galleries/History/WW2/Ads/Ad-IAF-Bonds.jpg.html.
[108] 'Protectors Today, Pioneers Tomorrow' Accessed July 17, 2015. http://www.bharat-rakshak.com/IAF/Galleries/History/WW2/Ads/IWI05.jpg.html.
[109] Khan, *The Raj at War*, p. 171.

Figure 1.7 'Protectors today—Pioneers tomorrow'. The IAF embarked on an intensive propaganda campaign aimed at attracting recruits to the force. Posters like this one promised a future career in civil aviation after the war. Via Jagan Pillarisetti

India. It would open up new questions within the force about what form the nation would take and who would represent the new national air force after the war. For the time being, the Government of India had indicated that it was willing to recruit men with nationalist views provided they served the IAF loyally for the duration of the war.

Despite launching the most intensive propaganda campaign among the three uniformed services, the IAF was forced to take a series of desperate

Figure 1.8 This card is an example of the use of patriotic themes by the colonial government in its recruitment propaganda. Appeals to Indians to join the IAF to protect India and 'Make India Strong' were common in wartime propaganda. Via Jagan Pillarisetti

measures to deal with its manpower shortage. Six of ten IAF squadrons had to accept a significant foreign component to remain functional.[110] Recruitment standards had to be reduced and stop-gap measures such as Recruit Education Boards had to be relied on. As physical standards

---

[110] Doe, *Fighter Pilot*, p. 163; Also see for instance: MoD (I), 601/9621/H, ORB No. 8 Squadron, 12 November 1944.

were reduced the IAF was eventually forced to sanction the provision of milk to bring recruits close to the necessary physical standard.[111] There is also reason to believe that less savoury methods were used to recruit IAF personnel. Several IAF tradesmen, for instance, were told that they would fly planes in the IAF despite the fact that they were by definition ground crew personnel.[112] The incomplete expansion of the IAF would have a series of destabilizing political consequences especially once India was plunged into the uncertainties of the post-war political settlement.

The 1946 RIAF Strikes

In 1946 the RIAF was wracked by a series of non-violent strikes across India and Burma. Though the strikes were non-violent and were quickly resolved, they combined with other events that year including the RIN Mutiny and the RAF strikes to hollow out British military power in India. The strikes had a series of causes, nearly all of which could be traced back to the rapid wartime expansion of the force. These included slow demobilization rates, poor working conditions, racial discrimination, and sympathy with the RIN mutineers. The strikes revealed that older scripts of colonial military control which emphasized the need for loyalty to the colonial state in order to win the war and deliver Indian self-government in its aftermath, had seriously broken down. While this undermined British rule it also contributed to a major divide between the officers and airmen of the RIAF.

The RIAF strikes were a consequence of the rapid infusion of educated Indians into the IAF. A report from AHQ (I) fretted that the force had been forced to rely on pilots and airmen drawn 'entirely from the Middle classes of India' whose 'political ideas are uniformly radical'.[113] Despite this, incidents of nationalist protest among RIAF men were vanishingly rare during the war.[114] This was partially because staunch nationalists were not likely to serve in the colonial armed forces and partially because the expansion of the RIAF had, as seen above, positioned its expansion in

---

[111] NMML, *Air Force Instructions* (New Delhi, 1940), p 75.
[112] Saigal, *Birth of an Air Force*, p. 171.
[113] TNA, AIR 23/1973, Expansion … IAF, p. 16.
[114] TNA, AIR 23/5423, AHQ (I) to AHQ (Bengal), All Gps and Independent Units, 1 September 1942.

nationalist terms. The war had necessitated a new script of military control that emphasized the extent to which the growth of the RIAF served the interests of the Indian nation. Educated Indians were promised a strong India in return for wartime service in the RIAF. The rapid expansion of the IAF over a very short period and the instability following the war put this script under great stress.

The year 1946 was a year of profound instability in the Indian subcontinent. Nationalist agitations and communal violence put the Government of India on the defensive. The trials of officers of the Indian National Army, which had fought alongside the Japanese, led to widespread and often violent waves of nationalist protest.[115] The Raj's ability to respond to widespread disturbances was also seriously undermined by indiscipline in its armed forces, both Indian and British. Airmen of the RAF would launch a 'strike' on the 19 January 1946 that would grow to become the largest mutiny in military history, involving 50,000 men from 60 stations from an estimated 60 RAF units from the Suez to Singapore.[116] The 'strikers' demands for faster demobilization would be quickly conceded by the British government and was identified, by both contemporary observers and historians, as a cause for the RIN Mutiny, which occurred only a month later.[117] In February 1946, RIN ratings at Bombay mutinied against harsh working conditions. Like the RIAF, the RIN had also been expanded tenfold to meet wartime needs and much like the RIAF, RIN personnel by the end of the war were deeply disillusioned by their poor treatment. The mutiny would rapidly take on political undertones, melding with wider civilian unrest against wartime measures eventually engulfing over 10,000 RIN men and 66 ships and naval establishments throughout the country. The revolt was eventually put down by

When, in the wake of the Quit India Movement, Aircraftsman Chandra Dutt tendered his resignation to the Officer Commanding, Vizagapatam Air Force Station on 18 August 1942, he was quietly discharged without a court martial. A subsequent order from AHQ (I) read 'The greatest care must be taken by Station and Unit Commanders to ensure that advantage is not taken of this policy by personnel, who do not, in fact hold such political views'. For a similar incident at the RIAF Walton Station see: Saigal, *Birth of an Air Force*, p. 181.

[115] Khan, *The Raj at War*, p. ix–x.
[116] David Childs, *Britain since 1945* (London: Routledge, 2001), p. 20.
[117] Loveday, *RAF and Raj*, p. 100; Spence, 'Beyond Talwar', p. 501.

force, resulting in the deaths of several RIN ratings and perhaps over 250 civilians.[118]

Conditions within the RIAF also made trouble likely. A 1945 joint report by two Indian monarchs tasked with liaising with RIAF men, the Maharaja of Jodhpur and the Nawab of Bhopal, painted a bleak picture of life in the service. 'The treatment of IAF men in mixed squadrons is invidious' the report noted, referring to the racism that many IAF personnel were forced to endure in units in which they served alongside the British. Social mixing between RAF and IAF personnel was essentially non-existent and IAF officers had few opportunities for promotion. The pay gap between RAF and IAF personnel was considerable. IAF airmen were often given poor clothes, living quarters, and salaries. The conditions of Indian Other Ranks (IORs) compared especially badly to their British counterparts who received more leave, railway allowances, and better rations despite doing the same work. The situation was further inflamed by the uncertainty about the force's future that hung over its personnel.[119] Though AHQ (I) was able to address some of these concerns there is little doubt that tensions within the force remained high, as subsequent events would prove.[120]

The first serious strike by RIAF personnel occurred at RAF Station Headquarters, Vizagapatnam on 6 January 1946. The trouble began over a dispute over a music concert. When about one hundred RIAF IORs, seconded to the RAF as part of the substitution scheme, refused to attend an English musical concert on 2 January, this was treated as an act of defiance by their British commanders. The IORs claimed that they were unable to attend the concert since the cost of admission for the concert was very high. British personnel however believed, perhaps rightly, that the IORs were in fact snubbing them since music remained a controversial issue in mixed air force stations. For IAF men the playing of Hindustani music was a means of asserting their national identity while RAF personnel often insisted on playing English music as a means of showing

---

[118] The exact number of RIN personnel and civilians killed during the mutiny is unknown due to its widespread nature and also because no real count was taken at the time by the Government of India. Deshpande, *Hope and Despair*, p. 60.

[119] MMA, Household Records No. 6, Their Highnesses of Bhopal and Jodhpur-Report on Indian Air Force.

[120] MMA, Household Records No. 6, Air Vice Marshal M. Thomas to Air Commodore His Highness the Maharaja of Jodhpur.

their dominance. In these circumstances the seemingly trivial decision of the IORs not to attend an English music concert could be interpreted as a challenge to the British racial dominance of the Air Force Station. The next day RAF officers openly abused the RIAF men as 'silly bastards' and 'black brethren' in front of the British Other Ranks.[121] The RIAF IORs responded by staging a hunger strike to protest racial abuse on 4 January. To punish them for their insubordination, British officers forced the IORs to parade at the double in the afternoon heat, causing many of them to collapse from exhaustion. On 6 January the IORs refused to report for duty. Indian army troops were called in to arrest the strikers who were held for three days. An RAF Group Captain was dispatched to enquire about Indian grievances and managed to allay these enough for IORs to return to work by 8 February. The Station CO was subsequently trans-ferred and several RAF officers were reduced in rank for their inept hand-ling of the affair. No further action was taken against the 'strikers' despite the fact that they had flouted military rules.[122]

The Vizag strike would be indicative of the wider characteristics fol-lowed by the RIAF strikes. First and foremost, the 'strikes' which in re-ality were acts of mutiny were kept scrupulously non-violent. Couching military insubordination in terms of industrial disputes signalled the willingness of RIAF personnel to negotiate returning to work with AHQ (I). Secondly, like the Vizag strike which was led by the IORs, the RIAF strikes were usually limited to airmen. This would have the eventual ef-fect of causing a divide between RIAF officers and airmen. Thirdly, RIAF strikes would be resolved by the government through negotiation rather than force. The Government of India would choose a moderate approach in dealing with strikers. Even in situations, like Vizag, where troops were initially called in to arrest strikers, the government would choose to rely on compromise rather than force in resolving RIAF strikes. This was in stark contrast with the RIN strike which was put down by force. AHQ (I) moderation was, as we shall see, both a consequence of the strikers embrace of non-violent tactics and a consequence of the increasing diffi-culty of enforcing military discipline. This is perhaps best demonstrated

[121] Loveday, *RAF and Raj*, p. 154.
[122] Loveday, p. 157.

by what was by far the most serious wave of RIAF strikes in response to the RIN mutiny.

Strikes broke out among RIAF units at Bombay, Jodhpur, Cawnpore, and Allahabad in response to the RIN mutiny in late February 1946. In Bombay, the rumour that RIAF men might be called upon to bomb the RIN sailors set off serious concerns and resulted in a peaceful laying down of tools and a refusal to work.[123] Peaceful strikes in which RIAF men refused to combat RIN mutineers occurred even at stations as distant from the scene of the RIN mutiny as Kohat in the North West Frontier Province and Madras in the South.[124] Air Marshal Roderick Carr informed Lieutenant General R.M.M. Lockhart, the commander put in charge of confronting the RIN mutineers at Bombay, that he could only rely on RAF squadrons in case it became necessary to sink RIN vessels since RIAF units throughout India were in the midst of a 'sympathetic strike'.[125] While this extreme measure did not ultimately prove necessary it is an indicator of the extent to which British military control in India had been hollowed out. The RIAF strikes along with indiscipline in the RAF and RIN likely contributed to hastening the end of colonial rule. To be sure the Indian army remained loyal and disciplined till the end of the Raj, despite the trials of INA personnel and the communal violence of 1946–1947.[126] It is also true that decolonization was not solely occasioned by the erosion of military control since factors like Britain's adverse balance of payments, the labour victory in British elections, nationalist pressure and the demands of its wartime allies also played a part. Nevertheless, the RIAF strikes along with the RAF strikes and the RIN mutiny showed the limits of Britain's ability to maintain colonial rule in the subcontinent.

While RIAF personnel clearly demonstrated support for what many of them saw as a patriotic mutiny by their colleagues in the RIN, they themselves never chose the path of violent revolt. This lack of violence is explained by a series of factors. First, the RIAF was commanded mostly by Indian officers as opposed to the RIN which was commanded largely by British officers. This is significant since, in the case of the RIN mutiny,

---

[123] RAFM X003-6159/001/002, Bad effect of RIN mutiny, p. 4.
[124] Edwards, *Spitfire Singh*, p. 283; Loveday, *RAF and Raj*, p. 102.
[125] RAFM X003-6159/001/002, Position in Bombay improves, p. 3.
[126] Marston, *The Indian Army and the End of the Raj*, p. 136.

there is some evidence to show that vessels commanded by Indian officers were less likely to mutiny violently.[127] Second, RIAF airmen were better educated than RIN ratings due to the technical demands of the force. The educated recruits, whom AHQ (I) had so dreaded, proved to have more moderate demands and methods than the RIN ratings. RIAF airmen had already begun using strike actions as a means of expressing dissent as early as 2 January 1946, with some success and had little reason to escalate 'strikes' into mutinies.

The RIAF strikes had multiple causes, nearly all of which can be traced back, albeit in complex ways, to the hasty wartime expansion of the force. In addition to sympathy for RIN mutineers, these included grievances over low pay and working conditions, racial discrimination occasioned especially by 'substitution' of RIAF personnel into RAF units. One of the largest strikes, the RIAF strike at Rangoon, is indicative of this. When 140 personnel of the No. 2 Forward Equipment Unit (F.E.U) refused to work on 23 February they put forward a series of demands that were by then common; faster demobilization, higher pay, and better working conditions. As a unit that was forced to work side by side with the RAF, the airmen of the FEU also made a series of demands for more equal treatment. These included equal rights and equal distribution of duties. When the men were assured that their demands would be taken into consideration, provided that they first returned to work, they assented to do so on 28 February.[128] The Rangoon strike is significant not only for its size and foreign location but also for the fact that despite coinciding with the RIN mutiny, the strikers framed their grievances in terms of a labour negotiation rather than a revolt.

In evaluating the causes behind the RIAF strikes both contemporary writers and later historians have implied that they were largely precipitated by the strikes of the British RAF in early 1946. A signal from AHQ (I) tallying the ill effects of the RAF strikes in January 1946 warned that, 'Already their example is being followed by the RIAF'.[129] More recently Daniel Spence has, somewhat puzzlingly, referred to RAF and RIAF personnel going on strike at Drigh Road, Karachi.[130] This despite the fact

---

[127] Spence, 'Beyond Talwar', p. 499.
[128] RAFM X003-6159/001/002, Position in Bombay improves, p. 5.
[129] RAFM, X003-6159/001/001, 'A Brief History of events associated with disaffection and "strikes" among personnel in RAF units, South East Asia Command', p. 16.
[130] Spence, 'Beyond Talwar', p. 501.

that the source he uses to argue about common action between RAF and RIAF personnel, an essay by Norman Harding, makes no mention of the latter.[131] While the RAF strikes no doubt influenced the RIAF strikes, it is important not to overstate the degree of this influence for a number of reasons. First, RIAF strikes in many cases preceded strikes by RAF personnel meaning that the former were not necessarily imitating the latter. The strike at Vizag in the South on the 6 January 1946 coincided with the first known instance of an RAF strike at Bamrauli in the United Provinces and there is no evidence that these were linked.[132] More significantly the Vizag strike preceded the largest and most well-known RAF strike action which began on 19 January 1946 at Mauripur. While major RAF strikes lasted from 17 to 27 January, RIAF strikes, as shall be seen, occurred in sporadic bursts throughout the year.[133] Second, the RIAF strikes were differentiated from the RAF strikes by their utilization of hunger strikes as a major tactic. If British personnel were 'skilled civilians in uniform' drawing from the arsenal of industrial protest to dissent against poor working conditions, then RIAF men were deploying methods gleaned from the arsenal of Gandhian protest.[134] Third, there were no instances of combined strike action by Indian and British personnel. When for instance RIAF IORs came out on strike at the same time as RAF British Other Ranks at Mauripur station on the 23 January 1946, the latter were quick to distance themselves from the former claiming they 'had not incited the IORs to strike and also that they (BORs) were not in sympathy'.[135] The tendency to closely link the RIAF strikes with the RAF strikes prevents a better understanding of the latter, not least by denying the agency of RIAF airmen.

A grave cause for concern within the RIAF was the degree to which the force itself was fragmented on the lines of rank. When Wing Commander Mukherjee, the highest-ranking Indian officer, visited RIAF men striking

---

[131] Norman Harding, 'Odd Events: In 1945–6 and now', Accessed April 17, 2017. https://stayingred.files.wordpress.com/2012/03/odd-events-labour-1945-63.pdf.

[132] RAFM, X003-6159/001/001, 'A Brief History of events associated with disaffection and "strikes" among personnel in RAF units, South East Asia Command', p. 15.

[133] D. Duncan, *Mutiny in the RAF: The Air Force Strikes of 1946* (London: Socialist History Society, 1998), p. 32.

[134] N. Harding, 'Odd Events: In 1945–6 and now', Accessed April 17, 2017. https://stayingred.files.wordpress.com/2012/03/odd-events-labour-1945-63.pdf.

[135] RAFM X003-6159/001/002, 'The Story of the Mutiny at "notorious" Mauripur', p. 2.

in Delhi for better pay since 15 February 1946 he was greeted with hostility. If the avowedly communist *People's Age* newspaper is to be believed, Mukherjee was unpopular with the men for opposing increases in their increment and was seen as a pro-establishment figure. The newspaper further alleged that Mukherjee threatened the men with 'reprisals, prison, beatings and the rest' to no avail. It was only after repeated entreaties from Congress leader Asaf Ali, and another more popular Indian officer, possibly Sq. Ldr Harjinder Singh, that the men resumed work on 21 February. Increasingly, the divisions between high-ranking officers and airmen were playing out in public, in a series of newspaper articles. *People's Age* ran articles praising the discipline of the strikers and lambasting Wing Commander Mukherjee for justifying British policies.[136] The *Bombay Sentinel* responded by criticizing the 'Indiscipline and Discontent' that had manifested itself among the ranks. The paper claimed that the need for armed forces discipline at a time when the nation was subject to cleavages on political and religious lines was of the utmost importance, and that while the government was considering increases in pay, service was of higher importance than pay.[137] An anonymous 'high ranking officer' interviewed by *The Evening News of India* stated that India would soon have its national government and its national army and in these conditions it was imperative that discipline be maintained. Blaming the 'insidious propaganda' on 'misguided and misinformed individuals' he went on to ask whether it was not a great pity that the men who had built up the IAF and 'are at the top of it are being maligned by their own countrymen'.[138] Cleavages on the lines of rank were also increasingly taking ideological undertones, with Communist newspapers supporting RIAF strikes and Congress politicians like Asaf Ali urging patience. This was in keeping with the increasing tension between the Congress Party and the Communists that resulted in a number of violent confrontations between the two parties from 1946 onwards.[139] Daniel Marston has argued that Congress leaders were increasingly concerned about preventing damage to the discipline and reputation of the Indian armed forces they would soon be in command of while the Communists took a more radical

---

[136] PC (JRN), *People's Age*, October 6, 1946.
[137] PC (JRN), *The Bombay Sentinel*, July 11, 1946.
[138] PC (JRN), *The Evening News of India*, June 23, 1946.
[139] See for instance; Times of India, January 30, 1946.

stance. Communist leaders had encouraged violent protests against the trials of men from the Indian National Army, which had sided with the Japanese, while Congress had distanced itself from these despite its apparent support of the INA.[140] The split between nationalist officers and communist ranks in the RIAF also recalled the RIN mutiny where the Communist Party had supported the mutineers while the Congress had called on them to surrender.[141] The clash over working conditions, racial discrimination, and pay reveals a growing gap between high ranking officers, who were prone to taking a longer-term view about the need to establish the IAF as a strong national institution, and the ranks for whom this view was symptomatic of a leadership that had no sympathy for their more immediate needs.

Squadron leader Harjinder Singh, whom we have encountered before, emerged as an intermediary between the upper echelons of the IAF and its ranks. Singh's rise through the ranks would eventually take him to the rank of Air Vice Marshal and his experience of this conflict would make him ideally suited to act as a 'trouble shooter' resolving strikes across the country.[142] At a meeting with the Commander-in-Chief of the Air Forces in India Air Marshal Sir Roderick Carr, Singh suggested a series of measures to combat disaffection among the ranks. He concluded that the airmen were of the 'right type' and needed encouragement from senior Indian officers. The lack of promotions, partly as a result of racial discrimination in mixed units, for Indian Non-Commissioned Officers had caused a breakdown in the chain of command. Further, he asserted that Indian officers 'had ignored the needs of the Indian airmen very badly' and would need to pay more attention to them. Singh also called for measures for greater racial equality, including the raising of pay for Indian airmen, which had fallen well below what their RAF counterparts received for the same work.[143]

The RIAF strikes were caused by a series of factors which can be traced back to the messy expansion of the force during the war. The sheer speed of the expansion had led to a series of inequalities between Indian

---

[140] Marston, *The Indian Army and the End of the Raj*, p. 140.
[141] Meyer, 'The Royal Indian Naval Mutiny', pp. 46–69.
[142] Saigal, *Birth of an Air Force*, p. 221.
[143] PC (JRN), 'Important points raised by Sq. Ldr. Harjinder Singh for discussion with AOC-in-C', 23 June 1946.

and British personnel and between officers and other ranks. The RIAF strikes point to the breakdown of older scripts of colonial military control. During the war the Government of India had accepted the need to appeal to Indian patriotism in order to recruit RIAF personnel from the educated middle classes. Drawing on the rhetoric of Indian nationalists in the interwar years, AHQ (I) had indicated, albeit in ambiguous terms that service in the force would lead to national development and even self-government after the Axis forces were defeated. By the end of the war this script of colonial military control had broken down. Though many officers in the RIAF still considered the force to be the foundation of a free India, airmen were increasingly disillusioned with poor service conditions and racial discrimination. They were also more radical in their support of the RIN mutineers. In a sense by 1946 the anticipation of political independence had outstripped the older argument for institutional loyalty. For many among the new generation of airmen the RIAF's officers were simply 'British toadies'.[144]

The wave of RIAF strikes would last well beyond Indian independence in August 1947.[145] They would eventually sputter out as a result of demobilization and harsher disciplinary action. Prime Minister Jawaharlal Nehru permitted Thomas Elmhirst, Air Marshal Commanding RIAF, to use his powers after saying that 'in an Armed Force there must be discipline and subordination'. Several officers and 'the odd thousand' airmen were sacked. Measures were also taken to increase pay and promotion opportunities. Elmhirst also later implied that the outbreak of war in Kashmir in 1947 helped restore discipline in the RIAF.[146] The war in Kashmir is the subject of the next chapter. Here it is worth noting that the Indian state was only able to restore military control over the RIAF after its transformation from colony to dominion. The RIAF strikes, coming alongside other acts of indiscipline in both the British and Indian military in India, signalled the extent to which the colonial Government of India could not rely on military force to retain control, making the eventual transfer of power inevitable. Rapid IAF expansion had been necessary for

[144] Saigal, *Birth of an Air Force*, p. 220.

[145] *ToI*, October 25, 1947. As late as October 1947, a month after India attained independence, RIAF non-combatant personnel at Cawnpore went on a hunger strike to protest their poor pay and rations.

[146] Chinna, *The Eagle Strikes*, pp. 262–3.

winning the war but also served to rapidly erode British military control in India.

Conclusion

Established as a concession to Indian opinion, the IAF was kept small and limited to policing the Northwest Frontier. The colonial government also did little to support the development of Indian airline companies. The war changed all this. Not only was the IAF expanded but the colonial government itself adopted much of the rhetoric of Indianization. Confronted by the need to wage an unprecedented, highly technologized conflict from a colony, the Indian government was forced to reverse its policies constraining Indian aviation. The IAF expanded tenfold and performed well in the war. Civil aviation would also be mobilized for a conflict without precedent in the subcontinent, portending a major post-war boom.

Despite this the broader structures of colonialism inhibited the expansion of the IAF. Aircraft and recruits were in short supply in the educationally and industrially backward colony. The IAF's manpower woes were further compounded by policies that compensated its personnel poorly and 'substituted' them into RAF units. The IAF's difficult and ultimately incomplete expansion would contribute to a series of peaceful 'strikes' in 1946 that substantially undermined British military control in India.

The war played a foundational role in the establishment of the Indian aviation sector. It left behind a series of complex legacies, many of which were not apparent at the time. What was clear however that the stresses of wartime transformation had resulted in the irreversible decline of the colonial state, not least because of the destabilization of its armed forces. The imminent demise of the colonial state created an atmosphere of grave uncertainty that was to have enduring consequences on aviation. It is to this that we now turn.

2

Ittehad Mein Shakti (Strength in Unity): Aviation and the Partition of India 1946–1947

Some of the most striking images that convey the scale of the Partition of colonial India into the dominions of India and Pakistan were taken from the air. Aerial photographs taken show sprawling rehabilitation camps and winding refugee columns. The aeroplane was an important presence in the story of Partition. However just as in the aerial photographs, the aeroplane is a constant albeit unexamined presence in the wider historiography of Partition.[1] There are a number of reasons for this. The sheer scale of Partition which saw twelve million people displaced from their homes and perhaps as many as two million killed means that several historical perspectives remain to be explored.[2] The immensity of Partition also marginalizes the scale of aviation's contribution to shaping events. Of the 12 million refugees who fled from India and Pakistan the overwhelming majority travelled on the ground, vastly dwarfing the 41,000–50,000 who were flown out.[3] This means that aviation accounts for less

---

[1] See for instance: Gopal Das Khosla, *Stern Reckoning: A Survey of the Events Leading up to and Following the Partition of India* (New Delhi: OUP, 1952); Yasmin Khan, *The Great Partition The Making of India and Pakistan* (New Haven: Yale University Press, 2007); Ayesha Jalal, *The Sole Spokesman: Jinnah, the Muslim League, and the Demand for Pakistan* (Cambridge: CUP, 1985); Joya Chatterjee, *Bengal Divided: Hindu Communalism and Partition* (Cambridge: CUP, 1994); S. Wolpert, *Shameful Flight: The Last Years of the British Empire in India* (Oxford: OUP, 2006); Haimanti Roy, *Partitioned Lives: Migrants, Refugees, Citizens in India and Pakistan, 1947–65*, (Oxford: OUP, 2012); I. Talbot and Singh, *The Partition of India* (Cambridge: CUP, 2009); Wazira Zamindar, *The Long Partition The Long Partition and the Making of Modern South Asia: Refugees, Boundaries, Histories* (New York; Chichester: Columbia University Press, 2007); Venkat Dhulipala, *Creating a New Medina: State Power, Islam, and the Quest for Pakistan in Late Colonial North India* (Cambridge: CUP, 2016).

[2] U. Butalia, *The Other Side of Silence: Voices from the Partition of India* (New Delhi, Penguin books, 1998), p. 3.

[3] The total number of Indians and Pakistanis evacuated by air is difficult to calculate with certainty. Three major evacuations occurred between 31 August and 30 November. RAF aircraft evacuated approximately 9,200. 'Operation Pakistan' involved the evacuation of 6,300 people.

The Aeroplane and the Making of Modern India. Aashique Ahmed Iqbal, Oxford University Press.
© Oxford University Press 2023. DOI: 10.1093/oso/9780192864208.003.0003

than 1 per cent of the total number of those who were evacuated from one dominion to another during Partition. In this context it is worth asking why a study of the role of aviation in Partition should be undertaken?

This chapter argues that the aeroplane played a small but highly crucial role during the division of British empire in India into the independent dominions of India and Pakistan. The elite nature of aviation is uniquely revealing of the actions and anxieties of states dealing with, the violence of Partition, a catastrophe of almost incomprehensible magnitude. Aviation offered a relatively safe and extremely rapid means of transport to the governments of India and Pakistan. However, aircraft were limited in number and expensive to fly, meaning that both governments had to carefully prioritize who was evacuated. Moreover, the versatility of aircraft meant that refugee evacuation was only one of many tasks to which limited aviation resources had to be assigned. Control of aviation was critical in the struggle of the newly independent states of South Asia to emerge as legitimate governments with a monopoly on violence. The extensive use of aircraft in the restoration of order in the face of mass violence in 1947 would inextricably intertwine aviation technology with novel centripetal notions of sovereignty in both India and Pakistan. If the aviation sector affected Partition in important ways, then it was fundamentally reconstituted and transformed by the events of 1947. Partition created the postcolonial Indian and Pakistani air forces and put the private aviation sector on the path to terminal decline.

This chapter is divided into two broad sections. First it will look at the consequences of Partition on both civil and military aviation. From 1946 onwards, the political confrontation between the Muslim League and the Congress over Partition undermined carefully laid post-war plans for the regulation of civil aviation. Once the decision to partition the subcontinent was taken in June 1947, the Royal Indian Air Force (RIAF) was 'reconstituted' at break-neck speed into the independent air forces of India and Pakistan. The second half of this chapter will focus on the role aviation played in Partition. The RIAF would be playing a vital role in quelling disorder and aiding refugee evacuation, serving as an important

'Operation India' resulted in the evacuation of 35,000. It is not possible to make a total however since RAF aircraft took part in both Operation India and Operation Pakistan. Some overlaps are therefore likely to have occurred. Further, there is some variance in the figures themselves due to the often ad-hoc nature of the mass evacuations.

force multiplier for independent states confronted with increasingly militarized mass violence. Civil aviation meanwhile was pushed to breaking point by the mass evacuations made necessary by Partition. The eventual decision by the governments of India and Pakistan to hire foreign airlines in 1947 to expedite the transfer of government officials critical to the refugee evacuation effort was as much a grudging acceptance of the failure of Indian civil aviation as it was of the unforeseen need to exchange populations as a consequence of Partition.

Aviation played a small but critical role in the state-making that accompanied independence and Partition. Little work has explicitly dealt with this aspect of Partition despite the constant presence of the aeroplane in literature on the subject. This chapter will as such attempt to trace the ways in which aviation transformed South Asia and was itself reconstituted in 1947. In doing so it seeks to provide a more holistic understanding of the ways in which Partition played out by recovering the centrality of aviation in both technological and institutional terms. In order to understand these processes however the story of the aeroplane in India must be located in the post-war context of increasing instability.

Prelude to Partition: The Failure of the Tymms Plan

The Second World War was a period of difficulty for civil aviation companies since their planes and pilots were effectively commandeered by the colonial state to serve the war effort. Wartime conditions placed severe strains on airlines as planes and the personnel to operate them became increasingly scarce. The war absorbed nearly all pilots and trained ground personnel and the suspension of flying training meant that it became difficult to replace them. However, as seen in the previous chapter, the war was not entirely detrimental to the civil aviation sector. The Indian government would come increasingly to understand the critical importance of civil aviation as for wartime communications. Consequently, the government dedicated resources to ensure that the civil aviation sector remained functional. Steps were taken to provide the two largest civil aviation companies, Tata Air Lines (TAL) and Indian National Airways (INA), with additional aircraft and personnel before the end of the war.[4] An aviation wing of the Central Public Works Department (CPWD) was set up exclusively to provide infrastructural support for civil aviation. By the end of the war INA and TAL were flying more routes with more planes and personnel than they had ever before.[5]

The war's end would usher in an unprecedented boom for Indian civil aviation. Indian airline companies gained access to a large pool of experienced aviators being demobilized by the RIAF and to cheap aircraft left behind by the departing United States Army Air Force.[6] In 1946 the Indian government purchased all aircraft and equipment designated as surplus by the United States Army and Navy Liquidation commission. Tata Aircraft Ltd were then designated as Government Agents for the sale of aircraft to companies and individuals.

Arguably the most important aeroplane left behind by the Americans was the Douglas DC-3 Dakota transport aircraft (see Figure 2.1). The Dakota, or 'Dak' for short, was a remarkable twin-engine passenger aircraft that had taken part in the famous 'Hump' operations, aimed at flying supplies over the Himalayas from India to Nationalist China during the Second World War.[7] Designed to fly long distances at high altitudes, the Dakota would become ubiquitous in India after the war partly because of its relative cheapness and partly because of its durability. It would, as shall be seen, play a critical role in the history of the subcontinent over the next decade. Dakotas rapidly replaced Beechcraft C-45 Expeditors and De Havilland 89 Dominies in the inventories of Indian airline companies on most air routes in 1946.[8] Tata Air Lines, purchased 12 DC-3 aircraft for itself from the liquidation commission in January 1946 and placed an order for ten more.[9] Later that year TAL went public with a

---

[4] TNA, BT 217/32, DCA to Secretary for Posts and Air, 31 August 1945.
[5] TCA, T53-DES-AVI-A2-2, Wartime Operations.
[6] *Centenary of Aviation in India*, p. 17.
[7] J.D. Plating, *The Hump* (College Station, Texas A & M University Press, 2011), Accessed online on April, 18, 2017. https://ebookcentral.proquest.com/lib/oxford/detail.action?docID= 3037902, -.
[8] *Flight*, 5 December 1946.
[9] These included orders for a number of variants of the aircraft including eight C-47s, two C-53s, and two C-58s. *Flight*, 10 January 1946.

Figure 2.1 A Douglas Dakota Aircraft belonging to TAL being serviced in the hangar. Purchased from the United States Army Air Force, the Dakota or Dak for short play a key role in Indian aviation history transporting refugees during partition and troops during the Kashmir conflict. Courtesy: Tata Central Archives.

capital of 50 million rupees (3.75 million pounds) and was renamed Air India Ltd.[10] INA meanwhile not only acquired a fleet of Dakotas but commenced an ambitious programme of expansion by ordering six Vickers Viking VC 1 aircraft from Britain. With its 24-passenger capacity the Viking could carry nearly double the number of passengers as the 14 passenger Dakota. The first of six Viking aircraft, christened *Jumna*, was dispatched to India in August 1946.[11] Its purchase is indicative of the highly optimistic, even bullish, outlook for civil aviation at the time.

---

[10] TCA, Tata Sons Air India Formation Papers.
[11] *Flight*, 15 August 1946.

Table 2.1   Air routes operated by Indian airline companies in April 1939

Airline Company	Air routes
Air Services of India	Bombay-Kathiawar and Bombay-Poona-Kolhapur.
Indian National Airways	Karachi-Lahore and Lahore-Delhi.
Indian Transcontinental Airways*	Karachi-Jodhpur-Delhi-Allahabad-Gaya-Calcutta.
Tata Sons Ltd	Karachi-Bhuj-Ahmedabad-Bombay-Hyderabad, Hyderabad-Madras-Trichinopoly-Colombo, Trivandrum-Trichinopoly, Bombay-Goa-Cannanore-Trivandrum and Bombay-Indore-Bhopal, Gwalior-Delhi.

Note *: Indian Transcontinental Airways was owned partly by Imperial Airways and partly by Indian National Airways as a link of the trans-imperial air route.

Table 2.2   Air routes operated by Indian airline companies in June 1946

Airline company	Air route
Air India	Karachi-Ahmedabad-Bombay, Bombay-Hyderabad-Madras-Colombo, Delhi-Ahmedabad-Bombay and Bombay-Nagpur-Calcutta
Indian National Airways Ltd	Calcutta-Allahabad-Cawnpore-Delhi, Delhi-Lahore-Rawalpindi-Peshawar, Delhi-Jodhpur-Karachi, Lahore-Quetta-Karachi, Lahore-Jodhpur-Bikaner-Ahmedabad and Delhi-Rampur-Lucknow
Air Services of India	Bombay-Jamnagar-Bhuj-Karachi, Bombay-Bhopal-Gwalior-Cawnpore-Lucknow, Porbandar-Jamnagar, Jamnagar-Ahmedabad and Bombay-Bhavnagar
Deccan Airways	Delhi-Gwalior-Nagpur-Hyderabad-Madras and Hyderabad-Bangalore
Mistri Airways	Bombay-Nagpur-Calcutta

By the end of 1946 India's four major airlines were operating over 14 routes totalling 11,608 miles. This marked an unprecedented expansion of the number of air routes being operated by Indian companies. Below are two tables of air routes operated by Indian airline companies. Table 2.1 covers air routes operated in 1939, the year before the outbreak of the war and arguably the zenith of pre-war Indian aviation.[12] Table 2.2 is a

[12] *Flight*, 27 April 1939.

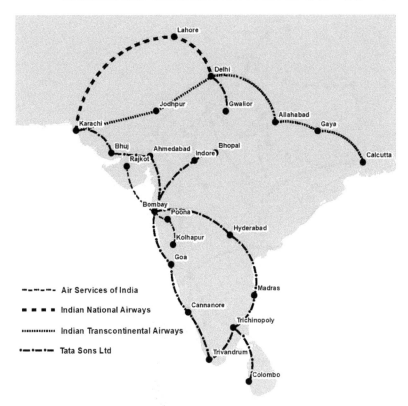

Figure 2.2 Air routes operated by Indian airline companies in April 1939.
Figure created by Prashant Arya.

summary of air routes operated by Indian commercial airline companies in 1946, the year following the war.[13]

Clearly the number of routes under operation had grown greatly from 1939 to 1946 (see Figures 2.2 and 2.3). The frequency of flights also increased. Bombay emerged as India's leading air hub with flights twice daily to Karachi and Delhi. A passenger boarding at Santa Cruz aerodrome could fly with Indian airlines to destinations as varied as Calcutta, Karachi, and

---

[13] TNA, BT 217/32, Joint Secretary (GoI) to Undersecretary of State, 11 October 1946.

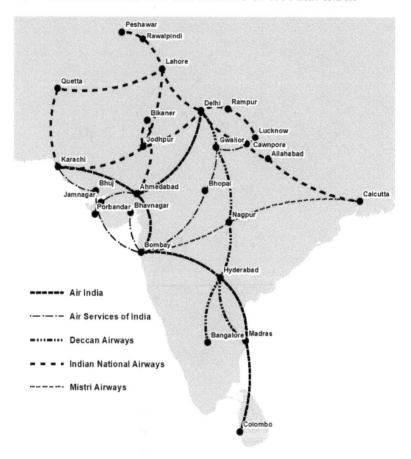

Figure 2.3 Air routes operated by Indian airline companies in 1946. Figure created by Prashant Arya.

Madras. INA began flying 34 Hajj pilgrims from Karachi to Jeddah in late 1946 under an agreement with the Government of India.[14] This marked a break with the colonial government's pre-war policy of limiting the services of Indian airline companies to India and Burma. It is likely that the government granted permission for this since Indian civil aviation had in any case been used during the war to ferry British personnel to West Asia.[15]

---

[14] TNA, BT 217/32, Secretary (GoI) to Undersecretary of State, 21 May 1947.
[15] Lala, *Beyond the Last Blue Mountain*, p. 107.

While Air India and INA remained the premier airlines with some 63 per cent of all Indian air traffic, Deccan Airways, founded in 1946 to represent Hyderabad State, also became prominent along the North-South route.[16]

Indian airline companies were not the sole beneficiaries of the end of the war. The Director General of Civil Aviation (DGCA) came to possess aerodromes, equipment, and greater regulatory authority following the war. The Harewood Overseas Air Terminal Committee, set up by the government, recognized the growth in the stature of the office of Director of Civil Aviation by recommending that it be raised to the DGCA. It also advised the bifurcation of the DGCA into two divisions—aircraft (operations and engineering) to oversee technical matters and an airways branch to manage civil aviation.[17] The DGCA was offered its pick from the vast network of aerodromes constructed during the war. It took over 28 aerodromes in 1946 bringing the total number of aerodromes at its disposal to 50. These included 2 international, 7 major, 14 intermediary, and 27 minor aerodromes.[18] Radio stations along the trans-India route, which had been controlled by the British Overseas Airways Corporation (BOAC), were handed over to the DGCA as the British personnel manning them were repatriated. Indeed, the DGCA came into possession of so many communications facilities, aerodromes, and navigational aids that it simply did not have the personnel to man them. Consequently, staff from the Department of Posts and Communications were transferred to help the DGCA in its new responsibilities.[19] As the DGCA grew in size it took on new responsibilities including the establishment of an Air Transport Licensing Board in order to bring aviation in India in line with international standards.

Deciding which airline would operate which routes was critical to ensuring the continued profitability and therefore the viability of civil aviation and had been at the centre of the DGCA's post-war planning. The increasing profitability and falling costs of investing in commercial aviation drew a number of new players. Several of these were established

---

[16] The airline receives detailed treatment in a subsequent chapter and as such it will suffice to state here that the Tata's had a stake in Deccan Airways and that it was founded as a department of the Nizam's State Railway. See: Reddy, *Aviation in the Hyderabad Dominion*.

[17] *Centenary of Civil Aviation in India*, p. 19.

[18] *The Aeroplane*, April 7 1947.

[19] TNA, BT 217/32, Secretary (GoI) to Undersecretary of State, 21 May 1947.

industrial magnates looking to invest wartime profits made in fields other than aviation.[20] These included established business families not unlike the Tatas, such as the Dalmia Jain family and the Birlas who had prospered greatly during the war. Also represented were much smaller operators such as the proposed Varadaraja Airways based out of Tiruppur in Southern India and Kalinga Airways based in Cuttack. The latter of these two, Kalinga airways, was founded by the famed aviator and future chief minister of the Indian state of Orissa, Biju Patnaik. A former RIAF pilot who had earned a two-year jail term in 1943 for aiding Indian nationalists against the British, Patnaik would become a national icon after a daring flight, in July 1947 to fly Indonesian nationalists to Delhi in the teeth of resistance from that country's Dutch colonizers.[21] Biju Patnaik's story is an interesting example of the pan-Asian solidarities forged by anti-colonial movements. His decision, like that of many other small operators, to set up an airline, in 1947, is reflective of the sense of promise the airline business inspired at the time. The Air Transport Licensing Board, which came into existence in October 1946, was flooded with applications for the establishment of airline companies, receiving a total of 97 applications from 20 companies for 78 proposed routes. In the normal course of affairs most of these would have been rejected by the DGCA in keeping with what came to be called the Tymms plan.

When he retired in 1947, Sir Frederick Tymms had headed India's Civil Aviation Directorate for over 15 years. Tymms had begun flying with the Royal Flying Corps in the Great War in 1918 and had worked for the Air Ministry after the war where he had among other things helped set up air routes in Africa.[22] Arriving in India as Director of Civil Aviation in 1931 he had played an active part in encouraging the growth of civil aviation in the country and was particularly close to both J.R.D. Tata and Neville Vintcent of Tata Airways.[23] As early as 1943, while the Second World War was still raging, Tymms had taken 18 months leave from the post of Director of Civil Aviation in order to begin planning for the future of

[20] For a discussion of wartime fortunes see: Khan, *The Raj at War*, p. 118.

[21] 'Biju Patnaik: the two time Odisha chief minister who was a RAF pilot in World War 2', *The Print*, https://theprint.in/theprint-profile/biju-patnaik-the-two-time-odisha-chief-minister-who-was-raf-pilot-in-world-war-2/201326/, Accessed 9 July 2021.

[22] Ernest A. Johnston, *To Organise the Air* (Cranfield: Cranfield University Press, 1995), p. 29.

[23] CUL, RCS/RCMS/1/2/1/6, Neville Vintcent, CBE, DFC.

civil aviation after the war.[24] The result of his efforts was a paper entitled 'Post-War Civil Aviation in India', usually referred to as the Tymms Plan. The plan aimed to reduce operating costs so that the thus far unprofitable commercial aviation sector could become self-supporting. This was especially important because until airlines became self-sustaining, the government would have to bear not only the costs of maintaining aviation infrastructures such as aerodromes, signals, and meteorological facilities but also have to pay subsidies to keep aeroplanes flying. Though post-war profitability was certainly rising, airlines continued to lose money and continued to require government support. The Tymms plan called for four key measures to be taken to reduce costs. First, airlines would have to conduct more frequent operations, flying at least daily on routes designated as trunk routes and operating by night whenever possible. Second, airlines would have to operate the largest and most modern aircraft that they could. This would allow them to adopt the most recent technical methods that enabled cost reduction. The durability and relatively low maintenance costs of the DC-3 Dakota aeroplane which was being widely adopted at the time could play a role here. Third, airline companies would have to operate a series of essential air routes ranked according to priority as Trunk, links between Trunks and local air service routes (see Figure 2.4) listed as follows:[25]

Trunk Routes

1. Karachi-Bombay-Madras-Colombo
2. Calcutta-Allahabad-Cawnpore-Delhi-Peshawar-Kabul
3. Delhi-Nagpur-Hyderabad-Madras
4. Calcutta-Cuttack via Madras-Colombo
5. Bombay-Nagpur-Calcutta
6. Karachi-Jodhpur-Delhi
7. Bombay-Ahmedabad-Delhi

---

[24] Johnston, *To Organise the Air*, p. 97; For other accounts of the Tymms plan see, Singh, *History of Aviation in India*, p. 59; Nayyar, *The State and International Aviation in India*, pp. 52–3.
[25] NMML, G. Rajadhyaksha et al., Report of the Air Transport Enquiry Committee 1950, (New Delhi, 1950), p. 8.

8. Bombay-Indore-Bhopal-Cawnpore-Lucknow
9. Calcutta-Akyab-Yenangyaung-Rangoon

Essential Links between Trunk Air Routes

10. Karachi-Quetta-Lahore
11. Calcutta via Sylhet-Tezpur-Dinjan
12. Madras-Bangalore-Cochin-Trivandrum

Local Air Services

a) Ahmedabad-Kathiawar states
b) Hyderabad-Bombay
c) Hyderabad-Bangalore
d) Lahore-Srinagar

This would 'constitute a route mileage of 11, 280 miles involving a total capacity of approximately 17 million ton-miles a year', significantly reducing costs.[26]

Perhaps most importantly for the ton-miles being envisioned as ideal the total air fleet would need to consist of no more than 35 planes, 60 to 70 aircrews and 400–500 engineers and mechanics.[27] While other planes could be accommodated, particularly in short hops or taxi flying, it was important to keep the number of routes limited to the above number. This, combined with the eventual adoption of better aircraft and the prioritization of passengers, mail, and freight in that order, would mean that within a period of five years the cost per ton-mile could be reduced from Rs 2 to Rs 1/8. Airlines could thus reasonably expect to move from a combined loss of Rs. 160 lakh to a profit of Rs. 13 lakh in five years; more than doubling revenue.[28]

---

[26] NMML, G. Rajadhyaksha et al., Report of the Air Transport Enquiry Committee 1950, (New Delhi, 1950), p. 9.
[27] CUL, GBR/00115/RCS/RCMS 20/1/2/1/6, Frederick Tymms, *Post War Civil Aviation in India.*
[28] NMML, Rajadhyaksha et al., *Report of the Air Transport Enquiry Committee*, p. 8.

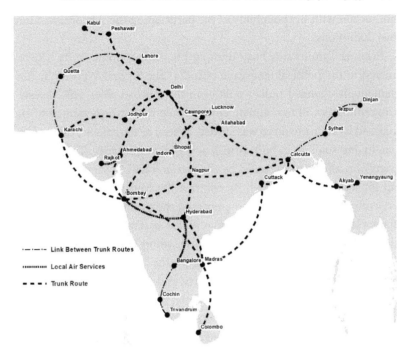

Figure 2.4 Air routes proposed by the Tymms Plan 1946. Figure created by Prashant Arya.

Finally, Tymms advocated continued private control of commercial aviation with adequate safeguards, since he felt that it afforded the still young aviation sector a fair degree of flexibility. In order to technically and commercially regulate private commercial aviation, he proposed the formation of an Air Traffic Licensing Board in 1944, which would eventually be formed in 1946.[29] This final point of the Tymms plan was remarkable for the foresight with which it approached the difficulties likely to occur from the grant of excess licenses. In the words of Tymms' biographer: 'In report after report, paper after paper written in the decades to follow, tribute was paid to the eminent soundness of these plans.'[30] However the Tymms plan was aimed at services in a united India and did

---

[29] CUL, E.A. Johnston, GBR/00115/RCS/RCMS 20/1/3, *Life and Tymms*, (Manuscript), p. 553.
[30] Ibid., p. 563.

not reckon with the possibility of the partitioning the subcontinent into two dominions.

Even as Tymms was busy drafting his plan, tectonic shifts had occurred in the political landscape of India. The Second World War fundamentally changed Indian politics in three broad ways. His Majesty's Government's will to maintain colonial rule was severely dented by the war and its ability to do so was eroded, as seen in a previous chapter, inter alia by indiscipline in both British and Indian militaries. The Congress party was effectively silenced by the war and had to scramble to make up for lost political capital. By contrast the Muslim League had been enormously strengthened and embraced the goal of a separate Muslim state. Elections held in March 1946 revealed an unprecedented divide between Hindus and Muslims with the latter voting overwhelmingly for the Muslim League and the former voting for the Congress.[31] Negotiations, between the British, the Congress party, and the Muslim League, failed to yield a consensus on the constitutional future of India. The need for such a consensus became greater as communal violence on an unprecedented scale erupted in several parts of Northern India from August 1946 onwards. An attempt at a compromise between the Congress and Muslim League was made in October 1946, with the entry of Muslim League politicians into the Congress-led interim government that had been formed to govern India as British rule came to an end. The entry of Muslim Leaguers into the interim government proved fateful for aviation as Abdur Rab Nishtar, a Muslim League politician, was made minister for Posts and Air. Nishtar's entry into office in October 1946 coincided with the establishment of the Air Transport License Board and he therefore became responsible for overseeing the Tymms Plan.

According to the plan, air services which existed on 1 July 1946 were to automatically receive route licenses for the routes operated by them from the ATLB on 1 October, the date from which the ATLB began functioning. The Tymms Plan's requirement for about four airlines had thus been largely catered to by the existence of INA and Tata Airways as well as the formation before July 1946 of Air Services of India, owned by the

---

[31] For an accessible introduction to Indian politics in 1946 see: Sumit Sarkar, *Modern India 1885–1947* (New Delhi: Macmillan, 1983).

magnate Walchand Hirachand, and Deccan Airways.[32] Nishtar however granted licenses to 21 companies with an authorized capital of 42 crores and a government authorized issue of 97 crores.[33] Instead of the compact fleet of 35 aircraft that Tymms had visualized, by early 1947 India had 115 aeroplanes operating a plethora of routes run by 11 companies including those that existed in July 1946.[34] These included:

1) Air India
2) Indian National Airways
3) Air Services of India
4) Deccan Airways
5) Dalmia-Jain Airways
6) Bharat Airways
7) Airways (India)
8) Mistri Airways (Later Indian Overseas Airways)
9) Orient Airways
10) Ambica Airways
11) Jupiter Airways

Aviation became a zone for speculation and profits dropped so greatly in future years that both Jupiter and Ambica Airways were forced to shut down by bankruptcy. To point to just one example of how steeply operating costs had risen, Ambica Airways which was liquidated in 1947, estimated that it spent Rs. 3/9/6 per mile greatly diverging from Tymm's hope that costs would decrease from Rs. 2 per ton mile to Rs. 1/8.[35] Nishtar's decisions as minister for Posts and Air disregarded the Tymms plan and plunged the aviation sector into a long-term crisis.

Nishtar's reasons for granting a large number of licenses are impossible to establish with certainty. It is possible that he was attempting to keep airlines from earning excessive profits and establishing monopolies. His Congress predecessor as Minister Syed Ali Zaheer had argued

---

[32] Walchand also has the distinction of starting India's first aircraft, automobile, and ship building factory. He features prominently in chapter IV.
[33] NMML, Rajadhyaksha et al., *Report of the Air Transport Enquiry Committee*, p. 12.
[34] Ibid., p. 13.
[35] NMML, Rajadhyaksha, p. 20.

that the interim government would attempt to curb monopolies. Unlike Nishtar however Zaheer had warned against the proliferation of airlines and warned that permission to set up an airline was by no means a guarantee of being assigned a route.[36] It is also possible that Nishtar was concerned about the low number of 'Muslim companies' and sought to prepare for the eventuality of Partition which might necessitate airlines to serve Pakistan. Mohammed Ali Jinnah, leader of the Muslim League, had met with Mirza Ispahani in June 1946 to discuss the possibility of the establishment of an airline that could later serve as Pakistan's flag carrier. Orient Airways was provided with a license in June 1947 and went into operations on the Calcutta-Akyab-Rangoon route in 1947 with two DC-3 Dakotas. This tiny airline would form the nucleus of the flag carrier of independent Pakistan; Pakistan International Airways.[37] Along with Pakistan's fledgling air force, it would constitute the air bridge between the two units of the new state, East and West Pakistan, separated by over 1000 miles of Indian territory.

What cannot be ignored, however, is the context of extreme distrust and violence in which Nishtar served as minister. The Muslim League-Congress coalition was underpinned by extreme distrust as Hindu-Muslim violence swept North India. When Nishtar discussed the possibility of nationalising private airlines in the legislature, he was confronted by fellow Muslim Leaguer A.R. Siddiqui, who enquired what nationalization might mean when the nation was a yet undefined entity. As the *Times of India* reported, 'Mr A.R. Siddiqui confessed that nationalisation created a terror in him, because it raised among other things questions about the meaning of a nation and so on.'[38] Nishtar served in a government that many in his party saw as representing Congress and therefore Hindu interests. It is not as such unlikely that Nishtar sabotaged the Tymms plan in order to deliberately damage the interim government in pursuit of the Partition of the subcontinent.[39] Damaging the civil aviation sector could have served to wreck the working of the

---

[36] 'No Monopolies in Civil Aviation' *Times of India*, October 1, 1946. Proquest.

[37] 'PIA History', Accessed April 18, 2015. http://www.piac.com.pk/pia_about/pia-about_history.asp,.

[38] 'Nationalisation Principle is Salutary', *Times of India*, November 18, 1946. Proquest.

[39] This is the view of Tymms biographer Ernest A. Johnston who in turn attributes it to J.R.D. Tata. See: Johnston, *To Organise the Air*, p. 129.

interim government moving Congress and the British closer to Partition. There is some evidence for this view. Nishtar had strained relations with Frederick Tymms and refused to designate a successor for the critical office of the Director of Civil Aviation when the latter retired. He also refused to fill in other critical DGCA posts such as those of two Deputy Generals.[40] Nishtar would not be the only Muslim League minister in the interim government to enact policies aimed at making Partition inevitable. Liaquat Ali Khan's interim 'socialist' budget of the same year deliberately hamstrung Congress ministries in the interim government and targeted many of that party's wealthy supporters.[41] The interim budget, like Nishtar's jettisoning of the Tymms plan, signalled the unwillingness of the Muslim League to work with Congress in a unified India after independence, speeding up Partition.

The failure of the Tymms plan was a serious blow to the profitability and hence the viability of private commercial aviation companies in India. The failure to adopt it severely hurt the prospects for the establishment of a profitable civil aviation sector in India and would, as a later chapter will show, contribute to the eventual nationalization of the sector in 1953. However, it is important here to note that the plan was not without its shortcomings not the least of which was its rigid conceptions of the post-war order. It refused to consider the possibility that colonial India might be divided into several successor states as evidenced by Tymms' insistence in 1945 that an independent Hyderabad could not be accommodated.[42] It assumed that private operators were most well suited to conduct commercial aviation in India. This was partly a result of Tymms closeness to private operators such as the Tatas with whom he had worked in 1942 on an abortive project aimed at setting up an aircraft factory in India.[43] Tymms opposition to nationalization was also underpinned by his 15 years of experience in India, during which the government had made minimal investments in aviation. Tymms could simply not have conceived of the enormous state investment in aviation that the

---

[40] CUL, GBR/00115/RCS/RCMS 20/1/2/1/6, Tymms to Nishtar, 27 March 1947.

[41] Raghabendra Chattopadhyay, 'Liaquat Ali Khan's Budget of 1947–48: The Tryst with Destiny.' *Social Scientist*, vol. 16, no. 6/7 (1988), 77–89.

[42] CUL, GBR/00115/RCS/RCMS 20/1/2/1/6, Frederick Tymms, *Post War Civil Aviation in India*, p. 19.

[43] Johnston, *To Organise the Air*, p. 96.

Congress Party would undertake after independence. Still the failure of the plan as a side effect of the politics of Partition was indicative of the dysfunction that had come to characterize relations between India's two largest political parties. In late 1946 and early 1947 it was unclear what shape a postcolonial state or states might take, though it was increasingly certain that India's two greatest parties, and the communities they claimed to represent, were heading for a confrontation.

The Reconstitution of the RIAF

Dysfunction among India's leading parties and mass violence between its largest religious groups convinced the newly appointed British Viceroy Lord Louis Mountbatten on 3 June 1947 to announce the Partition of colonial India into two independent dominions. Both the Indian National Congress and the Muslim League had been persuaded to accept the 'Mountbatten plan' in an effort to avoid further bloodshed. This would lead to the creation of two new states and two new air forces on the Indian subcontinent. Before discussing the process of the reconstitution of the RIAF into two separate air forces, it is important to locate the process in its wider historical context.

The end of the Second World War was a period of both great promise and great instability for the RIAF. As seen in a previous chapter, 1946 was characterized by a number of 'strikes' and a widening rift between officers and the ranks revealed itself. If the force had been affected adversely in certain ways by the war, it was also larger and more entrenched than ever before. The RIAF had grown from one to ten squadrons between 1939 and 1946. A paper put forward to the Consultative Committee on the Defence of India in September 1946 outlined plans to maintain and build upon this growth. While it was optimistic about the prospects of nationalization and expansion, the paper also noted that this expansion would be impossible without the RAF's help. Because of the speed of its wartime expansion the RIAF had been unable to develop its own maintenance organization. The short period of time available as well as the quality of recruits to the RIAF during the war prevented this.[44] The

---

[44] See Chapter I for a discussion of manpower shortages afflicting the IAF.

RIAF's 15000 strong force of airmen hid the fact that it was desperately short of skilled Group I tradesmen and Non-Commissioned Officers (NCOs).[45] If the RAF withdrew from the subcontinent the RIAF would find it difficult to maintain even one of the ten squadrons it had.[46] As such the paper suggested that the nine RAF squadrons present in India at the time be liquidated and their personnel transferred to help train the RIAF. The committee hoped that the RIAF would be able to help turn out Group I tradesmen and NCOs in about five years. It recommended that an apprentice school should be opened in India and Indian personnel ought to be sent to England for training. India would publish terms of service for RAF personnel who chose to stay on after independence. If enough volunteers were not found Britain would have to consider forcing its personnel to stay on in India.

Not unexpectedly the RAF response was one of shock and dismissal. Service in India was 'intensely and universally unpopular' in the RAF, Air Chief Marshall John Slessor wrote to Hugh Walmsley the Air-Officer-Commanding, Air Forces in India. Only a year earlier some 50,000 RAF personnel had staged perhaps the largest military mutiny in modern British history by going on strike in order to protest the slow rate of demobilization.[47] As seen in the previous chapter this mutiny was highly successful in speeding up the rate of repatriation of British personnel from India while making it clear that RAF personnel had no appetite to police the empire. Once the state of war with the Axis powers which was in force was repealed there would be no way to force RAF personnel to serve in India.[48] There was also the pressing need to redeploy the available RAF personnel at a time when the force was rapidly demobilizing. Nevertheless the RAF in particular and HMG were not totally unresponsive to the needs of the RIAF. Recognizing that 'India has no hope whatever of building an Air Force without outside assistance' Slessor emphasized the benefits and indeed the necessity of supporting the RIAF through its transition.[49] HMG's attitude to the Indian proposal 'must be

---

[45] BL, Mss Eur IOR Neg 15538, Slessor to Ismay, undated.
[46] BL, Mss Eur IOR Neg 15538/1, Paper presented to the defence consultative committee, undated.
[47] See Duncan, *Mutiny in the RAF.*
[48] BL, Mss Eur IOR Neg 15538, Slessor to Walmsley, 21 January 1947.
[49] BL, Mss Eur IOR Neg 15553, Mountbatten to Ismay, 9 October 1947

governed by the fact that it is very much in our interest to link India to us strategically and to see that she looks to the RAF to help her in building the RIAF.[50] Central to the British stance on helping train the RIAF was the hope that India would stay in the Commonwealth and would continue to provide Britain with the same military support that it had before independence.[51] British military planners plainly saw the Commonwealth as a military alliance in which the Dominions would continue to serve Britain's needs.[52]

Moreover, HMG was especially concerned about the possibility of leaving Indian defences weak. Undivided India abutted the Soviet Union, sparking British Cold War fears. If the 'ludicrously small' RIAF was unable to protect India it might well fall on the RAF to send its own squadrons to protect India from Soviet aggression.[53] British fears of the Soviet Union intervening were fundamentally misplaced but they shaped policy nevertheless. Thus while the scheme to volunteer a large part of the RAF in India for training the RIAF was rejected the RAF had good reasons to provide support to the RIAF for several years after independence.[54] India would not receive large numbers of RAF personnel, particularly since it was believed that this would only perpetuate the existing imbalance of expertise in the RIAF.[55] However the RAF would take what measures it could to support the growth of the RIAF.

Any plans to expand the RIAF had to be shelved when, in June 1947, Field Marshall Claude Auchinleck, the Commander-in-Chief of the Indian army, was ordered to preside over the division of the armed forces

---

[50] BL, Mss Eur IOR Neg 15553, Mountbatten to Ismay, 9 October 1947.
[51] Chandrashekhar Dasgupta, *War and Diplomacy in Kashmir* (New Delhi: Sage, 2002), p. 13. Undivided India's strategic Western airfields were especially attractive to British strategists since they offered facilities at which to base aircraft to attack the USSR.
[52] BL, Part I (b), Mss Eur IOR Neg 15542, Defence of India and Pakistan. India would provide airbases to the United Kingdom and provide troops for Commonwealth military operations. In return she would could use British scientific knowledge, resources, and experience. British planners were especially concerned about the possibility of a future Soviet nuclear weapons attack against a badly defended India.
[53] BL, Mss Eur IOR Neg 15538, Slessor to Walmsley, 21 January 1947.
[54] Ibid.
[55] Harjinder Singh, who would later rise to the rank of Air Vice Marshal, vehemently contested this view and believed that Indian ground crews were capable of maintaining their own aircraft. The fact that independent India's first RIAF commander-in-chief Air Marshal Sir Thomas Elmhirst requested a contingent of no more than seven RAF personnel to help organize the RIAF indicates that Singh may not have been mistaken. See: Saigal, *Birth of an Air Force*, p. 227.

of colonial India. Auchinleck had been a proponent of the widely held view in British Indian military circles that if Partition were to occur the armed forces ought not to be divided for a period of a few years since the logistical challenges of separating the Indian military between the dominions would be formidable.[56] He would later turn down a peerage for his role in dividing the armed forces since he considered this to be a fundamentally dishonourable task.[57] Moreover, there were compelling reasons from the British perspective to oppose the division of the Indian military. A united Indian military would be better able to defend the sub-continent from the Soviet Union. It would also be able to serve as a more cohesive expeditionary force for the Commonwealth, which British military planners saw as a military alliance.[58]

The prospect of dividing the RIAF was particularly unappealing given its still relatively small size. In the words of the Air Vice Marshal Robert Blucke, Mountbatten's acting air officer:[59]

> It is considered that the Partition of the RIAF into two forces to serve the independent states of Pakistan and Hindustan will lead to the dis-integration of the RIAF as it now exists to an extent that will leave India well-nigh defenseless against air attack for a period of years which cannot be estimated.

The non-communal organization of RIAF units down to the lowest levels meant that it would be hard to reform units with any level of functionality after they were separated.[60] The communal composition of the force presented distinct problems, especially to Pakistan. The following Table 2.3 is demonstrative.

Only 28 per cent of the officers and 24 per cent of the airmen were Muslim. Assuming that all Muslims would opt for Pakistan, far from a certainty, it was unclear how many Sikhs and Hindus would opt for

---

[56] Shahid Hamid, *Disastrous Twilight* (New Delhi: Lee Cooper, 1993), p. 163.

[57] Hamid, *Disastrous Twilight*, p. 258.

[58] Sharmila Singh, *Partition of the Indian Armed Forces between India and Pakistan*, PhD thesis, Jawaharlal Nehru University [hereafter JNU]), 1994, p. 84.

[59] Mss Eur IOR Neg 15538, Planning for partition-Armies of Hindustan and Pakistan.

[60] This was in contrast to the Indian army which due to the martial races doctrine featured 'class' based units that could be more easily divided on communal lines. See: S. Wilkinson, *Army and Nation*, (Cambridge, 2015).

Table 2.3 Composition of the RIAF on 1 March 1947

	Officers	Men
Hindu	588	9657
Muslim	230	3041
Sikh	142	790
Non-Muslim (Anglo-Indians, Parsees etc)	320	3205
Total	1380	16693

Source: Mss Eur IOR Neg 15538, Future of Air Forces in India.

Pakistan. The position of the 'non-Muslims' such as the Anglo-Indians was also ambiguous. Pakistan was unlikely to be able to possess the personnel required to man the equipment allotted to it. This was especially bound to be the case when taking into consideration the skill of the ground crews available. Pakistan could at most count on the services of three Engineering officers and four signals officers. There were no Muslim armament officers. India by comparison could count on considerably larger reserves of Hindu, Sikh, and other 'non-Muslim' technical personnel available.[61]

The ultimate decision to split the armed forces in time for independence was taken at the insistence of the Muslim League once the overarching principle of Partition was accepted. Writing to Mountbatten in April 1947, Liaquat Ali Khan had opposed the scheme of nationalization of the armed forces on which the interim government had embarked, arguing that this would lead to a reduction of Muslim personnel in the army even as Muslim representation in the RIAF and Royal Indian Navy (RIN) remained low. He famously said that, 'Without its own Armed Forces Pakistan would be a house of cards.'[62] Khan would later circulate a plan that he had written for the division of the armed forces. Mohammed Ali Jinnah insisted to Mountbatten that 'the begin all and end all' for Pakistan was to have its own army, and nothing short of this could possibly satisfy

---

[61] Mss Eur IOR Neg 15538, Future of Air Forces in India.
[62] Liaquat Ali Khan to Mountbatten, 7 April 1947. Quoted in Nicholas Mansergh eds, *Transfer of Power*, vol X (New Delhi, Stationery Office, 1970–83), p. 151.

them. At least one historian has argued that the demand for the division of the military was a stratagem aimed at securing tacit British acceptance for the principle of separate states and perhaps it was.[63] However it is also worthwhile remembering that Muslim League leaders came from a broader Indian political tradition that saw control of the armed forces as the ultimate marker of sovereignty. They had witnessed and taken part in the Indianization debates of the interwar years and understood the armed forces to be both symbolic and instrumental embodiments of the sovereignty of India. Jinnah had, along with Motilal Nehru, been one of the key members of the 1926 Skeen committee which had recommended, among other things, the entry of Indians into the air force as a means to guarantee eventual self-rule in India.[64]

There was considerable opposition to the division of the Indian armed forces from both the Congress and the British, as represented by Lord Mountbatten. A united Indian military would be better equipped to aid Britain in its confrontation with the Soviet Union as part of the Commonwealth.[65] Congress for its part opposed any plans for the division of the armed forces until Partition itself was finally agreed upon. Jawaharlal Nehru compared the division of the army to the failed dyarchy system that had caused administrative dysfunction during the war.[66] The decision to partition the armed forces was only arrived at during a meeting on 25 April 1947, following the acceptance of the principle of Partition by both Mountbatten and the Congress leadership.[67] The armed forces of colonial India would cease the process of nationalization and begin to be divided on the lines of 'class' a euphemism for religion. Significantly, Jinnah was adamant that personnel ought to be permitted to opt for which dominion they wished to serve, regardless of religion, with the sole caveat that a Hindu from India could not serve in Pakistan and a Muslim from Pakistan could not serve in India.[68] This was

---

[63] Singh, *Partition of the Indian Armed Forces between India and Pakistan*, p. 89.

[64] BL, Andrew Skeen et al., *Report of the Indian Sandhurst Committee* (London, 1927).

[65] Singh, *Partition of the Indian Armed Forces between India and Pakistan*, p. 84. Not all British policy makers opposed the division of the armed forces. Sir Francis Tuker, perhaps the commander with most experience of combating communal violence in India drew up a Partition plan as early as 1946. See: Mary Wainwright, 'Keeping the Peace in India 1946–47; The role of Lt General Tuker in Eastern Command', C.H. Philips eds, *Partition of India: Policy and Perspectives 1935–47* (London: Allen and Unwin, 1970), pp. 127–147.

[66] Singh, *Partition of the Indian Armed Forces between India and Pakistan*, p. 91.

[67] Ibid., p 93.

[68] Hamid, *Disastrous Twilight*, p. 185.

in keeping with Jinnah's belief that Pakistan would be a multi-religious state as well as the fact that even as late as June 1947 no exchange of populations had been seriously envisioned. Further, Jinnah was almost certainly aware of the significant gaps in Pakistan's military that would be caused by the departure of all non-Muslim elements to India. Since the RIAF was expected to suffer heavy losses to civil aviation a questionnaire regarding RIAF personnel's plans was sent out and the government considered compelling men to stay if it felt there was going to be too large an exodus. RIAF personnel, like other government servants, were asked whether they would serve the dominion of India or Pakistan.[69] In order to prevent the demoralization of the Indian military, the expert committee that would oversee the division of the armed forces was euphemistically named the Armed Forces Reconstitution Committee (AFRC) rather than the Armed Forces Partition Committee.[70]

The reconstitution of the RIAF under the AFRC has been the subject of scholarly attention.[71] As such a summary of the negotiations followed by a brief analysis will suffice. The AFRC was set up under the chairmanship of Field Marshal Auchinleck and consisted of four committees dealing with the army, the RIN, the RIAF, and financial details. Chaired by Air Vice Marshal Perry Keene the Air Force reconstitution committee's members included Air Commodore G.W. Birkenshaw, Air Commodore S. Mukherjee, Group Captain A.M. Engineer, Wing Commander M.K. Janjua, and Squadron Leader M.A. Khan. It also included Wing Commander Arjan Singh and Flight Lieutenant H.U. Bhatty as Joint Secretaries while S. Jayashankar and Mumtaz Mirza were recruited as advisers for the committee later.[72]

The subcommittee decided that on 15 August 1947 two new air forces, the RIAF and the Royal Pakistan Air Force (RPAF) would be created with separate headquarters based at New Delhi and Rawalpindi.[73] Air Headquarters, Supreme Command based at New Delhi would continue to administer a number of joint subjects until they could be devolved

---

[69] MoD (I), 601/14476/H, *Partition Proceedings,* vol. V, Third meeting of Partition council, 5 July 1947.
[70] Singh, *Partition of the Indian Armed Forces between India and Pakistan,* p. 97.
[71] Ibid.; Kumar, *An Incredible War;* Hussain, *History of the Pakistan Air Force 1947–82.*
[72] Kumar, *An Incredible War,* p. 14.
[73] The RPAF did not actually move to Rawalpindi and its Air Force Headquarters remained at Peshawar well into the 1970's. Hussain, *History of the Pakistan Air Force 1947–82,* p. 26.

piecemeal to the air forces of the Indian Union and Pakistan. Since both dominions would retain specialized maintenance facilities it was agreed that the Indian Union would continue to repair its Tempests in Pakistan while Pakistan would be permitted to have its Dakota aircraft repaired at Bangalore.[74]

However, disagreements cropped up over the division of equipment for fighter squadrons. Indian Union representatives on the sub-committee claimed that India was due eight out of ten squadrons' shares of equipment, in keeping with the communal composition of the RIAF in which non-Muslims outnumbered Muslims 80:20. Pakistani representatives argued that Pakistan ought to receive enough equipment to constitute five squadrons since Pakistan would have to defend the vulnerable North West Frontier. At the heart of the dispute was the question of whether squadrons ought to be divided on the basis of the communal make-up of the forces that they were drawn from or whether strategic necessities should dominate redistribution of the forces. G.S. Baljia, the Additional Defence Secretary, stated that communal ratios should ultimately determine the division of equipment though details could be negotiated. Pakistani representatives countered by stating that the communal ratio represented nothing other than the composition of the RIAF in 1947 and that this was hardly immutable.[75] Vice Admiral Geoffrey Miles who chaired the naval sub-committee weighed in by pointing out that the RIN had received more ships than the numbers of her non-Muslims merited because of the fact that India had a larger coastline and hence needed vessels for strategic reasons.[76]

A committee comprising Wing Commander Janjua, Air Commodore Mukherjee, and Group Captain Barnett found the problem intractable. Hence it was sent to the Provisional Joint Defence Council (PJDC) to resolve. A series of solutions to Pakistan's vulnerability on the North West Frontier were considered by the PJDC including the possibility of India lending two squadrons to Pakistan in case of an emergency. This proposal, brought by Mountbatten before Mohammed Ali Jinnah and Vallabhbhai Patel, failed when Patel insisted that RIAF squadrons could

---

[74] Kumar, *An Incredible War*, p. 15.
[75] MoD (I), 601/14476/H, *Partition Proceedings*, vol. V.
[76] Kumar, *An Incredible War*, p. 17.

not be used to bomb tribals in the North West Frontier since Congress was opposed to this policy. Jinnah responded by pointing out that ammunition from Indian ordnance factories, which Congress had agreed to provide Pakistan, would doubtless be used against the tribesmen.[77] Eventually the impasse around the division of equipment was resolved when Mountbatten suggested that Pakistan be allotted enough equipment for one transport and one fighter squadron. In addition to this, equipment would be gathered for it from all-India stores for a third fighter squadron. While this was bound to reduce the overall number of spares that were available it would allow Pakistan to field three squadrons while India would receive eight.[78]

Negotiations conducted around the reconstitution of the RIAF are remarkable for their inconsistency. Once Partition was accepted in principle, negotiators on both sides jockeyed to maximize the military resources their state could gain from the negotiations. A consequence of this is the inconsistent negotiating positions adopted by Indian representatives. In the case of the RIN where the presence of a large number of Muslim seamen made communal ratios relatively disadvantageous as a basis for reconstitution, Indian representatives argued that India's large coastline meant it should receive more sloops, mine sweepers, and survey ships. In the RIAF where Muslim representation was lower, the communal ratio was treated as the key basis for arguing for a larger share of squadrons. This was representative of the widespread inconsistency that characterized much of Partition from the negotiations around office supplies to those around princely states. The absence of agreed principles governing the division of assets meant that bilateral negotiations between India and Pakistan had to proceed without the benefit of either precedent or mediation. Needless to say, this was a recipe for conflict since it meant that both India and Pakistan could make competing claims to an asset with little regard to consistency. Whereas the vast majority of bilateral negotiations between the two nascent states, including those over the RIAF, produced acceptable resolutions, when deadlocks occurred there was simply no mechanism to resolve these amicably. The future confrontation

---

[77] MoD (I), 601/14476/H, *Partition Proceedings*, vol. V
[78] Kumar, *An Incredible War*, p. 20.

between India and Pakistan over Kashmir would see two states ruled by former lawyers arguing over the finer points of a non-existent law.

Whatever the relative gains, both air forces suffered as a consequence of reconstitution. The independent RIAF would not have access to the majority of pre-independence equipment depots since these were based in Pakistan. The RPAF would be unable to use its old training bases, with the exception of the Chaklala parachute training school, since these were based in India.[79] That these two air forces proved ready for operations in the coming months is a tribute to both their professionalism and improvisational skills.

Independent Air Forces

The day of India's independence, 15 August 1947, was suffused with deep ambiguity for the men of the two newly created air forces. The process of completely separating the two air forces had not been completed and many of the newly re-designated Indian and Pakistani airmen found themselves in the wrong country. The ceremonial fly past over India Gate and the Red Fort, a symbolic assertion of Indian independence and sovereignty, was not solely an Indian affair. Photographs from that day show what appear to be B-24 Liberator bombers flying over the Red Fort. The RIAF had no heavy bombers in its inventory at the time, meaning that British planes with British crews played an important part in India's Independence Day ceremony. The British presence in India was far from ended by the grant of formal independence and as later chapters will show decolonization took considerably longer than is understood. More remarkably a number of planes flown over New Delhi as part of the Independence Day parade were piloted by Muslim pilots from Ambala air station, who were waiting to be sent to Pakistan. Some of these were part of a 'JAI HIND (Victory to India)' formation flown overhead millions of cheering Indians.[80]

The date 15 August 1947 not only marked the creation of a new dominion but also the creation of two new successor air forces. The RIAF

---

[79] Kumar, *An Incredible War*, p. 23.
[80] Zafar A. Chaudhury, *Mosaic of Memory* (Lahore, Z.A. Chaudhury, 1985), p. 14.

and RPAF were new air forces with new staff headquarters. The RPAF self-consciously defined itself as a new air force in keeping with the wider narrative of Pakistan as a new homeland for South Asia's Muslims. As Faisal Devji has argued that Pakistan, like Israel, made claims to being a new nation forged through a common ideological will rather than through more traditional claims of geographical and cultural contiguity.[81] The RIAF and its histories have, in contrast, often stressed continuities with the colonial Indian Air Force. The force continues to celebrate 8 October 1932 as Indian Air Force day.[82] This is in keeping with a wider narrative that emphasizes the continuities between independent India and the colonial state. Partha Chatterjee for instance has argued the postcolonial state appropriated the 'universal rationality' enshrined in the colonial state by retaining 'in a virtually unaltered form the basic structure of the civil service ... and the armed forces as they existed in the colonial period'.[83] Independent India in this view retained colonial institutions with the addition of a new programme of 'development' which legitimated the new state and differentiated it from its colonial predecessor. Chatterjee is correct in pointing out the many continuities between colonial and postcolonial institutions such as the military. There is no doubt that the post-independence RIAF, like the RPAF, inherited personnel, equipment, and doctrine from the pre-independence RIAF. However, it is worth examining ruptures in addition to continuities. Indeed, it can be argued that the post-independence RIAF was in several respects a new institution. The RIAF like its Pakistani counterpart had a new headquarters, whose staff had been largely Indianized, which began operations shortly after independence. Based in 'temporary hutments' in the defence ministries H Block the RIAF had to raise new Group Headquarters from scratch in order to run independent India's air force.[84] Of the original ten senior squadrons from before independence the RIAF lost four. No. 2 Squadron,

---

[81] Faisal Devji has shown how Indian political philosophers in the period before the Second World War considered the nation-state to be an unsatisfactory model around which to organize an independent Indian polity because of its exclusionary nature. Indeed, the colonial period permitted more expansive thinking on the nature of the state due to the necessarily multi-ethnic nature of Empire. Devji, *Muslim Zion*, p. 71.

[82] 'Air Force Day 2019: Here's what you can expect from 87th IAF day'. *NDTV.com*. Accessed 29 August 2020.

[83] Chatterjee, *The Nation and Its Fragments*, p. 203.

[84] Kumar, *An Incredible War*, p. 26.

the second oldest of the RIAF's units, was disbanded in December 1947 after it left its equipment behind in Pakistan following Partition.[85] No. 6 Squadron, which was training to serve in air transport, was also disbanded in 1947 when it left behind its Dakotas in Pakistan.[86] Both units would subsequently be 're-raised' in India in the 1950s. No. 9 Squadron would become the sole RIAF squadron to be maintained by the RPAF.[87] The most distinguished unit of the RIAF, No. 1 Squadron was disbanded by the RPAF, as will be seen.[88] Many of the IAF's most important stations, including Drigh Road, Karachi, where the IAF had first been raised in 1933, would not lie in India. Perhaps most importantly the force's religious composition underwent an important shift as a consequence of Partition. While the IAF remains arguably the most inclusive of the independent India's armed forces, the proportion of Muslims in the force underwent a radical reduction during its reconstitution.[89] It is also possible to argue that the inclusiveness of the force underwent a qualitative change. This is demonstrated by the change of the motto of No. 1 Squadron IAF.

As a result of Partition, No. 1 Squadron IAF was allotted to the RPAF. The squadron was the first and for long the only squadron of the colonial RIAF. It had served two tours of duty with in the Second World War and it is no exaggeration to say that it was the most distinguished squadron in the force. Instead of adopting the squadron after independence however Pakistan disbanded it on 14 August 1947, the day before the RPAF was created, in a deliberate attempt to distance itself from the RIAF. The story of No. 1 Squadron did not end there however since independent India re-designated No. 15 Squadron as No. 1 Squadron in 1953, with much of the same regalia. One minor change however was revealing. The pre-independence No. 1 Squadron's motto had been *Ittehad mein Shakti*

---

[85] Bharat Rakshak, 'No. 2 Squadron'. Accessed August 29, 2020. http://www.bharat-rakshak.com/IAF/units/squadrons/2-history/2-squadron-winged-arrows.html#gsc.tab=0

[86] Bharat Rakshak, 'No. 6 Squadron'. Accessed August 29, 2020. http://www.bharat-rakshak.com/IAF/units/squadrons/6-6-squadron.html#gsc.tab=0.

[87] Kumar, *An Incredible War*, p. 20.

[88] Chhina, *The Eagle Strikes*, p. 252.

[89] The first post-independence study of figures for the number of Muslims in the Indian Air Force was conducted in 2006. The Sachar committee report's findings on Muslims in the Indian armed forces were withheld on the request of the Ministry of Defence. See: Rajinder Sachar et al., *Social, Economic and Educational Status of the Muslim Community in India: A Report* (New Delhi, 2006), p. xiii.

Figure 2.5 The crest of No. 1 Squadron RIAF. The squadron's motto was changed from '*Ittehad Mein Shakti*' (Unit in Strength) which combined Urdu and Sanskrit to the more Sanskritized '*Ekta Mein Shakti*' after independence. © USI of India

or 'Unity in strength' (see Figure 2.5). This combined the Urdu *Ittehad* meaning unity with the Hindi *Shakti* meaning strength. This was especially significant in the context of the Hindi-Urdu controversy which had pitted Urdu speaking Muslims against Hindi-speaking Hindus at the turn of the century.[90] Attributed variously to both Sir George Cunningham, the Governor of the North West Frontier Province where it had first served and to Wing Commander Karun Krishna Majumdar, the motto, that included both languages, the IAF's first squadron clearly signalled the unity and equality of India's two largest communities.[91] When No. 1 Squadron was raised after independence its motto was changed to *Ekta mein Shakti*.[92] While the meaning of the motto remains the same, the complete shift to Sanskritized Hindi is revealing of the less inclusive nature of the independent Indian Air Force even at the peak of Nehruvian secularism. This was even as the IAF remained arguably the most inclusive of independent India's armed forces, having featured multiple commanders-in-chief from India's minorities. By extension the change in No. 1 Squadron's motto is also illustrative of the ruptures between the postcolonial Indian state and its predecessor of the same name.

Indian independence, as a result of Partition, was imbued with an inescapable poignancy for air force men that statistics barely capture. RIAF personnel had been given a choice in July 1947 to choose which dominion they wished to serve with. A total of 896 officers, 10,350 airmen, and 820 non-combatants opted for the RIAF while 224 officers, 2189 airmen, and 407 non-combatants chose the RPAF.[93] Not all men went where their communities were the majority. Idris Latif, a Hyderabadi chose to stay in India even though his Muslim colleagues told him he would be unsafe in India and would receive great promotions in Pakistan. He would later hold the distinction of being the first and only Muslim commander of any Indian armed service, when he was appointed as Chief of Air Staff in 1978.[94] Two Hindus remained in the RPAF.[95] For many of the smaller

---

[90] Sekar Bandopadhyay, *From Plassey to Partition* (New Delhi, 2004), pp. 242–3.

[91] Sapru, *Combat Lore*, pp. 561–2.

[92] Bharat Rakshak, 'No. 1 Squadron'. Accessed August 29, 2020. http://www.bharat-rakshak.com/IAF/units/squadrons/1-squadron-tigers.html,.

[93] Hussain, *History of the Pakistan Air Force 1947–1982*, p. 21.

[94] Reddy, *Aviation in the Hyderabad Dominions*, p. 92.

[95] Kumar, *An Incredible War*, p. 34.

'non-Muslim' communities it was unclear as to which country to choose. In at least one case two brothers from an Anglo-Indian family opted for different air forces.[96] Parsees however overwhelmingly chose to serve India and one of them, Aspy Engineer would become the second Indian to hold the position of Chief of the Air Staff in the IAF.

Partition often had a personal impact on RIAF and RPAF personnel. It was near impossible even for men in the armed services to avoid being affected by the violence, that by August 1947 had engulfed much of North India. Zafar Chaudhury, was stationed as a flying instructor at Ambala air station in September 1947 while awaiting the move to Pakistan. He was instructed by his family to travel to Calcutta to extricate his aunt and her three daughters, one of whom was his fiancé, from the riots that were affecting the city. Chaudhury flew to Allahabad from where he took the train to Calcutta. He was relieved that although the passengers abroad the train, 'endlessly talked of the racial violence in India and Pakistan and gave accounts of what they had seen and heard, the journey itself was uneventful.'[97] The newly married Sergeant A.L. Saigal, aged 24, had to leave his native city of Lahore along with his wife as the communal situation worsened in August 1947. After a short 20-mile journey, during which Saigal feared the worst, they arrived in Amritsar to find that the red brick railway station had transformed into a refugee camp.[98] S.M. Ahmad's plane would crash land at Halwara on his way to Ambala. There he would find himself stranded in a Muslim village 'where the injured, maimed and mutilated bodies were pouring in at intervals'. For four days Ahmad would organize the village defences and himself conduct patrols armed with a *danda* (big stick), before being rescued.[99] No doubt many men lost loved ones to the violence accompanying Partition. Squadron Leader O.P. Mehra's uncle Barkat Ram Mehra, for instance, was stabbed to death in Lahore in early 1947.[100]

The increasingly embittered communal relations in the force manifested themselves in a variety of ways, especially during the 'reconstitution'. Wing Commander M.K. Janjua invited six RIAF officer cadets to

[96] 'Derek O'Brien on minorities of India and Pakistan', *India Today*. http://indiatoday.into day.in/story/derek-obrien-minorities-of-india-and-pakistan/1/212816.html,-accessed 20/4/15.

[97] Chaudhury, *Mosaic of Memory*, p. 15.

[98] Edwards, *Spitfire Singh*, p. 303.

[99] S.M. Ahmad, *A Lucky Pilot: Memoirs of Wing Commander Lanky Ahmad* (Lahore: Ferozsons, 1997), p. 25.

[100] Mehra, *Memories Sweet and Sour*, p. 64.

a party celebrating Pakistan's independence on the 14 August 1947 at Risalpur. When the same six cadets approached the officers mess the next morning they were allegedly confronted by Janjua and two Sten gun-wielding guards. Janjua ordered the Indians of the base exclaiming 'Gentlemen! The officer's mess of the Pakistan Air Force is off limits to Indian pigs'. If the men had left Risalpur by train they would very likely have been attacked. The tense situation was only defused by the arrival of Wing Commander Asghar Khan, the most senior RPAF officer on the station. Asked what was happening RIAF officer Verghese Kurian responded, 'Sir, We would prefer to be killed right here on the airbase rather than be butchered on the way back in the trains'. After harshly reprimanding Janjua, Khan had the Indians airlifted back to India that day.[101]

Pakistanis would complain that the RIAF never quite delivered all the aircraft and equipment that had been allotted to the RPAF by the AFRC. Of the 35 Tempest aircraft assigned to Pakistan 5 never arrived. Three aircraft were found to be unserviceable and two simply disappeared.[102] RIAF ground crews were also alleged to have filled the tanks of RPAF aircraft with sugar as they made their way to Pakistan.[103]

Partition's consequences were especially tragic for the RIAF because they created a rift between Muslim and non-Muslim personnel who had served together in a force that had always celebrated inclusivity. From its formation the RIAF had been envisioned as an All-Indian service. Indian legislators who had lobbied the RIAF into existence had consciously sought to distance the force from the earlier martial races policy and even the colonial authorities had conceded the unacceptability of recruiting exclusively from the 'enlisted classes'.[104] The RIAF had been first among the Indian forces to have mixed messes for its officers and had served as a symbol of a modern India in which men from different communities served together for the national good. Visiting No. 6 Squadron during the Second World War *The Bombay Chronicle*'s war correspondent propounded that view when he noted:[105]

[101] Bharat Rakshak. George Verghese Kurian, 'Partition Troubles', Accessed 29 August 2020. http://www.bharat-rakshak.com/IAF/history/1950s/1208-kuriyan.html#gsc.tab=0.

[102] Singh, *Partition of the Indian Armed Forces between India and Pakistan*, p. 133.

[103] BL, MSS Eur D670/6, Diary entry, 21 September 1947; M. Ahmad, *A Lucky Pilot*, p. 30.

[104] CS, *Council of State Debates* (New Delhi, 1933), p. 354.

[105] Dosabhai Framji Karaka, *The Bombay Chronicle*. Quoted in T.S.R. Chinna, *The Eagle Strikes*, pp. 138–9.

Out there where our men are doing a first-class job in the shape of eliminating a powerful enemy they do not speak the language of our communal leaders. This is gratifying for it lays the foundation of the new India. This India, which is out there on the airstrips of Burma and Arakan, is on the march—a disciplined India of that newer generation which is growing up from a conglomeration of communities into a nation.

Indeed, the inclusivity and diversity of the RIAF had been advertised during the Second World War to ensure recruitment.[106] To be sure claims of inclusivity in the RIAF had always papered over politico-religious differences. Harjinder Singh recalled an instance where he was forced to complain about an Indian officer who was maligning a particular religion, most likely Islam, for being 'nothing but barbarism'.[107] Politico-religious differences in the force that had always simmered came to the surface with the drawn-out reconstitution of the air forces. These circumstances make those instances when the men from the air forces aided each other all the more remarkable.

Wing Commander Asghar Khan was living with his wife in Ambala air force station awaiting his transfer to Pakistan in late August 1947. A South Indian technical officer named Nair was allotted Khan's house and pending his departure for Pakistan agreed to live with Khan as his guest. The Khans spent a few pleasant days with Nair and his wife before preparing to depart on 23 August 1947. Nair insisted that trains were too unsafe for Khan to take and personally requested RPAF chief Air Marshal Perry Keene to fly Khan and his wife out of Ambala. Khan would later learn that Muslims evacuated by train on 23 August had been massacred and that in insisting that he be flown out Nair had almost certainly saved his life.[108] Even more remarkable is the story of Harjinder Singh's journey to Pakistan to pick up spares for Indian aircraft in October 1947. RIAF Tempest aircraft lacked critical tools to service their Centaurus engines which had not yet been moved to Karachi. Singh therefore rang up his RPAF counterpart M.K. Janjua, who agreed to permit Singh to fly in and

---

[106] See for instance: NFAI, *Planes of Hindustan* (Film, 1940); NFAI, *Cavalry of the Clouds*, (Film, 1941).
[107] Saigal, *Birth of an Air Force*, p. 31.
[108] Asghar Khan, *My Political Struggle* (Oxford: OUP, 2008), pp. 5–6.

take the tools he needed. When Singh flew in to Karachi on 22 October however Janjua met him at the air field and warned him that tribal raiders backed by Pakistan had invaded Kashmir. War could very well break out between the two dominions and Singh was not safe in Pakistan. Instead of sending Singh back to India empty-handed, however, Janjua merely asked Singh to send his plane back. Singh was then locked in a hangar where he spent the day dividing the tools. His RIAF plane would return in the evening to fly him back to Amritsar with critical equipment that would then be used in the conflict in Kashmir between India and Pakistan.[109] While the incident is remarkable in itself, what makes it nearly incredible is the fact that Janjua was the same RPAF commander alleged to have ejected Indians from Risalpur air station the day after independence. Given Janjua's co-operation with Singh in the matter of the Centaurus tools it appears unlikely that he did indeed eject the RIAF cadets from Risalpur in 1947. However, there is no way to establish this and given the contradictory nature of much of Partition, it is possible that the same man who threatened Indians the day after independence was willing to provide them with military equipment for use against his country at a later date.

Reconstitution of the two air forces would give way to war in October 1947 and this is the subject of a later chapter. Much of the writing on Partition, perhaps rightly, emphasizes the shift from unity to war when discussing the Indian military in 1947.[110] However it is also worth emphasizing that the division of institutions was a longer process with often contradictory results. Pallavi Raghavan's assertion that partition was characterized by co-operation alongside conflict is borne out in the case of the reconstitution of the Indian Air Force.[111] India and Pakistan continued to remain in the Joint Defence Council well into 1948, not least to ensure that reconstitution was a success. The governments of both countries were forced, partly as a result of reconstitution, to work together despite deep mutual hostility. Another factor that compelled the governments to co-operate was the threat of being consumed in chaos by

---

[109] Saigal, *Birth of an Air Force*, pp. 230–1.

[110] For a sentimentalist instance of this see: Dominic Lapierre and Larry Collins, *Freedom at Midnight* (London: Granada, 1983), p. 234.

[111] Pallavi Raghavan, *Animosity at Bay: An Alternative History of the India-Pakistan Relationship, 1947–1952* (London: Hurst and Company, 2020).

the communal violence accompanying Partition and it is to this that we now turn.

Indian Aviation in Partition

There is a growing consensus in recent scholarship emphasising the continuities between Partition and the Second World War. This strand demonstrates how the Second World War militarized Indian politics and society and shaped the violence accompanying Partition. Daniel Marston convincingly argues that the demobilization of the Indian Army led to the release of thousands of men with military experience who came to be closely associated with 'various political militias'.[112] Mary Wainwright has shown that rioters in 1947 could count on vast stocks of arms and ammunition, much of which was left behind by the departing Allied armies.[113] William Gould has shown how sectarian militias, better armed than ever before, inflicted unprecedented levels of mass violence on the 'Other' in pursuit of explicitly political goals. Militias such as the Rashtriya Swayam Sevak Sangh, the Muslim League National Guard, the Khaksars, the Akalis, and the Ahrars had been drilling to 'defend' their communities in the political uncertainty that followed the war.[114] It was only a matter of time before the many political agitations that rocked India in 1946 gave way to widespread communal violence, in August that year. Heavily armed militias conducted organized campaigns aimed at cleansing their regions of minorities. This had the effect of embittering and accelerating constitutional negotiations. The final acceptance of the decision to partition colonial India by major political parties would in large part be explained by their hopes that this would stem the flow of violence that by June 1947 was already dangerously widespread.

The division of the subcontinent led to unprecedented violence as majorities in both India and Pakistan turned on minorities in order to

---

[112] Marston, *The Indian Army and the End of the Raj*, p. 279. There is also evidence that a number of rioters were serving personnel in the military of the princely states, many of whom actively abetted mass violence. Hamid, *Disastrous Twilight*, p. 163.

[113] Wainwright, 'Keeping the Peace', pp. 127–147.

[114] William Gould, *Hindu Nationalism and the Language of Belonging in India* (Cambridge: CUP 2004), pp. 165, 235.

ethnically cleanse their states. Little stopped them from doing so. As a consequence of decisions taken considerably before Partition, British forces were not used in order to maintain law and order in the dominions. This was ostensible because the dominions were independent and the use of British forces would be seen as an attempt to prolong imperial rule.[115] Civilian organs of the state such as the judiciary and the police were often too overwhelmed by the violence to deter it on those occasions when they did not actively sympathize with the mob. In these circumstances the independent Indian state was reduced to those of its organs that continued to function, the largest of which was the Indian military. As a contemporary observer would note, the Indian Army was now the 'Super Police Force'.[116] It was a designation that might well have suited the RIAF.

Over the course of nearly three months the RIAF would perform a number of critical roles from protecting refugee columns to dropping leaflets on rioters. If the riots were akin to civil war then the RIAF played a crucial role in successfully conducting a series of military operations that helped retard the spread of violence and bring about a return of order within a relatively short span. Due to its small size and the relatively sophisticated nature of many of the tasks it performed however the RIAF has thus far received little attention from scholars. This section will therefore point to the critical role of the RIAF played in saving thousands of lives during the Partition.

The first RIAF aircraft to be deployed to aid the army during Partition were a flight of Auster aircraft from the 659 Artillery Observation Post Squadron, stationed in August 1947 as part of the short-lived Punjab Boundary Force. The planes were reconnaissance aircraft whose task was to scout disturbances and relay news of them to ground troops who could then rapidly move in to restore order. Punjab was an ideal space in which to use aircraft since landing spaces were easy to find meaning that pilots could liaise with ground troops very quickly after performing reconnaissance.[117] In the acclaimed Hindi novel *Tamas* (Darkness) by

---

[115] It has been suggested that this was not the case. See for instance: Khan, *The Great Partition*, p. 128.

[116] Hamid, *Disastrous Twilight*, p. 163.

[117] MoD (I), 601/14185/H, Rajendra Singh, *Draft History of the Military Evacuation Organisation*, pp. 120–21.

Bhisham Sahni the arrival of the aeroplane saves the lives of Sikhs whose Gurudwara is about to be torched:

The plane flew over the village thrice before it went away. The atmosphere of the village changed. People ventured out. The fighting seemed to have stopped and dead bodies were being disposed of. People went back to their houses to assess their losses in terms of clothes and ornaments ... The villages over which the plane had flown stopped beating their drums.[118]

There may be some truth in fiction since early on the 'mere presence' of aircraft was found to have a deterrent effect, dispersing mobs, and giving villages time to prepare their defences. A similar effect was also observed with the deployment of tanks and wheeled personnel carriers.[119] The aeroplane likely evoked earlier memories of state violence in India. The Royal Air Force had bombed rioters at Gujranwala during the nationalist agitation that followed the Great War in 1919.[120] It had also been used extensively to crush the Quit India agitation in 1942. Low flying RAF aircraft had strafed crowds during the agitation and a measure of the fury that this gave rise to can be gained from the vicious murders of RAF personnel whenever they were unlucky enough to fall into the hands of enraged Indian mobs.[121] During Partition where large bodies of men acted as militias in order to violate the state's monopoly on violence, a potent means to restore order was through the deployment of the high technologies of violence. As the Hunter Commission had noted about a previous crisis where the state was faced with mass violence, 'We are not prepared to lay down as a charter for rioters that when they succeed in preventing the ordinary resources of Government from being utilized to suppress them, they are to be exempt from having to reckon with such resources as remain.'[122] The democratization of violence that characterized Partition

---

[118] Bhishm Sahni, 'Tamas' (Jai Ratan translation), Accessed 5 May 2022. https://archive.org/details/Tamas-English-BhishamSahni/page/n135/mode/2up?q=plane+flew&view=theater, 16.

[119] MoD (I), 601/14185/H, Singh, *Draft History of the Military Evacuation Organisation*, p. 120.

[120] Disorder Inquiry Committee 1919–1920 (Calcutta, Superintendent of Government Printing, India, 1920), pp. xxvii–xxviii.

[121] B. Chandra, *India's Struggle for Independence* (New Delhi: Penguin books, 2016), p. 462.

[122] Disorder Inquiry Committee 1919–1920, p. xxvii.

could effectively be resisted by the state through a demonstration of its ability to resort to technologized forms of violence on which it had the monopoly. Aviation resources deployed by the Indian state until August 1947 however were grossly inadequate to stem the tide of carnage.

The possibility that Partition might lead to an exchange of populations had not been considered, let alone planned for by the governments of the two new states. Consequently, measures to combat mass violence on an un-precedented scale as well as to expedite the transfer of minority populations from affected regions were grossly inadequate. Mass violence moved from Punjab to consume New Delhi itself. Levels of violence were so great that they imperilled the continued functioning of states that were still recovering from the division of nearly all their assets and personnel. Nehru later wrote to the chief ministers of provinces that the disturbances might well have spread from the western United Provinces to engulf all of India. If that happened then apart from the butchery and the destruction of property they would face, 'the wholesale disruption of communications, disorganisation of food supplies and the spread of epidemic diseases.'[123] Fears that India might be overwhelmed by Partition were reflected in the aviation world with the BOAC's 'Operation By-Pass' which aimed to fly aircraft around India rather than land in the chaos.[124] In order to pacify the violence the governments of India and Pakistan were forced to concede that millions of citizens would have to be evacuated as part of an exchange of populations. This would entail working together on a very large scale and led to the raising of the Military Evacuation Organisation (MEO) on 1 September 1947.[125]

The MEO had its headquarters in Lahore in order to liaise between the Pakistani armed forces and East Punjab Area Command which in-cluded the entirety of the 4th Division under General K.S. Thimayya with a larger RIAF contingent. The MEO represented a much larger military and diplomatic commitment than its predecessor, the Punjab Boundary Force. Aeroplanes would begin flying every morning at dawn to provide tactical reconnaissance and would be sent out every three hours to overfly railway tracks on which trains were scheduled to

[123] Nehru to Chief Ministers, 15 October 1947, in G. Parthasarathi eds, *Letters to Chief Ministers 1947-64* (Oxford, 1985), p. 2.
[124] TNA, BT 217/1887, Appendix 'A'.
[125] MoD (I), 601/14185/H, Singh, *Draft History of the Military Evacuation Organisation*, p. 14.

travel.[126] Aeroplanes were used to ensure that trains were not ambushed by mobs in a variety of ways. Planes would search for breaks or obstructions in the tracks. They would look out for armed men and would report on the progress of the mobile columns of troops that often travelled alongside the train to protect it. RIAF planes could communicate with trains in a number of ways. The most conventional of these was the use of wireless radio transmissions. However, if this was not available planes could use flare guns to communicate with engine drivers. Red flares would signal the train to stop, green would signal 'GO' and white flares were used to acknowledge messages from the train. If for whatever reason the pilot was unable to communicate with the train through these means then he could use more physical methods. To indicate a mob or obstruction a pilot could dive over a point multiple times before flying towards the train to signal it to halve speed until reinforcements could arrive. This might be followed by a message dropped near the engine. To stop the train pilots were ordered to fly low over the train twice from rear to front. In order to make trains easy to spot from the air they were painted with white Xs on the front bogey of each train.[127]

Pilots flying over Punjab in September 1947 reported spotting foot columns of 20–30,000 refugees extending 17 to 25 miles. Reconnaissance by RIAF aircraft acted as force multipliers by spotting mobs waiting to ambush refugees on foot and reporting their positions to military patrols.[128] The RIAF had specialized in tactical reconnaissance during the Second World War and was therefore well suited to this task, especially on the flat terrain of Punjab.[129] Pilots flying over the region at the time reported seeing pillars of black smoke rising from scores of burning villages.[130] If one flew low enough it was possible to see the bodies floating through Punjab's famous canal system.[131] Some of the photographs of refugee camps spreading out as far as the eye can see could only have been taken by aircraft at high altitudes.[132]

---

[126] It remains unclear which squadrons RIAF aircraft, deployed as part of the MEO, were drawn from.

[127] MoD (I), 601/14185/H, Singh, *Draft History of the Military Evacuation Organisation*, p 77.

[128] Ibid., p 34.

[129] See for instance: MoD (I), 601/9621/H, ORB No.8 Squadron.

[130] Chaudhury, *Mosaic of Memory*, p. 20.

[131] Ahmad, *A Lucky Pilot*, p. 25.

[132] BL, *Millions on the Move* (New Delhi, Ministry of Information Broadcasting, 1948), p. 72.

In addition to tactical reconnaissance RIAF aircraft performed a number of other critical tasks. RIAF planes flew one and a half million doses of cholera vaccine from Delhi to Karachi in September 1947.[133] That widespread disease did not follow on the heels of mass violence despite the squalid conditions in refugee camps is owed partly to the speed with which aircraft could deliver vaccines. Dakotas from the RIAF's No 12 squadron flying from Delhi and Amritsar air dropped cooked food, sugar, and oil for refugee columns at Joranwalla, Lyallpur, Churkhana, Dhabhansinghwala, and Bhai Pheru.[134] When the Government of Pakistan (GoP) proved unable or unwilling to feed non-Muslim refugees in refugee camps in its territory RIAF aircraft air dropped food supplies at Wah, Jaranwallah, Balloki, Khudian, and Chunian. Both India and Pakistan agreed to the use of aircraft to drop leaflets warning rioters to cease violence or face dire consequences.[135] Given the small size of the RPAF and the increased cooperation between the dominions in the MEO it is not unlikely that RIAF aircraft dropped leaflets in both dominions.

The extent to which the crisis of Partition pushed the state's resources to breaking point is revealed by the decision to use RIAF personnel for law enforcement in New Delhi. Air Marshal Elmhirst promised the deployment of a 150 armed airmen at Palam airport where Muslim refugees were boarding flights for Pakistan.[136] These would have served alongside a motley collection of forces put together by the Indian government to restore order in New Delhi drawn from the military, the police, the Home Guard, and irregular volunteers. RIAF personnel were also posted to ground duties with relatively little connection to aviation. As thousands of Muslim refugees flocked to Purana Quila and Humayun's tomb to escape the violence, the Government of India came to rely on loud speakers to organize the refugee camps. The wires to these speakers were repeatedly cut by anti-Muslim elements in order to cause chaos in the camp. RIAF men were deputed to protect and operate the speakers, a task they accomplished despite wires being repeatedly cut.[137]

---

[133] MoD (I), 601/14476/H, *Partition Proceedings*, vol. V, Emergency committee meeting, 12 September 1947.

[134] BL, *Millions on the Move*, p. 5.

[135] Ibid.

[136] Ibid. It is unclear if the airmen were deputed since, as I will show, airfield security in Delhi was disorderly at best.

[137] BL, Mss Eur IOR Neg 15542, Emergency committee of the cabinet, Part I, 13 September 1947.

Dakotas from No. 12 Squadron RIAF would take part in refugee evacuation operations alongside the RAF, Indian and foreign chartered aircraft. These operations are discussed in detail below. However it is important here to point out that the RIAF's final contribution to Partition relief was the evacuation of non-Muslims from distant pockets of Pakistan such as Multan, Bannu, and Peshawar up to November 1947.[138] These relatively distant communities were often too far away from railway lines and their evacuation, often from regions that had experienced relatively little communal violence, represented India's commitment to the evacuation of as many non-Muslims from Pakistan as possible. A near-complete exchange of populations, on the Western frontier, was effected in less than three months, between the acceptance of the principle of population exchange in September and the final flights out of Pakistan in November 1947.

The Limits of Indian Civil Aviation in Refugee Evacuation

Indian and Pakistani politicians had conceded the possibility of an exchange of populations after Partition. As Muhammad Ali Jinnah noted in May 1947 'sooner or later an exchange of populations will have to take place … wherever it might be necessary and feasible.'[139] What the political leaderships of both dominions did not expect was the speed and scale of the population exchange. The possibility that millions of people would leave behind their homes over the course of less than half a year was neither thought about nor planned for by the national leaderships of both new states.[140] When the unthinkable finally began to happen New Delhi and Karachi had to scramble to organize a gargantuan evacuation in which the aeroplane would play a minuscule but highly critical role. Whereas aviation would account for less than 1 per cent of evacuees, a significant proportion of these would be government officials and their families. These officials included an entire plethora of public servants, from military officers to postal officials, who were critical to successfully

---

[138] MoD (I), 601/14185/H, Singh, *Draft History of the Military Evacuation Organisation*, p. 82.
[139] TNA, FO 371/63533, *Speech by Muhammad Ali Jinnah on 4th May 1947*.
[140] Khan, *The Great Partition,* p. 122.

overcoming the logistical bottlenecks involved in moving millions to the dominion of their choice. Later Indian aircraft would be dispatched to West Pakistan to evacuate non-Muslim refugees living in distant corners of Pakistan from which ground evacuation was simply too dangerous. Indian civil aviation companies would play a critical role in this process, often risking planes and pilots to move as many people as they could. However, the sheer numbers of people who needed to be evacuated as well as the lack of facilities in the cities in which they were functioning would force Indian civil aviation companies to scale down refugee evacuations. The governments of India and Pakistan eventually employed a fleet of foreign aircraft to complete the most urgent refugee evacuations. This had important long-term effects.

The earliest crisis facing the Indian government in East Punjab was the restoration of communications in August 1947. Air services were organized between Delhi, Amritsar, and Jullundur, all of which were in Indian territory, in order to efficiently coordinate state efforts. Subsequently an attempt was made to speed up the evacuation of refugees by air from Pakistan through the establishment of daily services to Quetta, Rawalpindi, and Peshawar as well as additional services to Lahore and Karachi. Charter facilities were provided for private individuals to hire aircraft to move them from Sialkot, Sarghoda, Lyallpur, and Dera Ismail Khan.[141] A Controlling Air Transport Authority for refugees was appointed to coordinate air services under Rai Bahadur N.C. Ghosh.[142] A major decision that confronted the governments of India and Pakistan with regard to using aircraft in refugee evacuation was whether scheduled flights ought to be continued in light of the emergency. A precedent for controlling civil aviation did exist in the form of controls placed on Indian commercial airline companies during the Second World War. The Emergency Committee of the Indian cabinet briefly discussed the possibility of diverting flights from Pakistan to Ambala rather than New Delhi in order to avoid the gathering of large numbers of refugees in the capital, since these often served to exacerbate the communal situation and placed pressure on relief facilities. However, the committee concluded that most passengers who came by plane were wealthy and therefore did not stay

---

[141] BL, *Millions on the Move*, pp. 3–4.
[142] BL, Mss Eur IOR Neg 15542, Emergency committee of the cabinet, Part I, 9 September 1947.

in camps. Indeed, many of the passengers on planes did not even stay in New Delhi but rather moved on to other destinations. A move to divert scheduled services to Ambala would also mean that aircraft would have to return to Pakistan empty. Consequently, scheduled services which had operated before 14 August 1947 would be permitted to continue.[143] Non-scheduled services however would now be diverted to Ambala. Air services were to be intensified between Delhi on the one hand and Quetta, Karachi, Lahore, Rawalpindi, and Peshawar on the other. All available civil aircraft that were not plying scheduled routes were used to ferry refugees from Pakistan to India. Ten planes became available for government use and on most days seven of these flew from Delhi to Sarghoda, Lyallpur, Multan, and Rawalpindi.[144]

A number of measures were taken to expedite air evacuation, especially of government officials. A Subcommittee of the Cabinet for Air was formed under the joint leadership of the DGCA and the Air Marshal Commanding RIAF. The sub-committee was tasked with centralizing the evacuation effort and effectively subsuming the Controlling Authority for Air Transport of Refugees. Indian Air Liaison officers were appointed at Pakistan aerodromes in order to better coordinate refugee evacuation.[145] Two Royal Air Force transport squadrons deployed in India to evacuate British nationals were pressed into service by Lord Mountbatten, for the evacuation of Indian government officials from Pakistan.[146] A total of 12,000 people would be transported between India and Pakistan by these aircraft along with the tiny RAF communication flight in India. Only 2,790 of these would be British personnel. The rest were government personnel including railway, post, telegraph, and military personnel with their families.[147] Many of these officials would go on to play a central role in the wider exchange of populations happening on the ground. The use of aircraft therefore enabled the rapid constitution of the independent Indian state in the crucial first months after independence.

---

[143] BL, Mss Eur IOR Neg 15542, Emergency committee of the cabinet, Part I, 8 September 1947.
[144] BL, *Millions on the Move*, p. 6.
[145] BL, *Millions on the Move*, p. 6.
[146] BL, Mss Eur IOR Neg 15553/2, Royal Air Force Dakota Squadrons (September 1947–January 1948).
[147] *Flight*, October 23 1947, p. 484.

The airfields of Delhi and Punjab became scenes of great danger and desperation in August 1947. Typically, refugees would be confined to camps abutting the airfield and would rush the planes as soon as they were permitted, crowding the airfield. More often than not the number of passengers who could be carried on aircraft was limited and passengers desperate to be flown out of danger offered aircrews bribes in the form of money, gold, and jewels for a chance to board the plane.[148] A photograph from the period depicts a Dakota aeroplane in Multan surrounded by refugees with different kinds of luggage. Some have large trunks, while others stand next to sacks and mats while a man in uniform, presumably a pilot, desperately shouts at a group of passengers right next to the plane's wing.[149] Flight tickets were expensive and it was not uncommon for passengers to be charged 150 Rupees for a one-way journey.[150] Black market sales of marked-up tickets were also not unheard of nor were attempts to pay large sums in order to board an aeroplane.[151] Strict restrictions on luggage, usually restricted to 44 pounds, permitted passengers to carry only a fraction of their possessions. Forced to prioritize what she would carry, Alia Hyder, a Muslim from Hyderabad carried only her Koran with her to Pakistan.[152] Other refugees are reported to have carried a 'small and rather battered child's cane chair; a moth-eaten-looking- parrot' and a 'length of fine suit material worn round the shoulders like a shawl'.[153] Refugees attempting to board planes were particularly vulnerable to being harassed and robbed by the police who would check their belongings before they got onto flights. While it was not uncommon in India for 'unauthorized persons' to search Muslim refugees before they boarded planes, harassment of refugees in Pakistan was particularly pronounced. In one case refugees' belongings were stolen by a District Magistrate.[154] Searches continued to be seen as necessary by authorities in both governments however especially since refugees had on occasion been spotted

[148]   Reddy, *Aviation in the Hyderabad Dominions*, p. 157.
[149]   BL, *Millions on the Move*, (New Delhi, 1948), p. 74.
[150]   'From Orient to PIA', Accessed April 19, 2015. http://defence.pk/threads/frm-orient-to-pia.232677/.;
[151]   Khan, *Great Partition*, p. 144.
[152]   Collins and Lapierre, *Freedom at Midnight*, p. 373.
[153]   PC (AR), *Indian Aviation*, 'Operation India', April 1948, p. 116.
[154]   BL, Mss Eur IOR Neg 15538, Meeting between representatives of Air Operating Companies and GoI, 9 September 1947.

smuggling weapons.[155] When refugees got past the searches and boarded the planes they were subjected to enormous overcrowding. Seating and carpets in aeroplanes were removed by airline companies to accommodate as many refugees as possible. Dakota DC-3 aircraft meant to carry 21 passengers often carried five times that number. Deccan Airways technician Allen Joseph Francis was issued with a pair of knuckledusters by his pilot for crowd control. When the plane had been filled, Francis would punch his way to door collect the under-carriage pins of the plane and punch his way back into the plane before firmly locking it. Only once the doors were firmly closed the engine would start. Then the 'crowd would automatically vanish due to the slip stream of the engines'.[156] Despite all the travails of flying, however, once refugees were aboard an aeroplane they could be certain of reaching their destination quickly and without facing any of the dangers confronting the millions making the journey on land.

It is remarkable that no major crashes were reported despite the massive overcrowding of aircraft. Refugees often crowded airfields before planes landed because of the lack of security.[157] Matters were not helped by the hostility authorities displayed to aircrews of the 'other' country. Pakistan officials, for instance, refused to provide ground crew support to Indian planes flying out refugees forcing them to carry their own technical crews. This degraded the efficiency of the plane and reduced the number of refugees that could be evacuated. Indian aircrews were often not allowed to deplane in Pakistan and when they did were treated with extreme suspicion.[158] Ground crews and pilots were often threatened and as a group of airline representatives explained to the government were 'definitely in danger'.[159]

[155] BL, MSS Eur 670/23, Cunningham papers, Fortnightly report, 15 October 1947. There had been considerable concern in both states about refugees bearing arms. What no doubt seemed to be a survival strategy for refugees was seen by the governments to be another barrier to the restoration of law and order. See: Bal Ram Nanda eds, *Selected Works of Ballabh Pant* (New Delhi: OUP, 1993), p. 88.

[156] Reddy, *Aviation in the Hyderabad Dominions*, p. 152.

[157] BL, Mss Eur IOR Neg 15538, Meeting between representatives of Air Operating Companies and GoI, 9 September 1947.

[158] A key reason why Deccan Airways was able to function longer in Pakistan than other airlines was because of its White and Muslim personnel. Reddy, *Aviation in the Hyderabad Dominions*, p. 150.

[159] BL, Mss Eur IOR Neg 15538, Meeting between representatives of Air Operating Companies and GoI, 9 September 1947.

Even in Delhi, which by all accounts was the most well-organized site of evacuation, airport security could be remarkably lax. Palam airport, which had a large Muslim staff, was woefully unprotected at the height of Partition. The chaos of Partition meant that forces to protect vital zones like airfields were stretched thin. A company of Royal Scots Fusiliers officially in New Delhi to protect British lives was posted at the airport on the 6 September 1947. Matters would be so dire that the airport would be closed down the next day.[160] The tiny platoon defending Willingdon airport was withdrawn forcing ground crews to absent themselves. Burmah Shell petroleum complained, 'The a/c (aircraft), the petrol installations and the staff on duty are at the mercy of unruly mobs.'[161] Refugee evacuation to and from the city was further complicated by the absence of facilities to house and feed air service personnel. Trains carrying food were having difficulty getting into Delhi forcing INA staff at Palam to live on hard rations.[162] It was also far too unsafe for Muslim personnel to live in private accommodation in New Delhi as Deccan Airways learnt. Its Muslim technicians had to move out of Lodhi colony next to Willingdon aerodrome due to the violence there.[163] Various attempts were made to properly house air service personnel based in New Delhi for refugee evacuation numbering 500, including an attempt to house them at Constitution house where only a month earlier India had been declared independent.[164] However all these attempts failed partially due to safety concerns and partially because the near-total breakdown of the economy meant that food and furniture were simply not available.

Just as pressing as worries about crews were concerns about the sustainability of the tempo of operations due to the serviceability of the aircraft, which was seriously affected by the continued lack of servicing facilities provided to planes at many of the airfields they visited, especially in Pakistan. Engines were not being serviced as often as needed and it was likely that the continued tempo of operations might well result in crashes or at the very least the grounding of aircraft. If this state of affairs continued India could well risk the gains that had been accrued in civil

---

[160] Hamid, *Disastrous Twilight*, p. 246.
[161] BL, Mss Eur IOR Neg 15542, Emergency committee of the cabinet, Part I, 9 September 1947.
[162] PC (AR), *Indian Aviation*, 'Operation India', April 1948, p. 116.
[163] Reddy, *Aviation in the Hyderabad* Dominions, p. 153.
[164] BL, Mss Eur IOR Neg 15542, Emergency committee of the cabinet, Part I, 9 September 1947.

aviation over the last decade. Airline companies felt that the 'conservation of aircraft and personnel for civil aviation and communications in India as a whole was a matter of greater importance than this attempt at tackling a problem which was really a problem of mass evacuation which can only be done by rail and road'.[165] The sheer size of the problem confronting the airline industry was crushing. According to airline operators evacuation by air had 'utterly failed' to achieve any tangible results. It had 'not even touched the fringe of the problem when lacs (sic) of people had to be evacuated'.[166] While Indian aircraft would continue to take part in refugee evacuation operations well into December 1947, operators became increasingly reluctant to risk aircraft and personnel for what seemed like an increasingly impossible task. It became clear that Indian aviation alone could not carry out air evacuations.

'Operation Pakistan' and 'Operation India'

The Pakistan government, perhaps because of its much smaller aviation sector, had realized early on that it would need foreign help in order to move the relatively large numbers of government officials and their families. An urgent request was sent to the BOAC for aircraft and crews to evacuate government officials and their families totalling seven thousand from New Delhi to Pakistan's new capital Karachi. A BOAC Lancastrian arrived in Karachi the following day while other aircraft were mobilized for this effort from BOAC itself as well as a number of other British companies including Scottish Airlines, Silver City Airlines, and Westminster Airways. After briefly calling off the request, most likely to consider the costs of the operation, the Pakistani cabinet gave what came to be called 'Operation Pakistan' the go-ahead. In order to maximize the speed of operations the arriving British aircraft carried as many extra crews as possible.[167] They also took special permission from the British Air ministry to fly aircraft without any seats so as to maximize the number of

---

[165] BL, Mss Eur IOR Neg 15538, Meeting between representatives of Air Operating Companies and GoI, 9 September 1947.
[166] BL, Mss Eur IOR Neg 15538, Meeting between representatives of Air Operating Companies and GoI, 9 September 1947.
[167] *Flight*, 2 October 1947.

passengers that could be evacuated. Over the next 15 days, 21 British aircraft working nearly non-stop would move about 6,300 people from Delhi to Karachi. They also carried 45,000 kilograms of food, tents, and vaccines for Muslim refugees stuck at Delhi's aerodromes.[168] On their way back to India aircraft also brought 1,500 fare paying non-Muslim passengers. The breakneck pace of operations can be gauged from the fact that these non-Muslims were often dropped off at the airport before planes taxied back 500 yards to prepare to take off again.[169] Operation Pakistan was extraordinarily successful and there is no doubt that its success played a critical part in ensuring that Pakistani personnel were in place to commence the task of organising the exchange of populations.

By October 1947 the Indian government had come to realize that it too needed to airlift its government personnel stranded in Pakistan who were in danger of being massacred. It also saw the need to evacuate non-Muslims in distant pockets of Pakistan's Northwest in order to protect them from the violence they would likely face on the long land journey to India. The independent Indian government also knew by this point that Indian civil aviation, even with the aid of the RIAF and RAF, could not complete these tasks with speed. However there appears to have been a certain measure of reluctance on the part of the Government of India to request British aid. In early October 1947 Indian officials inquired with the US Ambassador to India Henry F. Grady if the United States could provide India with aircraft and crews for the evacuation of 50,000 non-Muslims from the North West Frontier Province. The US State Department responded that it was willing to do so on the condition that the Pakistan government was willing to acquiesce to the scheme and also that full protection be provided for its air service personnel.[170] American conditions would multiply over time to include the demand that all violence cease before any evacuation was undertaken. It is likely that the State Department was making impossible demands largely as a means of staying out of operations the United States did not, at this point,

---

[168] Several accounts at the time cite 7000 as the number of people evacuated. However, 6300 is the official BOAC estimate. TNA, BT 217/ 1793, Chairman to Brackley, 17 September 1947.

[169] *The Aeroplane*, 1947, p. 507.

[170] TNA, BT 217/ 1793, Secretary for Commonwealth relations to United Kingdom High Commissioner (UKHC) India, 12 October 1947.

have any interest in undertaking.[171] This does not explain Indian reluctance in calling on the services of BOAC however. The Indian Ministry of Refugees and Rehabilitation resented the possibility of having to pay over a million pounds a month to British companies to carry out relatively small evacuations at a time when the money was badly needed elsewhere.[172] There is also some evidence that New Delhi was irked by what it saw as Britain's pro-Pakistan stance. Its reluctance to rely on British airlines was strengthened by the belief that BOAC would charge India more than it had Pakistan.[173] The pressing need for evacuation of Indian government personnel as well as non-Muslims stranded in remote regions in Pakistan however eventually compelled India to accept an offer to assist in refugee evacuation from BOAC.

'Operation India' was conducted under the leadership of Air Commodore H. G. Brackley, assistant for Special duties to the chairman of BOAC, who had conducted 'Operation Pakistan'. As BOAC refused to lend any aircraft plying its famed 'Speedbird' routes several British companies—Westminster Airways, Air Contractors, Air Charter, Sieverwright Airways, Scottish Aviation, Channel Islands Air Transport Charter, Kearsley Airways, and Silver City Airways—had to be approached for aircraft and crews.[174] Brackley would eventually successfully assemble an air fleet consisting of twenty Dakota and one Wayfarer aircraft. Over the course of six weeks between 19 October and 30 November 35,000 people and over 1,500,000 lb of baggage were flown between Pakistan and India.[175] The British companies used the same tactics used with great success during 'Operation Pakistan'. British airlines brought their own personnel with them to Palam aerodrome. Some 170 air service personnel were flown in from Britain and two barrack blocks were taken over from the RAF. The DGCA also handed over a terminal building to serve as offices. Still there was simply no food and furniture available. A total of 200 camp beds, 40 wardrobes, 30 dressing tables, 250 chairs, linens, and even charcoals for fires were flown in from Calcutta

---

[171] TNA, BT 217/ 1793, Commonwealth Relations Office (CRO) to UKHC India, 11 November 1947.
[172] TNA, BT 217/ 1793, UKHC Pakistan to CRO, 22 October 1947.
[173] TNA, BT 217/ 1793, UKHC India to CRO, 23 October 1947.
[174] PC (AR), *Indian Aviation*, 'Operation India', April 1948, p. 113.
[175] TNA, BT 217/ 1793, H.G. Brackley, 1 December 1947.

and Karachi.[176] Eggs from Quetta, cigarettes from Karachi and poultry from Calcutta were also transported by aircraft to New Delhi.[177] The Government of India directed operations by deciding everyday where planes would be sent, since aircraft often needed to serve distant regions. They would then be sent from Palam aerodrome in New Delhi to pick up points all over India and Pakistan. These included Peshawar, Risalpur, Rawalpindi, Chaklala, Multan, Der Khan, Quetta, Lyallpur, Khanpur, Amritsar, Ambala, and Lahore. Aircraft would land in groups and each plane's captain would then let as many passengers as he felt his plane could handle on board. A photograph from the period shows a British captain screaming at a Dhoti clad villager, most likely about luggage permitted on board the aeroplane in the background.[178]

Some 14,000 people flown out during Operation India were transported to Pakistan from India, while some 21,000 were flown from Pakistan to India. There are three reasons for the relatively low number of people flown out to Pakistan. The first of these is technical. Planes had to take off with full fuel tanks due to the lack of refuelling facilities. Much of this would be burned on the journey making the plane lighter. This meant that they could carry fewer loads flying out than when flying in.[179] Secondly 'Operation India' followed 'Operation Pakistan' during which the most urgently needed Pakistan personnel had already been flown out of India, meaning that the need for more Pakistan personnel had reduced. Third and perhaps most important was the fact that Pakistan was beginning to be overwhelmed with refugees. As the head of the BOAC wrote, 'They have little space for and limited resources with which to feed their greatly swollen population.'[180] The exchange of populations, while accepted by both dominions in principle could never actually be total. Pakistan could never evacuate India's vast Muslim population with the same thoroughness with which India evacuated West Pakistan's non-Muslim minorities. Pakistan was never meant to be a refuge for all Muslims

[176] *Flight*, 25 December 1947.
[177] PC (AR), *Indian Aviation*, 'Operation India', April 1948, p. 116.
[178] *Flight*, 25 December 1947.
[179] BT 217/ 1793, Evacuation in India-Proposal to waive safety regulations.
[180] BT 217/ 1793, Head of BOAC, undated; For a detailed view of Pakistan's difficulties accommodating Muslim refugees see: Zamindar, *The Long Partition*.

and the view that India was attempting to overwhelm Pakistan with waves of Muslim refugees began to take root in Karachi. This would have grave consequences for the later conflict in Kashmir which also saw mass migrations by Muslims from Indian to Pakistani territory.[181] Significantly the Indian government held similar views about East Pakistan. While refugees were evacuated en-masse from West Pakistan, similar attempts were not made in East Pakistan. There were several reasons for this but perhaps the most significant was the sheer numbers of evacuees this would have involved. Indian administrators found it extremely challenging to resettle the millions evacuated from West Pakistan and would have found it impossible to also settle those from East Pakistan. India would instead attempt to coerce Pakistan into protecting its Hindu minority and this, as shall be seen in a later chapter, would nearly plunge the two states into war.

Operation India is illustrative of the difficulties faced by the Indian government. Indian civil aviation could simply not conduct evacuation operations on the same scale as British companies, which could deploy far greater resources. British companies could also deploy white personnel who did not have to fear for their lives because of their religious identities. Nonetheless it is critical to point out that Operation India took part with the aid of the RIAF, the DGCA, and INA all of whom made important contributions.[182] The Indian Ministry of Refugees and Rehabilitation and the Pakistani government were critical to getting evacuees to aerodromes safely. The Indian and Pakistani states despite their hostility, which at this point was plunging them into war, understood the need to co-operate in order to prevent being swept away by violence unleashed by their majorities. Further, the experience of Operation India would inculcate an understanding of the importance of mobilizing a national aviation sector. This would have critical implications for the next major airlift; the Bengal airlift of 1950, as well as for the nationalization of Indian airline companies in 1953.

---

[181] BL, L/WS/1/1144, UKHC Pakistan to CRO, 18 November 1948.
[182] TNA, BT 217/ 1793, H.G. Brackley, 1 December 1947.

Conclusion

The two years after the Second World War were characterized by dysfunction in high politics and mass violence at the local level. There is an argument to be made that the instability unleashed by the Second World War in India ultimately manifested itself in mass violence between three of the subcontinent's largest religious communities. Nationalist Indian histories of the decade often drew a straight line from the Quit India movement of 1942 to Indian independence.[183] Perhaps a better way to understand Partition is to draw a shorter line from 1945 to 1947. The Second World War led to a crisis of legitimacy in the colonial military not seen since 1857. Indian army soldiers had defected to the Axis and subsequently became national heroes after the war, ratings of the RIN mutinied in 1946 and the RIAF staged a series of 'strikes'. Even as the colonial military was haemorrhaging legitimacy, militia groups organized on military lines were mobilizing to 'defend' their communities. That they could draw on demobilized military personnel and abandoned weaponry to do so is incidental to the broader democratization of violence based on the increasing loss of state legitimacy. Organized violence drove high politics into dysfunction as India's two leading parties, the Congress and the Muslim League failed to come to agreement on the constitutional issue.

The two parties were unable to work together in the short-lived interim government to implement plans towards long-term profitability and viability of Indian civil aviation. Their failure to implement the Tymms plan would have critical long-term implications and set the private airlines of India on a course that would lead eventually towards nationalization. As mass violence increased in a context of constitutional deadlock British and Indian politicians became convinced of the need to Partition colonial India into two dominions. This would lead to the reconstitution of the colonial RIAF into two new air forces, the RIAF and the RPAF.

The RIAF, which was itself in the throes of a difficult reconstitution, was deployed to assist with the refugee crisis of 1947. Through the deployment of high technology, the Indian state sought to reclaim its monopoly on violence from militias. Indian airline companies also stepped in to help with the refugee crisis. Ultimately however the sector proved to

---

[183] See for instance: Chandra, *India's Struggle for Independence*.

be too small to handle the magnitude of the evacuation, though they did continue evacuations well into December 1947.[184] The governments of India and Pakistan therefore had to rely on chartered British aircraft for Operation Pakistan and later Operation India, which saw the evacuation of 6,300 and 35,000 people respectively. This would serve as a key lesson for the newly independent Indian government about the importance of aviation in general and state control of it in particular.

[184] Reddy, *Aviation in the Hyderabad Dominions*, p. 154.

3

War in Kashmir 1947–1948

Indian aviation literally shaped both India and Pakistan in the 1947–1948 Kashmir war. The present-day 'Line of Control' between India and Pakistan represents the furthest point that Indian aircraft could keep advancing ground troops supplied during the war. The war confirmed and deepened the hostility between the Congress and the Muslim League and the dominions that they had come to rule. Though a relatively modest conflict by the standards of the 20th century, the war came to define the self-image of India and Pakistan.[1] As an ideological struggle between Indian secularism and Pakistani two-nation theory the war nationalized the dispute between the Congress and the Muslim League over the shape of post-colonial South Asia. It also unravelled British plans to closely integrate the Indian and Pakistani militaries in service of the Commonwealth in the broader context of the Cold War.

Indian aviation played a substantial role in the Kashmir war. The conflict signalled the elevation of the Royal Indian Air Force (RIAF) to the national stage. While the RIAF had played a junior role to the Allied air forces operating against the Japanese in the Second World War, in Kashmir it was second in importance only to the Indian Army. Indian aviation in general, and the RIAF in particular, helped initiate, sustain, and escalate the conflict. Aircraft effectively initiated the Kashmir conflict by enabling independent India to rapidly deploy its army in the mountainous Kashmiri terrain in the winter of 1947. This allowed the

---

[1] For the wider Kashmir conflict also see: Sukhwant Singh, *India's Wars since Independence* (New Delhi: Vikas Publishing House, 1980):Alastair Lamb, *Incomplete Partition: The Genesis of the Kashmir Dispute* (Hertingfordbury: Roxford Books, 1997); Sudhir S. Bloeria, *The Battles of Zojila* (New Delhi: Har-Anand Publications, 1997); Christopher Birdwood, *Two Nations and Kashmir* (London: Robert Hale, 1956); Dasgupta, *War and Diplomacy in Kashmir 1947-48*; M.N. Gulati, *Military Plight of Pakistan: Indo-Pak War, 1947–48* (New Delhi: Manas Publications, 2000); Sumit Ganguly, *The Origins of War in South Asia: Indo-Pakistani Conflicts since 1947* (Oxford: Westview, 1994); Lionel Protip Sen, *Slender Was the Thread* (New Delhi: Orient Longman, 1969): Arjun Subramaniam, *India's Wars: A Military History, 1947–1971* (Noida: Harper Collins, 2016).

The Aeroplane and the Making of Modern India. Aashique Ahmed Iqbal, Oxford University Press.
© Oxford University Press 2023. DOI: 10.1093/oso/9780192864208.003.0004

Indian government to contest what Pakistani strategists hoped would be a military fait accompli. Subsequently the Indian government's small fleet of civilian and military aircraft would enable the Indian government to sustain a conflict in which India suffered from grave logistical disadvantages. Limited aviation resources and nearly unlimited military needs meant that the Indian government led by Jawaharlal Nehru had to carefully strategize the use of aircraft in ways that best fulfilled Indian political objectives. This prioritization of the use of scarce aircraft helps improve our understanding of Indian political objectives in a conflict where these have often been occluded by controversy. Aviation also gives us an insight into the independent Indian and Pakistani governments' notions of their newly won sovereignty. Over the course of the conflict, airpower would emerge as an important component of the calculus of escalation that the Indian and Pakistani leaderships were required to manage. The Kashmir war was a conflict that both states had an interest in limiting. I argue here that the escalatory potential of air power in the Kashmir conflict has been misunderstood by both historians and contemporaries. Whereas much of the writing on escalation has focused on the possibility that the Indian and Pakistani air forces would drag the two states into a wider full-scale war by clashing in the air, I argue that this was not in fact the case. The true danger of escalation emerged instead from the possibility of continued conflict in a theatre which the Pakistani government, saw increasingly, in existential terms. This chapter then is, in part, an attempt to understand the escalatory role of air power in the Kashmir war.

This chapter is not intended to be a comprehensive account of air operations in the Kashmir war. Part of the reason for this is the existence of well researched operational histories.[2] Rather it builds on existing operational histories in order to situate air power in the broader politics and diplomacy of the war through an analysis of three events during the war in which air power played a significant role; the Srinagar airlift, the siege of Punch, and the bombing of Palak. This analysis emphasizes the degree to which the conflict was an exercise in the management of escalation. Both the Indian and Pakistani governments along with their British military

---

[2] S.N. Prasad ed, *Operations in Jammu and Kashmir 1947–48* (New Delhi: Natraj, [1987] 2005); Kumar, *An Incredible War*; Chhina, *The Eagle Strikes*; Mirza Aslam Beg, *The Pakistan Army 1947–49* (Dehra Dun: Natraj, [1977] 2003).

commanders sought to prevent the war from developing into a broader conflict that might prove ruinous. This makes a more holistic reading of military actions, than those that concern operational histories, necessary. The war was limited for a number of reasons.[3] An increase in the scope of the conflict, by its spread to West Punjab for instance, would severely affect armed forces recently divided between two dominions. It would also potentially provoke great power intervention against the side seen as the aggressor. Both India and Pakistan were reliant on Britain, and to a lesser extent the United States, for military and diplomatic support meaning that they could not afford to antagonize them. Moreover, Cold War paranoia meant that Britain and the United States were deeply concerned about the possibility of Soviet interference in the subcontinent and might have intervened actively to prevent it.[4] The most pressing reason for India and Pakistan to avoid full-scale war, however, was due to the need to protect minorities in both countries. When war broke out in October 1947, the transfer of populations was still in progress and violence had yet to be brought totally under control. As I will demonstrate the war was in many ways an extension of the ethnoreligious violence of partition. Neither the Indian nor the Pakistani governments were willing to risk unleashing the mass violence that had so recently convulsed their heartlands. Aviation therefore had to be utilized in ways that enabled both states to contest each other's sovereignty over Kashmiri territory while simultaneously avoiding the outbreak of a conflict that might irreversibly damage their nascent polities.

There were also other reasons why the war was limited. The highest echelons of both dominions' forces were incompletely indigenized as a consequence of the slow pace of nationalization as seen in a previous chapter. Independent India and Pakistan simply did not possess officers of an appropriate level of seniority to conduct sophisticated military operations. Indians had only begun to enter the higher echelons of the officer corps in both the army and air force during the Second World War. Consequently, the highest commanders of both dominions' armed forces were British and large numbers of British officers continued to serve

---

[3] The following paragraph draws from: Raghavan, *War and Peace in Modern India*, p. 121.

[4] Rajendra Kumar Jain, *US-South Asia Relations 1947–1982* (New Delhi: Radiant, 1983), p. 5. We now know that Joseph Stalin did not prioritize South Asia and left it in a state of 'benign neglect' until his death in 1953.

in technical and staff positions.[5] This was to have the effect of eventually pitting British officers against each other, as will be discussed subsequently in this chapter. More immediately however the reliance on both sides of British officers provided the British government with a great deal of power to influence the war. Both dominions were also handicapped in their own ways. Pakistan suffered the worst effects of Partition on its armed forces. Not only did it receive a smaller proportion of the armed forces than its Indian counterpart but Pakistani authorities often complained that their rightful share of armaments was being withheld by the Indian government.[6] India's problems are best encapsulated in a single word; overextension. The Indian military, though larger and better organized than its Pakistani counterpart had myriad commitments that stretched it to breaking point. When war broke out in Kashmir, Indian troops were committed to a variety of other duties which detracted from larger deployments in the Kashmir theatre. Indian forces were concentrated on the Punjab border to prevent Pakistani forces from attacking East Punjab in case of the outbreak of a wider conflict.[7] They were also deployed around Hyderabad to project power against the Nizam who had not acceded to India after independence. As will be seen in a later chapter the RIAF was at the time deployed to prevent weapons from being flown into the state by gun runners. Further, Indian troops were committed to internal security, which was a pressing requirement in order to restore peace and disarm the bevvy of private armies that had emerged as a result of Partition.[8]

The Kashmir war would thus emerge as an archetypally limited war, fought in fits and starts, as the Indian and Pakistani leaderships did their best to attain their political goals without provoking a larger conflict. Both sides sought to impose their sovereignty on the entirety of the princely state of Kashmir for strategic and ideological reasons. This shaped the way that they utilized military power in general, and air power in particular, in the course of the conflict. While it remained a limited regional conflict between two newly decolonized states, the Kashmir conflict is

---

[5] In 1948 the Pakistani military fielded about 800 British officers while India employed around 350. Andrew Whitehead, *A Mission in Kashmir* (New Delhi: Penguin books, 2007), p. 204.

[6] TNA, DO 134/1, AH Reed to H.S. Stephenson, 21 March 1948.

[7] NAM, 7901-87-6-1, Bucher to H.M Patel, 15 March 1948.

[8] NAM, 7901-87-6-1, Chiefs of Staff Paper 48/1.

reflective of the emergence of a new global order following the Second World War premised on nation-states rather than on older forms of organizing sovereignty such as the semi-autonomous princely rule represented by Kashmir state. The following chapter deals with the collapse of the princely order in the context of the new order of nation-states. What is worthwhile pointing out here however is the extent to which in engaging with each other, even through the mode of conflict, the Pakistani and Indian states recognized each other's sovereignty while ignoring that of the princely state they each ostensibly laid claim to.

The Srinagar Airlift

The state of Kashmir was created as a consequence of the sale of a number of territories, including the Kashmir valley, to the *Raja* (King) of Jammu, a Dogra Rajput named Gulab Singh, by the British East India Company in 1846.[9] Like several other princely states, Kashmir saw the emergence of popular movements in the 20th century which aimed to limit the power of its monarch. Led by Sheikh Abdullah, the National Conference party began an agitation in 1931, demanding greater rights for subjects of the state.[10] Politics in Kashmir state was complicated by the fact that the ruling dynasty was Hindu, while the majority of the populace, some 78 per cent, was Muslim.[11] Moreover, opposition to Dogra rule was informed by the view that the Dogras were only the latest in a line of foreign occupying powers dating back to Mughal rule. Between 1931 and 1947 popular agitations against Dogra rule were routinely met with state repression, further widening the gulf between the Kashmir government and its people.[12]

By 1947, the prospect of independence was beginning to have its impact on the state. Both India and Pakistan sought to integrate Kashmir. Jawaharlal Nehru the soon-to-be prime minister of India was making

---

[9] For the political backdrop to the Kashmir war see: Mridu Rai, *Hindu Rulers, Muslim Subjects: Islam, Rights, and the History of Kashmir* (London: Hurst & Co, 2004), p. 19.

[10] Ajit Bhattacharjea, *Sheikh Abdullah: Tragic Hero of Kashmir* (New Delhi: Roli books, 2008), p. 3.

[11] Suranjan Das, *Kashmir and Sindh* (Kolkata: Bagchi and Co, 2001), p. 28.

[12] Rai, *Hindu Rulers, Muslim Subjects*, p. 294.

overtures to Ram Chandra Kak, prime minister of Kashmir as early as June 1947 well before independence.[13] Sumit Ganguly has shown the Indian government was aware of the immense strategic importance of Kashmir, a state with several international frontiers that would also be critical to India economically.[14] When Kashmir offered India a stand-still agreement on the same lines as it was offering Pakistan in 1947, the Government of India made signing of the agreement conditional on accession.[15] The Pakistani leadership, for its part, assumed that Kashmir would be integrated into Pakistan due to its Muslim majority and its contiguity to Punjab. When by the time of independence the state had not acceded, Pakistan signed a standstill agreement with Kashmir agreeing to continue to provide services for which the state had earlier relied on British India.[16] Relations between Pakistan and Kashmir however severely deteriorated after independence once the Kashmir government accused Pakistan of blockading it in order to force it to accede to Pakistan.[17] Mohammed Ali Jinnah, the Governor-General of Pakistan, responded by accusing the Kashmir government of trying 'to join the Indian Union by coup d'etat'.[18]

Caught between having to choose between Indian rule, which would most likely see a hollowing out of his considerable power in Kashmir through democratization, and accession to the Muslim dominion of Pakistan, Maharaja Hari Singh gave serious consideration to the possibility of independence. In order to entrench Dogra rule, the Kashmir government embarked on a campaign of mass violence aimed at the states' Muslim majority. Claims that up to two hundred thousand Muslims were killed are impossible to establish, though there is little doubt that violence in the state became entangled in the wider partition conflagration and resulted in mass migrations out of the state, which in turn destabilized

---

[13] Abdul Gafoor Noorani, *The Kashmir Dispute* (New Delhi: Tulika books, 2013), p. 15.

[14] Ganguly, *The Origins of War in South Asia*, p. 50.

[15] Noorani, *The Kashmir Dispute*, p. 17.

[16] Lamb, *Incomplete Partition*, p. 122.

[17] At least one scholar has argued that the transport situation in Pakistan was dire in Pakistan due to both partition violence and disorder in Kashmir itself. However, given the bitterness of exchanges between the two governments at the time it is not unlikely that a blockade was in fact in place. Victoria Schofield, *Kashmir in Conflict: India, Pakistan and the Unending War* (London: I.B. Tauris, 2003), p. 45.

[18] NMML, *White Paper on Kashmir* (New Delhi, 1948), Jinnah to PM Kashmir, 19 October 1947.

the region.[19] Dogra repression in Punch district resulted in the outbreak of an armed rebellion in August 1947. Evaluations of the success of the rebellion vary with some historians claiming that it was crushed quickly by the Dogras, while others have claimed that Punchi rebels controlled the countryside trapping Dogra forces in the towns.[20] Whatever the rebellion's military consequences, politically it would become implicated with the tribal invasion of Kashmir.

Alarmed by the prospect of Kashmir's possible accession to India and certain a military fait accompli could be achieved in Kashmir, elements of the Pakistani government organized a military operation codenamed 'Operation Gulmarg' aimed at overrunning the state with the aid of tribal proxies. The invasion of Kashmir began on 22 October 1947. Tribesmen from Pakistan's Northwest Frontier province (NWFP) and beyond descended from West Punjab onto the Kashmir Valley. The tribal force was well-armed, travelled in trucks at a time of petrol rationing, and had faced no resistance traversing the length of the NWFP and West Punjab to reach Kashmir. Pakistan's government would maintain the position that the invasion was not in fact supported by it until May 1948, though planning for the invasion was largely carried out by the provincial government of the NWFP with Jinnah's tacit acceptance.[21] The resort to irregular forces to impose Pakistan's will on an increasingly hostile Kashmir government was a consequence of Pakistan's own military weakness.[22] Its army was yet to be properly reorganized, stores due from India were yet to arrive and Jinnah's own control over British officers commanding the Pakistani armed forces was limited.[23] The decision to use the tribal forces in the conflict signalled its internationalization, as for the first time a number of tribes from Afghanistan were inducted into what had essentially been mass violence between rival South Asian religious communities. This can

---

[19] Christopher Snedden, 'What Happened to Muslims of Jammu? Local Identity, "the Massacre" of 1947 and the Roots of the "Kashmir Problem"', *South Asia*, 2001, vol. 24, no. 2, pp. 111–34.

[20] For an instance of the Punch rebellion being treated as a success see- Christopher Snedden, *The Untold Story of the people of Azad Kashmir* (London: Hurst, 2012). For the claim that the rebellion was quickly suppressed see- Raghavan, *War and Peace in Modern India*, p. 105.

[21] When he discovered plans for the invasion Jinnah is alleged to have said, 'Don't tell me anything about it. My conscience must be clear.' BL, MSS Eur D670/6, (Cunningham papers).

[22] The decision to invade was by no means unanimous and prominent GoP leaders such as States Minister Agha Shahid Bad Shah correctly predicted that invasion would drive Kashmir into acceding to India. Noorani, *The Kashmir Dispute*, p. 8.

[23] Noorani, *The Kashmir Dispute*, p. 10.

be read as both a departure from and an expansion of the partition violence that had fed into the increasing instability of the Kashmiri state at the time of independence.

The tribal raiders were supported by a motley assortment of forces. This included a number of regular Pakistani army officers sent to oversee and direct them, former members of the *Azad Hind Fauj* (Indian National Army), Muslim deserters from the Kashmir state forces, and the Gilgit scouts.[24] The last of these was a militia raised by the British to protect the Gilgit agency and had under the leadership of one Major William Brown revolted against the governor of the region and declared their allegiance to Pakistan. In the months of fighting to follow they would prove to be formidable opponents to the Indian army.

The tribal forces streamed down the valley seizing Domel, Uri, and Muzzafarabad. Their immediate objective was the capture of Kashmir's summer capital Srinagar, though in the longer term they hoped to push all the way South to Jammu. At Baramullah tribal forces engaged in an orgy of rape, looting, and violence. Though some of the claims about the sacking of Baramullah's Catholic mission made by the Indian government in its 'White Paper on Jammu and Kashmir', have been shown to have been exaggerated there is no doubt that the town was violently sacked.[25] In Baramullah, and elsewhere, the lack of discipline of the raiders led to indiscriminate violence though it is clear that non-Muslims were the prime targets. The sacking of the town would significantly slow down what was meant to be a rapid advance on Srinagar.

Srinagar was important for a number of reasons. It was the summer capital of the Dogras and the heart of the most populous region in Kashmir state, the valley of Kashmir. Perhaps more important, in the context of the tribal invasion, however is the fact that it had the sole airstrip in the Kashmir valley. Interestingly the fair-weather airstrip had been constructed for the private use of the Maharaja and is representative of the significant if understudied contribution of the princely states to aviation in India. This was especially important given the paucity of connections between Kashmir and Indian territory, which consisted solely of

---

[24] O.P. Sharma, 'How Pakistan Occupied Gilgit: A First Hand Account', in M.L. Kumar (ed), *Maharaja Hari Singh* (New Delhi: Har Anand Publications, 1995), pp. 115–132.

[25] Whitehead, *A Mission in Kashmir*, p. 231.

a road from Pathankot to Srinagar. Nehru understood the importance of the airfield for maintaining communications with the state as evidenced by a letter he had sent to the state's Prime Minister, M.C. Mahajan, prior to the invasion, in which he had requested that the airfield be prepared for service in winter conditions.[26]

The Indian government's reaction to the tribal invasion of Kashmir was swift. The Indian Defence Committee of the Cabinet met on 25 October and decided to dispatch V.P. Menon, the Secretary of the Ministry of States, to Kashmir. Menon would later claim that he was flown to Kashmir in a British Overseas Airways Corporation (BOAC) aircraft chartered to fly British refugees out of Srinagar where he was alarmed by the 'atmosphere of impending calamity'.[27] Air Marshal Hari Chand Dewan however claimed to have personally arranged for Menon's aircraft and flown it to the city.[28] Assuming both these claims are in fact true, Menon was flown to Srinagar by a BOAC plane piloted by a RIAF officer, a highly unorthodox measure but not one that was unlikely given the urgent circumstances. Menon returned to Delhi with the Kashmiri Prime Minister M.C. Mahajan after urging Maharaja Hari Singh to leave Srinagar for Jammu—his winter capital. The Maharaja's haste to vacate Srinagar was such that he did not leave behind transport for Menon and Mahajan so that they and their aircrew had to be bundled into an old jeep to travel to the airfield.[29] The process of Kashmir's accession was expedited by the use of aircraft to quickly transport negotiators from Delhi to an Indian State capital.

The tribal invasion had driven Kashmir to accede to India and Mahajan informed the Indian cabinet of this. The decision was made on 26 October to airlift troops to Kashmir. The accession of the state on the wishes of the Maharaja would be accepted 'provisionally' with a plebiscite to be held in the state to ascertain its people's wishes once the *lashkars* (Pathan columns) were driven out. Moreover, the Maharaja was instructed to form a provisional government with Sheikh Abdullah, who had until September 1947 been imprisoned, as its head. Menon would once again be flown to

---

[26] S. Gopal, *Selected Works of Jawaharlal Nehru* (New Delhi: Orient Longman, 1972), Nehru to M.C. Mahajan, 21 October 1947, p. 274.

[27] V.P. Menon, *Integration of the Indian States* (New Delhi, Orient Longman, 1985), p. 273.

[28] Kumar, *An Incredible War*, p. 41.

[29] Menon, *Integration of the Indian States*, p. 274.

Kashmir to receive the signature of the Maharaja on the instrument of accession, though this was almost certainly signed on 27 October shortly after the first Indian troops had landed in Srinagar.[30] India's reasons for accepting the accession were manifold. As seen above the Indian leadership had strong integrationist ambitions in Kashmir for strategic reasons and India's ruling party, the Congress, had strong affinities with the National Conference. A further factor prompting Indian intervention in Kashmir was the need to maintain communal harmony in India. Nehru was keenly aware that the fall of Kashmir and the atrocities against non-Muslims that would most likely follow it would have catastrophic consequences in India, leading almost certainly to large scale reprisals against India's substantial Muslim minority. As V.P Menon would later note 'the only alternative to sending troops would be to allow a massacre in Srinagar, which would be followed by a major communal holocaust in India.'[31]

Even as Menon was gauging the situation in Srinagar on 25 October an Army Airlift Committee (AAC) was formed to prepare for the airlift of Indian army troops to Srinagar on an emergency basis. By the time orders were received to airlift troops to Srinagar the next day, RIAF planes had been begun to ferry much-needed ammunition from Jabalpur to New Delhi and arrangements for the airlift had been finalized. Oxford training aircraft, the only planes available for reconnaissance, were sent to scout the airfield on 26 October. The AAC included Air Chief Marshal Thomas Elmhirst, Air Commodore Subroto Mukherjee, Group Captain Mehar Singh, the Joint Secretary, Ministry of Defence H.C. Sarin, and significantly the Director-General of Civil Aviation (DGCA) N.C. Jain.[32] As seen in the previous chapter the DGCA had served not only as the primary government officer responsible for civil aviation but had also been central to supporting government during emergencies such as the Second World War and the Partition airlift. When it was realized that the RIAF's planes would be inadequate for the task at hand, the decision was taken to have the DGCA commandeer planes from the civil airline companies such as Dalmia Jain, Air Services of India, and Deccan Airways.[33]

[30] Raghavan, *War and Peace in Modern India*, p. 108.
[31] Menon, *Integration of the Indian States*, p. 276.
[32] Kumar, *An Incredible War*, p. 41.
[33] Reddy, *Aviation in the Hyderabad Dominions*, p. 158.

An emergency broadcast was made on All India Radio by Indian Home Minister Vallabhbhai Patel requiring civilian aircraft from airline companies to report at aerodromes in New Delhi. Some 25 aeroplanes, mainly DC 3 Dakota transport aircraft, which had been purchased by Indian airline companies in the aftermath of Second World War from the United States Army Air Force, responded to the call. Many of these were actually in the midst of ferrying partition refugees to and from Delhi.[34] Significantly many of the civilian pilots who would undertake the perilous airlift had only recently been demobilized after serving in the RIAF during the Second World War.[35]

The Srinagar airlift coincided with 'Operation India', the BOAC led operation aimed at evacuating Indian government officials and non-Muslims stranded in Pakistan, discussed in Chapter 2. Alastair Lamb has suggested that 'the presence of a large number of civil aircraft as part of a project to fly Muslim refugees from India to Pakistan' provided 'an admirable cover' for Indian military plans to intervene in Kashmir.[36] This was however not the case. Both London and Karachi were deeply concerned by the possibility that BOAC aircraft might be used by the Government of India to airlift its troops to Srinagar.[37] Air Commodore H.G. Brackley who was heading the relief effort was instructed by the Commonwealth Relations Office (CRO) not to permit BOAC aircraft to be used in the Kashmir operations. Consequently, an Indian request on 31 October 1947 for the use of BOAC aircraft in airlifting Indian troops was denied.[38] While HMG could easily limit BOAC involvement in the conflict it was much more difficult to prevent British personnel flying aircraft for Indian airline companies from taking part in the Srinagar airlift. A number of foreign pilots had been recruited to fly for Indian companies and many of these were now flying as part of the Kashmir operations. These included 30 British, 1 Canadian, 5 Australians, 3 Ceylonese, 1 Burmese, 3 Americans, and 2 Poles most of whom worked for Indian National Airways. According to the CRO at least half the aircrews flying Indian troops into Kashmir were British European subjects from Australia and

---

[34] Kumar, *An Incredible War*, p. 44.
[35] Subramaniam, *India's Wars*, p. 127.
[36] Lamb, *Kashmir*, p. 145.
[37] TNA, DO 142/482, Kashmir: Aircraft and Air Crews.
[38] TNA, DO 142/482, UK representative New Delhi to CRO, 31 October 1947.

the United Kingdom. The Australian High Commission in India had advised Australian pilots not to take part in Kashmir operations and the British CRO considered following suit, though it was clear that there were no legal tools whereby foreign, and particularly British personnel, could be restrained from flying in Kashmir if they wished to.[39] By mid-November 1947 however HMG decided not to request the Indian government to advise British personnel from taking part in the Kashmir operations. This was partly because of the legal difficulties of doing so and also because the most dangerous phase of the Srinagar operations appeared to have passed.[40] The British government's quandaries over the employment of British pilots in Kashmir is indicative of the difficulties of separating military and civil aviation. It is also demonstrative of the broader internationalization of the conflict which, as we have seen already involved a number of tribesmen from Afghanistan.

British commanders of the Indian armed forces and Lord Mountbatten opposed the airlift to Srinagar since this was fraught with military risks. Indian planes would have to fly over the Zanskar mountain range, whose lowest point was 9300 feet, to a city that might well have fallen into enemy hands, bearing a full load to land on a short airstrip that pilots had never before seen.[41] Moreover, Srinagar airfield was a fair-weather field with little in the way of signals and refuelling facilities for aeroplanes.[42] Their objections however were overridden by the Indian cabinet considering the urgency of the situation. A land column would be forced to travel via the Banihal pass and simply could not be expected to arrive in time to defend Srinagar. Consequently, troops of the first Sikh battalion, who were policing Gurgaon in the immediate aftermath of the Partition riots, were ordered to rapidly embark the impromptu air fleet assembled for them in the early hours of the morning of 27 October.[43] Their commander, Lieutenant Colonel Ranjit Rai was famously ordered to circle the airfield

[39] In at least one case a British pilot expressed his willingness to undertake operations in Kashmir provided there were no legal consequences in the United Kingdom. TNA, DO 142/482, UKHC India to CRO, 4 November 1947.

[40] TNA, DO 142/482, CRO to UKHC India, 15 November 1947.

[41] Sen, *Slender Was the Thread,* p. 45.

[42] CAC, GBR/0014/ELMT 3-1, 'Kashmir, Winter 1947'.

[43] Prasad, *History of Operations in Jammu & Kashmir, 1947–48,* p. 28.

Figure 3.1   Indian troops deplaning at Srinagar in November 1947. The aircraft in the background is likely one of the Dakotas commandeered from airline companies for the airlift. © USI of India

to make sure that it had not fallen to the tribesmen before disembarking his troops.[44]

A total of 22 aircraft were able to make the landing on Srinagar airfield on 26 October 1947.[45] Over the next weeks the tempo of flights bearing Indian troops to Srinagar would remain steady (see Figure 3.1). The AAC met every day to decide on the number of sorties that could be delivered utilizing between 25 and 30 civil aircraft to transport troops and supplies from New Delhi's Willingdon airport to Srinagar. Aeroplanes, dedicated purely to the airlift, made two trips daily from Delhi to the Srinagar airfield. Planes would have to quickly taxi on Srinagar's increasingly dusty airfield in order to make the rapid turnaround required to make the ten hours flying in daylight.[46] Others would continue flying their designated

[44] NAM, 7901-87-6-1, 'Army Headquarters India Operational Instruction No 3', 26 October 1947.

[45] NAM, 7901-87-6-1, 'Army Headquarters India Operational Instruction No 3', 26 October 1947.

[46] CAC, GBR/0014/ELMT 3-1, 'Kashmir, Winter 1947'.

routes in the mornings and do one flight to Kashmir in the afternoon. In the three weeks after the airlift began Indian planes flew 750 flights, carried 13 million pounds of load and flew about 600,000 miles in journeys to Kashmir.[47] Somewhat ironically the Indian Union owed its large reserve of planes to a Muslim Leaguer, Sardar Abdur Rab Nishtar, who as seen in a previous chapter, had as member of communications in the 1946 interim government India granted licenses to a large number of airline companies. Though in the long term this led to the bankruptcy of many of the commercial airlines, in 1947 it provided India with a sizable pool of civil aircraft for operations in Kashmir.

An unexpected outcome of the airlift was the evacuation of a large number of holidaymakers who wished to flee the imminent capture of Srinagar by the tribals. Lieutenant General L.P. Sen recalled the way in which large numbers of tourists simply abandoned their vehicles at the airfield when they were informed that the army would not take care of them. Troops eventually had to be used to clear close to one hundred vehicles clogging the route to the airfield.[48] Nearly four hundred British citizens, mainly retirees and families of British government officials based in India, resided in Srinagar. Their evacuation from what would soon become a war zone was a key concern for the British government. The British Royal Air Force asked for and received permission to evacuate them. This was done using RAF squadrons that Mountbatten had demanded in the face of opposition from the Air Ministry, to deal with just such a contingency.[49] This added an extra layer of complications an extremely difficult logistical operation for the RIAF as the precious daylight time for landing planes in Srinagar had to be shared with the RAF.

Though transport aircraft dominated the Srinagar airlift they were also accompanied by combat aircraft. The RIAF found itself in a disorganized state at the commencement of the Srinagar operations. There were severe shortages of spares, transportation, and ammunition. RIAF Air Marshal Thomas Elmhirst noted that 'equipment staffs hardly knew what was

---

[47] *Hindustan Times*, December 19, 1947. Quoted in Kumar, *An Incredible War*, p. 57.

[48] Sen, *Slender Was the Thread*, p. 61.

[49] BL, IOR Neg 15538-67, Dickson to Ismay, 20 October 1947. Negotiations to this end were still on when the Kashmir war broke out. The RAF had firmly indicated it considered the maintenance of two transport squadrons in India for the evacuation of British personnel an extravagance, despite the fact that it would permit Mountbatten to maintain his own communications squadron in case the situation in India deteriorated, necessitating his evacuation.

available and where it was.[50] Srinagar airstrip also posed a problem, as it was too short for the RIAF's frontline plane, the Tempest. Nevertheless, the RIAF improvised rapidly. Harvard trainer aircraft were equipped with guns and the flown to Jammu by flying instructors. Later they would be fitted with makeshift bombing racks. Soon Spitfires used for training at the Ambala Elementary Flying Training School were rearmed with guns and sent to Srinagar to provide fire support for the Indian troops defending the airstrip, much to the horror of the civilian pilots for whom it made an already risky flight more dangerous.[51]

A number of problems with the Srinagar airfield had to be overcome by the RIAF. This included the lack of communications, repair, and re-fuelling facilities. A RIAF headquarters was flown into Kashmir airfield including a jeep to serve as a 'communications car' to enable better coordination between New Delhi and Srinagar. Pilots conducted turnaround repairs on their own before the arrival of ground crews. The lack of re-fuelling facilities at Srinagar was offset by the draining of excess fuel from transport aircraft until a Dakota was refitted solely to carry fuel to the airfield.[52]

With the help of the RIAF, the Indian army managed to hold onto Srinagar and its all-important airfield despite bitter fighting at nearby Badgam on 3 November 1947. RIAF Spitfires and Harvards were based at the airfield and sent into action against the invaders. Interestingly the small contingent of four Spitfires and three Harvards based at Srinagar was temporarily designated as No.1 Squadron, perhaps as a rebuke to the Royal Pakistan Air Force (RPAF), which as seen in a previous chapter had disbanded the famous No. 1 Squadron which it had inherited at the time of Partition.[53] Tempests based at Ambala helped destroy columns of raiders moving about by trucks in the open during daylight hours.[54] By 6 November, India had 3500 troops in Srinagar.[55] The long-awaited column of armoured cars from Punjab had also arrived over the perilous

[50] CAC, GBR/0014/ELMT 3-1, 'Kashmir, Winter 1947'.
[51] CAC, GBR/0014/ELMT 3-1, 'Kashmir, Winter 1947'.
[52] Ibid. This unorthodox practice was the cause of much fury, when airline companies presented their bills to the Government of India's finance department as the latter protested that forms measuring fuel transfer had not been filled.
[53] Kumar, *An Incredible War*, p. 69.
[54] CAC, GBR/0014/ELMT 3-1, 'Kashmir, Winter 1947'.
[55] Prasad, *History of Operations in Jammu and Kashmir 1947–48*, p. 40.

road from Pathankot. Harvard reconnaissance aircraft and other Indian scouts detected a build-up of thousands of raiders at Shalateng. Indian forces were ordered to attack the raiders from three sides with full air support on 7 November. In their concentrated numbers they offered perfect targets for RIAF Tempests and Spitfires from Nos. 1, 7, and 10 Squadrons. The battle was over in 12 hours. The raiders were routed, leaving some 500 dead on the field for only three Indian casualties.[56] Indian forces drove them all the way to Uri in the next three days effectively securing the Kashmir valley.

Mohammed Ali Jinnah was furious when he heard about the Srinagar airlift and immediately ordered the Pakistani army to go into action against the Indians in Kashmir. General Messervy, Commander-in-Chief of the Pakistan army, was unwilling to do this since it would effectively mean war with India. Consequently, he called, Field Marshal Claude Auchinleck, the supreme commander, to talk Jinnah out of military action. Auchinleck flew to Lahore on the morning of 28 October and forced Jinnah to withdraw his orders by threatening a 'stand down' of all British officers serving in the Pakistani military which, given its post-partition disorganization it could scarcely afford.[57] This by no means meant that Pakistan accepted Kashmir's accession to India and the Pakistan government stepped up its support for the raiders. The Kashmir war had begun in earnest.

Indian aviation had played a central role in initiating the conflict in Kashmir. While the war between India and Pakistan was not unexpected over another disputed princely territory, Junagadh, the speed with which aircraft could facilitate both diplomacy and war in Kashmir was critical to beginning the Kashmir conflict.[58] Indeed, the speed and success of the airlift was so great that it convinced Pakistani observers and later historians that India had planned it well in advance.[59] By initiating a limited conflict in Kashmir aircraft enabled the Indian government to avoid a full-scale war, since that would have been the only meaningful option left

---

[56] Gulati, *Military Plight of Pakistan*, p. 243.
[57] The 'stand down' order would lead to a withdrawal of British forces from the armed forces of dominions that went to war with each other and was aimed at preventing British soldiers from being pitted against each other. Raghavan, *War and Peace in Modern India*, p. 109.
[58] Raghavan, *War and Peace in Modern India*, p. 57.
[59] Bharat Kumar has convincingly refuted the allegations of Alastair Lamb that the airlift was pre-planned. Kumar, *An Incredible War*, p. 208. Also see Lamb, *Incomplete Partition*, p. 145.

to it if it was unable to intervene in Kashmir. From the beginning therefore, aviation served as a crucial tool for Prime Minister Nehru to manage the escalation of the Kashmir conflict.

The roots of India's ability to project air power in a spectacular and sustained way must be traced to the Second World War. Not only was the RIAF's sole transport squadron, No. 12, raised as part of the wartime expansion of the force but the sale of aircraft to airline companies in its aftermath provided India with a large strategic reserve.[60] As noted above the size of this reserve was a product of the politics of partition. The airlift stands out as one of the myriad instances of the blurring of civil and military aviation during the decade. Aircraft are an excellent example of what would be later called dual-use technology and the ways in which India made use of its scarce aviation resources is illustrative of how poorer states throughout the world would seek to exploit this dual-use capability in what have, somewhat ethnocentrically, come to be called 'regional conflicts'.

The Siege of Punch

As Indian troops and Pakistan backed *Azad* (freedom) forces clashed in Kashmir, negotiations between the Indian and Pakistani governments commenced.[61] On 1 November 1947 Lord Mountbatten, in his capacity as Governor-General of India, met with his Pakistani counterpart M.A. Jinnah. Jinnah was offered a U.N conducted plebiscite to be preceded by the withdrawal of Azad and then Indian forces. Jinnah's dismissal of the offer is ironic in hindsight since all subsequent negotiations to this day have broken down on the issue of plebiscite and the withdrawal of Indian troops from Kashmir.[62] Besides the obvious need to prevent a

---

[60] TNA, AIR 27/180, No 12 Squadron Operations Record Book.

[61] The Government of Pakistan used the term *Azad Kashmir* for those zones that had broken free from Dogra control. Consequently, the umbrella term Azad forces was used to address the diverse forces ranged against the Dogras and later the Indians. See for instance: NMML, *Pakistan Times*, October 22 1947.

[62] Nehru may have changed his mind on conducting a plebiscite as early as November 1947. Talks between India and Pakistan over a plebiscite in Kashmir ever since have stumbled on the question of withdrawing Indian troops. Noorani, *The Kashmir Dispute*, p. 40.

subcontinent wide conflagration, Mountbatten was moved by one other major consideration.

British planners had hoped to integrate India and Pakistan into a Commonwealth that they envisioned as a military alliance primarily aimed at the Soviet Union. British Chiefs of Staff penned a paper titled 'British Defence Requirements in India', according to which India would provide Britain with bases in the Indian Ocean and manpower, while Pakistan would provide it with forward strategic airbases aimed at the USSR. Both dominions were to have the closest defence cooperation whose basis lay in the Joint Defence Council.[63] At least one bureaucrat involved in planning compared the proposed Indo-Pak military arrangements to those of New Zealand and Australia.[64]

The proposed Commonwealth defence alliance was a casualty of the war in Kashmir. Mountbatten presented a paper on joint defence arrangements against external aggression to the Indian and Pakistani governments at the Joint Defence Council meeting held on 22 December 1947. India and Pakistan were unanimous in stating that foreign policy convergence had to precede defensive alliances. Vallabhbhai Patel, the Indian Home Minister, tersely stated that the joint defence council had not been constituted for this purpose.[65] Mountbatten failed to convince the Joint Defence Council to invite the British chiefs of staff before his departure from the subcontinent despite attempting, as late as January 1948, to secure some form of tripartite military agreement.[66] Cold War paranoia underpinned much British thinking during the Kashmir war often at the cost of ignoring the depth of the ideological conflict between Pakistan and India.[67]

That ideological contest was nowhere more clearly borne out than around the siege of Punch. The Kashmiri town, besieged by Pakistan backed forces early on in the conflict, would become a major flashpoint.

[63] BL, Mss Eur IOR Neg 15542, Defence of India and Pakistan Part I (b).

[64] BL, Mss Eur IOR Neg 15542, Defence of India and Pakistan Part I (a); It is also worth noting that given his staunchly internationalist position Nehru, would most likely have steered clear of military alliances. For a discussion on Nehru's internationalism see: Zachariah, *Nehru*.

[65] NAI, Vallabhbhai Patel Papers, File2/180, Vallabhbhai Patel to Jawaharlal Nehru, 22 December 1947.

[66] BL, Mss Eur IOR Neg 15542, Defence of India and Pakistan Part I (b).

[67] This is a point first raised by C. Dasgupta. His view however vests excessive agency in British hands at the cost of ignoring Indian decision making. Dasgupta, *War and Diplomacy in Kashmir 1947–48*, p. 13.

In a telegram to the CRO, British High Commissioner to India, J.S.H. Shattock noted that 'To Indians the Punch siege was somewhat parallel to the siege of Tobruk or Kut'.[68] The Indian leadership was not initially certain that military efforts should be concentrated around Punch since it was located in the mountainous region where the rebellion against Dogra rule had first begun.[69] Proposals were even mooted for the early evacuation of state forces and the non-Muslim population of Punch town and the eponymous district.[70] However, Indian military reverses in November 1947 fundamentally changed the tenor of the Indian government's position on Punch.

The fall of nearby Kotli and severe attacks against the town of Uri, which served as the gateway to the Kashmir valley, nearly pushed the Indian military in Kashmir to desperation in December 1947.[71] The Indian leadership actively considered an offensive into the Punjab to relieve pressure on its forces in Kashmir, a move that would certainly have heralded full-scale war with all its attendant problems noted earlier.[72] Though Uri would be held and the situation would be stabilized, the Azad offensives of December had two key effects. First it led India to place its case ahead of the UN largely in the hopes of placing pressure, short of full-scale war, on Pakistan. Second it led to the decision to hold Punch town.

Holding Punch for the Indians was critical on a number of important lines. Non-Muslim refugees had fled to Punch to escape from rebels who were targeting them.[73] Punch was one of the granary districts of Kashmir state.[74] The most important reason for holding Punch however was, as Srinath Raghavan has argued, that Nehru was well aware of 'the link between military operations and diplomacy'.[75] Control of Punch would convince Pakistan and the world that India was serious about its military commitment in Kashmir precisely because the region was difficult to hold.

---

[68] TNA, DO 133/82, Shattock to CRO, 19 October 1948.
[69] Raghavan, *War and Peace in Modern India*, p. 114.
[70] Ibid., p. 117.
[71] Prasad, *History of Operations in Jammu & Kashmir, 1947–48*, p. 87.
[72] Dasgupta, *War and Diplomacy in Kashmir 1947–48*, p. 97.
[73] Whitehead, *A Mission in Kashmir*, p. 116.
[74] TNA, DO 133/96, Military Situation (hereafter Milsit) 28 September to 4 October.
[75] Raghavan, *War and Peace in Modern India*, p. 120.

Figure 3.2 Indian troops landing at the besieged town of Punch. The IAF helped India keep the town supplied despite enemy encirclement and the incredibly harsh terrain that is visible in the background. © USI of India

Punch town had been under siege before Indian troops landed in Kashmir. Its Kashmir state force garrison had been reinforced by an Indian battalion led by Lt. Col. Pritam Singh on 21 November 1947, though a larger accompanying force had been prevented from relieving the town by a combination of enemy action and sheer bad luck.[76] Some 3000 troops had to defend a civilian population of 40,000 non-Muslims. They were cut off from all relief and in a particularly vulnerable position as the lines of communication of the Punch garrison with friendly forces faced the enemy. Only the air link now connected Punch with the outside world.

Lt. Col. Singh realized that the town could not be supplied by airdrops and the decision was made to put the able-bodied population of Punch to work, constructing a landing ground that could support transport aircraft by extending the J & K militia parade ground. Construction

---

[76] Prasad, *History of Operations in Jammu & Kashmir, 1947–48*, p. 58. A bridge meant to carry over the relief column of vehicles was burnt by friendly state forces who mistook it for a raider column.

was done in full view of besieging forces and with only RIAF aircraft fire support for cover.[77] The 600-yard Punch airstrip was completed in little over six days and was carefully tested with lighter planes, to see if it was capable of accepting fully loaded transport aircraft. A trial Harvard plane piloted by Baba Mehar Singh was followed by an Oxford aircraft test before fully loaded Dakota aeroplanes landed bearing critical supplies from 12 December onwards.[78] Dakotas from No. 12 squadron RIAF flew in petrol, medicines, ammunition, flour, rice, sugar, matches, fruit, whisky, cigarettes, and even champagne (see Figure 3.2).[79] As they had in Srinagar, civil aircraft also played their part, flying in despite the extreme danger of Punch's very short airfield.[80] The air fleet began bringing in a regular stream of supplies while evacuating those refugees, particularly women and children, whose labour was not considered necessary for the garrison. Over the course of six days 4,27,000 pounds of supplies and a battery of mountain guns were flown into the town as part of what would later become known as 'Operation Punching'.[81]

Azad forces constantly shelled and sniped at Punch. Full-scale attacks were not launched at least partly because of the difficulty in concentrating troops in the face of constant RIAF tactical reconnaissance though the town's fortifications also discouraged offensives.[82] The siege of Punch on the ground was thus an action in which the garrison constantly streamed out in an effort to capture strategically critical points in keeping with the belief that it was facing irregular forces.[83] The besiegers meanwhile fought often to defend positions that they held while avoiding concentrations that might be easily spotted from the air. Indeed, by March 1948, the situation had sufficiently been alleviated by evacuations of civilians and the flying in of supplies that the Punch garrison moved to the fields out of the town to cover civilians from Punch as they harvested grain fields.[84]

In order to bombard Indian pickets outside the town and disrupt the landing of planes at Punch airfield the raiders moved up 3.7-inch guns

[77] Chhina, The Eagle Strikes, p. 270.
[78] CAC, GBR/0014/ELMT 3-1, 'Kashmir, Winter 1947'.
[79] MoD (I), 601/14292/H, Air Drops.
[80] MoD (I), 601/14418/H, AO 70, 6 January 1947.
[81] Chhina, The Eagle Strikes, p. 271.
[82] TNA, DO 133/95, Milsit 12 to 18 February 1948.
[83] TNA, DO 133/95, Milsit 24 February to 1 March 1948.
[84] TNA, DO 133/95, Milsit, 2 March to 9 March 1948.

against the town later that month. Indian forces would later learn that the Azad forces were in fact backed by the 3rd Mountain Battery of the Pakistan army.[85] The consequences of the bombardment were grave. RIAF Dakotas tasked with supplying Punch from Jammu were forced to suspend landings and to resort to the far less effective method of airdropping in order to supply Punch. As the British military adviser in Pakistan noted, 'Food is said to be running short in the town which is packed with refugees, the morale of the troops is low and without more substantial assistance than the Indians can provide by parachute the town is expected to fall in a month at the outside.'[86]

It was in this context that General Roy Bucher, commander-in-chief of the Indian army, approached his Pakistani counterpart, General Douglas Gracey, to negotiate possible safe passage for refugees from Punch and a limiting of military action.[87] The negotiations are representative of the influence of British commanders in de-escalating the Kashmir conflict. They are also significant to a degree not previously realized in the context of the RIAF resupply of Punch. According to the agreement the RIAF would limit its bombing of hostiles around Punch while the Azad forces would stop their increasingly effective artillery bombardment of the town. Bucher pursued two interconnected objectives in the negotiations that were begun on 19 March 1948, two days after the 3.7-inch guns were inducted to bombard Punch. He believed that the Indian political leadership was intent on holding Punch to protect its large non-Muslim population. Therefore, he sought to ensure that civilians were withdrawn from Punch so he could convince the Indian government to eventually withdraw its forces from Punch. Bucher assumed mistakenly that the Indians were committed to holding Punch primarily to defend its non-Muslim civilian population and once civilians were evacuated the 'commitment of the Indian Army would be less'.[88] He was also at least partially concerned about the adverse supply situation caused by the arrival of the Pakistani artillery.[89] Bucher eventually ended the talks with Gracey, claiming that

---

[85] TNA, DO 133/95, Milsit, 22 to 28 April 1948.

[86] TNA, DO 134/1, A.H. Reed to H.S. Stephenson, 25 March 1948.

[87] Dasgupta's reading of these talks has been contested. See; Dasgupta, *War and Diplomacy in Kashmir 1947–48*, p. 141; Raghavan, *War and Peace in Modern India*, p. 115.

[88] BL, L/WS/1/1141, Shone to CRO, 28 March 1948.

[89] BL, L/WS/1/1141, Shone to CRO, 28 March 1948.

Azad forces were not capable of implementing a scaling down of action due to their poor communications. Talks between the British commanders of both dominions broke down partially because Bucher took a stridently pro-India position and Gracey supported Pakistan. There is also reason to believe that the Indian government was displeased with Bucher for overstepping his brief.[90] Further it is very likely that the RIAF's delivery of artillery to Punch, took the pressure off Bucher to negotiate de-escalation.

RIAF aircraft famously flew in two 25 pounder guns along with ammunition and artillery crews to counter the 3.7-inch guns that the Azad forces were bombarding Punch with on 21 March 1948.[91] This eventually stabilized the situation in Punch. By the end of April, the town could boast a battery of four 25 pounder guns as the Azad commitment to attacking it seemed to decrease, partly because Punchi rebels needed to return to their fields in order to harvest their crops. Meanwhile over twenty thousand refugees of the original refugee population of forty thousand were evacuated by air.[92] Indeed the situation for India improved so greatly that the reinforced garrison of Punch was able to fan out and capture positions around the town, even briefly linking up with friendly troops from Rajauri.[93]

India had committed to holding Punch in December 1947 to ensure its prestige in Kashmir. Holding Punch would not only convince rebellious Kashmiris and Pakistan but also Hyderabad, as shall be seen in an upcoming chapter, was holding out for independence, of India's commitment in the broader context of negotiations. India's position before the United Nations would be more secure if it claimed sovereignty over all Kashmir in keeping with its broader case that all of Kashmir state was 'provisionally' Indian territory. It did so primarily through the work of the RIAF which both provided the Punch garrison with air support and kept it supplied.

As Azad forces increasingly showed signs of disintegrating from the force of the imminent Indian spring offensive of 1948, Pakistan inducted

[90] Dasgupta, *War and Diplomacy in Kashmir 1947–48*, pp. 141–2.
[91] For a detailed account of the delivery of 25 pounder guns to Punch see: Kumar, *An Incredible War*, p. 189.
[92] TNA, DO 133/95, Milsit, 22 to 28 April.
[93] Prasad, *History of Operations in Jammu & Kashmir, 1947–48*, p. 246.

its regular forces into combat, considerably upping the stakes of the Kashmir war.[94] Following the failure of the Indian spring offensive and the arrival in the subcontinent of the United Nations Commission for India and Pakistan (UNCIP), Indian military activity in Kashmir wound down considerably. Pakistan made use of the opportunity to infiltrate troops into Ladakh and to encircle Punch. For Pakistan the capture of Punch was important not only for prestige reasons. Over 12,000 personnel in the Pakistani army were from Punch and the integrity of the Pakistani army depended on forestalling further Indian moves in Punch.[95] Perhaps more importantly the full scope of the refugee crisis created as Muslims fled from the Indian army was making itself apparent to the government of Pakistan. Karachi's concerns on this count are apparent from the fact that the Pakistan army's ceasefire plan, hoped to gain Indian permission to use roads as far as Uri as well as the Jhangar crossroads in order to get supplies to homeless Punchi refugees who were wandering between Punch district and the Jhelum river.[96]

Confronted with the imperative of capturing Punch, Pakistan deployed a large force to surround the town. By late September nine battalions of Pakistani and Azad troops had surrounded Punch in a semi-circle.[97] A 25 pounder gun was transported with great difficulty from Kohala in Pakistan to Punch being towed by hand for 35 miles before being broken down into man loads and then being carried by 400 men for 16 miles.[98] It matched the heaviest Indian guns in Punch and could rapidly change position to avoid counter-battery action. The Pakistani artillery piece was able to put the airfield out of action, effectively dooming Punch unless a link up by land was effected. Indian planes continued to airdrop supplies around Punch but these supplies would not be adequate, particularly with the onset of winter. Even Pakistani army officers who insisted that the bombardment of the Punch airstrip did not constitute a major provocation, since they argued that Punch likely had stocked up provisions for months, conceded that 'the (Indian) Union troops must have been handicapped greatly by their inability to evacuate casualties'.[99]

[94] Nawaz, *Crossed Swords*, p. 67.
[95] TNA, DO 134/3, A.H. Reed to H.S. Stephenson, 16 May 1947.
[96] TNA, DO 134/4, A.H. Reed to S.J. Olver, 2 August 1948.
[97] TNA, DO 133/96, Milsit 28 September to 4 October.
[98] TNA, DO 134/4, J.F. Walker to UKHC Pakistan, 23 September 1948.
[99] TNA, DO 134/5, A.H. Reed to UKHC, 7 December 1948.

The cutting off of Punch is illustrative of the limitations of air supply against a determined enemy. India was able to sustain Punch by air for a year thanks to the heavy and often ingenious commitment of its air force but this could not be maintained continuously. Consequently, the Indian army was forced to launch a major ground offensive to relieve the Punch garrison in the winter of 1948.[100] While in the long term the decision to hold Punch proved politic, the link up alarmed the Pakistani military which was convinced that India was seeking to conquer all of Kashmir, pushing forward an unsustainable mass of refugees into Pakistan. As a British observer at Pakistan Army Headquarters noted following the Indian link up on 20 November 1948, 'The general opinion here is that the Union Government is dedicating all its energies to achieving a fait accompli in Kashmir as soon as possible ... For their part the Pakistan Government is equally determined this shall not come to pass.'[101] Pakistan was in the midst of deploying nearly its entire army in Kashmir with the intention of launching an offensive against India's line of communications in late November 1948 and the Punch link up seemed to offer them a reason to do so.

Indian aviation had enabled the holding of Punch but it had done so at the cost of escalating the artillery duel there with Pakistan, a duel that could not in the long term be won given the determination and superior logistics of the enemy. To be fair it is worth noting that the initial decision to hold Punch was made under the assumption that regular Indian forces would be combating irregular forces rather than the Pakistan army.[102] Ultimately however the continued Indian presence in Punch, which was heavily dependent on air supply, came to be seen as escalatory by Pakistan which dedicated ever greater resources to besieging the town. This in turn necessitated a dangerously escalatory Indian ground assault. The Indian ground offensive to link up Punch, launched after the failure of the RIAF to keep the town supplied, was seen very differently in New Delhi and Karachi. What to Nehru appeared to be 'defensive measures ... assuring supplies to Punch' could appear to be 'impending offensives' to Liaquat Ali Khan.[103] By December 1948 full-scale war looked as likely as it had

---

[100] Subramaniam, *India's Wars*, p. 153.
[101] TNA, DO 134/5, A.H. Reed to S.J. Olver, 23 November 1948.
[102] Prasad, *History of Operations in Jammu & Kashmir, 1947–48*, p. 73.
[103] TNA, DO 133/82, Nehru to Menon, 19 November 1948; TNA, DO 134/5, Liaquat Ali to Clement Atlee, 8 December 1948.

been in December 1947. As the next section will reveal the RIAF mechanisms to manage escalation were under serious pressure by the end of the war.

Managing Escalation

The acceptance by both India and Pakistan of the need to limit the war meant that explicit and often highly detailed arrangements were worked out between the armies of the two countries. As seen earlier, even before the Pakistani army was officially inducted into combat, the commanders-in-chief of both armies were working on ways to prevent escalation. Managing escalation between the Indian and Pakistani ground forces usually amounted to localising combat and conveying clear signals about military intentions. The case of the air forces of the two dominions however was more complex.

The RPAF was remarkably small at the time of the Kashmir conflict and was still going through the process of reorganization following Partition. George Cunningham, governor of the NWFP, was 'struck by the smartness and good appearance of its officers' at a parade but noted that 'it is a little disturbing that this was the whole of the Air Force of Pakistan'[104] Its participation in the early phase of the war was a secret, though there is some evidence that Harvards and Spitfires of the RPAF undertook reconnaissance for the Azad forces.[105] This secrecy around its early deployment and the small size of the RPAF meant that there was little need to evolve a framework around managing its escalatory potential.

The RIAF in contrast was central to India's war in Kashmir. Consequently, the Indian political leadership restricted its actions to prevent escalation. As was the case with the army, despite claiming sovereignty over the entirety of the territories of the state of Kashmir, the Indian government limited the areas in which the RIAF could attack the enemy. Pilots were ordered not to bomb the Lachman Pattan and Kohala bridges due to their proximity with Pakistan and not to attack the Mangla irrigation headworks. Any violation of these restrictions or any attacks on

---

[104]   BL, MSS Eur D 670/6, Diary entry, 14 January 1948.
[105]   Hussain, *History of the Pakistan Air Force, 1947–1982*, p. 33.

Pakistan territory by gun, bomb, and rocket would result in immediate court-martial.[106] Indeed bombing restrictions were heavy enough to draw complaints from high-ranking Indian army commanders who felt severely constrained. Lt. General Cariappa called for the bombing of the Lachman Pattan bridge, arguing that if the RIAF did not bomb the bridge the build-up of enemy forces would be so great as to threaten Indian territorial gains and hence endanger the very political goals for which aerial bombardment was being held back.[107] He was swiftly rebuffed by the Indian military's British commanders who were especially keen to avoid escalation. Air Marshal Thomas Elmhirst claimed that over half of all bombs dropped on the bridge would fall in Pakistan territory.[108] General Roy Bucher meanwhile warned of the 'incalculable political repercussions' of such an action ending any possibility it would be undertaken.[109]

Despite this, the RIAF was accused of indiscriminate and occasionally provocative bombing, not least by its own commander. Air Marshal Thomas Elmhirst, Commander-in-Chief of the RIAF, wrote to his deputy that he was alarmed at the 'apparently indiscriminate' attacks by Tempest aircraft on houses. This did not fulfil the military objective of supporting the advance and 'would cause locals not to vote for the accession to India'.[110] Air Vice Marshal Subroto Mukherjee, to whom the letter was addressed, was instructed to consider the matter and to pass orders he thought were necessary to control indiscriminate bombing. Consequently, restrictions on bombing were further increased by a fresh directive for pilots in Kashmir. Attacks on buildings and civilians were to be avoided as the 'Air Force is fighting within the territory of India'.[111]

The RIAF also received complaints from the East Punjab Red Cross for bombing its hospitals and shooting up its vehicles. One Miss Macqueen, niece of the West Punjab governor who worked for the East Punjab Red Cross, accused the RIAF of bombing the Bagh hospital once and the Kotli

[106] MoD (I), 601/14247/H, Directive to AOC No 1 (op) Group for conduct of air operations in Kashmir, 26 June 1948.
[107] NAM, 7901-87-6-1, K.M. Cariappa to Chief of General Staff, 19 June 1948.
[108] NAM, 7901-87-6-1, T.W. Elmhirst to R. Bucher, 23 June 1947.
[109] NAM, 7901-87-6-1, R. Bucher to H.M. Patel, 24 June 1948.
[110] MoD (I), 601/14247/H, Elmhirst to Mukherjee, 21 June 1948.
[111] MoD (I), 601/14247/H., Directive to AOC No 1 (op) Group for conduct of air operations in Kashmir, 26 June 1948.

Figure 3.3 Air Marshal Thomas Elmhirst, first Commander-in-Chief of the Royal Indian Air Force after independence. Elmhirst oversaw the RIAF during the 1947 war in Kashmir and grew increasingly worried about the possibility of its escalation into all-out war. © USI of India

hospital twice despite her repeated complaints.[112] Elmhirst consequently launched investigations that revealed that Kotli hospital had indeed been bombed, though he defended the bombings by claiming that it was inadvisable to place hospitals in forward areas without markings visible from the air. Since 'under no circumstances would RIAF pilots deliberately attack' a Red Cross building, Elmhirst claimed that 'the lady in question must be in quite an imbalanced state of mind'.[113] Nevertheless restrictions were made ever tighter and Pakistani radio intercepts in November

[112] MoD (I) 601/14420/H, Telegram from Miss MacQueen, Red Cross Chairman, West Punjab, 9 October 1948.
[113] MoD (I) 601/14420/H, Elmhirst to H.M Patel, 25 October 1948.

1948 showed that RIAF planes were reporting back to headquarters on whether towns under reconnaissance had any visible Red Crosses on them.[114] Attacks on Red Cross hospitals opened India to international pressure as they could bring with them the scrutiny of the International Committee of the Red Cross. They also gave Pakistan valuable propaganda material. Pakistani newspapers were running stories on the Indian bombing of hospitals as early as November 1947.[115] The RIAF's sensitivity to allegations of bombing Red Cross buildings is indicative of the ways in which air action was being adapted to ensure that both international and Kashmiri opinion did not turn against India. It was also informed to a degree by the leadership of Air Marshal Elmhirst who appears to have been personally shocked by the actions of the force (see Figure 3.3).

More alarming for the Indian government however were those instances when Pakistani territory was bombed by RIAF planes. Bombing Pakistani territory was dangerous for a number of reasons. Attacks on Pakistan might lead to a full-scale escalation of the war, which the Indian leadership was keen to avoid. The RIAF attacked Pakistan on multiple occasions. Some, such as the attack on Kohala bridge, occurred before strict orders were enforced. Others such as the attacks on Garhi Habibullah and Murree were caused inadvertently.[116] The bombing of Murree is revealing of the difficulty of preventing RIAF bombings of Pakistan territory despite heavy restrictions. It is also revealing of the mechanisms in place for managing escalation between Pakistan and India over the bombing of Pakistan territory.

As seen earlier, the RIAF had managed to severely constrain enemy forces by attacking motor convoys during daylight hours. This meant that most Pakistani convoys then travelled by night when RIAF strike aircraft could not fly. Lacking aircraft designed for night bombing the RIAF improvised by loading its Dakota transport aircraft which could fly at night time with twelve 250-pound bombs which were then rolled out of the plane. One such 'Dakota bomber' meant to carry out a bombardment of Muzzafarabad bridge on the night of 19 August 1948, overflew its target. Mistaking the lights of the Pakistani hill station town of Muree for their

[114]   TNA, DO 134/5 A.H. Reed to UKH C Pak, 21 November 1948.
[115]   NMML, *Pakistan Times*, 5 November 1947.
[116]   TNA, DO 134/3, Grafftey Smith to Carter, 7 June 1948.

target the IAF pilot T.N. Ghadiok dropped two bombs before realizing his mistake. T.N. Ghadiok, who would rise to be an Air Marshal, called off the bombing run when he recognized the town from its Great Mall road, since he had gone to college in Murree.[117]

The Pakistan army was quick to condemn the action. General Gracey, its commander, was 'wild' with Air Marshal Elmhirst, as his wife was 'summering' in Murree when the bombs fell.[118] Pakistani authorities also went on to claim that the bombing had been accompanied by a machine-gunning of the town, though this was later proven to be untrue.[119] India's response to the complaint was conciliatory. The claim was investigated, and when found to be true, apologies were made to Gracey by Elmhirst. Pakistan Army Headquarters accepted the apology though anti-aircraft batteries were dispatched along with their British staff to Northern Punjab as a precaution against further air raids.[120] Pakistani military authorities were willing to make allowances for attacks that were clearly inadvertent, caused no casualties and were not aimed at targets of military importance, even if these occurred in Pakistan itself. In contrast when the RIAF bombed the Northern town of Gilgit, Pakistan not only claimed that a hospital had been hit but also threatened to execute Indian prisoners of war being held there.[121] India was quick to cease bombing Gilgit town and Nehru ordered that no towns located behind Pakistani lines should be bombed by the RIAF.[122] Clear signalling by both governments of the thresholds of escalation communicated primarily through the British military commanders of the Indian and Pakistani armies went some way in ensuring that the RIAF would be used in limited ways.

The Government of India sought to prevent bombings of Pakistani territory for a number of reasons. Bombing Pakistani territory would almost certainly provoke Pakistan into escalating the conflict into a large-scale war that would be ruinous for both countries. Indiscriminate bombing would also paint India as a callous invader in a political setting where the legitimacy of its intervention was under question. This

---

[117] Kumar, *An Incredible War*, p. 175.
[118] CAC, GBR/0014/ELMT, 5/5 A, 22 August 1948.
[119] TNA, DO 134/4, Anonymous to Symons, 23 August 1948.
[120] TNA, DO 134/4, A.H. Reed to S.J. Olver, 24 August 1948.
[121] MoD (I) 601/14422/H, Gracey to Bucher, Telegram 10007, undated.
[122] TNA, DO 134/4, UKHC India to CRO, 6 September 1948.

would severely weaken India's standing among the Kashmiri populace and also potentially invite international opprobrium, especially from the United Kingdom and the United States with its attendant consequences. Finally, there was the not inconsequential concern that directly attacking Pakistani territory would alienate British commanders of the Indian armed forces leading potentially to their resignations at a time when their experience was critically necessary both for the conduct of military operations and for the organization of independent India's armed forces.

A key consequence of India's unwillingness to bomb Pakistan was the almost painstaking observance of Pakistani territorial sovereignty by the RIAF. Its pilots, as seen above, were strictly forbidden from attacking or even flying close to Pakistani territory. This was in gross contrast to contemporary Indian actions in Hyderabad where RIAF aircraft not only routinely violated the princely state's air space but were also ordered to attack aircraft smuggling arms into the state, even if they sighted them on the ground. Indian restraint with Pakistan and aggression in Hyderabad is emblematic of independent India's emerging notions of sovereignty. Indian recognition of Pakistani territory was consistent with its wider notions of sovereignty that located it in a global order based on international legal sovereignty.[123] Despite disagreements over Kashmir, the Government of India recognized Pakistani sovereignty, in large part because there were concrete international repercussions to violating it, whereas such disincentives were absent in the Hyderabad case. This is less revealing in certain ways of Indian notions of sovereignty than it is of the international system that emerged from the Second World War. That world was one constituted by a set of nation-states that were simultaneously distinct and modular.[124] Overt violations of territorial sovereignty in this system were treated as a threat to global stability, particularly in the context of the Cold War, whereas violence aimed at consolidating the domestic sovereignty of the nation-state was not. These seemingly abstract notions had concrete military consequences in Kashmir where RIAF aircraft were prevented from risking escalation through attacks on Pakistani territory.

---

[123] For a discussion of international legal sovereignty see: Krasner, *Sovereignty*.

[124] A growing body of work has critiqued the inevitability of the emergence of the nation state as the sole means of organizing sovereignty. See for instance: Devji, *Muslim Zion*, p. 71.

Another source of anxiety related to the use of air power in the region was the possibility that Indian aircraft might intercept Pakistani aircraft beginning a cycle of escalation that would end in full-scale war between the two countries. The eventual clash of the RIAF and the RPAF in Kashmir altered the mechanisms evolved to keep the conflict limited, but not by very much. It is unclear when exactly the RPAF was inducted into Kashmir though Dakotas of the RPAF may have begun supply dropping missions as early as December 1947. These missions were carried out in radio silence to avoid detection by the Indians and were flown over some of the most mountainous terrains of the world.[125] By October 1948 with the open participation of the Pakistan army in Kashmir, the RPAF took on ever-increasing supply duties. RIAF planes sought to suppress this and made attacks on airfields behind Pakistani lines in places such as Bunji, Gilgit, and Chilas which were then heavily patrolled from the air to prevent repair.[126]

It was on one such patrol that RIAF Tempests from No. 7 Squadron, spotted an RPAF Dakota dropping supplies on 4 November 1948. The RIAF had been authorized by the Defence Committee of the Cabinet to intercept any Pakistani aircraft flying over Kashmir territory. On spotting an RPAF plane the Indian pilot was to signal it to land at a nearby airfield failing which he was to open fire across the planes bow. If even this did not work the plane was to be shot down. When they spotted the RPAF plane the Indian pilots followed their orders.[127] Unwilling to surrender, despite being pursued by considerably faster Tempest fighter aircraft, the Pakistani pilot, Flying Officer Mukhtar Ahmad Dogar flew low into the Chilas valley. Dogar used a tactic that the RIAF, which he had been a member of before Partition, had used in the face of faster Japanese aircraft during the Second World War. He flew so low and so slow that it became difficult for Tempests to successfully shoot down his plane. F.O. Dogar managed to evade the Indians who were chasing him despite losing two crew members to Tempest firing and was subsequently awarded the Sitara-e-Jurat for his actions.[128]

---

[125] Hussain, *History of the Pakistan Air Force, 1947–1982*, p. 30.

[126] MoD (I), 601/14302/H, No. 206, 3 November 1948.

[127] MoD (I), 601/14302/H, No. 207, 4 November 1948.

[128] Hussain, *History of the Pakistan Air Force, 1947–1982*, p. 35.

The sole aerial engagement of the war precipitated a flurry of diplomatic correspondence as British officials in the CRO, members of the Indian government and the Pakistan cabinet tried to defuse what they saw as an act of escalation.[129] Air Vice Marshal Subroto Mukherjee, the deputy commander of the RIAF, would fly to Karachi to negotiate a 'gentleman's agreement' with the commander of the RPAF, Air Vice Marshal Perry Keene whereby he essentially restated the Indian government's policy of only shooting down transport aircraft if they refused to surrender at the nearest Indian airfield.[130]

Chandrashekhar Dasgupta has argued that British High Commission officials and commanders, working in conjunction, prevented escalation and robbed India of a chance to seriously disrupt Pakistani supplies by attacking Dakotas. In making this argument he appears to share the belief of contemporary British officials that RIAF attacks on Pakistani Dakota transport aircraft would naturally escalate the conflict into a full-scale war. If Pakistan protected its transports with fighters, this thesis assumes, India would ultimately be forced to attack Pakistani airbases triggering an inter-dominion war. The British government would then have to issue a stand-down order to its officers serving in the armed forces of one or both of the dominions. This assumption ignores a point put forward in the very files Dasgupta quotes. A note most likely written by Sir P. Patrick of the CRO says:

Even if the RPAF and RIAF did become engaged in desultory fighting (for it would, I think be no more) I do not see why this should be any more reason for the sounding of the Stand-down than the indisputable fact that the Indian and Pakistani armies are at this moment fighting each other.[131]

A similar argument was echoed in a letter by the British High Commissioner to India, Terence Shone, to the Air Marshal Thomas Elmhirst of the RIAF dated 16 November 1948. Elmhirst had spoken to Shone informing him that he was wracked by guilt at the possibility of

---

[129] Dasgupta, *War and Diplomacy in Kashmir 1947–8*, p. 175.
[130] Kumar, *An Incredible War*, p. 131.
[131] BL, L/WS/1/1144, BGS 8 November 1948.

fighting breaking out between the RIAF and RPAF. He might find himself in the position of advising the Indian government to attack RPAF bases in Pakistan thus being forced to wage war against his fellow-RAF officers.[132] The Air Marshal bemoaned the fact that the His Majesty's Government had not issued the stand-down order as soon as Pakistani regular troops were found to be fighting India. Finally, he had hinted that he would put in his resignation if he found himself in the position of fighting the RPAF.[133]

Shone replied that thus far Elmhirst had not put in his resignation despite the long-standing public knowledge that Pakistani regular forces commanded by British officers were operating in Kashmir. Shone felt that 'the fact that you wear a blue hat and the soldiers wear khakhi hats is a matter of mere detail'. So long as any air operations took place 'in the confines of Kashmir' the conditions under which Elmhirst operated would not 'have changed one iota'.[134]

Shone wrote to Elmhirst that, 'If you did give such advice it does not necessarily follow that the Indian Government would accept it, because the political implications of such an action, not only locally but throughout the world, would be very grave indeed.' However, if such a recommendation was given and accepted 'it seems to me an entirely different situation would be created.' Shone also said that an identical situation would emerge if India decided to launch a land attack on Pakistan.[135]

Thus, it appears that both contemporaries and historians overestimated the escalatory potential of air-to-air combat in the Kashmir war. A clash between the RIAF and the RPAF would not lead with any certainty to the bombing of air bases inside Pakistan or for that matter to an order to stand down from Her Majesty's Government. While it is true that in keeping with the broader policy of not engaging in provocative actions the Indian government ceased operations aimed at downing Pakistani transports it is likely that even if there had been aerial confrontations between the RPAF and RIAF, it would not have led to full-scale war as long as the Indian government was committed to keeping the war

---

[132] The RPAF had a large contingent of British officers and technicians and it is likely Elmhirst feared that Indian bombings of Pakistani bases might harm them.
[133] CAC, GBR/0014/ ELMT 3-1, Shone to Elmhirst 16 November 1948.
[134] Ibid.
[135] CAC, GBR/0014/ ELMT 3-1, Shone to Elmhirst 16 November 1948.

localized. It is worth noting here that British commanders in India had by late 1948 made it clear that they were neither willing nor able to prosecute an advance on the Pakistani border in Kashmir, let alone a full-scale war against Pakistan in the Punjab.[136] For its part the Indian leadership understood that there was no hope for a military solution in Kashmir and did not intend to expand the conflict into a full-scale war.[137] What would turn out to be the only clash of Indian and Pakistani aircraft in the war simply did not merit an escalatory response.

The Indian political and military leadership had created a number of mechanisms aimed at restraining air power from providing its adversary with propaganda as well as preventing the escalation of the conflict. Air power was used sparingly, India's military intent was clearly signalled by its primarily British general staff and an attempt was made to prevent the repetition of any action that Pakistan held out as overtly provocative. Though it was believed by both contemporaries and historians to be a grave escalation, air to air combat merely underlined the fact that as long as it was localized, the fighting in Kashmir would not lead to full-scale war. By the end of 1948 however this situation began to change as Pakistan deployed the bulk of its army in an offensive posture in Kashmir.

Inadvertent Escalation: The Palak Bombings

By December 1948 Pakistan considered its military situation to be desperate. Indian troops had linked up with the besieged towns of Punch and Leh. Like Punch, Leh was a strategically critical town, which served as an important junction and as the capital of the Ladakh region. Also, like Punch, it had been besieged by rebels, the Gilgit scouts, and had relied on the air link to survive a siege that lasted from May to November 1948. Just as in Punch, the air link had remained tenuous and Indian troops had been forced to take the offensive to relieve the town before it ran out of supplies.[138] Combined with the Punch link up, the Indian march on Leh, and the capture of the strategically vital towns of Dras and

---

[136] NAM, 7901-87-6-1, R. Bucher to H.M. Patel, 23 November 1948.
[137] BL, L/WS/1/1144, UKHC India to CRO, 24 November 1948.
[138] TNA, DO 133/96, Symon to CRO, 6 November 1948.

Kargil had pushed Pakistani forces back considerably. In some sectors, Pakistani defensive positions were not more than 20 miles away from the East Punjab border.[139]

The Pakistani leadership was alarmed by these developments and redeployed nearly its entire army to reinforce its troops in Kashmir from late November 1948.[140] The Indian advances were the cause of alarm for two reasons. First, the Indian army had advanced into striking distance of the canals that watered much of the Punjab. The capture of the Jhelum and Chenab headworks would give India control over four-fifths of the water necessary to feed the Punjab. Pakistani policymakers were convinced that their capture would mean the effective end of Pakistan's independence.[141] Perhaps more immediately troubling for Pakistan was the possibility that further Indian advances would cause an influx of Muslim refugees that the country simply could not cope with. As the High Commissioner for Pakistan noted, 'they believe that an influx of no more than another one or two hundred thousand refugees would crack the provincial economy and mean the end of Pakistan.'[142]

The calculus of the war in Kashmir shifted in fundamental ways from the end of November onwards. Pakistan no longer saw Kashmir as a theatre in which it was waging a limited war with India. Instead due to the threat to its water supplies and the influx of refugees, Pakistan's leaders felt that it was possible for 'India to destroy Pakistan by action in Kashmir alone'.[143] Indian forces were extremely vulnerable to an attack by the Pakistani army and RPAF in Kashmir due to their exposed communications lines and their reliance on air supply. It is likely that a Pakistani offensive in Kashmir with the full weight of its army and air force would have been catastrophic for Indian forces.[144] The Indian leadership would then likely be forced to counterattack in Punjab where Pakistan's reduced defences would make East Punjab vulnerable to invasion unleashing the worst effects of full-scale war.[145] A Pakistani offensive was slated for 7 December 1948 and subsequently postponed to the 11 December. Only

---

[139] TNA, DO 134/5, A.H. Reed to S.J. Olver, 23 November 1948.
[140] BL, L/WS/1/1144, UKHC Pakistan to CRO, No 1322, 18 November 1948.
[141] Ibid.
[142] BL, L/WS/1/1144, UKHC Pakistan to CRO, No 1392, 18 November 1948.
[143] BL, L/WS/1/1144, UKHC Pakistan to CRO, No. 1395, 18 November 1948.
[144] BL, L/WS/1/1144, UKHC India to CRO, 5 November 1948.
[145] TNA DO 134/5, H.S. Stephenson to Grafftey Smith, 26 November 1948.

the prospect of a diplomatic breakthrough by the UNCIP sent to Kashmir convinced Karachi to postpone the offensive[146]

On 13 December 1948 eleven RIAF Tempests from No. 1 Wing, dropped 500 and 1000-pound bombs on enemy supply dumps in two waves near Palak in Mirpur district. They strafed three trucks spotted in the area and ended the raid with incendiary bombs. The next day two Tempests dropped incendiary bombs on the area. Further, raids were called off when Bofors anti-aircraft guns were encountered in the area. In order to prove that it was attacking legitimate military targets and to show that the nearby village was not attacked, the RIAF was careful to aerially photograph the aftermath of the Palak bombings.[147] The attack was among the largest and most well planned RIAF air raids launched during the war.[148]

In Pakistan, the Palak bombings caused some alarm. General Gracey ordered Pakistani artillery to bombard the Beri Pattan bridge and adjoining supply dump in retaliation. A 24-gun field regiment and an 8 gun medium battery fired at the Indian depot at Beri Pattan from the morning of 15 December to the evening of the 18 December. RIAF planes that attempted to attack the gun batteries were driven away by sustained anti-aircraft fire. The bombardment devastated the Indian supply dump at Beri-Pattan, scored a direct hit on the critical bridge situated there, destroyed a 25 vehicle Indian convoy, and led some Indian troops to flee from their positions in panic. In light of Pakistan's decision not to launch an offensive this artillery bombardment was not as heavy as it would have been a few days previously when it would also have been followed up with attacks by Pakistani armour and infantry.[149] The artillery bombardment came as a shock to the General Bucher who called up General Gracey to ask why Pakistani gunners 'had put 25,000 rounds into his supply dump'. When he was informed that this was retaliation for the Palak bombing he confessed that he was unaware of the bombing, which later emerged had been carried out on the orders of Air Marshal Thomas Elmhirst.[150]

---

[146] Raghavan, *War and Peace in Modern India*, p 144.

[147] MoD (I), 601/14314/H, No 135, Air OPSUM, December 1948.

[148] Bharat Kumar has also written about the Palak bombings though some of the details in his account vary from those of the sources that I have consulted. He also shows how, like many other RIAF raids, the Palak raid was portrayed as an attack against civilians and the Red Cross by Pakistani newspapers. Kumar, *An Incredible War*, pp. 193–194.

[149] BL, L/WS/1/1145, A.H. Reed to S.J. Olver, 21 December 1948.

[150] Ibid.

Ironically, as seen earlier, Elmhirst had been concerned, to the point of threatening resignation, about the possibility of plunging the subcontinent into war through air action.

General Gracey claimed that the RIAF bombing of Palak had been a violation of an earlier agreement between himself and Gracey whereby Indian forces would make take no major actions following the linkup with Punch and Leh.[151] Moreover, the Pakistan government pointed to a more recent agreement drawn up between Air Vice Marshal Mukherjee of the RIAF and Air Commodore Janjua of the RPAF, that India would reduce the number of Tempest squadrons based in Kashmir and, in the aftermath of the Giligit bombings, that no towns would be attacked. India had in this view violated the agreement, meaning that Pakistani military forces were no longer obligated to limit themselves to defensive operations. The telegram sent by Gracey to Bucher when the bombardment eventually ceased was revealing, 'All is now quiet on the Western front. *Nemo impune me lacessit* (No one cuts me with impunity).'[152]

The Palak bombings and subsequent repercussions were occasioned by a number of factors. Agreements drawn up between Indian and Pakistani military authorities continued to be coloured by their political views on the conflict, meaning that the British chiefs of the Indian and Pakistani militaries had increasingly internalized the convictions of the countries they had been seconded to serve. Earlier during negotiations over de-escalation of Punch, General Bucher had maintained the Indian government's position that the Indian army was operating in its own territory against raiders while Gracey had insisted on inducting Pakistani troops into the district in keeping with Pakistan's broad position that it had at least as much right to maintain forces in Kashmir as India.[153]

Thus, Gracey's reading of the most recent agreement to limit hostile operations included large scale air operations while Bucher had clearly not taken these into consideration.[154] The Indian agreement not to bomb towns was read by the RIAF as meaning that it would not attack populated towns and the photographic evidence gathered by it during the Palak raid clearly indicated that it had not indeed done so. Another reason for the

---

[151] BL, L/WS/1/1144, UKHC India to CRO, 23 December 1948.
[152] BL, L/WS/1/1145, UKHC Pakistan to CRO, 19 December 1948.
[153] Dasgupta, *War and Diplomacy in Kashmir 1947–8*, p. 141.
[154] BL, L/WS/1/1145, UKHC India to CRO, 22 December 1948.

way in which the Palak bombings clearly escalated the conflict was the sheer complexity of the military structures involved. Though Bucher had agreed to restrain Indian military actions in the aftermath of the Punch linkup, he could hardly be expected to prevent all military actions at a time when the Indian and Pakistani armies were in close proximity. His clear surprise on being informed of the Palak bombings by the Pakistan army reveals that he had not considered the possibility that air attacks would be escalatory.[155] Indeed the RIAF was also not aware that its operations were likely to have escalatory effects.

The Palak raid may have been a large raid but it was similar to other air interdiction operations that the RIAF had carried out in the Kashmir theatre. RIAF commanders continued to believe that operations carried out in Kashmir would not lead to escalatory action by Pakistan as long as they continued to remain within a framework that the RIAF had evolved over the course of the war by adapting its actions to the signals sent to it by the Pakistani military. The RIAF had entered the war with a long list of restrictions which had over time expanded in response to Pakistani objections and its own understanding of what actions were provocative. The bombing of what RIAF commanders knew to be an enemy supply dump located within Kashmir territory away from major population centres did not appear to be a provocative action that would invite escalation. Given the changed tenor of Pakistani military policy in Kashmir however it led to an inadvertent escalation.

The response in New Delhi to the shelling of Beri Pattan was furious. As the British High commissioner there noted, 'there are very strong and bitter feelings in all responsible circles as a result of the recent action at Beripattan (sic), which has roused feelings of indignation to a degree which I would not have thought possible in apparently reasonable people.'[156] Jawaharlal Nehru was enraged and renewed calls he had earlier made for British officers in Pakistan to be given a stand-down order since they were no doubt involved in the planning of the bombardment.[157] The British government would not acquiesce to this for a battery of reasons. These included concerns that a British stand down order aimed

---

155 TNA, DO 134/5, A.H. Reed to S.J. Olver, 21 December 1948.
156 BL, L/WS/1/1145, UKHC India to CRO, 22 December 1948.
157 BL, L/WS/1/1145, UKHC India to CRO, 22 December 1948.

at Pakistan would potentially throw the country into chaos opening the door to communism and also endanger the lives of British citizens present in Pakistan.[158] Nehru also again implied that the conflict would be escalated by threatening to take whatever steps were necessary to check the 'offensive' against the Indian army on its own territory.[159]

Nevertheless, India did not militarily respond to the Beri Pattan shelling. Indeed, Bucher assured Gracey that there would be no repeat of the Palak bombing, after speaking with Elmhirst. There were several reasons for this apparent de-escalation. Nehru knew that a military victory was no longer possible in Kashmir.[160] India controlled most of Kashmir and had little to gain from the capture of predominantly Muslim regions where the populace considered it to be a hostile power. Though Nehru had long given up on the prospect of a plebiscite he was willing to accept a ceasefire followed by negotiations on plebiscite as an alternative to full-scale war.[161] It is not unlikely that the Beri Pattan action, among other events, convinced him that the prospect of a stand-down by British officers in the Pakistan army, which would have given India a significant advantage, was distant, prompting him to settle for what effectively amounted to a partition of Kashmir.[162] Confronted with British unwillingness to call for a stand-down order, Indian Prime Minister Jawaharlal Nehru found himself facing a decision on whether to go to war with Pakistan or conclude a ceasefire. He chose the latter ending the war.

---

[158] BL, L/WS/1/1145, CRO to UKHC Pakistan & UKHC India, 20 December 1948,
[159] BL, L/WS/1/1145, Nehru quoted in CRO to UKHC India & UKHC Pakistan, 20 December 1948.
[160] TNA, DO 133/82, UKHC India to CRO, 19 November 1948.
[161] Raghavan, *War and Peace in Modern India*, p. 145.
[162] This is not to ignore other military developments that the prime minister was concerned about such as the shelling of Sadabad and the Pakistani army's construction of roads towards Akhnur. See: NAM, 7901-87-6-1, Nehru to Bucher, 23 December 1948; There are also some indications that the Indian government's decision in favour of a ceasefire was taken suddenly. General Bucher sent General Gracey a telegram on the 30 December 1948 that began, 'In view of political developments my government thinks continuation of moves and counter moves due to misunderstanding accompanied by fire support seems senseless and wasteful in human life besides only tending to embitter feelings.' The Pakistani government accepted the proposal and what later telegrams between the two armies referred to as an 'informal ceasefire' came into existence the next day on 31 December 1948 ending the war in Kashmir. See: NAM, 7901-87-6-1, Bucher papers.

Lessons from the Kashmir War

The Kashmir war is illustrative of the political potential of air power. At least one historian has compared the Kashmir airlifts to the 1948 Berlin airlift which occurred at the same time.[163] While not as large as the Berlin airlift, the political consequences of the mobilization of Indian aviation, both civil and military, in Kashmir have been no less enduring. The Indian government drew critical lessons on air power, its political importance and its role in escalation from the Kashmir war. This was reflected in the higher government thinking on aviation. Civil aviation came to be seen increasingly as a strategic asset too important to leave in the hands of private operators.[164] Paying tribute to Indian airline companies on the eve of their nationalization in 1953, G.L. Bansal, a prominent legislator reminded parliament of the indispensable role civil aviation had played in Kashmir. He asked if any could 'forget those hectic days when we Kashmir was attacked by the barbarians from the other side, and when civil aviation of the country, which was completely in private hands came to the rescue at a moment's notice'.[165] The RIAF in India meanwhile remained central to defence planning.

The emphasis in Indian defence planning before the Kashmir war had been heavily on reducing expenditure on defence in order to focus on a programme of social welfare and industrial development. Jawaharlal Nehru had envisioned a major reduction in the size of the Indian army after independence with a view to reducing military spending which accounted for more than half of all expenditure by the Indian government. For Nehru, India's defence ultimately rested on the country's ability to build up its industrial and scientific base which would in turn reduce reliance on foreign arms imports. Doing this would necessitate the retrenchment of the army. Interestingly, the Prime Minister saw the Indian Air Force as a key means of effecting savings since it could strike 'quickly and effectively' and was cheaper to maintain than a large army.[166] Nehru's thinking on the subject was no doubt affected by British interwar policies

---

[163] Subramaniam, *India's Wars*, p. 123.
[164] More on this in Chapter V.
[165] 'Air Corporations Bill' 21 April 1953, *Parliament of India Digital Library*, https://eparlib. nic.in/bitstream/123456789/56065/1/lsd_01_03_21-04-1953.pdf, Accessed 9 July 2021.
[166] S. Gopal, *Selected Works of Jawaharlal Nehru*, Nehru papers, 16 September 1947, p. 483.

that had also attempted to reduce heavy expenditures by substituting relatively cheap air power for more expensive ground forces.[167] The importance of aviation technology had also not been lost on Nehru. His father, Motilal Nehru, had played an instrumental role in the founding of the Indian Air Force as part of the Skeen Committee in the interwar years. Both Nehrus held the view, popular in the interwar years, that air bombing would play a key role in future wars, making air forces the most important of the military services. This view is likely to have been further reinforced with the advent of the atomic bomb. As Nehru noted 'the development of the air arm' was likely to be 'most important to the defence forces in the future'.[168] As such the Indian prime minister hoped to maintain a relatively small army while investing in air power.

The Indian Air Force's performance in the Kashmir war appeared to validate the Nehru's faith in military aviation. Paying tribute to the pilots and airmen of the RIAF at Safdarjung aerodrome on 20 November 1947, less than a month after the Srinagar airlift, Nehru declared:

> Indian pilots and crews compared favourably with those of the air force of any nation in the world but we do not have a sufficient number of them at present and we must try to train more young men for this work. Aircraft will be bought and I hope we will soon begin to manufacture them in India. But the more difficult task is to train an adequate number of men to work them.[169]

Expenditure on the RIAF continued even as the Indian government sought to gradually reduce the size of the army after the war. The Indian budget of 1949–1950 set aside a substantial grant for air force expansion with a view to training more technicians who could help build a force better balanced between its air and ground crews.[170] The Indian cabinet

---

[167] For a detailed discussion on this see: Priya Satia, 'The Defense of Inhumanity: Air Control and the British Idea of Arabia', *The American Historical Review*, vol. 111, no. 1 (February 2006), pp. 16–51.

[168] S. Gopal, *Selected Works of Jawaharlal Nehru*, 16 September 1947, p. 483.

[169] S. Gopal, *Selected Works of Jawaharlal Nehru*, 20 November 1947, p. 327.

[170] Expenditure on the army did not in fact reduce as tensions between India and Pakistan continued to remain high. What I point to here however is the belief that the air force ought to continue to be funded even as expenditure on the army was reduced. 'Speech of Dr. John Matthai, Minister of Finance, Introducing the Budget for the year 1949–1950', 28 February 1949, *Parliament of India Digital Library*, https://eparlib.nic.in/handle/123456789/218?view_type= search, Accessed 28 June 2021.

remained united in its view that the Indian Air Force ought to be expanded. In a letter to Nehru in January 1950, Baldev Singh, the Minister for Defence, pushed for the expansion of the IAF to ten squadrons by insisting that the Indian Air Force had put India in a superior position in any future conflict with Pakistan. The Indian leadership's commitment to air power, inherited partly from the British, was deepened by the war in Kashmir. Indeed, air power gained new significance in a context in which the Indian leadership saw future clashes with Pakistan as something of an inevitability. As Singh noted in the same letter to Nehru that 'the next year or two are the anxious times from the point of view of our relations with Pakistan'.[171] He was proven right as India and Pakistan would once more come close to all-out war, this time in Bengal.

Conclusion

Aviation was central to India's 1947 war in Kashmir. Aircraft initiated, sustained, and eventually escalated the conflict. The airlift of Indian forces to Kashmir changed the course of the princely state's history and is responsible for the present-day Line of Control. Aircraft were used to compensate for India's geographical disadvantages in the conflict, enabling it to hold politically crucial objectives like Punch without inflaming the military situation on the ground for some time. The caution with which the Indian Air Force was forced to act in the conflict was not only a result of the Indian government's wish to keep the conflict limited but also a recognition of the territorial sovereignty of Pakistan outside of Kashmir. Measures to prevent the conflict from escalating by limiting it to Kashmir proved unsustainable in the long term, as the rapid escalation following the bombing of Palak showed. The conflict underlined the pivotal role of both civil and military aviation for the Indian government. It contributed to the eventual decision to nationalize Indian airline companies and also reinforced the view that the IAF would play a key role in India's national defence.

---

[171] NAI, File 2/369, Sardar Vallabhbhai Patel papers, Defence Expenditure, Baldev Singh to Jawaharlal Nehru, 5 January 1950.

4

Of Princes and Planes: Aviation in the Indian States 1931–1948

The 'Indian' or 'Native' states covered two-fifths of the British Raj on the subcontinent. Consisting of some 600 odd states of varying sizes, the Indian states were indirectly ruled by the paramount power, the Government of India. The Indian states spread over half a million square miles and included some 90 million subjects of the British Empire.[1] Also known as the princely states after the collection of monarchs who headed their governments, the Indian states pledged allegiance to the Government of India in return for a measure of autonomy in internal affairs.[2] Indirect rule had the benefit of entrenching colonial power with the support of a native elite, securing revenues cheaply, and served in important ways to underpin the ideological justification for colonialism. Moreover, the ambiguous relationship between the Government of India and the princely states meant that the former could freely interfere in the affairs of the princely states even when such intervention was often technically illegal. Despite this, the governments of the princely states had greater freedom to frame policy than their counterparts in the provinces of British India. This meant that they were able to make innovative interventions in a number of important fields such as aviation.

The princely states played a critical role in the establishment of the Indian aviation sector. They encouraged aviation both within and outside of their territories contributing extensively to the setting up of aerodromes, flying clubs, and airlines. An Indian prince, Maharaja Bhupinder

---

[1] The total number of Indian states remains contested since historians do not agree on the precise definition of what constitutes a princely state. Ian Copland, *The Princes of India in the Endgame of Empire 1917–1947* (Cambridge: CUP, 1997), p. 1

[2] This could refer to a widely different set of political arrangements that usually involved the bearing of financial and military obligations towards the colonial state on the part of the Indian states.

The Aeroplane and the Making of Modern India. Aashique Ahmed Iqbal, Oxford University Press.
© Oxford University Press 2023. DOI: 10.1093/oso/9780192864208.003.0005

Singh, had the distinction of becoming the first Indian, and perhaps the first Asian, to own aircraft when in 1910 he sent Patiala state's chief engineer to Europe to purchase two Farman biplanes and a Bleriot monoplane.[3] Over the next four decades India's semi-autonomous princely states would play a major role in the establishment of the Indian aviation sector. Hyderabad and Nawanagar would establish their own airline companies.[4] Bhopal, Jodhpur, Travancore, Patiala, and Cochin would come to feature some of India's most sophisticated aerodromes. A 'confederation of Indian chiefs' offered to fund a programme of glider training in 1934 to make Indians more 'air minded.'[5] Mysore State would set up India's first aircraft factory, Hindustan Aircraft (Private) Limited for the manufacture of planes during the Second World War. Some of India's smallest states, with no aircraft of their own, insisted on donating money for the purchase of aeroplanes for the Royal Air Force (RAF) during the war. Sirmur state, for instance, paid 50,000 rupees towards the purchase of a Vickers Valentia while Khairpur paid 1,40,000 rupees for a Hawker Hurricane.[6] Maharaja Kunwar (prince) Paljor Namgyal the heir apparent of Sikkim state died in an air crash at Peshawar on the 20 December 1941 while serving in the Indian Air Force (IAF).[7] A telegram from his father, the Maharaja of Sikkim to the political officer poignantly noted that pilot officer Namgyal had 'sacrificed his life in attempting to serve the King and the country.'[8]

Indeed, the princely contribution to aviation is so expansive as to be challenging to summarize. This chapter therefore raises and seeks to answer three questions about the princely engagement with aviation in India. Why did the Indian states pour substantial resources into the development of aviation? What were the political implications of the aeroplane for India's monarchical order? How did aviation inform the broader engagement between princely India and the colonial and post-colonial Indian state?

[3] *Flight*, 'A Lane Farman Biplane for a Maharajah', 17 December 1910.
[4] PC (AR), James B. Muff files (1916–1977).
[5] *Legislative Assembly Debates* (New Delhi, 1940), p. 208.
[6] NAI, 8740/229/40/AIR, Donations by princely states.
[7] MoD (I), 601/9616/H, ORB No 1 Squadron, 20 December 1941.
[8] NAI, 1941_200_X_41, F&P, Progress report of Maharaja Kunwar Paljor Namgyal, Maharaja of Sikkim to Political Officer, 21 December 1941.

It will be argued that the princely investment in aviation was part of a broader struggle to maintain and exert sovereignty by the monarchical order in the face of increasing pressure from the colonial state on the one hand and Indian nationalists on the other. Significantly the challenge to the legitimacy of princely rule was framed by both the colonial Government of India and Indian nationalists in terms of a lack of modernity. In the eyes of both the colonial state and nationalists the princely states did not, and indeed could not, possess modernity and therefore had little authority to govern. As Manu Bhagwan has pointed out 'colonial modernity' was built, at least partly, in opposition to the idea of an unchanging princely India. In this view the princely states stood for tradition and stagnation whereas British India stood for modernity and progress.[9] This tendency, which had long been a defining characteristic of the colonial state, only deepened as it increasingly embraced developmentalist ideas of improvement, to counter an increasingly confrontational mass nationalist movement.[10] Even when Indian states attempted to modernize, this process was seen by the colonial power as being a failed imitation of Western methods. Racialized notions that underpinned ideas of the modernity of British India meant that though Indians might adopt Western methods this adoption was doomed to imperfection due to racial difference. Indian states, in other words, were seen as being incapable of modernization at a time when modernity was held to be the basis of British rule. The tendency to delegitimize strategies of modernization in the Indian states by the colonial government had serious consequences in the form of constant and often illegal interference in the affairs of the Indian states. As will be seen the Government of India, in its role as the 'paramount power', would make use of an ambiguously defined paramountcy to intervene in the affairs of the princely states. In these circumstances the need to modernise and to modernize credibly would push several of the larger princely states to embrace aviation technology.

If the colonial state made claims that princely states lacked legitimacy because they stood outside modernity and were only capable of imperfectly

---

[9] Bhagwan, *Sovereign Spheres*, p. 4.

[10] See for instance: Debdas Bannerjee, *Colonialism in Action* (Hyderabad, Orient Longman, 1999). For discourses on improvement see: Frank Luggard Brayne, *Village Uplift in India* (Gurgaon: Rural Community Council, 1928); Frank Luggard Brayne *Socrates in an Indian Village* (New Delhi: OUP India Branch, 1937).

mimicking 'colonial modernity', nationalists argued that the princely rule was illegitimate because it was unrepresentative. According to nationalists' princely governments were both simultaneously undemocratic and incapable of modernizing. Indeed, the inability to modernize sprang from the anachronistic form of government that monarchy represented. This is not to argue that nationalists always or even consistently opposed princely rule. Several nationalists looked to the Indian states for inspiration for their dream of an independent India and some monarchs such as the Gaekwad of Baroda maintained close links with the nationalist movement.[11,12] Moreover for a series of complex reasons India's leading nationalist party, the Indian Nationalist Congress, eschewed active political interventions into the affairs of princely states until 1938. Nevertheless, elements of the party could display a marked antipathy towards princely governments. Jawaharlal Nehru famously began his 1929 Congress Presidential speech by saying:

> I must frankly confess that I am a socialist and a republican and am no believer in the order of kings and princes, or in the order which produces the modern kings of industry, who have greater power over the lives and fortunes of men than even the kings of old, and whose methods are as predatory as those of the old feudal aristocracy.[13]

The speech is remarkable more for its dismissal of the princely order than for its socialist emphasis. The 'old feudal aristocracy' is contrasted with 'modern kings of industry' as though the monarchical order which existed at the time was an anachronism. Congress pressure on the princes steadily increased in the years following 1938, as links were forged between the party and a number of organizations within the princely states seeking greater representation. Indian states were increasingly accused by nationalists of lacking modernity because they were undemocratic.

The Indian states were thus confronted by two distinct challenges to their sovereignty framed in modernist terms. The colonial state maintained that it was the sole agent of modern developmentalism in the

---

[11] Fatehsinhrao Gaekwad, *Sayaji Rao of Baroda: The Prince and the Man* (Bombay: Popular Prakashan, 1989) p. 183.

[12] For a survey of the relationship between the princes and Indian nationalists see: Barbara Ramusack, *The Indian Princes and Their States* (Cambridge, CUP, 2004), p. 216.

[13] *Congress Presidential Addresses 1911–1934* (Madras: G.A. Natesan, 1934), p. 894.

subcontinent since Indian states were incapable of possessing true modernity. Indian nationalists on the other hand took an increasingly strident tone, allying with subjects of the princely states, to claim that the Indian states were not modern because they were unrepresentative. The challenge to modernity thus translated to a challenge to the legitimacy of the princes to rule.

The princely response in several of the larger states was to pursue a sophisticated programme of modernization. This had two main thrusts aimed at meeting the twin challenges of an exclusive colonial modernity and a nationalist vision of modernity premised on representation. Indian states would not aspire merely to mimic Western modernity but to craft their own 'native modernity' that could successfully confront 'colonial modernity' despite labouring under colonial constraints.[14] To be sure native modernity was not solely reliant on technology. An Indian state could make claims to modernity by adopting more modern social policies such as the Mysore government's decision to ban the religio-sexual services of the *Devadasi* (servants of god) order.[15] However technology in general and high technology in particular loomed large in visions of native modernity as they did in most visions of modernity at the time.

In order to counter nationalist criticism about the unrepresentative nature of their rule the Indian states made use of a variety of strategies. The most common of these was to increase, or provide the perception of increasing, popular representation. Indeed, in the years between the end of the Second World War and independence, the Indian states made enormous strides in developing representative institutions.[16] Nevertheless other strategies could be adopted instead of or in addition to the provision of representation. Some of India's larger states sought to offer an alternative vision of modernity where representation would be replaced by governance as the basis of state legitimacy. Once again high technology served as an important means of realizing such modernity.

In these circumstances the aeroplane, arguably the pre-eminent symbol of modernity, offered larger Indian states a means to leverage their wealth and autonomy to produce 'native modernity'. Aviation

---

[14] Bhagwan, *Sovereign Spheres*, p. 8.

[15] Janaki Nair, *Mysore Modern: Rethinking the Region under Princely Rule* (Minneapolis, University of Minneapolis Press, 2011), p. 218.

[16] Copland, *The Princes of India in the Endgame of Empire 1917–1947*, p. 212.

served to strengthen princely claims of legitimacy on two levels. First the strategic potentialities of the aeroplane could be tapped, as I shall demonstrate, in order to legitimate princely rule. The mobility of the aeroplane and the technical impact it had on princely governments served to undergird princely power in a number of ways. Just as importantly, aviation could serve a number of ideological ends by reconstituting the image of the princely state as a site of modernity.

The princely engagement with aviation was broadly characterized by an attempt to utilize technology to constitute a 'native modernity' that could then be used to entrench the sovereignty of the Indian states. However, the manner in which states operationalized this could vary depending on a number of factors including the size of the state involved, its goals and in the context of aviation, its location. This chapter will analyse the role of aviation in three princely states; Jodhpur, Hyderabad, and Mysore. While all three states share some commonalities such as large size, wealth, and consequently an advanced administrative apparatus they are also adequately diverse to represent the very different ways in which aviation was approached by the Indian states. Jodhpur constituted a new paradigm that combined traditional notions of martiality with the modernity of the aeroplane in the person of its Maharaja. Mysore sought to use the aeroplane to begin a broader process of industrialization that catered to its developmentalist view of modernity in the course of the Second World War. Hyderabad meanwhile sought to entrench its sovereign status through the establishment of an airline and when this failed resorted to utilising aeroplanes for the purpose of blockade running.

The princely engagement with aviation would have important consequences for the process of state formation in 20th-century South Asia. It would in important ways affect not only the legitimating ideologies of the Indian states but also their own self-image. Moreover, aviation played an important role in the events surrounding the dismantling of the princely order or as it was euphemistically termed the 'integration of the princely states'. The long-term consequences of the princely engagement with aviation would continue to be felt long after the demise of the monarchical order in 1949 as the new Indian Union came into possession of, among other things, the aircraft, aerodromes, and institutions previously patronized by the princes. Before undertaking an analysis of aviation in the princely states under discussion however it is important to ground the study in historiographical and chronological context.

The Indian States: A Background

The British East India Company (EIC) established the system of indirect rule over large swathes of India from 1759 to 1856. The process of transforming Indian kingdoms into subordinates of the EIC was long and complex, relying as often on constant renegotiation between the EIC and the kings as it did on treaties and other agreements.[17] As a reward for their loyalty during the 1857 rebellion, the princes were assured by Queen Victoria that 'all Treaties and engagements made with them by or under the Authority of the Honourable EIC are by Us accepted and will be scrupulously maintained'.[18] The proclamation had the effect of stabilizing indirect rule. The political map of India from 1858 would remain largely unchanged for the duration of colonial rule.[19] Despite the Queen's proclamation, however, Government of India interference in princely affairs continued.[20]

With the outbreak of the First World War the stance of the colonial government regarding the princes softened. The Indian states contributed large amounts of personnel, funds, and materiel to the war effort. The rulers of Bikaner, Patiala, Cooch Behar, Rutlam, and Jodhpur even served directly in the war.[21] Consequently, the Indian government looked upon princely demands with favour and permitted the setting up of a representative institution for the princes of India in the war's aftermath; the Chamber of Princes (CoP). The CoP was aimed at representing princely interests to the Indian government and was focused around two key

---

[17] Ramusack *The Indian Princes and Their States*, p. 59.

[18] *Proclamation of the Queen in Council to the Princes, Chiefs and People of India* (Published by the Governor-General at Allahabad, November 1st 1858). Accessed 4 May 2022. https://dsp ace.gipe.ac.in/xmlui/bitstream/handle/10973/35193/GIPE-014321-Contents.pdf?sequence= 2&isAllowed=y.

[19] Barbara Ramusack has shown how in practice territorial transfers continued to occur. Ramusack, *The Indian Princes and Their States*, p. 106.

[20] For a discussion of British interference in Indian states see: John McLeod, *Sovereignty, Power, Control: Politics in the States of Western India 1916–1947* (Leiden: Brill, 1999), p. 183.

[21] Sanatanu Das, 'Responses to the War (India)', Accessed June 28, 2016. http://encyc lopedia.1914-1918-online.net/pdf/1914-1918-Online-responses_to_the_war_in dia-2014-10-08.pdf.

objectives. It sought to develop a united and coherent princely front to pressure the government to redress grievances, especially surrounding the lack of definition of 'paramountcy', which enabled interference into the Indian states.[22]

At the Round Table Conference on 12 November 1930 held in London to discuss India's political future, the representative of the princes, Sir Tej Bahadur Sapru, proposed an All-India Federation. According to the proposal, British India and the princely states would join a Federation which would be legislated for by a bicameral house. This legislature would feature elected Indian representatives as well as the representatives chosen by the governments of the princely states. The idea of Federation was appealing to the princes since it would lead to a formal recognition of their powers by the British and might eventually bring about an end of the dreaded paramountcy as Indian states affairs would be handled by a central government.[23]

In the long term however, Federation would turn out to be a failure as a number of factors would militate against its implementation. These included the disunity of the CoP, the decision by larger states such as Hyderabad and Mysore to stay away from the scheme, and the fear of smaller states that they would not be represented in a federal legislature.[24] Ultimately too few Indian states would join the Federation, ensuring that the scheme was a failure. When the Indian government finally dropped plans for federation in 1939, due to the outbreak of the Second World War, opinion in government circles held that the princes had failed to implement a plan that they had been at the forefront of proposing.[25]

The princes came to the aid of the British Empire in the Second World War in much the same way as they had during the Great War. Their contributions to the war, at a time when the Indian National Congress rebelled against colonial rule, did much to regain the princes some of the favour they had lost due to the failure of Federation. The wartime chancellors of the CoP from 1938, Digvijaysinhji of Nawanagar and Nawab

[22] Barbara Ramusack, *The Princes of India in the Twilight of Empire: Dissolution of a Patron Client Relationship* (Columbus, Published for the University of Cincinnati by the Ohio State Press, 1978), p. 23.

[23] Copland, *The Princes of India in the Endgame of Empire*, p. 80.

[24] McLeod, *Sovereignty, Power, Control: Politics in the States of Western India 1916–1947*, p. 124.

[25] Copland, *The Princes of India in the Endgame of Empire*, p. 191.

Hamidullah of Bhopal, worked hard to reinvigorate the organization and to press the princely cause in Britain and India. A sophisticated strategy involving political agreements with India's leading parties and an attempt to push states to provide greater representation to their subjects in decision-making and the amalgamation of several of the smaller states into rationalized administrative units was evolved.[26] By 1946 the princely order appeared to be prepared for constitutional negotiations that would follow the war. Despite this however the CoP continued to suffer from a number of weaknesses. The speed of reform while unprecedented was still very slow in many of the Indian states and it was also severely weakened by the failure to strike an alliance with the Muslim League. Though Hamidullah hoped to strike a collective bargain that would maintain at least some of the autonomy of the princely states in an independent India he was to ultimately fail.[27] The vast majority of princes therefore acceded to India in 1947, only to be pensioned off in 1949.

The princely order that had been constituted, if not created, by the British from 1759 onwards came to an end two centuries later in 1949. The princes collapsed in part because they had failed previously to gain a secure position in the constitutional apparatus emerging in 20th-century India. They were also in great measure thwarted from defending their interests by a failure to act, outside of the first Round Table Conference, with unity. The speed of decolonization also clearly caught them off guard ensuring the end of their order. Further, as I will argue Cold War calculations meant that British planners withdrew their support from the princely order since they wanted strong centralized states in South Asia.

The overwhelming academic consensus is that the princes were able to exercise sovereignty, though this was often precarious and limited.[28] It is largely in the details of the circumstances of individual states then that there is variance in academic analyses. Specificity mattered in the ways in which states exercised their sovereignty. It is these specificities,

---

[26] Ibid., p. 210.

[27] Ibid., p. 233.

[28] See: Robin Jeffrey ed, *People, Princes, and Paramount Power: Society and Politics in the Indian Princely States* (Delhi: OUP, 1978); Ian Copland, *The British Raj and the Indian Princes* (Bombay: Orient Longman, 1982); Ramusack *The Princes of India in the Twilight of Empire*; Ramusack, *The Indian Princes and Their States*.

this chapter will argue, that shaped the princely encounter with aviation in the princely states of Jodhpur, Mysore, and Hyderabad.

Jodhpur: Aviation as Modern Martial Tradition

Jodhpur state was located in the Indian north-western region of Rajputana. The Rathore dynasty that ruled over the state traced its lineage back to the 8th century A.D., though the kingdom of Marwar or Jodhpur came into its own in the 15th century.[29] Pressed by the Marathas and the Pindaris and riven by a series of violent dynastic conflicts, Jodhpur concluded a treaty with the EIC in 1818 that inaugurated British indirect rule over the state. British rule had a stabilizing effect on what had been a highly conflicted region despite the EIC's tendency to intervene in state affairs. Consequently, Jodhpur's rulers were swift to come to the aid of the British during the 1857 rebellion and were rewarded for their services with the grant of a *sanad* (deed), recognizing their right to rule, by the Viceroy, Lord Canning in 1861.[30] The Government of India intervened often in Jodhpur state's internal affairs. It appointed the state's prime ministers or *Dewans*, restricted the ruler's powers and imposed a minority administration on the state from 1895 to 1898.[31] Despite or perhaps because of this the period of indirect rule led to significant legal, social, and economic reforms. Land, excise, and customs were reformed, slavery and *Sati* (widow immolation) were outlawed, new systems of famine relief were introduced, and railways were constructed extensively.[32] Jodhpur also played its part in the suppression of anti-British dissent in the state and contributed military forces to the British Empire's global project. Jodhpur state forces served on India's Northwest Frontier province, in China during the Boxer rebellion of 1900, and in the Great War.[33]

---

[29] Rima Hooja, *A History of Rajasthan* (New Delhi: Rupa & Co, 2006), p. 373.

[30] This recognized the right of the Rathore dynasty to adopt children in order to continue the dynastic line. Nirmala M. Upadhyay, *The Administration of Jodhpur State, 1800–1947 A.D.* (Jodhpur: International Publishers, 1973), p. 57.

[31] Maharaja Takht Singh for instance was punished for leaving the Ajmer Durbar of 1870 in anger for having been seated below the kings of Udaipur and Jaipur whom he considered to be his inferiors. The act incensed the Viceroy Lord Mayo and led to his eventual abdication. Upadhyay, *The Administration of Jodhpur State*, 1800–1947 A.D., p. 63.

[32] Sahdev Singh Kheeche, *Economic Reforms of Maharaja Umaid Singh's Reign* (Jodhpur: Maharaja Mana Singh Pustak Prakash Research Centre, 2004), p. 29.

[33] Upadhyay, *The Administration of Jodhpur State, 1800–1947 A.D.*, p. 64.

Maharaja Umaid Singh ascended to the throne of Jodhpur state in 1919, a century after indirect rule had been established. The state that the 15-year-old king would have to eventually administer encompassed an area the size of modern-day Hungary and a population of some 212,000 people in 1921.[34] It was also passing through a period of great turbulence.[35] As a consequence of the reforms passed by his predecessors under British guidance, and the more recent shocks of the Great War, the boundaries separating Jodhpur from British India had turned increasingly porous. This had led increasingly to the entry into the state of political ideas from British India. As early as 1921, a no rent agitation launched in coordination with the Non-Cooperation movement had to be put down by the Jodhpur military. A series of organizations such as the *Marwar Seva Sangha* (Marwar Service Union) and the *Marwar Hitakarani Sabha* (Marwar Welfare Gathering) sprang up through the decade demanding increased civil rights for the people of Jodhpur. Interestingly these organizations did not directly attack the Maharaja but claimed to be protesting misgovernment by subordinate officials. They nevertheless alarmed the state administration, which understood that the movements were ultimately subversive of both colonial and princely power. Repressive legislation was introduced and political leaders such as Jai Narain Vyas, Banwar Lal Shraff, and Madan Mohan Sarda were jailed.[36] The 1930s were even more disturbed and several new organizations demanding civil rights and the extension of representative government emerged in the state including the Marwar State People's Conference, the *Praja Mandal* (Subjects Board), and the *Marwar Lok Parishad* (Marwar People's Council).[37] These organizations were often repressed by the government but it was increasingly clear that the state would have to continue to contend with movements that at the very least subverted the Maharaja's sovereignty.

In these taxing circumstances Umaid Singh adopted a complex strategy to bolster his regime's legitimacy. A vast programme of administrative

---

[34] Kheeche, *Economic Reforms of Maharaja Umaid Singh's Reign*, pp. 25–26.
[35] Umaid Singh took on formal powers in 1923 as he was deemed too young to rule. His uncle Sir Pratap Singh was appointed to rule in his stead as regent. Dhananajaya Singh, *The House of Marwar* (New Delhi: Lotus Collection, Roli Books, 1994), p. 151.
[36] Upadhyay, *The Administration of Jodhpur State, 1800–1947 A.D.*, p. 204.
[37] Singh, *The House of Marwar*, p. 173.

reforms was inaugurated and the land revenue, excise, customs, agriculture, and legal departments were rationalized in order to increase their efficiency.[38] The value of architecture as a means of representing power and promoting welfare was not lost on the Maharaja who constructed such iconic buildings as the Jubilee Court, Ajeet Bhawan, and Umaid Bhawan palace. He also constructed a number of 'modern' facilities in Jodhpur city itself such as the Windham hospital, Umaid Female hospital, Sardar Museum, Sumair Public Library, Willingdon stadium, Willingdon Garden, and a mental hospital. Perhaps more significant, for a land that routinely suffered droughts and famines, were the waterworks constructed by the Maharaja's government. These included the Umaid Sagar dam, Jawai Bandh, Sumer Samandh Jodhpur water supply dam, and Takhat Sagar Dam.[39] This replicated and in certain ways exceeded the colonial state's claims to 'colonial modernity' through programmes of 'improvement' and 'development'.[40]

The Maharaja of Jodhpur was perhaps the first Indian monarch to grasp the idea that the aura of modernity surrounding aircraft could be used to legitimize his rule. During the first decade of his reign he oversaw the transformation of the aeroplane from a luxury object to an instrument of policy. This is not to argue that the modern appeal of aircraft had escaped other rulers such as the Maharaja of Patiala, who as seen previously, was the first Indian to purchase aeroplanes in 1910. Nevertheless, the advances in aviation technology between 1910 and 1931, the year Jodhpur aerodrome was built, were extensive making it possible for aviation to become a matter of state policy. Umaid Singh poured more resources into aviation, at an earlier time than any of his counterparts in the princely order. The Maharaja established a Flying Department in his state, the first of its kind, to oversee the construction of aerodromes in 1924. One of India's most sophisticated aerodromes was constructed at Jodhpur between 1924 and 1931 at a cost of rupees 1,36,830 while a satellite aerodrome was constructed at Utterlai for rupees 9,610. By 1933

---

[38] Kheeche, *Economic Reforms of Maharaja Umaid Singh's Reign*, p. 29.

[39] Ibid., p. x (Introduction).

[40] For a detailed discussion on colonial and nationalist ideas on developmentalism see: Benjamin Zachariah, *Developing India: An Intellectual and Social History 1930–50* (New Delhi: Oxford University Press, 2012).

the Department had completed the construction of 15 aerodromes throughout the state.

Jodhpur state's heavy investment in aviation is possibly explained by the nature of the state's revenues. Railways generated between 20 and 30 per cent of the state's revenues in the years of Umaid Singh's rule.[41] Jodhpur State Railway served to traverse hostile terrain in a state bordering the Thar Desert and leveraged the state's then central location in British India for the generation of customs and excise taxes. Similarly, investments in aviation also sought to use Jodhpur's prime strategic location to bolster the state's income. While precise figures on revenue generated by aviation remain unavailable, there is reason to believe that revenues generated by aviation were not insubstantial, especially in the context of the Great Depression. This can be deduced from the fact that the number of aircraft landing at the Jodhpur aerodrome more than doubled from 418 in 1932–1933 to 863 in the year 1935–1936.[42] Further evidence that the state profited from aviation can be found from a letter by the state's Chief Engineer after the Second World War which alluded to 'the heavy loss of income due to the main foreign lines . . . now overflying Jodhpur.'[43]

To be sure much there is little doubt that the Maharaja's enthusiasm for aviation was genuine. Maharaja Umaid Singh was himself a graduate of the RAF academy at Cranwell and one of the first Indians to qualify for a flying license. As 'Flight Magazine' claimed, the young ruler was 'intensely keen on aviation.'[44] Another observer noted the royal family's enthusiasm for aviation by quipping that, 'There are probably more Jodhpur royals in the air than on the ground at any given point in time.'[45] Nevertheless the decision to invest heavily in aviation was explained by a number of other motivations. Jodhpur state's terrain and administrative structure made investments in transportation attractive. Like Hyderabad it could draw on a sophisticated railway system for the necessary skilled

---

[41] Kheeche, *Economic Reforms of Maharaja Umaid Singh's Reign*, p. 93.
[42] The Report on the Administration of the Jodhpur State for the year 1932–33 (Jodhpur: Jodhpur Government Press, 1934), p. 81; The Report on the Administration of the Jodhpur State for the year 1935–36 (Jodhpur: Jodhpur Government Press, 1938), p. 106.
[43] MMA, M-KHAS AVIATION-NO-13 P-3 FN-C-3 B-NO-02-YEAR-1947, Chief Engineer Jodhpur to Development Secretary, Jodhpur, 1 May 1947.
[44] *Flight*, 'The Log of the Astraea', 16 November 1933.
[45] 'The Real Zubeida', *Rediff.com*. Accessed on 7 July 2016 http://www.rediff.com/movies/2001/jan/17zub.htm.

personnel required to service aircraft and aerodromes. Besides serving to buttress the state's claims to modernity, earning it revenues and, as we shall see, granting the state a degree of prominence, aviation also allowed the Maharaja to pay quick visits to those parts of his state that required attention. Thus, for instance the Maharaja flew to the city of Ladnu to open a hospital on the 4 March 1938 and revisited it by air later in the year on 14 November 1938 in order to inspect famine relief work taking place in the region.[46]

Jodhpur state further moved to promote flight as a state prerogative with the establishment of princely India's first flying club in 1931. The club made use of the aerodrome established near the Maharaja's Chittar palace in Jodhpur city. Umaid Singh had been closely associated with the New Delhi Flying club, from where he had earned his license and hoped to encourage flying in his own state. For this he hired Geoffrey Godwin, a South African aviator who had served in the RAF and expanded Jodhpur aerodrome to include a longer runway for larger planes, night landing gear, and a control tower costing around rupees 1,28,000 combined.[47] A moat and a barbed-wire fence surrounded the aerodrome to keep wild boars away and a roof viewing area surrounded by canvas was set up so that the ladies could view the planes without being seen.[48]

Jodhpur aerodrome benefitted from the critical location that Jodhpur city occupied on the trans-India imperial air route. What this meant was that planes flying on the trans-India route from Karachi to Calcutta would have to fly via Jodhpur. Jodhpur thus became an important transit point for planes from a number of international airlines such as KLM, Imperial Airways, and Air France flying the 'Imperial air route' from London to Sydney, a journey at the time of several weeks.[49] Given the fact that planes at the time sometimes needed to stop over during nights for maintenance, a red stone hotel 'with appropriate carving winged horses' was constructed close to the airfield for passengers to rest in.[50] This had the effect not only of earning Jodhpur aerodrome a transit fee but also of placing Jodhpur city in the constellation of notable cities in India and the

[46] Kheeche, *Economic Reforms of Maharaja Umaid Singh's Reign*, p. 19.
[47] Ibid., p. 128.
[48] Vacher, *History of the Jodhpur Flying Club,* p. 15.
[49] Alexander E.W. Salt *Imperial Air Routes* (London: J. Murray, 1930), p. 32.
[50] *Flight*, 'The Log of the Astraea', 16 November 1933.

world. Thus, Jodhpur a medium-sized state was able to place itself on an international map that included not only prominent Indian cities such as Karachi and Calcutta but also London, Cairo, and Sydney. Due to its advanced facilities and central location Jodhpur emerged as a critical stop not only for international airlines but also one for what was arguably the first Indian operated air route; the Delhi Flying Club's mail delivery route from Karachi to Jodhpur to Delhi which had been established in 1932.[51]

As Jodhpur emerged as the leader in aviation among the Indian states it became involved in the question of formulating aviation laws for princely India. This was a complicated matter as aviation law in India had to operate on three different levels. First the British Empire and Her Majesty's Government were signatories of the 1919 Paris convention relating to the regulation of air navigation and the 1929 Warsaw convention for international carriage by air respectively. This meant that India would be required to accept certain international aviation laws regarding aircraft safety and air sovereignty in order to bring them in line with international norms. Secondly British India had a number of aviation laws including the 1911 Indian Aircraft Act and the Carriage by Air Act of 1934 which had no binding power over the princes. Third South Asia had hundreds of princely states who could pass whatever laws on aviation they wished.

The Government of India could pass laws to bring aviation regulations in British India in line with international standards but lacked the power to pass said laws in the princely states. As the princely states began to become increasingly involved in aviation from the late 1920s, the responsibility for bringing their aviation laws fell on the colonial government which faced legal hurdles in legislating aviation laws for the princes. This in certain ways reflects the anomalous nature of the relations between British India and the princely states in international law. Matters were complicated though by the fact of impending Federation. As noted above from 1930 onwards the princes and the Government of India hoped to form an All-India Federation. The prospect of Federation however meant that laws passed by the princely states might well have to be rescinded or rewritten once it was achieved necessitating negotiation. New Delhi consequently felt that it would be best for the princes not to pass additional laws.

---

[51] *Flight*, 'Indian Air Mails', 8 December 1932.

The Jodhpur government, represented among others by Godwin, was consulted by the Director of Civil Aviation and the Secretary for the Department of Industries and Labour to evolve certain general principles regarding aviation in 1931.[52] In doing so the government effectively recognized Jodhpur as the leader in aviation among the Indian States at the time. The regulations discussed included the decision to register aircraft and provide them with certificates of airworthiness, to require pilots to have flying licenses, to use common sign language for aircraft, and to jointly investigate air accidents on Jodhpur territory. Significantly the state was permitted to declare certain areas as prohibited zones for flying though it was urged not to use this power excessively.[53] With the sole exception of the 'Jodhpur Carriage by Air Act' of 1935, the state would not pass any further aviation-related legislation. The act sought to bring Jodhpur's laws into line with the Warsaw Convention of 1929 since Jodhpur was a major international hub and as such had to conform to international standards.[54] Jodhpur played a central role in evolving aviation regulations for the princely states, a role that becomes even more critical when it is understood that federation never occurred and as such the rules relating to aviation that were crafted in consultation with Jodhpur effectively remained the rules of all of the Indian states with major investments in aviation until the outbreak of the Second World War.[55] It was only in 1939 after the war had broken out and Federation was effectively shelved that the Government of India made some moves towards encouraging the states to legislate on aviation matters under the Defence of India Act.[56]

With the outbreak of the Second World War, Jodhpur's aerodrome became a critical for the transfer of air supplies and reinforcements from the West to the Burma front. The RAF took over Jodhpur aerodrome in 1942 and designated it as an RAF station. The United States Army Air Corps also set up a base at Jodhpur for flights to pass on to the 'Hump'

[52] NAI, F&P-Reforms Branch-72 (21)-R/1931, General Principles for Flying in Jodhpur.
[53] NAI, F&P-Reforms Branch-72 (21)-R/1931, General Principles for Flying in Jodhpur.
[54] KSA, Industries and Commerce file 20, Legislation of Aircraft rules in Jodhpur.
[55] Jodhpur itself reversed its early pro-Federation position when it became clear that the state would suffer significant financial losses as a result of Federation. Copland, *The Princes of India in the Endgame of Empire*, p. 103.
[56] KSA, General and Revenue Secretariat file 26, Secretary to the resident to Chief Secretary of Mysore state, 22 June 1940.

operations aimed at supplying Nationalist China. This in turn meant that Jodhpur would also host the crews and planes of the Chinese Air Force.[57] Jodhpur state forces were deployed to protect the station and their numbers were rapidly increased with the outbreak of the Quit India movement later that year. Rooms in the state hotel next to the aerodrome were reserved for air crews ferrying aeroplanes to the Burma front.[58] This involved among other things the flying in of planes from Europe and the United States which were then fitted at 317 Maintenance Unit based out of RAF station before being dispatched to Burma. This process could involve the fitting of up to 50 planes at a time at the station.[59]

Even as Jodhpur aerodrome was pressed into service with the RAF, Jodhpur Flying Club was given over to the training of Indian pilots. The club was initially designated as Jodhpur Air Training Centre and later as No. 2 Elementary Flying Training School, IAF for the training of cadets recruited from India.[60] Several IAF pilots who would serve in Burma in the following years received their training at Jodhpur's Flying training school which was second in size only to the one at Hyderabad.[61] Like several others, the Elementary Flying Training School would be affected by high rates of trainee wastage as rapid wartime expansion of the IAF had an adverse impact on the quality of recruits. By 1943 the school was suspending the training of those cadets considered to be unfit for flying early in order to concentrate on those who displayed an aptitude for the task.[62]

Jodhpur state also made a number of other contributions to the war in the air. The Maharaja's personal plane, a Lockheed Electra was donated for the use of Lord Wavell, then commander of the Allied or ABDA (American-British-Dutch-Australian) forces.[63] The Shri Maharaja Umaid Singhji Air Defence fund, begun in 1942 collected 58.5 lakhs by the end of the war for the purpose of buying aircraft and paying for Jodhpur State Forces.[64] It also donated funds towards the purchase of a

---

[57] TNA, AIR 28/406, Operations Record Book (ORB) Royal Air Force Station Jodhpur, 28 August 1942.
[58] TNA, AIR 28/406, 11 August 1942.
[59] TNA, AIR 28/406, Establishment of RAF personnel
[60] Vacher, *History of the Jodhpur Flying Club*, p 100.
[61] TNA, AIR29/616, ORB No 2 Elementary Flying Training School, April 1943.
[62] Ibid., November 1943.
[63] Vacher, *History of the Jodhpur Flying Club*, p. 107.
[64] NAI, Home Political I 1946 NA F-13-6, Review of the Administration of Jodhpur State for the year 1945.

Halifax bomber for the RAF and 400,000 rupees towards the Viceroys War Purposes fund for the purchase of four fighter planes for the IAF.[65]

Maharaja Umaid Singh himself volunteered for active service at the front in the RAF, in which he had had been granted the honourary rank of Air Commodore since 1939.[66] He was bitterly disappointed when the colonial government refused to permit this for political reasons, since his elder brother and predecessor, Maharaja Sumer Singh had served in combat during the Great War.[67] Though the Maharaja was prevented from serving on the front he was appointed to serve on the staff of Air Marshal Sir Richard Peirse along with Nawab Hamidullah Khan of Bhopal.[68] The two Air Commodores were expected to serve as liaisons between the Indian personnel of the Air Forces in India and Air Headquarters (India). Both Umaid Singh and Hamidullah Khan toured the country extensively to check on the welfare of Indian airmen and communicated their grievances to the government.[69] A report by them on the poor service conditions suffered by Indian Other Ranks helped improve service conditions and salaries in the IAF after the war.[70] Umaid Singh's commitment to the welfare of the men of the IAF and RAF was such that he went on to donate 100,000 rupees, a quarter of which was drawn from his own privy purse, for the welfare of the IAF men.[71] Maharaja Umaid Singh also played an important role in publicizing the IAF in India by addressing audiences at war services exhibitions and regularly inspected the passing out parades of the IAF cadets at the Elementary flying training school.[72,73] The Maharaja's lavish parties and entertainments for RAF and IAF men stationed at Jodhpur with such prominent guests as the Duke of Gloucester

[65] Copland, *The Princes of India in the Endgame of Empire*, p. 185; Upadhyay, *The Administration of Jodhpur State, 1800–1947 A.D.*, p. 197.

[66] TNA AIR 2/4912, India: Regulations regarding the grant of honourary commissions in the RAF.

[67] Sumer Singh was 17 when he led the Jodhpur Lancers into battle in Flanders. Singh, *The House of Marwar*, p. 148.

[68] Chhina, *The Eagle Strikes* (New Delhi, 2006), p. 77.

[69] MoD (I), ORB No 1, 10 November 1944.

[70] MMA, Household Records No. 6, Their Highnesses of Bhopal and Jodhpur-Report on Indian Air Force.

[71] Vacher, *History of the Jodhpur Flying Club*, p. 118; Upadhyay, *The Administration of Jodhpur State, 1800–1947 A.D.*, p. 197.

[72] TNA AIR 29/481, 1 IAF exhibition unit formed at New Delhi (India) in March 1942, 1 March 1942.

[73] See for instance; TNA, AIR 29/616, ORB No 2 Elementary Flying Training School, April 1943, December 1942.

served to raise the morale of men battling the heat, overcrowding, and malaria to keep the war effort going.[74] As a reward for his services during the war, Umaid Singh was granted the honourary rank of Air Vice Marshal of the RAF along with Nawab Hamidullah, making them the first Indians to receive that rank.[75]

After the war Umaid Singh backed the Cabinet mission plan, which would have granted his state a degree of autonomy in an independent India.[76] However the negotiations were to prove to be futile with the announcement of the Mountbatten plan on 3 June 1947, according to which British India was to be divided between India and Pakistan. Maharaja Umaid Singh died six days later of a ruptured appendix and was succeeded by his son Hanwant Singh.[77] Maharaja Hanwant Singh would eventually accede to the Indian Union. However before he did so he famously discussed the possibility of joining Pakistan with Mohammed Ali Jinnah.[78] Though the negotiations have since been considered as the naïve acts of an inexperienced prince or explained away as a wily negotiation tactic that strengthened the hands of Jodhpur in its negotiations with the Indian Union, there might well have sound reasons for them.[79] Jodhpur's demands for access to the port of Karachi, control of the Jodhpur-Hyderabad (Sindh) railway line, grain for famine relief, and freedom to import arms reflect the historical concerns of the state. The demand for access to control over the Jodhpur-Sindh line is especially relevant in the context of a state revenue structure that depended on earning from the railways. It shows a clear preoccupation, and one not exclusive to Jodhpur, with the possibility of the state being encircled by an independent and possibly hostile Indian Union. Significantly demands for overflight did not feature among Jodhpur state's priorities in the negotiations reflecting the many uncertainties over the how flight and

---

[74] TNA, AIR 28/406, Operations Record Book (ORB) Royal Air Force Station Jodhpur,

[75] TNA AIR 2/4912, India: Regulations regarding the grant of honourary commissions in the RAF.

[76] Singh, *The House of Marwar*, p. 177.

[77] Ibid., p 179.

[78] The meeting was to have far reaching consequences because of its implications for the Kashmir dispute. If Jinnah could court Jodhpur despite its Hindu majority then the Indian government could claim the right to interfere in Kashmir, a state with a large Muslim population. Noorani, *The Kashmir Dispute*, p. 7.

[79] For a view of the former see: Menon, *Integration of the Indian States*, p.117. For the latter view see: Singh, *The House of Marwar*, p. 182.

sovereignty might operate in South Asia after independence. It is possible to speculate that the state's strong aviation position might very well have been one of the factors that convinced the Maharaja that it could come to an agreement with Pakistan, ensuring a degree of internal autonomy. Whatever the case, Hanwant Singh was eventually persuaded by Viceroy Lord Mountbatten, Home Minister Vallabhbhai Patel, and Secretary of the Indian states ministry V.P. Menon to accede to India.[80] Hanwant Singh would go on to become the first of India's successful democratic princes, trouncing the Congress party in elections held in 1952. He would however not live to see the victory as his Beechcraft Bonanza aeroplane crashed while he was travelling through his state to check election results, killing him and his wife, the film actress Zubeida Begum.[81] Though Jodhpur state was merged with the Indian Union in May 1949 several of its legacies in the field of aviation remain. Jodhpur aerodrome continues to serve as a major international civil airport and Jodhpur air force station is an important air base.

Maharaja Umaid Singh of Jodhpur represents a new model of 'martial valour' that was taking root in parts of princely India. In common with other Indian princes, he sought to garner legitimacy as an enlightened monarch intent on bringing his state into the 20th century. Like other Indian states Jodhpur sought to deploy aviation technology to make claims to a 'native modernity' that would buttress its sovereignty against the criticism of both the paramount power and nationalist challengers. Jodhpur offers a distinct model, however in its particular approach to aviation. It combined the state's historical military tradition with the modernist appeal of aircraft to be embodied in the person of the Maharaja as combat pilot. This approach to aviation was a consequence of the distinct conditions prevailing in the state. Jodhpur was a desert state that drew much of its revenue from the railways and whose rulers had traditionally legitimated themselves through martial prowess. Closely associating aviation with the person of the Maharaja therefore served to paint him as a valorous leader who was keen to modernize his state. Aviation

---

[80] Maharaja Hanwant Singh, an amateur inventor and magician, had built a gun that could be disguised as a pen. When he finally agreed to accede, he is famously alleged to have threatened V.P. Menon with death in case his subjects were betrayed. For an account of the event see: Collins and Lapierre, *Freedom at Midnight*, p. 242.

[81] Hooja, *A History of Rajasthan*, p. 1143.

also served to leverage the central location of the state not only in India but also on the globe at a time when the technology's range was limited. Umaid Singh's early investment in aviation it would appear was a success. The critical importance of Jodhpur aerodrome and the Maharaja's exceptional wartime record served to legitimate the monarchy in the eyes of the colonial government, if the grant of the highly exceptional rank of Air Vice Marshall to Umaid Singh is taken as an indicator.[82] That the Rathore dynasty's legitimacy was intact with its subjects is indicated by Hanwant Singh's electoral success years after Jodhpur state merged with India. It is important here not to overstate the importance of aviation. Several other actions such as the provision of irrigation facilities and famine relief probably helped entrench dynastic legitimacy, yet there is no doubt that the aeroplane lent a degree of prominence to the Rathores of Jodhpur that they would likely not otherwise have enjoyed. Other states would choose different strategies to utilize aviation to uphold their sovereignty with very different results.

Mysore: Aviation as Development

Though the Wodeyar Dynasty that came to rule Mysore could trace its genesis to the 14th century, modern Mysore state was very much a British creation.[83] Following the defeat of its great enemy Tipu Sultan, the EIC annexed Mysore. In order to deny the territorial claims of their former allies Hyderabad and the Marathas, the British decided to hand over a portion of the conquered territory to the Wodeyars. The Wodeyars would then act as their surrogates, enabling the EIC to rule Mysore indirectly. This led to the formation of Mysore state, India's second-largest princely state in terms of population and third largest in terms of territory.[84]

---

[82] This did not however ensure British support for an independent Jodhpur though, as I will argue, that was a consequence of Cold War pressures and a larger policy of not supporting princely independence. Maharaja Hanwant Singh both before and after accession actively considered fighting the Indian Union for independence. Singh, *House of Marwar*, p. 181.

[83] For a complete history of the Wodeyar Dynasty that stresses the continuities of Mysore kingdom and Mysore state see: Vikram Sampath, *Splendours of Royal Mysore: The Untold Story of the Wodeyars* (New Delhi: Rupa & Co, 2008).

[84] Made Gowda, *Modern Mysore State 1881–1902: A Study of the Elite, Polity, and Society* (Mysore: Prasaranga, University of Mysore, 1997), p. 2.

Wodeyar Mysore thus signed a subsidiary treaty with the EIC in 1799. In 1831 the EIC took over the state on claims of misgovernment.[85] Mysore remained under direct colonial rule for 50 years until 1881 when it was returned to Maharaja Chamarajendra Wodeyar. As a consequence of its origins as a British client state and the long period of direct colonial rule, Mysore state developed an exceptionally powerful bureaucracy. Though Wodeyar rulers were hardly powerless, much of the responsibility for running the state fell on the state's prime minister or Dewan.[86] This affected what may broadly be termed as the states ideological underpinnings and would have significant consequences for the manner in which aviation was engaged with.

From the 19th century, Mysore's bureaucracy thus espoused an ideology of developmentalism that identified the economy as the primary site for state intervention. This drew from both the prevailing colonialist economic discourse, and the nationalist critique of this that emphasized India's inability to progress economically under colonial rule. As Chandan Gowda has shown, Mysorean developmentalism drew on a number of often contradictory economic ideas drawn from social evolutionism, neomercantilism, utilitarianism, and even orientalism.[87] This is not to argue that the justification for princely rule was drawn solely from Western intellectual formations. Indian ideas about the nature of kingship revolving around *Dharma* were often fused with developmentalist ideology.[88] Indeed the relative lack of ritual legitimacy of the Mysore Maharaja in comparison to smaller northern Rajput states was keenly felt by the Wodeyars, leading to the adoption of certain Rajput customs such as resort to a mythological lineage.[89] These ideas however were subordinated to developmentalist policy reflecting the wider subordination of a ritualized monarchy to the state's bureaucratic machinery. This had the effect of ensuring that modernity in Mysore was heavily, though not exclusively conflated with industrial development.

---

[85] Bhagwan, Sovereign Skies, p. 38.
[86] Nair, *Mysore Modern*, p. 13.
[87] Chandan Gowda, 'Empire and Developmentalism in Colonial India', in George Steinmetz (ed), *Sociology and Empire* (Durham: Duke University Press, 2013).
[88] Ibid., p. 355
[89] Nair, *Mysore Modern*, p. 12.

If a developmentalist ideology informed the agenda of the Mysore bureaucracy this was not solely a response to an overweening colonial power. Mysore, along with Baroda, was considered to be a 'model' Indian state, in part due to the fact that it had granted a degree of popular representation not seen elsewhere among the princely states. The state convened the first representative institution in princely India, the Mysore Representative Assembly in 1881 and the first legislature, the Mysore Legislative Council in 1907.[90] As the 20th century progressed however powerful forces emerged to challenge the legitimacy of the princely government to rule. A non-Brahmin movement challenging the dominance of the Brahmins in the state bureaucracy began in 1917. This was followed by the establishment of the Mysore Congress in 1920. By 1937 the two movements had united to demand greater representation from the government. Ironically the states 'modern' focus on education enabled the Congress to recruit volunteers from the students of the state's schools and colleges for their agitations. Unlike in Jodhpur however, the Mysore government was broadly supportive of the Congress and the Dewan of Mysore Mirza Ismail was highly successful in defusing the crisis by claiming that the Mysore government could not grant greater representation while the state was under indirect colonial rule.[91] Nonetheless political tensions with nationalists persisted. Confronted with a popular political movement the Mysore administration, as Janaki Nair has argued, sought to legitimate the state through governance rather than representation.[92] Mysore state officials would explicitly assert that development was the sole font of legitimacy for the state and that they, rather than elected representatives, were best placed to deliver it.

Since development and modernity were synonymous to a large extent with industrialization, the Mysore government would exert great efforts to industrialize. The state thus became the site of several of India's leading industries including steel, cement, fertilizers, coffee curing, and paper.[93] Opportunities for expanding the state's industrialization plans were however ultimately limited by the conditions of colonialism. This however

[90] Ibid., p 17.
[91] James Manor, *Political Change in an Indian State* (New Delhi: Manohar, 1977), p. 110.
[92] Nair, *Mysore Modern*, p. 16.
[93] Gita Piramal, *Business Legends* (New Delhi: Viking, 1998), p. 254.

was to change with the outbreak of the Second World War and the entry into Mysore of Walchand Hirachand.

Walchand Hirachand was an Indian industrialist and the founder of the Walchand group which had interests in construction, sugar, engineering, and sugar. Walchand had nationalist leanings and wished to be the first Indian to manufacture aircraft, ships, and automobiles. This had led him to establish the famous Scindia Steam Navigation Company in 1919, the first Indian ship building firm.[94] Walchand had also discussed the setting up of an automobile factory with Mirza Ismail's predecessor as Dewan of Mysore, Mokshagundam Visvesvaraya, as early as 1934. The plan to set up an automobile factory with the aid of the Congress government of Bombay in partnership with an American automobile firm had however failed due to a lack of support from the colonial government following the resignation of the Congress ministry in Bombay in 1939.[95]

In October 1939 Walchand Hirachand met American businessman William Pawley on an aeroplane from San Francisco to Bombay, an event that would lead directly to the establishment of India's first aircraft company.[96] Pawley represented the Intercontinental Aircraft Corporation, an American firm that had been involved in the assembly of aircraft for Nationalist China. He would play a critical role in the founding of the famed American Volunteer group, more popularly known as the Flying Tigers, which fought for Nationalist China against the Japanese. Pawley headed the Central Aircraft Manufacturing Company (CAMCO) based out of China's Wuhan province. When Wuhan was overrun by Japanese forces, with whom China had been at war since 1937, he moved the factory to Loiwing on the Sino-Burmese border.[97] This arrangement proved to be short-lived and further Japanese advances forced Pawley to consider moving his factory out of China in 1939 on the eve of his meeting with Walchand. On hearing of Pawley's predicament, Walchand offered

---

[94] For an overview of Walchand Hirachand see: Margaret Hardeck and Gita Piramal, *India's industrialists* (Washington: Three Continents Press, 1985).

[95] Raghavan, *India's War*, p. 93.

[96] Piramal, *Business Legends*, p. 242.

[97] William D. Pawley would go on to become the American ambassador to Peru and Brazil. He would also gain notoriety for his involvement in the Central Intelligence Agency's plans to overthrow unfriendly governments. See: Anthony Carozza, *William Pawley: The Extraordinary Life of the Adventurer, Entrepreneur, and Diplomat Who Cofounded the Flying Tigers* (Washington: Potomac books, 2012).

to help set up an aircraft factory in India.[98] Subsequently Walchand approached the Indian government with plans to set up an aircraft factory, offering to provide military aircraft made at the factory for the war effort.

The government response to Walchand's proposal however was unpromising or so much of the literature on the subject has assumed in the past.[99] However new work by Aparajith Ramnath has shown that the scheme to build aircraft in India was met with immense enthusiasm by both the Indian government, which had already been looking into the possibility of building aeroplanes in India, and by the Secretary of State, Leo Amery.[100] This supports a point I have previously made about fears that given the lack of air defences, India was open to air attack from the Soviet Union. For Amery, the construction of an aircraft factory, just like the expansion of the IAF, would not only better protect India but would also be widely popular, going some way to counter the claim that under colonial rule Indian air defences had been neglected.[101] The key obstacle in the way of the opening of an aircraft factory in India turned out not to be the sluggishness of the Indian bureaucracy, but rather the British Ministry of Aircraft production led by Lord Beaverbrook, who insisted that any Indian factory must not be allowed to claim vital production materials. Consequently, the British War Cabinet deferred a decision on establishing an aircraft factory in India till after the Battle of Britain was won, giving its blessing to the scheme in December 1940.[102] Walchand was summoned to Simla and given a 10-million-dollar contract and permission by the government to set up an aircraft factory.[103] He and Pawley would be permitted to set up the factory provided that it imported its own aircraft parts.

Despite this it was difficult for Walchand to raise capital for the venture at short notice. He wrote to the governments of Baroda, Gwalior, Mysore, and Bhavnagar for help.[104] While the others rejected Walchand's

---

[98]   *Life*, 'American Makes Planes in India', 22 March 1943.

[99]   See for instance: Carozza, *William Pawley*.

[100]   Aparajith Ramnath, 2016. 'International networks and aircraft manufacture in late-colonial India: Hindustan Aircraft Limited, 1940–47,' Working papers 205, Indian Institute of Management Kozhikode, p. 6.

[101]   Ramnath, 'International networks and aircraft manufacture in late colonial India', p. 7.

[102]   Ramnath, 'International networks and aircraft manufacture in late colonial India', p. 10.

[103]   BL, IOR/L/WS/1/496, Note dated 26 December 1940.

[104]   Piramal, *Business Legends*, p. 246.

approach, Mysore responded enthusiastically. Dewan Mirza Ismail offered Walchand very generous terms. The factory, which would come to be called the Hindustan Aircraft (Private) Limited factory or HAL, was to be set up in Bangalore on government land and private land would be acquired for it if this too was necessary. Electricity and water would be provided at subsidised costs. Machinery and plant required for the factory would not be charged customs or octroi when it entered the state from British India. State police would guard the factory at no additional cost. HAL would have a monopoly on aeroplane production in the state and would be given contracts by the state if it decided to ever train pilots or construct planes. The road to Bangalore was widened and tarred to allow heavy vehicles to move to the factory. Materials needed for factory construction were provided at a low cost and necessary steel structures were fabricated for the company at the state's Bhadravati steel works.[105] Perhaps most importantly, the company was not required to pay any taxes on profits on the 10-million-dollar contract it had received from the Indian government for the construction of aeroplanes.[106] The speed and vigour with which Mysore acted to erect the factory are indicative of the deep investment its administration had in the scheme. The paperwork for the company was rushed through and it was allowed to begin work within a week of being registered. The Belandur tank was acquired for the company to land seaplanes on before negotiations on compensation could be completed.[107] A 'Special Land Acquisition' officer was recruited to take measures to quickly acquire the 700 acres that the factory needed. This included rapidly reacquiring land that the state had earlier given to sixty lower caste *Voddar* families, for instance, who were only paid the paltry sum of five rupees per family to relocate their huts.[108] In addition to all of this, the state on its own initiative set up a chair of aeronautic and

---

[105] KSA, General and Revenue Secretariat file 205, Establishment of an aircraft factory in the state, The Hindustan Aircraft Limited.

[106] KSA, Industries and Commerce (I &C) file 25, Facilities to the Hindustan Aircraft Factory Limited.

[107] KSA, General and Revenue Secretariat file 205, Establishment of an aircraft factory in the state, The Hindustan Aircraft Limited.

[108] KSA, I & C file 130, Acquisition of Land for the Hindustan Aircraft Ltd, Deputy Commissioner Bangalore District to Chief Secretary, Government of Mysore, 1 February 1941.

automobile engineering at the Institute of Science, Mysore at a cost of 100,000 rupees with a recurring grant of fifty thousand rupees.[109]

Clearly the establishment of the HAL factory was central to the Mysore bureaucracy's developmentalist vision. The factory opened in 1941 with a capital of 75 lakhs to be divided equally between Walchand's company Messrs Walchand Tulsidas Khatau Limited, the Government of India, and the Mysore state government.[110] The company was thus a joint enterprise of a nationalistic businessman, a colonial government, and an Indian state. It had a contract worth 10 million dollars for the production of aircraft on an American license. Air Marshal Sir John Higgins became its resident Director, representing the Indian government, and the other two partners sent their representatives to the board of directors. HAL produced its first plane, a Harlow PC-5 trainer, in August 1941 and began producing the Curtiss P-36 in July 1942.[111] The factory did not function perfectly however as it fell behind schedule on the manufacture of Curtiss Hawks and Vultee Vengeances due to the difficulty of securing spare parts from America and because ships due to bring required parts from Europe, such as engines, were sunk by Axis forces on their journey to India.[112]

The outbreak of the war with Japan led the Indian government to propose the nationalization of the company at the beginning of 1942. This was partially because the American Lend-lease scheme was not allowed to be used in profit-making enterprises and partly because of fears that the factory could be bombed by Japanese aircraft.[113] The government also argued that it was better placed to run the factory on its own for a number of other reasons. Wartime production would require research and development that only it could provide. Moreover, the levels of secrecy required had now increased due to the entry of Japan into the

---

[109] KSA, General and Revenue Secretariat file 205, Establishment of an aircraft factory in the state, The Hindustan Aircraft Limited.

[110] KSA, I & C file 10, Agreement entered into between the Government of India, the Hindustan Aircraft Ltd and Messrs Walchand Tulisdas Khatau Ltd.

[111] Flight, 'Hindustan Aircraft Limited', 27 August 1954.

[112] KSA, General and Revenue Secretariat file 205, Establishment of an aircraft factory in the state, Walchand to Madhav Rao, 6 February 1942.

[113] Raghavan, India's War, p. 94; For the measures taken to protect HAL from air raids see: KSA, General and Revenue Secretariat file 22, Order under rule 51c of the Defence of India rules to be served on the Hindustan aircraft factory.

war.[114] Then there was the claim that the government would have to rapidly expand the factory in ways that might be found to be 'superfluous after the war' in order to meet military requirements and it would be unfair to saddle its partners with the costs of such an expansion.[115] Walchand was dismayed by the colonial state's decision to exclude him from an enterprise he had been instrumental in establishing. He was especially unhappy with what he saw as the lack of adequate compensation for the financial losses this would entail in profits and opportunity costs. Walchand claimed that his partners in Bombay were 'as shocked as I was at the idea of having to get out of this Industry'.[116] He asserted that the 12.5 lakhs he was being offered in lieu of profits were thoroughly inadequate. In addition to greater compensation for profits he demanded payment for his organization's role as managing agents highlighting the many concessions he had managed to secure from the Mysore government.[117] Walchand consequently asked to be paid between 34 and 38 lakh rupees in return for his share.[118] Ultimately the government bought out Walchand Hirachand's HAL shares for the cost of the original share capital plus 20 lakhs which included compensations of 12.5 lakhs for profits, 5 lakhs for managing agency fees, and 2.5 lakhs for goodwill.[119]

Mysore state's response to the Indian government's proposal to buy out its shares from HAL was markedly different. The state's new Dewan, Madhava Rao noted that:

> We have to look at the matter not only as investors but as a government which has promoted this enterprise on account of its indirect benefits,

[114] KSA, General and Revenue Secretariat file 205, Establishment of an aircraft factory in the state, The Hindustan Aircraft Limited.

[115] KSA, General and Revenue Secretariat file 205, Dewan's Minute, 2 February 1942.

[116] KSA, General and Revenue Secretariat file 205, Walchand to Secretary of Department of Supply, 3 February 1942.

[117] KSA, General and Revenue Secretariat file 205, Establishment of an aircraft factory in the state, The Hindustan Aircraft Limited.

[118] KSA, General and Revenue Secretariat file 205, Walchand to Secretary of Department of Supply, 24 January 1942; KSA, General and Revenue Secretariat file 205, McCann to Dewan, 24 March 1942.

[119] KSA, General and Revenue Secretariat file 205, McCann to Dewan, 24 March 1942; Gita Piramal has suggested that Walchand was relieved to leave HAL since he had undercapitalized the enterprise and India lacked the necessary ancillary industries required to manufacture aircraft. It is however extremely difficult to establish intentionality especially considering that Walchand Hirachand was widely acknowledged as one of the leading industrial propagandists of his times. Piramal, *Business Legends*, p. 248.

such as, stimulation of ancillary industries and provision of technical training for local men. It is, necessary therefore, to make sure that we can re-assume and if possible, improve our share in the management of the undertaking.[120]

Instead of focusing on compensation therefore Mysore state's representatives tried to negotiate the continued involvement of the state in HAL even if this could only be accomplished after the war. Madhava Rao made a concerted rebuttal of the government's arguments for taking over HAL completely. The state was interested in research, it had a record of maintaining the secrecy and it was not interested in profits accrued during the war.[121] Mysore state would be willing to relinquish decision making powers for the course of the war in return for only 12.5 lakhs in compensation for lost profits and the restoration of Mysore states' rights in the factory two years after the war. As Dewan noted, 'our interests in this matter are not identical with those of the Walchand group. The factory is within our jurisdiction and we can, in no circumstances, part with that jurisdiction.'[122] After an extended negotiation over the details of the agreement, New Delhi accepted Mysore's offer. An agreement was signed between the Mysore government and the Indian government on 5 August 1942, according to the terms of which Mysore would regain executive control of its share of HAL two years after the war. In the meanwhile, the Indian government would have a free hand to run HAL and the Mysore government would not gain any profits besides the 12.5 lakhs it received as compensation for wartime profits.

HAL was nationalized in 1942. In 1943 the firm was handed over to the United States Army for the assembly of aircraft being brought into India. The Americans hired 15,000 workers and began a three-shift system. In August 1945 with the end of the war, the factory was handed back to the Indian government. It was then repurposed temporarily to manufacture railway locomotives and finally handed over to Mysore state in 1947 just before for the *Mysore Chalo* (Go to Mysore) agitation.[123] The movement which was spearheaded by the Mysore Congress led to the end of

---

[120]   KSA, General and Revenue Secretariat file 205, Dewan's Minute, 2 February 1942.
[121]   KSA, General and Revenue Secretariat file 205, The Hindustan Aircraft Limited.
[122]   KSA, General and Revenue Secretariat file 205, Dewan's Minute, 2 February 1942.
[123]   *Flight*, 'Hindustan Aircraft Ltd', 27 August 1954.

Wodeyar rule as the state acceded to India on 24 October 1947.[124] Like many of its counterparts princely Mysore was swept away by the speed of independence and integration, though the state would only formally be liquidated with the formation of Karnataka in 1956.[125] HAL would go on to become independent India's largest factory. As a subsequent chapter will show it played an important part in pioneering Indian manufactured aircraft such as the HT-2 and HT 10. More importantly it would serve to repair B-24 Liberator bombers left behind by the United States Army Air Force thus immeasurably strengthening the IAF.

The question that remains however is how far the Mysore state bureaucracy was able to realize its developmentalist vision through HAL? As noted above, Mysore officials were motivated to aid the HAL project since they hoped that it would serve to aid in the goal of industrialization of the state. HAL would serve to train Mysore subjects in technical skills and provide the forward linkages necessary for the state to engage in advanced industrialization. Thus, following the establishment of HAL in 1940, Dewan Mirza Ismail turned to a project his predecessor M. Visvesvaraya had drawn up previously in conjunction with Walchand Hirachand; the Premier automobile factory.[126] As noted above Walchand hoped to produce India's first automobiles. That plan however had run into trouble with the Bombay government. Therefore, Walchand in conjunction with Ismail decided to establish an automobile factory in Mysore state. The planned car factory however was effectively blocked by the colonial government, which refused to release the requisite dollar credits and placed pressure on the Maharaja to withdraw support from the scheme.[127] It claimed not to be able to spare foreign exchange to import necessary machinery from the United States, where Walchand had been successful at securing a deal with car manufacturer Chrysler. However, Walchand and Ismail were convinced that the real reason behind this action was the unwillingness of the colonial government to allow Indian manufactured automobiles to compete with British made vehicles despite the exigencies of the war. Despite launching a bitter propaganda campaign that

---

[124] Manor *Political Change in an Indian State*, p. 159.
[125] Nair, *Mysore Modern*, p. 245.
[126] B.D. Sardesai, *Walchand Hirachand Diamond Jubilee Commemoration Volume* (Bombay, Walchand Diamond Jubilee Celebration Committee, 1942), p. 199.
[127] Ibid., p. 208.

saw him clash with government Commerce member and later member of the British war cabinet Ramasamy Mudaliar, Walchand was eventually forced to shelve plans for the automobile factory.[128] Walchand would ultimately realize his goal of building an automobile factory in 1947, rolling out the first car made in India's aptly named Premier Auto factory.[129] He would do so however under the aegis of the independent India headed by the Congress party, which embraced industrialization and development in what would come to be called the Nehruvian consensus.

Mirza Ismail was disillusioned enough by the failure of the automobile plan for it to contribute to his eventual resignation. To be sure, Ismail's resignation from the post of Dewan in 1941 was a consequence of his increasingly frayed relations with the new Maharaja of Mysore Chamarajendra Wodeyar, who keenly felt the dominance of the Dewan in a state with a particularly powerful bureaucracy.[130] Nevertheless the failure of the high prestige automobile plant certainly contributed to Ismail's resignation by highlighting the limits of the developmentalist vision under colonialism. Though the colonial government was willing, reluctantly to permit the establishment of an aircraft factory in order to make up for serious military weakness in 1940 it was unwilling to permit Mysore state to set up an automobile factory. The colonial state was unwilling to permit industrialization even in 'model' princely states, both since this would pose a threat to metropolitan interests as well as because this went too far in legitimizing Mysore's native modernity. Significantly the colonial state, the Mysore bureaucracy and even the nationalist movement shared similar understandings of modernity as development. As noted above, Mysore officialdom's notions of modernity drew heavily from colonial narratives of legitimacy. One consequence of this was that the colonial state recognized attempts to realize a native modernity through developmentalist policy as being ultimately subversive of its own legitimacy, even when this was carried out by its apparent allies.

The wartime industrialization of Mysore is indicative both of the enduring nature of developmentalist discourse and its limits under colonial conditions. As Janaki Nair has shown, nationalist criticisms of the

---

[128] NMML Walchand Papers- Subject File *Bombay Chronicle*, 14 September 1941.
[129] Piramal, *Business Legends*, p. 261.
[130] Manor, *Political Change in an Indian State*, p. 134.

Mysore government were based solely in the realm of representation rather than economic policy.[131] The construction of HAL is indicative of a number of other trends in the decade under discussion. HAL was very much a product of the internationalization of South Asia occasioned by the Second World War. It relied on American expertise, by way of China, for the establishment of an aircraft factory in Southern India. It also reveals the broader trend of the increasing association of the princely order with Indian capital which will be discussed at length in a later chapter. Here it is adequate to point to the fact that though Mysore's primary goal in setting up of HAL was not to make financial gains, the anticipated profits were handsome. Indian states could and in several cases did leverage state power in wartime to reap profits. Even, as in Mysore, when this was not the case the power of the Indian states to successfully intervene in the economic realm was a source of unease for both the colonial government and its independent successors.[132] Finally Mysore's engagement with HAL is illustrative of the different strategies that princely states could potentially embrace in using aviation as a means to legitimate state sovereignty. Mysore's actions were shaped by its historical context. As a wealthy state with a powerful bureaucracy and a complex strategy to nativize modernity, Mysore idealized aeroplanes and automobiles, though with different motives for doing so than, for instance, Jodhpur. The state's elite displayed a distinctly democratizing, though not democratic, vision aimed at uplifting its subjects economically, thus securing its authority to rule. In this it failed due to the traditional constraint it had faced since its formation; colonial rule.

Hyderabad: Aviation as Independence

Hyderabad came into existence as an independent kingdom when the Nizam-ul-Mulk Asaf Jah I, the Mughal governor of the Deccan defeated the forces of the emperor in 1724. British involvement in Hyderabadi affairs would begin in 1759 as British forces intervened in the succession struggles that affected the state to prevent the growth of French

---

[131] Nair, *Mysore Modern*, p. 15.
[132] Copland, *The Princes of India in the Endgame of Empire*, p. 185.

influence there. Hyderabad's independence would end with the signing of a series of subsidiary alliance treaties with the British EIC in 1798 and 1800. This would be followed in 1853 with the signature of a treaty that forced Hyderabad to pay for a British military contingent, ostensibly for Hyderabad's own defence by ceding several districts including the economically critical district of Berar. Though many of these were returned as a 'reward' for Hyderabad's support for the British during the rebellion of 1857, Berar would remain in British hands. The demand for the return of Berar was led by the state's famed *Dewan* (prime minister) Salar Jung, and the claim implicit in this, that Hyderabad was a sovereign state whose relations with the paramount power were defined by its treaties rather than its subordination would inform state policy in the long term.[133] Hyderabadi politicians from Salar Jung to Nizam Asaf Jah VII would argue, unsuccessfully but persistently, that Hyderabad had concluded its treaties with the British on equal terms as a sovereign state.[134]

Hyderabadi exceptionalism was also fuelled from the 19th century onwards by a keen awareness of the state's premier place at the head of the monarchical order established by the British in India.[135] The state was India's second largest in area and had a population of some 23 million at the time of independence, of whom the overwhelming majority were Hindu.[136] Hyderabad was also India's wealthiest princely state thanks to its size, location, and the administrative genius of a line of gifted administrators from Salar Jung to Akbar Hydari.[137]

Hyderabad's internal politics also served to distinguish the state from others in the princely order. Hyderabad did not have an analogue to the Congress or Praja Parishads that came increasingly to characterize other states. Instead it had a powerful nativist or *Mulki* (literally country)

---

[133] Michael Witmer, *The 1947–48 India-Hyderabad Conflict: Realpolitik and the Formation of the Modern Indian State* (PhD Thesis, Temple University, 1995), p. 54.

[134] The terms of the treaties signed with Hyderabad were indeed more equal, if not entirely so, than those that the British would subsequently sign with other Indian states as its position on the Indian subcontinent became more secure. Eric Lewis Beverly, *Hyderabad, British India and the World: Muslim Networks and Minor Sovereignty, C. 1850–1950* (Cambridge: CUP, 2015), p. 69.

[135] Hyderabad however consistently refused to join the Chamber of Princes as the Nizam refused to equate Hyderabad's relations with the Government of India to that of other princes. Copland, *The Princes of India in the Endgame of Empire*, p. 68.

[136] Lucien Benichou, *From Autocracy to Integration Political Developments in Hyderabad State, 1938–1948* (Chennai: Orient Longman, 2000), p. 13.

[137] For the career of Hyderabad's most prominent Dewan see: Vasant K. Bawa, *The Nizam between Mughals and British: Hyderabad under Salar Jung I* (New Delhi: S. Chand, 1996).

movement that was both anti-British and xenophobic towards non-Hyderabad subjects.[138] Significantly Mulki sentiment was not necessarily communal and meant in the long term that there were strong pressures on the government from below to uphold Hyderabadi nativism. Hyderabad was thus characterized by an elite that saw the state as sovereign and at least part of the populace that regarded it as distinct.

In 1874 the state would become the site of one of India's first railway lines leading later to establishment of the Nizam's State Guaranteed Railway (NSR).[139] The company would grow in size to become one of India's largest railway firms. It would also diversify operations into road transportation leading to the purchase of the curiously named NSR buses. More significantly, in 1938 it would become the first and only railway in a princely state to open an aviation department.[140] The Nizam's State Railways Air Department was created by an NSR takeover of the state's flying club, the Hyderabad Aero Club which had in turn been established in 1933.[141] The club and later the air department were placed under the supervision of two of the state's leading aviators; Pingle Reddy and Babbar Mirza. Reddy had been educated in mechanical engineering at the University of Leeds before completing an apprenticeship at Krupp industries in Germany in 1934 followed by an air instruction course in the United Kingdom in 1936. On his return to India he became chief pilot instructor at the Hyderabad Aero club and was subsequently made a flight instructor for the IAF at Hyderabad.[142] Babbar Mirza was the son of a local Hyderabad notable. After receiving flying training in England in 1930 where he had been sent to receive an education, Babbar returned to India to open the Hyderabad Aero Club on 5 August 1933.[143]

The Hyderabad government intended to use the NSR Air Department to start a service between Madras and Bangalore via Hyderabad before presumably expanding it. To this end the Aero Club's personnel and

[138] Karen Leonard, *Hyderabad and the Hyderabadis* (New Delhi: Manohar, 2014), p. 47.

[139] Ownership of the railway repeatedly changed hands going from the Great Indian Peninsular railway to the Nizam's Guaranteed Railway in 1885. It was then transferred in 1930 to the Nizam's State Railway. Vasant K. Bawa, 'Salar Jung and the Nizam's State Railway 1860-1883', *Indian Economic and Social History Review*, 2,307 (1964).

[140] APSA, 1942 Hyderabad Directory, H.E.H. Nizams State Railway, p. 200.

[141] APSA, H.E.H. The Nizams State Railway Annual report of the General Manager Financial year 1938-1939.

[142] Reddy, *Aviation in the Hyderabad Dominions* (Hyderabad, 2001), p. 34.

[143] Ibid., p. 39

machines were taken over and five aerodromes in the state were prepared.[144] However the service which had begun in 1938 had to be discontinued with the outbreak of the Second World War.

The state of Hyderabad, under Nizam Asaf Jah VII, won the title of
'Faithful ally' for its contribution to the British Empire's wars. During the
Great War, the Nizam had contributed towards the founding of an RAF
unit, No. 110 Squadron. During the Second World War, the Nizam paid
one hundred thousand pounds for the establishment of a RAF squadron
in October 1939. In June 1940 he sent the Crown fifty thousand pounds
for the establishment of another squadron.[145] This brought the total
number of squadrons contributed by the Nizam to three, the highest
number of squadrons paid for by any Indian princely state and second
in all of India only to the combined donation of four squadrons by the
entire populace of Madras state.[146] RAF squadrons No. 110, No. 152, and
No. 253 were designated the Hyderabad squadrons and bore specially designed crests as a tribute to the Nizam and his state.[147]

Besides providing money for squadrons Hyderabad state contributed
to the war effort in the air in a number of ways. Hyderabad's Begumpet
aerodrome, one of India's most advanced, was transferred to the DCA
and later the RAF to run as an Elementary Flying Training School.[148] The
Kachiguda training centre for flight trades also provided ninety *Mulki* or
Hyderabadi tradesmen to the IAF. These latter contributions were a result of the sophisticated aviation infrastructure that Hyderabad state possessed dating back to the years before the war. Employees of the Nizam
State Railway gathered Rupees 1,77,280 to pay for a Spitfire aeroplane.[149]

In addition to showering the Nizam with titles and praise His Majesty's
Government also gifted him with a curious memento, the ruins of a
downed enemy warplane. The Messerschmitt 109 in question had been
shot down over the English Channel and was sent to Hyderabad state
both as concrete proof that Hyderabad's money was vanquishing the en-
emies of empire as well as in order to raise more funds through fetes and

[144] *Flight*, 'State interests in India', 20 October 1938.
[145] Reddy, *Aviation in Hyderabad Dominions*, p. 97.
[146] Pushpindar Singh, 'India's Gift Squadrons', Accessed June 19, 2015. http://www.bharat-
rakshak.com/IAF/history/ww2/1203-gift-squadrons.html, -
[147] Reddy, *Aviation in Hyderabad Dominions*, p. 103.
[148] TNA, AIR 29/616, No. 1 EFTS Secunderabad.
[149] Reddy, *Aviation in Hyderabad Dominions*, p. 97.

exhibitions that the plane's display was likely to occasion. The *Deccan Chronicle* advertised the plane as a 'masterpiece of devilish Nazi ingenuity'. The 'King Kong of Germany gone criminally insane' was displayed at Secunderabad for a fee, which was treated as a contribution to the war effort.[150]

The Hyderabad government's contributions to the war effort were aimed at strengthening its position in negotiations with the paramount power on constitutional agreements after the war. In its view the departure of the British from India would end the system of paramountcy to which it had submitted through a system of treaties. This and its clear viability as an independent state in economic terms would mean that it would become independent with the passage of colonialism. In these circumstances Hyderabad needed to prepare for discussions on independence and on the retrocession of Berar which had been unfairly taken from it in 1853. Hyderabadi politicians were not blind to the obstacles this course of action would face. Thus, as early as 1942 Hyderabad's chief engineer Ali Yawar Jung handed over a memorandum to His Majesty's Government outlining Hyderabad's concerns. Most of these revolved around the possibility of the British handing power over to a central government that might also make claims to paramountcy. The most important point however, for the purposes of the present discussion, is Hyderabad's concern that if the British left without establishing constitutional safeguards for Hyderabad's independence then it would find itself defenceless and isolated. Vitally, it emphasized that Britain might have no strategic reasons for allying with such a state. Measures suggested to prevent this state of affairs from emerging included retrocession of lost territories, a new treaty with Britain that would effectively recognize Hyderabadi parity and an increase in Hyderabad's military potential.[151]

Nothing came of Hyderabad's negotiations with the colonial government as well as its talks with representatives of the British government such as Sir Stafford Cripps. As Michael Witmer has shown this did not however indicate that an independent Hyderabad was impossible at the end of the war. Hyderabad's position was reasonably strong in 1945. Its

[150] 'Warning Nazi fighter in Secunderabad', *The Deccan Chronicle*, September 28, 1941. Quoted in Reddy, *Aviation in Hyderabad Dominions*, p. 101.
[151] Witmer, *The 1947-48 India-Hyderabad Conflict*, p. 84.

military contributions to the war, not least in the air, had been signifi-cant.[152] Its rival at the national level, the Indian National Congress had in contrast been knocked out of the war with the arrest of its leadership in 1942. It also continued to receive mixed signals about independence from British representatives.[153] The notion that it would soon be inde-pendent once the British left and the treaties they had signed lapsed in-formed Hyderabad's aviation policy as well. Whereas Hyderabad had made a relatively limited attempt to form an air service before the war, towards the end of the war it made significant leaps towards establishing its own airline. It partook of the post-war boom in aviation by purchasing five Douglas DC-3 Dakota aircraft from the United States Army and Navy Foreign Liquidation Commission in early 1946.[154]

Deccan Airways was established on 21 September 1945. It was the lar-gest, though not the only, airline established by an Indian state.[155] Deccan Airways fleet would expand to include 19 aircraft including DC-3 Dakotas, De Havilland DH 89 Dominies, and Beechcraft C-45 Expeditors. Deccan Airways launched a Madras to Delhi service and a Madras to Bangalore service in cooperation with Indian National Airways four times a week via Hyderabad.[156] Though most of its personnel were drawn from Hyderabad and British India, the airline also drew personnel from abroad. At least four Polish pilots, R. Bobinski, K. Kuzubski, Garsetski, and S.Z. Zygnerski flew for Deccan, reflecting both the displacement caused by the war and the enormous financial reach of the Nizam's gov-ernment.[157,158] The increased presence of foreigners in India caused by the Second World War meant that the British grip even on forms of la-bour as specialized as aviation was weakening. Deccan Airways was also one of the first Indian airlines to feature air hostesses including a number drawn from Britain. The airline itself was headed by a retired RAF Air

[152] Hyderabad state forces had fought in the war. The Nizam had also paid for an Australian battleship, aptly named HMAS Hyderabad.

[153] Witmer, *The 1947–48 India-Hyderabad Conflict*, p. 86.

[154] *Times of India* (ToI) 'Deccan Air Services in Hyderabad', 2 January 1946.

[155] Jamair was established in 1946 in part by the Jam Sahib of Nawanagar in partnership with American pilots who had served in the China National Aviation Corporation. It was a consid-erably smaller concern than Deccan Airways and the Jam Sahib was bought out by his partners before the airline was eventually nationalized. PC, James B. Muff files (1916–1977).

[156] *Times of India*, 'New Air Services', 3 July 1946.

[157] Reddy, *Aviation in the Hyderabad Dominions*, p. 124.

[158] The Polish pilots would remain with Deccan until it was nationalized in 1953. Ibid., p. 158.

Commodore named Harold Arthur Fenton. It also had the distinction of hiring India's first female commercial pilot Prema Mathur. She was however not be permitted to fly planes as 'commander' and would subsequently quit Deccan Airways.[159] Deccan Airways would play a critical role in the crises of 1947. As seen in the previous chapter it was perhaps the last Indian airline to stop ferrying refugees to and from Pakistan during the partition violence. It also ferried Indian troops into Kashmir during the Kashmir conflict that year.[160]

The establishment of Deccan Airways was aimed at announcing Hyderabad's sovereignty as a free state. Though strategic considerations, aimed at connecting Hyderabad to the world in general and Pakistan in particular no doubt played a part in the establishment of the airline, it is also clear that the Hyderabad state prioritized the accumulation of reputational capital through the creation of the airline. The decision to kick-start the airline by rapidly buying aircraft and hiring personnel in the immediate aftermath of the war was clearly aimed at projecting a distinct Hyderabadi identity. This is especially salient when we return to the earlier point on modernity. In establishing Deccan Airways Hyderabad sought to construct its own variant of native modernity that had two simultaneous objectives. On the one hand the airline was clearly aimed at setting Hyderabad apart from any 'national' government that Britain might hand power to at the centre. On the other hand, the airline also proclaimed Hyderabad's long-cherished stance of parity with Britain, with which it had long maintained it was connected solely through treaties.[161] The foundation of Deccan Airways needs to be seen in the broader context of post-war actions taken by Hyderabad to ensure that with the passing of colonial rule it would resume its sovereignty.

Hyderabad drew what support it could from its closest ally in the colonial government, political advisor to the Crown representative Sir Conrad Corfield, to have restrictions on it eased in 1947. Hyderabad representatives travelled to the United Kingdom, France, and the United

---

[159] Mathur had been rejected by eight airlines before being hired by Deccan. When she asked P.M. Reddy for command of her plane she was told, 'If they know the pilot is a woman they will run away.' Mathur would later serve as industrialist G.D. Birla's pilot. 'High Fliers with nerves of steel', *The Hindu*, 17 March 2008.

[160] Reddy, *Aviation in the Hyderabad Dominions*, p. 152.

[161] On Hyderabad's insistence on parity see: Beverly, *Hyderabad, British India and the World*, p. 69.

States to commence diplomatic relations and raise support for its independence.[162] It hired Walter Monckton, the lawyer who had previously advised King Edward VII, to prepare its legal case for independence.[163] Keenly aware of being surrounded by British India, Mirza Ismail, who served briefly as the Dewan of Hyderabad, began negotiations to buy the port of Goa from the Portuguese. The Portuguese government claimed that it was unwilling under any circumstances to part with Goa, a claim that it would stand by for another 15 years, but would be willing to offer Marmagoa port for Hyderabad's use.[164] The ultimate failure of these talks however would force Hyderabad to make use of more desperate measures to import the arms necessary to protect its sovereignty. More immediately Hyderabad sought to leverage its enormous wealth as well as its existing aviation infrastructure by creating a Hyderabad Air Force.

In the first half of June 1947 Hyderabad's representative in London Mir Nawaz Jung approached retired RAF Air Chief Marshal Sir Christopher Courtney to enquire whether the latter would be interested in being employed by the Hyderabad government for the setting up of an air force for the state.[165] The initial plan was to form a Hyderabad air force consisting of a transport and a reconnaissance squadron. Since Hyderabad would not have the personnel to man such an air force it would recruit British personnel to begin with. The Hyderabad government would 'naturally wish that their Air Force should be organised on a British basis'.[166] If help was not forthcoming from Britain, as represented in this case by Air Chief Marshal Courtney, then Hyderabad would not rule out the possibility of approaching the United States for support in the project.[167] The proposal is remarkable in many ways for its underlying assumptions. Foremost among these is that Britain was likely to aid it militarily. The proposal would also appear to exhibit a lack of urgency since it focused

---

[162] Copland, *The Princes of India in the Endgame of Empire*, p. 251.

[163] See: BCA, Dep Monckton Trustees 25–52.

[164] Witmer, *The 1947–48 India-Hyderabad Conflict*, p. 144.

[165] There was some disagreement about Jung's official position since he claimed to be the Agent General for Hyderabad in the United Kingdom while the HMG only considered him to be a Trade Commissioner in keeping with the broader policy towards Hyderabad's sovereignty. TNA, AIR 8/1437, Air Force for Hyderabad, Hyderabad Provision of Air Forces: Report by the Joint Planning Staff, 15 July 1947.

[166] TNA, AIR 8/1437, Air Force for Hyderabad, Note by Air Chief Marshal Sir Christopher Courtney, 21 June 1947.

[167] TNA, AIR 8/1437, Air Force for Hyderabad, Note by Air Chief Marshal Sir Christopher Courtney, 21 June 1947.

on those arms of the air force that are least likely to be used offensively, though this could also be understood in pragmatic terms as indicating that Hyderabad would make use of infrastructure and personnel it already possessed for civil purposes. Moreover, the offer also acknowledged the passage of global power from Britain to the United States by invoking the possibility that Hyderabad would do business with the United States if Britain failed to oblige it.

Courtney, who had previously served on the British Air Council, was intrigued by the no doubt extravagant offer but wished to consult the British government before he answered Jung.[168] He therefore approached Sir David Monteath, Permanent Undersecretary of State at the India Office. Monteath advised him not to take up the Hyderabad offer as Hyderabad was likely to demand the retrocession of Berar when India became independent and that this would cause a tense situation in which the presence of retired British personnel would be seen by the 'Hindustan Government' as continued British interference in its affairs. Monteath subsequently confirmed this with his boss the Secretary of State.[169] Courtney however felt that 'there may very well be more than one view on the situation' and moved the matter to the Chief of Air Staff of the RAF, Arthur Tedder who in turn passed it on to the Joint Planning Staff.

In a note dated 15 July 1947, a month before Indian independence the Joint Planning Staff laid out reasons why Courtney should not take up the Jung's offer. These bear quoting at length:

"7. From the Political point of view, therefore, it would be undesirable to take any action that would lead to the 'Balkanisation' of India or which might encourage the Indian States to feel that they can stand on their own. We understand that the United States Government is in agreement with this policy.

8. From the Military point of view our primary aim remains to get satisfaction for our long-term strategic requirements from India and Pakistan. Military agreements with the Indian states are of little account in comparison with this and if in attempting to negotiate with them we

[168] Oxford Dictionary of National Biography. Accessed 6 May 2022. https://www.oxforddnb.com/view/10.1093/ref:odnb/9780198614128.001.0001/odnb-9780198614128-e-30975.

[169] TNA, AIR 8/1437, Air Force for Hyderabad, Note by Air Chief Marshal Sir Christopher Courtney, 21 June 1947.

make it harder to achieve our primary aim it would clearly be better to avoid any entanglements with the Indian states at this stage."[170]

To be sure the document also expressed some ambiguity about the possibility of agreements with the Indian states in case conditions were ideal and India proved unable to provide this.[171] However the note also showed that for HMG the process of decolonization was part of a larger Cold War policy. British planners believed that India and Pakistan would serve as military allies in the Commonwealth, continuing to play their old role as British military clients even after independence.[172] This belief would turn out to be badly misplaced, especially once India and Pakistan went to war in Kashmir. However, at the time it meant that the United Kingdom and the United States did not regard Hyderabad as a viable ally, actualizing the state's worst fears about the loss of sovereignty outlined in the 1942 memorandum.

India became independent in August 1947. In the months before and after this the newly constituted Ministry of States (MoS) led by Vallabhbhai Patel and V.P. Menon succeeded in securing the accession of the vast majority of princely states to India.[173,174] Several states however refused to accede to India including Junagadh, which had received some encouragement to stay independent from the Nizam and Kashmir where, as seen in a previous chapter, non-accession brought India and Pakistan to war in October 1947.[175] Hyderabad in keeping with its stance that it was resuming its sovereignty also chose to be independent after concluding a standstill agreement with independent India. Negotiations between New Delhi and Hyderabad were carried out from December 1947

---

[170] TNA, AIR 8/1437, Hyderabad Provision of Air Forces: Report by the Joint Planning Staff, 15 July 1947, p. 2.

[171] TNA, AIR 8/1437, Air Force for Hyderabad, Hyderabad Provision of Air Forces: Report by the Joint Planning Staff, 15 July 1947

[172] BL, Defence of India and Pakistan Part I (b), Mss Eur IOR Neg 15542.

[173] Menon, *Integration of the Indian States*, p. 7.

[174] Pakistan's integration of the princely states adjoining it would take longer. See: Yaqoob Khan Bangash, *A Princely Affair: The Accession and Integration of the Princely States of Pakistan* (Karachi: Oxford University Press, 2015).

[175] Interestingly the aeroplane had played a key role in the Junagadh crisis with Indian diplomats conducting shuttle diplomacy with the state's representatives. The Nawab of Junagadh would famously be dispatched from the state by Indian forces along with his large number of pedigree dogs. For a discussion of the Indian invasion of Junagadh see: Raghavan, *War and Peace in Modern India* (Basingstoke, 2010), p. 26.

to June 1948, on the latter's constitutional status. A vast corpus of literature has covered the Indo-Hyderabad negotiations and their subsequent
breakdown.[176] As such what follows is a brief précis. The Nizam's position
as we have seen contended that his state was resuming a legal sovereignty
ensured by the lapse of treaties with Britain and that it had the wherewithal to emerge as a viable independent state. The Indian leadership on
the other hand claimed that Hyderabad was an anachronistic despotism
that had no place in the modern world. Indian leaders pointed to the
Hyderabad government's close association with the *Majlis-e-Ittehadul-
Muslimeen* (Council of the Union of Muslims) Party and its paramilitary
wing the *Razakars* (Volunteers) to argue that Hyderabad was a communal
state in which a Muslim despot terrorized the Hindu majority.[177] Michael
Witmer has shown that despite being bitter, negotiations between India
and Hyderabad in June 1948 came close to succeeding with a compromise that would have seen a plebiscite carried out in the state to decide
on its future. He contends that these were not carried out largely due to
India's fears that Muslims, their numbers swelled by refugees fleeing communal violence in South India, would form an alliance with the state's
lower castes to ensure that Hyderabad did not join India.[178] Whether we
accept this admittedly controversial thesis or not, two other factors acted
to deeply complicate the Hyderabad imbroglio. India and Pakistan went
to war in Kashmir in October 1947 and Hyderabad's apparent friendship
with Pakistan, as seen in its grant of a 200-million-rupee loan to the latter,
served to paint it as a threat in Indian eyes.[179] Moreover Hyderabad itself was affected by a Communist insurgency which the Indian officials
feared would spread outside the state if it was not quickly stamped out.[180]

In order to pressure Hyderabad into acceding, the Indian government
imposed a blockade on the state from January 1948.[181] The blockade

[176] See: Menon, *Integration of the Indian States*; A.G. Noorani, *The Destruction of Hyderabad*
(London: Hurst and Co, 2014); Benichou, *From Autocracy to Integration*; Witmer, *Integration of
the Indian States*; Raghavan, *War and Peace in Modern India*.

[177] *White Paper on Hyderabad* (New Delhi, 1948).

[178] Witmer, *The 1947–48 India-Hyderabad Conflict*, p. 282.

[179] Witmer, *The 1947–48 India-Hyderabad Conflict*, p. 215.

[180] For the argument that independent India engaged in anti-communist actions
see: Benjamin Zachariah, *Nehru* (London: Routledge, 2004). See also: Paul M. McGarr, *The Cold
War in South Asia* (Cambridge: CUP, 2013), p. 32; Benichou, *From Autocracy to Integration*,
p. 209.

[181] Sunil Purushotham, 'Internal Violence: The 'Police Action' in Hyderabad', *Comparative
Studies in Society and History*, vol. 57, no. 2, 2015.

was apparently aimed at preventing the importing of arms into the state though there is some evidence to show that it was aimed at starving the state into submission paralleling Pakistan's actions in Kashmir in September 1947. English travellers to the state, for instance, were forbidden from carrying in parcels of potatoes and vegetables by the Madras government's customs department.[182] The weight of the blockade naturally fell heavily on Deccan Airways. Its provisional license was cancelled in July 1948 and all flights to Hyderabad were barred 'to complete the isolation of the Nizam's State from the air, which has hitherto proven a vital medium of traffic into Hyderabad'.[183] The decision to do this followed the collapse of talks between India and Hyderabad in June 1948, though the charge of arms smuggling was never proved. As a communique from Deccan Airways, dated 5 July 1948, pointed out, the airline had an impeccable record and in any case its Dakota planes were not suited for the long distance flights that would have been necessary to smuggle arms from Pakistan.[184] In the months preceding this Deccan Airways aircrews had been harassed by Indian authorities when landing at Indian aerodromes.[185]

The decision to suspend air services to Hyderabad while clearly aimed at pressuring the state also points to the broader underlying ideological conflict between India and Hyderabad. Hyderabad claimed to be returning to a sovereign status it had possessed before its subordination to colonialism. Its decision to issue its own currency, float an airline, arm its forces, and refuse to accede to India flowed from this conception of sovereignty. India vehemently denied Hyderabad's right to do so, signalling the radical new self-conception of sovereignty that it had crafted. Eric Beverly has called for an understanding of Hyderabad as a state possessing fragmented sovereignty that permitted it to surrender some functions of state to colonialism while maintaining others. In this view Hyderabad could emerge as a sub-Imperial sovereign space in which the relationship of colonial power with its subjects could be mediated by groups whose sovereignty, however limited, it was willing to

---

[182] BCA, Dep Monckton Trustees 36, Col. J.M. Graham to General Roy Bucher, 26 July 1948.
[183] 'Aim of India's blockade'. *Times of India*, 3 July 1948.
[184] 'Suspension of Air Services "Totally unwarranted"' *Times of India*, 5 July 1948.
[185] Beverly, *Hyderabad, British India and the World*, pp. 132, 156.

acknowledge.[186] The corollary of this then is that the nation-state that succeeded the colonial power sought to monopolize sovereignty and was intolerant of anyone that came between the Government and its citizens. I term this practice of sovereignty by the nation-state 'deep sovereignty' for its obsession with the penetration of state power to the people without the mediation of any other sovereign entity, however limited its claims. In this sense the adoption of state sovereignty in India was a radical departure from earlier colonial sovereignty whose acceptance of sub-imperial systems was anathema to the new regime. Thus, Hyderabad's claims to resume an old sovereignty were impossible for India to accept precisely because this in some ways validated the possibility that more than one sovereignty might dwell within a single state. Deep sovereignty prompted India's leadership, at a time of perceived existential crisis brought on by partition and the spectre of war with Pakistan, to consider any display of sovereignty including Hyderabad's operation of an airline as a threat.

The collapse of negotiations and the blockade of Hyderabad prompted the state to seek other means to acquire arms, that in the last resort would defend its continued existence. Hyderabad's legal advisor, Sir Walter Monckton contacted an Australian aviator Sidney Cotton to begin running arms to the state. Cotton agreed to fly required weapons into Hyderabad through his company the Aeronautical and Industrial Research Corporation (AIRC) in return for 400,000 pounds in May 1948.[187] Using a fleet of five Lancastrian aircraft Cotton began to bring much-needed equipment of various kinds from June 1948 onwards. Equipment flown in included pistols, rifles, machine guns, mortars, various types of grenades, and wireless sets.[188] Arms bought in Switzerland were flown via Karachi's Drigh road aerodrome, the birthplace of the IAF, to Bidar aerodrome, Hyderabad with the covert aid of the Government of Pakistan (GoP).[189] The operation had the support of Iskander Mirza, the Secretary of the Ministry of Defense. There is reason however to believe that relations between Hyderabad and at least parts of the Pakistan government were not always amicable.[190] Still Cotton was successful in

---

[186] Ibid., pp 64–69.
[187] BCA, Dep Monckton Trustees 36, Cotton to Monckton, May 1948.
[188] BCA, Dep Monckton Trustees 36.
[189] BCA, Dep Monckton Trustees 36., Bucher to Graham, 16 July 1948.
[190] BCA, Dep Monckton Trustees 36., (Sidney Cotton) to John (Graham), undated secret letter.

flying in over 400 tons of equipment to Hyderabad over the course of 39 trips and even expanded his fleet by purchasing two Canadian Lancaster aircraft.[191,192]

Needless to say, the Indian government was not pleased when it found out that AIRC planes had been flying to Hyderabad. It exerted both diplomatic and military efforts to stop the supply of arms by air to Hyderabad. Krishna Menon, India's High Commissioner to Britain made informal approaches to HMG in July 1948 but the latter chose not to share much of the information it had as this might compromise its intelligence sources on the sub-continent.[193] Further there were serious legal limits on what actions the United Kingdom could take to stop the flights. Evidence against Cotton was difficult to collate as long as his operations did not involve the United Kingdom. In terms of international aviation, the Chicago convention held that the carriage of weapons over a sovereign country was a crime but only prescribed a minor fine for the transgression. His Majesty's Government could not even legally hope to delay Cotton in the United Kingdom or impound his planes if they were landed in the country. Indeed, Cotton's lawyer's threatened to sue Air Marshal Elmhirst the commander of the Royal Indian Air Force (RIAF) for interfering with 'medical supplies' being flown by their client to Hyderabad![194] Cotton would eventually be prosecuted for gun running in 1949. Though he would plead guilty Cotton would pay a mere 1000 pounds in fines for his involvement in gun running to Hyderabad.[195] While the Cotton trial was a sensation in its time, for the purposes of the present chapter, it is revealing of the extent to which HMG was committed to aiding India against Hyderabad. As seen above the British government clearly considered the establishment of a centralized Indian state as being in its interests.

Attempts by the RIAF to stop the gun running were a failure. On 18th June 1948 two unarmed Tempest fighter aircraft of No. 2 Wing, were ordered to intercept any aircraft flying to Bidar from Karachi while

---

[191] BCA, Dep Monckton Trustees 36.
[192] TNA, DO 142/481, UK High Commissioner (UKHC) to India to Commonwealth Relations Office (CRO), 22 July 1948.
[193] TNA, PREM 8/1007, Krishna Menon's representations about the Flying of Arms into Hyderabad.
[194] TNA, DO 142/481, CRO to UKHC Pakistan, 17 July 1948.
[195] TNA, DO 1463/48, Evidence of specific instances of gun running in India.

patrolling. Such aircraft were to then be ordered to land in Santa Cruz in Bombay to face legal action. Aircraft were to be forced down through radio contact and were disarmed in order to prevent any incidents.[196] Less than a week later the Indian Defence Minister Baldev Singh was ordering fully armed planes to take 'offensive action' against AIRC planes. This alarmed RIAF Commander-in-Chief Thomas Elmhirst who noted that any such interception would for 'radar reasons' take place in the crowded area north of Bombay where a large number of American, British, and Indian four-engine aircraft, like the ones being operated by Cotton would be flying. Expressing his shock, he wrote, 'We are putting the responsibility of deciding a smuggler from other aircraft on to a young pilot of 22 or thereabouts of age.'[197] The order was subsequently rescinded but Indian leaders remained aggressive. Jawaharlal Nehru wondered how far radar could be used and whether smugglers could be brought down by 'offensive action'. The RIAF was ordered to launch Operation Radar Gunman, a dedicated hunt for the Lancaster planes flying arms into Hyderabad. The RIAF's No. 3 Fighter Squadron backed by two radar stations formed for the purpose at Deolali and Pune was to attempt to intercept the smugglers. An attempt was made to coordinate with the Directorate for Civil Aviation to ensure that no British Overseas Airways Corporation planes, which included Lancasters were shot down.[198] Matters had escalated so much that by July 1948 the RIAF was not only ordered to shoot down any Hyderabad planes that refused to land but also to attack Lancasters if they were spotted in Hyderabad's aerodromes.[199] Operation Radar Gunman failed for a number of reasons. Indian Tempests lacked the night flying capabilities possessed by the Lancasters which flew late in the night and left before daybreak.[200] The RIAF also lacked the equipment to trace the Lancaster's flight paths correctly. Finally, coordination between Indian intelligence in Karachi and the IAF was far too slow to make an impact.[201]

One of the key reasons that the Indian government was keen to cut off supplies of arms to Hyderabad was because it had begun to plan for

---

[196] MoD (I), 601/14238/H, Interception of intruder aircraft-Hyderabad 1948.
[197] MoD (I), 601/14238/H, Thomas Elmhirst to Baldev Singh, 24 June 1948
[198] MoD (I), 601/14238/H, OP Radar Gunman.
[199] MoD (I), 601/14238/H, H.M. Patel to Thomas Elmhirst, 6 July 1948.
[200] BCA, Dep Monckton Trustees 36.
[201] MoD (I), 601/14238/H, Interception of intruder aircraft-Hyderabad 1948, OP Radar Gunman.

Operation Polo, the invasion of Hyderabad. Jawaharlal Nehru had ordered the repositioning of Indian forces to the Hyderabad border as early as May 1948.[202] The IAF had been flying reconnaissance sorties over Hyderabad from at least July 1948. This demonstrated India's dismissal of Hyderabadi sovereignty, in comparison to Pakistan where during the 1947 Kashmir war, Indian planes were explicitly ordered from violating territorial sovereignty.[203] In July 1948 India requested and received ten battalions of Gurkhas from the King of Nepal to increase the amount of troops available to it.[204] For the Indian Union, the Hyderabad invasion was a calculated risk that could potentially plunge it into war with Pakistan. RIAF planners prepared for a worst-case scenario in which India would confront both Pakistan and Hyderabad even as its English officers were forced to step down by the British government. Consequently, Indian air defences were massed on Punjab while IAF units were divided between Kashmir and Hyderabad.[205]

Comprehensive accounts of the operation from the perspective of the RIAF have been provided elsewhere.[206] Once Indian forces began rolling across the border on 13 September 1948 the Polo Air Task Force which consisted of two Tempest squadrons, Squadron No. 2 and No. 3, along with two Dakotas modified for bombing, swung into action. Bidar aerodrome was bombed, Hyderabad troops were strafed, and leaflets were dropped proclaiming the end of the Nizam's rule.[207] The Hyderabad military collapsed within five days forcing the Nizam to surrender. This was not entirely unexpected. Not only were the Nizam's forces short on equipment, Cotton's interventions notwithstanding, but the Indian military had meticulously planned the operation for months. Pakistan did not respond militarily to the invasion of Hyderabad and so the greatest danger to the Indian intervention passed.

---

[202] Raghavan, *War and Peace in Modern India*, p. 84.

[203] MoD (I), 601/14238/H, Interception of intruder aircraft-Hyderabad 1948, Secretary of External Affairs Hyderabad to Secretary to the Ministry of States India, 20 July 1948.

[204] The Maharaja had sought instructions from the British government and when none were forthcoming he acquiesced to Indian wishes. PREM 8/1007, Kathmandu to Foreign Office, 3 July 1948.

[205] MoD (I), 601/14238/H, Interception of intruder aircraft-Hyderabad 1948, Air Defence Committee Paper No. 2, 29 July 1948.

[206] See for instance: R. Chhina, *The Eagle Strikes*; S.N. Prasad, *Operation Polo: The Police Action against Hyderabad 1948* (New Delhi, Manager of Publications, 1972).

[207] MoD (I), 601/1256/H, Summary of Operations Situation Reports-Hyderabad Operation.

Operation Polo resulted in 632 casualties for the Hyderabad forces. This was followed by the massacre of between 25,000 and 40,000 Muslims by Hindu mobs and Indian forces in Hyderabad.[208] It remains difficult to verify the numbers of those killed and the number quoted is a conservative estimate by the chairman of an Indian commission sent to the region.[209] The violence is explained by a number of factors including, among other things, the communalized discourse surrounding Hyderabad. Sunil Purushotham has pointed to the role of irregular Indian troops in atrocities in the state to argue that the Indian state had lost control of the monopoly on violence central to the exercise of sovereignty.[210] Consequently it sought to appropriate the violence of increasingly militarized irregulars in service of the state. Two questions about the aeroplane's role in the Hyderabad invasion are worth raising. Did control of high technology such as planes and tanks allow the state to claim to be the legitimating authority of violence? This becomes particularly pressing when we consider the blurring of lines between the military and 'militias', seen in the previous chapter, around the partition. Second, to what extent was the deployment of irregular forces an improvised response to the paucity of high technology?

While these questions cannot be authoritatively answered without further research, a couple of tentative answers can be offered. The widespread adoption of military tactics by armed militias who took part in the partition violence led, as seen in a previous chapter, to the increasing reliance of the state on high technology to re-establish its monopoly on violence. Attempts were also made, in Kashmir for instance, to integrate existing militias into state forces. In these circumstances state control of high technology was vital for providing the state with the legitimacy to decide which militias were a threat to order and which could be integrated to a degree with existing state apparatuses. As to the second question, the fact that the Indian militaries' high technology was at the time deployed against the more serious threat of a full-scale war against

---

[208] See: Raghavan, *War and Peace in Modern India*, p. 98; Purushotham, 'Internal Violence: The "Police Action" in Hyderabad'.

[209] 'Confidential Note attached to Sunderlal Committee Report'. Quoted in Noorani, *The Destruction of Hyderabad.*

[210] Sunil Purushotham, 'Destroying Hyderabad and Making the Nation', *Economic and Political Weekly*, 49, 22, 31 May 2014.

Pakistan in Punjab might explain why the state seemed willing to make use of the services of government militias such as the Home Guards. Ironically Deccan Airways would survive the collapse of the state it was meant to represent.[211] Its planes were briefly used by the commander of the Indian military governor of Hyderabad General J.N. Chaudhuri.[212] P.M. Reddy became the airline's general manager in 1948.[213] It would return to operating its old routes after the Indian invasion. With the integration of Hyderabad, the Indian government would take charge of the Nizam's shares in the company. Indeed, the company would come so heavily under the direct control of the Indian government, that at least one contemporary observer treated it as a partially nationalized enterprise.[214] In 1953 Deccan was nationalized along with a number of other airlines to form Indian Airlines Corporation.

Conclusion

The princely engagement with aviation presents an interesting view of the relationship between technology, modernity, and sovereignty in a colonial context. Confronted with claims by the colonial state on the one hand and nationalists on the other, that their rule was illegitimate because it was not modern, several Indian princes moved to embrace aviation technology to establish their credentials as modernizers. Indian states sought to construct their own distinctive 'native modernity' that would serve to legitimate their regimes and entrench their sovereignties. This was to have critical consequences for aviation, some of which endure into the present.

Though the three states under discussion invested heavily in aviation their reasons for doing so could vary widely resulting in very different approaches to the aeroplane. Jodhpur state sought to combine the Rathore dynasties' military traditions with the modernity of the aeroplane in the person of its monarch. In Mysore State aviation policy was tinged with a developmentalist agenda. The state's powerful bureaucracy hoped that

---

[211] APSA, Niz/ADM 20-1, Administrative report on Hyderabad State 1948–1950.
[212] Reddy, *Aviation in the Hyderabad Dominions*, p. 192.
[213] Ibid., p. 121.
[214] DO 35/ 4919, Confidential report, January 1953.

the establishment of an aircraft factory would instigate a larger process of industrialization in the state. Hyderabad's treatment of aviation was tied to its conception of itself as an equal of the British government which had temporarily abridged its sovereignty through legally binding treaties. When it became clear that colonialism was at an end, Hyderabad made a bid for independence on the understanding that Britain could not legally transfer its paramountcy to any independent central government.

The experiments of Jodhpur, Mysore, and Hyderabad with aviation varied widely. It is thus possible to argue that the princely states exhibited not one but several colonial modernities. Though these modernities proved abortive thanks to the overwhelming victory of the nation-state, this was in the circumstances of decolonization, not necessarily a foregone conclusion. Other historians have already drawn attention to the contingent nature of decolonization and the possibility that one or many princely states may well have achieved independence or autonomy if not for a complex series of outcomes that permitted the formation of the nation-state. This chapter points to some of those possibilities through the princely engagement with aviation. Even after the ultimate absorption of the Indian states into the triumphal Indian state, princely aviation has enjoyed a post-colonial afterlife. HAL rechristened as Hindustan Aeronautics Limited remains India's premier aircraft factory, Deccan Airways was absorbed into Air India and several of the aerodromes built by princes remain in use. Aviation in present-day India perhaps thus serves as an apt memorial to a long passed monarchical order that was obsessed with modernity.

5

Towards Sovereign Skies: Aviation in Independent India 1948–1953

The five years after India was granted formal independence mark a critical period of consolidation for both Indian aviation and the new state. Between 1948 and 1953 independent India took shape as a centralized republic with a commitment to unprecedented state power domestically and sovereign status abroad. This transformation of India from formally independent dominion to decolonized republic can be illustrated in the realm of aviation through an exploration of three major events that coloured the period; the establishment of external air services, the 1950 Bengal crisis, and the nationalization of civil aviation. Air India International (AII), India's flag carrier, made its debut in 1948, launching Indian civil aviation's long-delayed entry on the world stage. The 1950 confrontation between India and Pakistan over the rights of minorities in the new South Asian states contributed to the continuing entrenchment of the Indian Air Force (IAF) as a national institution. In 1953 the nationalization of civil aviation inaugurated a four-decade-long period during which aviation effectively became a state monopoly. The half-decade following independence was formative for aviation in independent India. A study of the period raises a number of important questions. What do the various views of aviation reveal about the nature of the independent Indian state? How did independent India 'territorialize the skies'? What was the vision for aviation expressed by independent India's government?

This chapter is divided into three broad segments studying the events that defined Indian aviation in the first five years after independence. Firstly, it studies the 1950 Bengal crisis, which put India and Pakistan on the path to war, to show that Indian state ideology came to be defined increasingly in opposition to Pakistan, thus belying the hope that the two countries could reconcile in the aftermath of the conflict in Kashmir.

The Aeroplane and the Making of Modern India. Aashique Ahmed Iqbal, Oxford University Press.
© Oxford University Press 2023. DOI: 10.1093/oso/9780192864208.003.0006

Secondly, it analyses the entry of India onto the international aviation stage with a specific focus on the negotiations between India and other countries that enabled this. I argue that India sought, from the very beginning of its diplomatic life to establish itself as a sovereign state in a post-war global order. It sought freedom of action, believing that the nation-state was the sole legitimate national formation, Thirdly, it traces the nationalization of the Indian civil aviation sector to historical trends dating to the Second World War. It will show that nationalization was part of a broader vision of unprecedented domestic state dominance that India's ruling elite saw as a necessary precondition to development and security.

While each of these events will be studied in some detail, a key aim of this chapter is to explore the origins of these events, the logic that underpinned them and the ways in which they related to each other. This is in service to an overarching argument that I make on the complex nature of the independent Indian state. The new state sought to enact new notions of sovereignty on multiple levels. It sought internationally to ensure that India was recognized as a sovereign state that enjoyed formal equality with the other nation-states that came to characterize the post-war global order. At the regional level India sought to impose its dominance vis-à-vis Pakistan, even as it recognized Pakistani sovereignty. Enacting new notions of sovereignty abroad meant that domestically the Indian state made unprecedented claims to state power and paradoxically sought greater control over the lives of its citizens, than the colonial state. Aviation reveals the different levels at which independent India exerted sovereignty, whether international, regional, and domestic, and the relationship between them.

Indian Aviation in the 1950 Bengal Crisis

The hope that the Partition of British India would result in the creation of two closely integrated states with common interests was dashed by the outbreak of a conflict in Kashmir that threatened to plunge the two newly independent dominions into full-scale war. The Kashmir war ended in a stalemate and would subsequently poison relations between India and Pakistan more than any other single issue. As I have argued, the Kashmir war was as much an ideological clash between India and Pakistan as it was a territorial conflict. Pakistan in keeping with the two-nation theory that had underpinned partition had based its claim on Kashmir on the fact that the majority of the state's population was Muslim. India meanwhile justified its intervention in the state, among other things, on its secularism with its implications that minorities could enjoy full rights as Indian citizens.[1] The stalemate in Kashmir did not resolve the wider ideological conflict between the two states and would return to threaten once more to plunge the two countries into a catastrophic conflict over the minorities question in Bengal a little over a year after the ceasefire in Kashmir. The Bengal crisis would have important consequences for both civil and military aviation, accelerating processes of expansion and nationalization. Moreover, the aeroplane would play a small but important role in the crisis.

By December 1947 an overwhelming majority of non-Muslims had been evacuated from West Pakistan. While relatively small minorities of non-Muslims would remain in West Pakistan, the two states could claim to have affected a transfer of populations in the West by December 1947.[2] The situation in the East however was different. Despite migrations effected by the violence of partition, a significant Hindu minority numbering some 12 million remained in East Pakistan while some 5 million Muslims remained in West Bengal.[3] The status of these minorities would be at the centre of the Bengal crisis.

The immediate cause of the 1950 Bengal crisis was a clash between East Bengal police and predominantly Hindu villagers in the province's Khulna district. Police searching for a communist fugitive had become involved in a fight on 20 December 1949 which had resulted in the deaths of two policemen. In retaliation, two days after this, East Bengal police along with a number of *Ansar* (helper) paramilitaries had surrounded several Hindu villages in the region and commenced a campaign of repression. Despite later Pakistani government claims, that the repression was aimed mainly at communists, the effect of the action was to begin a large Hindu exodus to India by January 1950.[4] These refugees carried

---

[1] For a detailed discussion of India's stance in the conflict see: Noorani, *The Kashmir Dispute*.
[2] TNA, DO 35/2989, Memorandum CRO 13 March 1950.
[3] Ibid.
[4] TNA, DO 35/2989, UKHC Pakistan to CRO, 24 February 1950.

with them a number of atrocity stories that were then magnified and widely disseminated by the West Bengal press prompting anti-Muslim violence in the city of Calcutta. As had happened during partition this set off a chain of retaliation which resulted in an exodus of Muslims to East Pakistan and prompted anti-Hindu violence in Dacca, the capital of East Bengal on 10 February 1950.

The outbreak of violence in Dacca prompted a rapidly increasing torrent of refugees travelling from East to West Bengal. Due to the shortage of railway facilities, several wealthier refugees made the short journey from Dacca to Calcutta by aeroplane. Air India and Orient Airways both flew shuttle services between the two cities, evacuating over a thousand refugees by 16 February. While not as large as the evacuations that had accompanied partition, the Bengal airlift was nevertheless coordinated by the Indian Deputy High Commissioner in Dacca.[5] As in 1947 clear figures for the number of refugees evacuated in the Bengal crisis are impossible to tally, for a number of reasons. It is difficult to calculate the number of those who fled East Bengal from the only uncontested numbers available at the time, which are of those who stayed in refugee camps. Most well-heeled refugees flying out of East Bengal, like those who fled West Punjab, could move into the houses of relatives if they did not have property of their own. Indeed, there was an element of speculative hedging that accompanied the Bengal air exodus as male members of affluent families often stayed behind to defend property while women and children were flown out.[6]

Whatever the actual figures, the numbers of Hindus fleeing East Bengal by air are likely to have been high since as the British High Commissioner estimated, some 300 were leaving everyday 'with no sign of slacking', as late as the 6 of March nearly a month after the riots in Dacca.[7] In the meanwhile large numbers of Muslims were flying out of Calcutta in the opposite direction. In a speech to Parliament, Indian Prime Minister Jawaharlal Nehru stated that in the nine days from 12 February to 21 February about 3,500 Hindus fled to India by air from East Pakistan while 2,100 Muslims made the journey in the opposite direction. If the Indian

---

[5] TNA, DO 35/2989, Weekly report number 7 for period ending 16 February 1950.
[6] TNA, DO 35/2989, Report on a visit to East Bengal by Horace Alexander, March 9 1950.
[7] TNA, DO 35/2989, UKHC Pakistan to CRO, 6 March 1950.

government's figures are accepted, then the number of those being evacuated by aircraft was a very high proportion of those being evacuated over the early ten-day period. Nehru estimated that a total of 16,000 arrived in Calcutta between 13 and 20 February.[8] This would mean that one in four refugees moving to India in the first ten days after the Dacca riots came in by air.

There are several likely reasons for the rush on aeroplanes. First, travel by train or steamer was likely to be dangerous. Dr Sita Ram, the Indian High Commissioner to Pakistan reported that there had been 'serious incidents' at Jamalpur and Bahadurabad railway stations' and that steamers had been attacked.[9] Memories of attacks on trains from partition may have encouraged those who could afford it to travel by aeroplane. Only one serious attack on an airfield took place in East Pakistan when a lorry full of rioters encountered a large number of undefended refugees at Kurmitola aerodrome, on 12 February killing 12 and injuring 30.[10] Subsequently all air operations were delayed till they were moved to the better defended Tejgaon aerodrome and no further incidents of violence were recorded.[11] Second, the availability of aeroplanes was far greater than it had been during partition. Indian airline companies had expanded since 1947 and do not appear to have suffered the same amount of attrition during the Bengal evacuations as they did during Partition.[12] The West Bengal Chief Minister Dr B.C. Roy, for instance, was able to charter 16 planes to ferry Hindu refugees into Calcutta.[13] Third, observers at the time have pointed to the presence of a large Hindu elite that sought to escape as the situation in Bengal worsened.[14] This elite could afford the high costs of air travel.

If the number of those travelling by aircraft was initially a high proportion of those fleeing India for Pakistan, and vice versa, then that proportion reduced as February turned to March. This was not because the numbers of those fleeing by air had reduced. It had not. As a report in the

[8] TNA, FO 371/84246, Supplementary Extract from Pandit Nehru's statement on 23 February 1950 about disturbances in Bengal.

[9] TNA, DO 35/2989., *Reuters*, 13 March 1950.

[10] TNA, DO 35/2989, Weekly report number 7 for period ending 16 February 1950.

[11] TNA, DO 35/2989, Allen Emerson to Ministry of Civil Aviation, 17 February 1950.

[12] *Flight*, 1 September 1949.

[13] Prafulla K. Chakrabarty, *The Marginal Men* (Calcutta: Naya Udyog, 1999), p. 27.

[14] *The Manchester Guardian*, 29 April 1950, Quoted in DO 35/2989.

Manchester Guardian would note in mid-March, 'hundreds of refugees flee everyday by every available airplane from Dacca and Chittagong, their places being taken by equal numbers of Muslim refugees from Calcutta.'[15] Instead those participating in the air exodus became a smaller fraction of the total numbers of those fleeing both states as over three hundred thousand refugees were displaced from their homes. This was partly a consequence of fear of communal violence being fanned in both countries by refugees and graphic tales in the press. It was also by March 1950, at least partly, a result of fears of the outbreak of a general war between India and Pakistan.

Srinath Raghavan has shown how the Indian government led by Jawaharlal Nehru coerced Pakistani authorities into coming to an agreement with India that would recognize the rights of minorities in Pakistan. Utilizing international relations theory he argues that Nehru made use of a 'compellence strategy' that eventually forced Liaquat Ali, the Prime Minister of Pakistan to offer him the best possible terms under the circumstances.[16] His work on the subject, the first of its kind, offers a detailed diplomatic history of the 1950 Bengal crisis rendering a narration of its events unnecessary. A brief precis of the crisis will therefore suffice.

Alarmed at the increasing numbers of Hindu refugees pouring into West Bengal and the growing anti-Muslim violence in India, that began in but was not limited to the province, Nehru wrote to Liaquat Ali, proposing a slew of measures aimed at restoring minority trust in both governments. This included the appointment of joint fact-finding committees, permission for High Commissioners of each country to tour riot-affected areas and also a proposal for both prime ministers to make joint visits to the worst affected areas to restore public confidence. When Liaquat Ali refused the last two of these Nehru, who was under considerable domestic pressure, ordered Indian military forces to begin mobilizing at the end of February on both of India's borders with Pakistan. By late March over 100,000 Muslims had fled India and 200,000 Hindus had fled Pakistan.[17] Unconvinced that an exchange of populations could

---

[15] *The Manchester Guardian*, 13 March 1950, Quoted in DO 35/2989.

[16] Raghavan, *War and Peace in Modern India*, p. 162.

[17] While these numbers are drawn from reports at the time they are difficult to verify since numbers provided by India and Pakistan vary and as the UK High Commissioner to Pakistan pointed out neither state had the means to perform a count given the chaotic atmosphere in which migrations took place. DO 35/2991, UKHC Pakistan to CRO, 22 July 1950.

realistically be affected and unwilling to plunge the subcontinent into a war that would be catastrophic for India, economically and communally, Nehru also attempted to press the United States and the United Kingdom to pressure Liaquat Ali to agree to his terms. Indian military moves and the apparent willingness of the USA and the UK governments to believe these were not aggressive finally convinced Liaquat to invite Nehru to Karachi for discussions. When Nehru instead invited him, Khan travelled to Delhi on 2 April 1950. After a week of negotiations an agreement was signed by the Prime Ministers of India and Pakistan assuring the citizenship rights of minorities in both countries. This would primarily be achieved through the appointment of minority affairs ministers, the establishment of committees of enquiry, the punishment of rioters, and the restitution of stolen property. In securing the agreement Nehru overcame not only the initial resistance of the Pakistani government to his terms but also an immense amount of domestic pressure for war with Pakistan from constituencies that included Hindu extremists, the Bengali press and a not inconsiderable segment of his party.

The IAF played a small but critical role in the 1950 Bengal crisis and was in significant ways transformed by it.[18] The force had made significant leaps in aircraft during the two years since independence. Under the supervision of Group Captain Harjinder Singh, the IAF had managed to recover 42 Consolidated Liberator bombers that the British had scrapped at Kanpur before their departure from the subcontinent (see Figure 5.1).[19] The bombers were flown one at a time by Jamshed Kaikobad 'Jimmy' Mistry, a Hindustan Aircraft Limited (HAL) test pilot with no previous experience flying four-engine aircraft from Kanpur to Bangalore, where they were repaired at the Hindustan Air Limited factory. Three Indian squadrons—No. 5, No. 6, and No. 16—would eventually be equipped with Liberator bombers. The RIAF would fly the bombers for nearly two decades, becoming the last air force in the world to fly the Liberator, which it only retired in 1967.[20] It also earned the distinction of becoming the first

[18] The Indian Air Force dropped the prefix 'Royal' on 26 January 1950 after India declared itself a republic.

[19] Saigal, *Birth of an Air Force*, p. 229.

[20] In a testament to the excellent engineering skills of the IAF, the Royal Air Museum would ask for and receive a Liberator aircraft for display at its museum. The Liberator, which was flown in 1974 from India to the United Kingdom, is still on display. K.S. Nair, 'Consolidated B-24 Liberator', *Warbirds of India*. Accessed 15 August 2020. http://warbirds.in/ovb24/227-consolidated-b24-liberator.html;

Figure 5.1 Prime Minister Jawaharlal Nehru shakes hands with Air Vice Marshal Harjinder Singh. Nehru was a keen proponent of air power and oversaw the eventual nationalization of airline companies. Singh has the distinction of rising from the lowest rank in the IAF, Hawai Sepoy (airman) to its second highest. © J.R. Nanda

Asian air force to field jet fighters when it inducted its first jet fighter, the De Havilland Vampire (see Figure 5.2).[21] Consequently, it outnumbered and, in significant ways outgunned, the Royal Pakistan Air Force to a far greater extent than it had during the Kashmir conflict. The force had also been able to learn from the lessons of the conflict.

When Nehru instructed the chiefs of staff to draw up plans for possible military action against Pakistan the new Commander-in-Chief of the IAF, Air Marshal Ronald Ivelaw Chapman, insisted that it would be impossible to keep military intervention by the IAF into East Pakistan localized.[22] Air Marshal Chapman, the penultimate British commander of the IAF, was restating the views of his predecessor, Air Marshal Thomas

[21] Seth, *The Flying Machines*, p. 39.
[22] Raghavan, *War and Peace in Modern India*, p. 169.

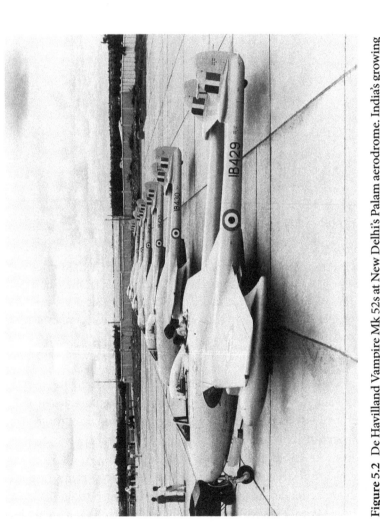

Figure 5.2 De Havilland Vampire Mk 52s at New Delhi's Palam aerodrome. India's growing inventory of aircraft likely played a role in bringing Pakistan to the table for negotiations during the 1950 Bengal crisis. © USI of India

Elmhirst, who previously sought to keep India out of a conflict with Pakistan, both since this was against the Cold War interests of the United Kingdom and also because it would potentially pit British personnel serving the two dominions against each other. Though Ivelaw Chapman was transparently disinclined to go to war with Pakistan for these reasons he was not misstating the possibilities of escalation inherent in what might at first be conceived as a localized military operation targeting parts of East Pakistan.[23] As I have argued elsewhere, air power had played an escalatory role in the Kashmir conflict despite the limited commitment of the RIAF there. Consequently, Chapman was not mistaken in arguing that IAF operations would be impossible to localize.

Two IAF squadrons were deployed as early as 3 March 1950 to the Bengal front, one of which was based at the Chakulia airfield dating back to the Second World War.[24] Plans were also put forward by Air Vice Marshal Subroto Mukherjee, the deputy Chief of Air Staff, for the establishment of advanced air headquarters in Punjab and operational centres at Bombay, Jammu, and Calcutta. This was in keeping with India's overall military plans which concentrated the bulk of army and air force units on the border with West Pakistan since that was where most Pakistani forces were based. Significantly Mukherjee acknowledged the possibility that senior British officers would be stood down in case of hostilities with Pakistan commenced.[25] This was also the second time that IAF squadrons had made plans for a potential conflict against Pakistan along the Western border. During Operation Polo in September 1948, most of India's operational squadrons had been placed on high alert to meet a possible Pakistani attack in support of Hyderabad. Plans for this had been drawn up in large part by Mukherjee.

Pakistani reactions to Indian military movements were initially restrained. The Defence Council of the Government of Pakistan did not at first take the threat of an Indian attack seriously since it was felt that India would not risk any action that would almost certainly lead to mass

---

[23] Chapman like Elmhirst expressed a willingness to resign rather than command the IAF in conflict against the Royal Pakistan Air Force. John Ivelaw Chapman, *High Endeavour: The Life of Air Chief Marshal Sir Ronald Ivelaw-Chapman, GCB, KBE, DFC, AFC.* (London: Leo Cooper, 1993), p. 150.

[24] TNA, DO 35/2989, UKHC India to CRO, 4 March 1950.

[25] TNA, DO 35/2989, UKHC India to CRO, 9 March 1950.

violence against the Hindu minority in East Pakistan.[26] This was not necessarily an irrational conclusion to draw and there is some evidence that much of the migration by Hindus out of East Pakistan had in fact been driven by the possibility of an Indian invasion that would result in Muslims massacring Hindus in large numbers.[27] Moreover, the Pakistani military did not expect an attack on the Western Frontier.[28] As it became clear by the third week of March that India had the means, if not the intention, to launch attacks in the West as well as the East, Pakistani General Headquarters scrambled its forces. The Royal Pakistan Air Force was ordered to prepare to move at 24 hours' notice.[29] India and Pakistan appeared to be on the brink of war to an extent not seen since the final month of the Kashmir conflict a year previously. As the *New York Times* noted late in March, 'It is the one place in the world today where war is a real possibility.'[30]

In the event, war did not begin and a pact between the two countries was signed in New Delhi in April 1950 in which Pakistan agreed to take measures to protect its minorities.[31] Despite the signing of the pact however it was unclear at the time whether war had been averted or merely postponed. Consequently, the Indian military mobilization was maintained and even increased. The Indian government in May 1950 approved the Defence Ministry's Plan *Shikar* (Hunt). Under Plan Shikar the IAF would be expanded to 15 squadrons as an emergency measure. This would enable it to deploy for a greater number of air operations if war with Pakistan did break out. For an air force that had planned to expand to no more than eleven squadrons, the plan caused serious attrition and threatened to dangerously undermine efficiency. Nonetheless by 1952 the IAF numbered fourteen and a half operational squadrons.[32]

The Pakistan government for its part moved to enlarge its own armed forces in the aftermath of the 1950 Bengal confrontation. Liaquat Ali Khan would leverage Pakistan's position as an ally of Britain and the United States in the Cold War to seek access to arms and equipment.[33]

---

[26] TNA, DO 35/2989, UKHC Pakistan to UKHC India, 16 March 1950.
[27] *Manchester Guardian*, 13 March 1950 Quoted in TNA, DO 35/2989.
[28] TNA, DO 35/2989, UKHC Pakistan to CRO, 11 March 1950.
[29] TNA, DO 35/2989, UKHC Pakistan to CRO, 23 March 1950.
[30] *New York Times*, 'Playing with fire', 29 March 1950 Quoted in TNA, DO 35/2989.
[31] Raghavan, *War and Peace in Modern India*, p. 184.
[32] MoD(I), 601/14513/H, Expansion of Air Force and Air Force matters.
[33] Raghavan, *War and Peace in Modern India*, p. 186.

Interestingly, the Pakistani government would also move to strengthen its civil aviation as a result of the crisis. Pakistan's Orient Airways relied on Dakota aircraft to connect East and West Pakistan but these had to land in Indian territory for refuelling. This gave rise to anxieties among Pakistani officials over the prospect that India might cut the two wings of Pakistan off from each other. Waqar Zaidi has argued that this led Karachi to acquire long-distance L-1049 Super Constellation airliners from the America and also to nationalize Orient Airways in order to better supervise the use of these aircraft. The United States for its part was increasingly willing to support Pakistani civil aviation since this enabled greater aerial co-operation with Pakistan in the context of the Cold War while also not upsetting relations with India.[34] In independent Pakistan as in India civil and military aviation were tied up in a number of complex ways.

Tensions between India and Pakistan would remain high despite the apparent resolution of the 1950 Bengal crisis. Another confrontation, this time over Kashmir, would once again result in refugee movements and military mobilization in mid-1951.[35] For much of the remainder of the decade the spectre of war would haunt South Asia.[36] The continuing hostility between the two states would provoke serious debate inside the Indian government on defence expenditure. In a letter to his chief ministers in late 1950, Jawaharlal Nehru had lamented that, 'It is in the long run, impossible for us to spend 50% of our Central budget on Defence'.[37] Nehru's concerns about defence spending sprang from several directions. Servicing enormous defence budget meant 'starving everything, health, education, development schemes and industrial growth'.[38] This would weaken India in fundamental ways by undermining the well-being of ordinary Indians and reduce industrial growth making the country reliant on western arms imports. India's international standing too would be damaged as the country came to be seen as a state in which all things revolved around the army.[39] The Indian government therefore sought

---

[34] S. Waqar Zaidi, 'Pakistani Civil Aviation and U.S. Aid to Pakistan 1950–1961', *History of Global Arms Transfer* 8, 2019, pp. 85–86.

[35] Raghavan, *War and Peace in Modern India*, p. 196.

[36] Haines, *Rivers Divided*, p. 53.

[37] Parthasarathi, *Letters to the Chief Ministers*, p. 45.

[38] NAI, File 2/369, Sardar Vallabhbhai Patel papers, Defence Expenditure, Jawaharlal Nehru to Cariappa, 28 December 1949.

[39] NAI, File 2/369, Sardar Vallabhbhai Patel papers, Defence Expenditure, Jawaharlal Nehru to Cariappa, 28 December 1949.

to reduce defence expenditure as far as possible. One means of doing so was to prioritize spending on the Indian Air Force rather than the Indian Army since the former was seen to be both a cheaper and more versatile military force. Nevertheless the steep demands of Plan Shikar would represent a substantial increase in defence spending.

The finance and defence ministries clashed in December 1953 about what was to be done about the squadrons, many of which were understrength, brought into existence by Plan Shikar. The finance ministry insisted on reducing the size of the air force in order to ensure that expenditure was kept below 35 crores. Tellingly, the defence ministry successfully argued that the results of Plan Shikar needed to be formalized even if it meant greater expenditure since Pakistan had received American military aid and had ordered 40 Gloster Meteors from the United Kingdom.[40] The decision to go ahead with a 15-squadron expansion of the IAF, taken on 23 December 1953, is illustrative of the extent to which the arms race with Pakistan was shaping Indian defence policy.

The expansion of the IAF to 15 squadrons in certain ways recalls similar plans from the Second World War. As seen before, when confronted with the need for air defences during the Second World War, the colonial government had considered expanding the IAF to 15 squadrons in 1941. Those plans had failed because of a shortage of personnel and experience stemming from India's status as a colony. A little over a decade later, despite the difficulties of Partition the IAF was on its way to reaching the 15-squadron goal. By then India could also boast a modest aircraft production infrastructure centred on the HAL factory in Bangalore and an armament wing at Kanpur. The first steps towards indigenous aircraft production were taken when HAL designed and produced the HT-2 trainer aircraft in 1953.[41] The next year, 1954 saw the total Indianization of the IAF as Air Marshal Subroto Mukherjee became the first Indian Commander-in-Chief of the IAF.

---

[40] MoD(I), 601/14513/H, Expansion of Air Force and Air Force matters, Statement of case for Defence Council Committee, 22 December 1953; For a detailed breakdown of squadron expansion see: Singh, *Himalayan Eagles*, p. 47.

[41] MoD(I), 601/14362/H, History of the IAF.

Figure 5.3 Air Marshal Subroto Mukherjee takes command of the IAF from Air Marshal Sir Gerald Gibbs on 1 April 1954. Mukherjee became the first Indian Commander-in-Chief of the Indian Air Force completing the two-decade long process of Indianization. © USI of India

This completed the process of Indianization that had been inaugurated with the founding of the IAF 20 years before (see Figure 5.3).[42]

The 1950 Bengal crisis served to demonstrate the political and military importance of the aeroplane in both India and Pakistan. This was part of a broader trend that I have traced back to the Partition riots and the conflict in Kashmir. The two newly independent states both understood the critical role civil and military aircraft had played in emergencies as demonstrated by their decision to expand their air forces and, eventually to nationalize their airline companies. Aviation's critical importance would also be confirmed by international negotiations over air routes between the two new dominions and the most advanced states in the world.

---

[42] Gerald Gibbs, *Survivors Story* (London: Hutchinson,1956), p. 171.

India and the World: The Establishment of External Air Routes

Post-war Air Route Negotiations

The establishment of AII in June 1948, less than one year after India attained its independence was a remarkable feat. The famed industrialist and aviator Jehangir Rattanjee Daddabhoy (henceforth J.R.D.) Tata who headed Air India Limited had made an application to the Ministry of Communications for the establishment of an international airline, that would fly Lockheed Constellation aircraft along a passenger route to London via Cairo and Geneva in September 1947. Government would hold 49 per cent of the companies' stock with an option to an additional 2 per cent while the Tatas would hold 25 per cent and the remaining 26 per cent would be publicly subscribed. Significantly, the proposal required the government to subsidise any losses incurred by the company over its first five years and these could be recouped from upto 50 per cent of future profits.[43] Despite the fact that New Delhi was at the time being convulsed by communal violence, the newly independent Indian government provided the company with permission to be set up within weeks. When decades later he was asked why permission for the founding of AII was rushed through, Jagjivan Ram, India's longest-serving cabinet minister, would quip 'We did not know any better then!'[44]

JRD Tata's offer to set up an external airline company was no doubt an attractive option for the Indian government. The Tatas could bring their considerable experience running Air India Limited by taking on the role of managing agents for AII. They could also establish the airline more rapidly than the Indian government could on its own since they had ordered three Constellation aircraft from Lockheed.[45] There is also no doubt that the Government of India saw having an airline as being an essential marker of India's independence and modernity and that it was keen to have a flag airline running as soon as possible. Certainly, other claimants to sovereign power were vying to set up airlines. As seen

[43] J.R.D. Tata 'The Story of Air Transport', *The Journal of the Royal Aeronautical Society*, 65, London: 1965, p. 11.
[44] Lala, *Beyond the Last Blue Mountain*, p. 113.
[45] *Flight*, 25 March 1948.

previously, the Nizam of Hyderabad had set up a state airline as early as 1945. Mohammed Ali Jinnah had met with Mirza Ispahani before Pakistan became independent in order to discuss the prospect of setting up the new state's flag carrier.[46] Additionally, as has been discussed, the Indian government was preoccupied by a number of crises in the first year of its birth and likely simply did not have the resources to spare to set up an international airline.

Yet the government's support for establishing an international airline was only possible in the context of a network of air routes transformed by the Second World War. While Indian independence certainly enabled and accelerated the founding of external services, the reconstitution of the pre-war international air route network was a necessary precondition that permitted the government of independent India to negotiate the setting up of its own international airline. JRD Tata had long hoped to establish an international airline that would fly west to London but it was only in the aftermath of the Second World War that AII could have been established.[47] While India's independence was no doubt crucial it was not the sole pre-requisite for the setting up of external air routes. Understanding how India went from being merely a link on the Imperial air route from London to Brisbane to the site of an international air service of its own requires us to turn to the period before the Second World War.

Confronted by competition with better subsidised French and German airline companies flying more advanced aircraft, Britain's Imperial Airways turned increasingly towards the Empire to maintain competitiveness during the interwar years. By effectively monopolizing what would come to be called the Imperial air route from Britain to Australia on the one hand, and South Africa on the other, Imperial Airways could continue to remain profitable. Ensuring that Imperial Airways maintained its monopoly meant restricting competition from the airlines of the dominions. His Majesty's Government (HMG) insisted that the dominions not form external services of their own since these might compete with Britain's international airline.[48] As has been discussed, Indian companies which were in their infancy at the time, actually benefitted

[46] Faizan Ali and Bidita L. Dey, *Is Pakistan International Airlines Up to the Mark?* (Bradford: VDM Verlag, 2011), p. 13.

[47] Tata, 'The Story of Air Transport', p. 11.

[48] Ewer, 'A Gentlemen's Club in the Clouds', pp. 75–92.

from the establishment of the Imperial air route since domestic carriers acting as feeders to Imperial Airways were able to avail subsidies in the form of the All-Up air mail scheme from 1938 onwards. By contrast the Government of India came increasingly to see its role in the Imperial air route as unprofitable. The company that it helped set up with the assistance of Imperial Airways and Indian National Airways was named Indian Transcontinental Airways but was considered to have been a failure. This was partially because of the failure of the company to hire Indian aircrews and partially because of what the government perceived as inequitable distribution of the All-Up Empire air mail scheme. New Delhi proposed a reorganization of the Imperial air route to permit Indian Transcontinental Airways to independently operate the Karachi to Calcutta leg of the route when war broke out in 1939.[49]

The Second World War, however, brought an end to the system of Imperial air routes. As Britain focused its wartime aircraft production largely on combat aircraft, it became increasingly clear that the United States with its vast fleets of transport aircraft and its growing civilian fleet would dominate post-war civil aviation. Alarmed by the prospect of being marginalized by aggressive American airline companies in the war's aftermath, British planners cast about a way to protect British dominance of civil aviation after the war. The idea of 'internationalization' gained immense prominence during the war in the highest echelons of the British government and was highly influential in defining Imperial aviation policy. As a propaganda pamphlet by Frederick Tymms explained, 'Under such a system international air services would be internationally owned and operated and no national or private service would operate outside its own country.'[50] At least one historian has argued that internationalization was in reality a highly ambiguous term with several, often contradictory, meanings. Nevertheless it came to enjoy widespread support across the political spectrum in the United Kingdom with prominent advocates including Winston Churchill, Anthony Eden, and Lord Beaverbrook and was the official policy of the British government until 1944.[51] When it

---

[49] BL, IOR L/E/8/6561, 'Post War Planning-External Air Services' (New Delhi, 1945), p. 3.

[50] CUL, GBR/00115/RCMS 20/1/2/1/6, *India and Aviation*, September 1944.

[51] S. Waqar Zaidi, '"Wings for Peace" versus Airopia: Contested Visions of Post-War European Aviation in World War II Britain', in M. Schiefelbusch & H. Dienel (ed.), *Linking Networks* (Farnham: Ashgate, 2014), pp. 151–168.

became clear that the United States, which advocated a laissez-faire 'Open Skies' civil aviation policy after the war, would not accept internationalization, HMG decided to drop many of the most idealistic components of its internationalization policy while continuing to campaign for an international organization that would be responsible for regulating air routes. Such an organization would help Britain maintain its Imperial air routes and limit American expansion into the Commonwealth and the colonies which Britain hoped would act as a single unit for purposes of aviation.[52] This stance was backed by the Indian delegation which was led by Sir Girija Shankar Bajpai at the Chicago conference on international civil aviation.[53]

While it enjoyed support from most of the Commonwealth and India, the United Kingdom was unsuccessful at the international negotiations that took place at the Chicago conference of November 1944.[54] The United States stubbornly defended its 'Open Skies' policy. Meanwhile, a joint Commonwealth front failed as the Canadian delegation played off the United States and the United Kingdom against each other so as to secure control over its own lucrative international air routes.[55] The Chicago Convention on International Civil Aviation, which resulted from the conference set up an International Civil Aviation Organisation to regulate aviation but left the question of fixing air routes to bilateral agreements between parties involved. In the new global order that the conference brought into existence, sovereignty over air space would be vested firmly in the national state, a fact that would be acknowledged by the United Kingdom itself when it signed the Bermuda Agreement with the United States in 1946. The agreement would see Washington use its financial muscle in bilateral negotiations to compel London to concede to a range of American demands, including fifth freedom rights. While it did not concede total freedom of the air to American aircraft, the Chicago Convention, was not a success for the United Kingdom.[56] The defeat of

---

[52] David R. Devreux, 'British Planning for Post-war Civil Aviation 1942–45', *Twentieth Century British History*, vol. 2, no. 1, 99, pp. 26–46.

[53] Johnston, *To Organise the Air*, p. 133.

[54] The USSR pulled out of the conference the day before it began and Axis states were not invited leaving the United States, Canada, and the United Kingdom to dominate the conference.

[55] R. Bothwell and J.L. Granatstein, 'Canada and Wartime Negotiations over Civil Aviation: The Functional Principle in Operation', *The International History Review*, 2, 4, pp. 585–681.

[56] Anthony Sampson, *Empires of the Sky: The Politics, Contests and Cartels of World Airlines* (London: Hodder and Stoughton, 1984), p. 72.

even its limited goal to form an international organization to regulate air routes at the Chicago conference caused HMG to fall back on another means of maintaining its competitiveness, namely a Commonwealth airline.

An airline operated jointly by the Commonwealth states, including India, would help offset American advantages especially through preferential route distribution and permit the United Kingdom to retain something of its status as a world leader in aviation. In recognition of changes in the political situation HMG offered to transfer operation of different parts of the proposed Commonwealth airline to the dominions and India. It also argued that the establishment of separate external services would merely serve to cause a competition between Commonwealth states and drive profits to non-Commonwealth airlines. At a Commonwealth conference held in Montreal in October 1944 however the dominions expressed their wish to establish their own international airlines independent of the United Kingdom.[57] David Devreux has pointed to the decision by Australia, New Zealand, and Canada to operate a Trans-Pacific Commonwealth airline jointly with the United Kingdom as proof that HMG wished to pursue a centralized aviation policy.[58] While there is some truth to this, the fact that the dominions asserted their independence by refusing to help establish a round-the-world Commonwealth airline demonstrates that Britain simply could not impose a centralized policy even if it wished. This not only meant the end of the proposed Commonwealth airline but also of the United Kingdom-India-Australia air route that Imperial Airways and then British Overseas Air Corporation aircraft had flown. As each section of the route came to be operated by the national airline involved, India was given permission to set up its own international airline to take up the United Kingdom segment of the old Imperial air route.[59]

[57] BL, IOR L/E/8/6561, 'Post War Planning-External Air Services' (New Delhi, 1945), p. 4.
[58] Devreux, 'British planning', pp. 26–46.
[59] BL, IOR L/E/8/6561, 'Post War Planning-External Air Services' (New Delhi, 1945), p. 4.

The Establishment of Air India International

In the aftermath of the Chicago conference, Frederick Tymms, the Director General of Civil Aviation (DGCA) of the Government of India drew up initial plans for the establishment of two international airlines to be based out of India. These would cater to four sets of routes:

a) Karachi to the United Kingdom
b) Karachi to the Middle East
c) Karachi to East Africa
d) Calcutta to China

The most important route proposed was India to United Kingdom route both for purposes of trade and also as a means of ensuring that both Britain and India could negotiate air routes without being crowded out by the services of other states operating between them. This was particularly critical since the defeat of internationalization at the Chicago conference had effectively vested the nation-state, as opposed to the international organization, with the power to negotiate air routes. From 1944 onwards, the principle that air routes would be determined by bilateral agreements between states became the norm, making the need for the United Kingdom and India to come to an agreement on air routes urgent.

Other routes were proposed to ensure that India had easy links with regions it had traditionally been connected with. A route to the Middle East from Karachi to Iraq, Iran, Palestine, Turkey, Syria, and Egypt had great traffic potential and would be logical for India to seek. The war had led to the creation of a short route to East Africa from Karachi via the Western Arab Desert possible. Wartime operations had also opened an air route from India to China. As the external services plan noted 'Shanghai is nearer to Calcutta than Cairo is to Karachi.'[60] It would be to India's advantage to demand reciprocal rights for her airlines to fly to China since the Chinese nationalist government's China National Aviation Corporation plied the China-India air route during the war.

The Directorate of Civil Aviation (DCA) proposed the formation of two corporations, one of which would carry traffic from India to its east, and

[60] Ibid., p. 1.

another which would carry traffic westward. The DCA proposed that the two companies provisionally named 'Indian Western Airways Limited' (IWAL) and 'Indian Eastern Airways Limited' (IEAL) be established as share companies in which the government would hold significant stocks amounting to about 20 per cent. A private airline or shipping firm would take up another 15 to 20 per cent of the stocks and be charged with running the airline. While this would be necessary to prevent competition between domestic commercial enterprises, other shipping firms and airlines would be permitted to hold up to 20 per cent of the shares of the international airline. The remainder would be subscribed by the public and strict limits would be placed on transferring ownership of shares. IWAL would have a capital of three crores since it would require long-range aircraft for the air route to the United Kingdom while IEAL's more modest needs would be met with two crores in capital.[61] The companies would begin external services as soon as possible in order to secure air routes though it was understood that it would take three years to raise the personnel and equipment to fly the United Kingdom-India route.

The plan noted that the establishment of international air routes would serve three purposes. First, it would ensure that India secured necessary air routes for itself before bilateral negotiations between other states weakened its negotiating position. Second, it would secure India's 'national aspirations to appear in the international air transport field'.[62] Third, it would increase India's necessary defence reserves. While the plan was never implemented, in large part due to the political instability leading up to Indian independence, it anticipates the formation of AII in significant ways. The plan was remarkably ambitious and points to the changes wrought by the war in India's relations with the United Kingdom. Unlike Australia and Canada, India was forced, as a consequence of its colonial status, to defer to the United Kingdom on the issue of air routes. Despite this the eventual collapse of British attempts to persuade the Commonwealth states to set up a Commonwealth airline caused the Indian government to consider seriously the establishment of its own independent international airlines. To be sure India would still have effectively been acting in the interests of the metropole by establishing

---

[61] Ibid., p. 4.
[62] Ibid., p. 11.

international airlines since these would help Britain secure reciprocal air routes to India. Nonetheless the fact that this would be an advantage to the United Kingdom, which less than a decade before considered the establishment of independent international air routes an act of defiance, is remarkable. It is indicative of how fundamentally the political terrain in which Britain and the Commonwealth operated had shifted.

When in September 1947 JRD Tata presented his plans to the independent Indian government to set up AII, it was to a government which no doubt inherited plans from the colonial DCA for the establishment of external air routes. Furthermore, as JRD Tata would note, his proposals were made in a transformed global context where air routes were 'regulated wholly by bi-lateral treaties between countries.'[63] The speed with which the government would move to approve Tata's plans is therefore explained not only by reasons of ease and the need for political representation noted earlier, but also by the existence of earlier plans to extend Indian airline services abroad. These in turn were a consequence of major political shifts in world politics, where Britain was being rapidly supplanted by the United States in the aftermath of the Second World War and by not entirely unrelated shifts in Commonwealth politics which saw leading dominions assert their independent aviation policies.

The Tatas had been closely following the air route negotiations and making their own plans for the post-war period. JRD Tata had been outraged to be excluded from the Indian delegation to the Chicago conference in 1944 due to pressure from other members of the Commonwealth who insisted that the Indian delegation be made up of government officials alone. In an exasperated letter written in October 1944 to the legislator F.E. James, Tata had commented that the exclusion of 'the very people who were going to run the air transport of the future' from the delegation was pointless unless 'it is the intention of these (Commonwealth) Governments to nationalise all air lines'. Later in the same letter he had noted that India's 'obvious lines of development' were 'to Burma, the Malay States and China on the one hand, and Persia, the Middle East and East Africa on the other.'[64] Tata would later state that he had laid some early plans for a possible air route to the United Kingdom during the

[63] Tata, 'The story of Air Transport', p. 11.
[64] TCA, T-53-DES-AVI-T9-4, JRD to F.E. James 24 October 1944.

war.[65] However he was also aware of the possibility that a Commonwealth airline might run the UK-India-Australia route and therefore appears to have expected to focus mainly on India's regional neighbourhood after the war.[66] The Tata air route to the United Kingdom was only made possible by a series of historically contingent developments. These included the final collapse of the attempt to set up a Commonwealth airline and subsequent plans for India to found its own international airline, authored by a close ally of Tata's, DGCA Frederick Tymms.[67]

The establishment of AII conformed closely with the plan to establish Indian Western Airways Limited. Independent India consented to invest heavily in AII and also to subsidise it for a period of five years. Further in keeping with the prescriptions offered in the external services proposal, AII would be managed by an Indian airline company; Air India Limited. Similarities can also be noted in the capital subscribed. Where the actual establishment of AII diverged most from earlier plans, however, was in the scale of government involvement. The independent Government of India eventually invested significantly more in establishing AII than the colonial government might have. Indeed, government share in the company was only kept below 50 per cent at the request of Air India Limited.[68] The heavy involvement of the government was indicative of two new trends ushered in by independence. Indian independence gave the Government of India the freedom to invest far greater resources in aviation which the colonial government would have not been able to afford. Perhaps more significantly it also pointed to the inclination of the new government to have greater state control of aviation.

The maiden flight of an AII plane to the United Kingdom was suffused with symbolism. On 8 June 1948 exactly a month after the formation of AII, the Lockheed Constellation *Malabar Princess* made the first international passenger flight by an Indian airline from Juhu airport, Bombay to Heathrow airport, London.[69] Tata himself would travel on the *Malabar*

[65] Lala, *Beyond the last Blue Mountain*, p. 115.

[66] TCA, T-53-DES-AVI-T9-4, F.E. James to JRD, 11 October 1944.

[67] As seen in Chapter II, Tymms had been loaned by the DCA to the Tatas after the death of Neville Vintcent during the war.

[68] Tata, 'The story of Air Transport', p. 14.

[69] The *Malabar Princess* was destined to have a tragic end. It would crash on Mont Blanc France on 3 November 1950 killing 8 crew and 40 passengers on board. Sixteen years later Air India Flight 101 would crash at the same spot on 24 January 1966. Among the 117 deaths caused by the accidents would be Homi Bhabha, the father of the Indian atomic programme.

Princess and would be received by the India's first High Commissioner to the United Kingdom, Krishna Menon, on his arrival. He was accompanied on the historical flight by the Jam Saheb of Nawanagar, famed for his interest in aviation, the wealthy industrialist Neville Wadia and the well-known film director K.K. Murthy.[70] Two other Constellation aircraft, the *Rajput Princess* and the *Mogul Princess*, would start flying the United Kingdom-India route via Geneva and Cairo that year. Over the next four years, with the minor exception of 1952, AII earned profits and was successful in doubling its level of operations.[71] The airline later expanded to include a DC 4 flight from Bombay, India to Nairobi, East Africa by way of Aden. It would have two Constellations costing one crore rupees on order from Lockheed by the time of nationalization in 1953.[72] The United Kingdom-India air route expanded to include Pakistan, Italy, and Germany. This was no mean feat for an airline that was now competing with some of the largest airlines in the world along with one of the world's most competitive routes.

AII was only the most remarkable of the Indian external services established after 1948. Himalayan Aviation flew regularly to Pakistan, Afghanistan, and Iran from Calcutta with its fleet of three Douglas DC-3s. Indian National Airways, also based in Calcutta, in keeping with its Eastern focus flew to Burma and Nepal in addition to Pakistan.[73] Bharat Airways meanwhile earned the distinction of opening long-range air routes to the East with weekly Douglas C-54 Skymaster flights from Calcutta to Bangkok in May 1949, to Singapore in 1950 and eventually to Jakarta in 1952.[74]

[70] Lala, *Beyond the Last Blue Mountain*, p. 114.
[71] Tata, 'The Story of Air Transport', p. 11.
[72] T53-DES-AV-A3-BO-1, AII Agenda and Minutes part I, 24 February 1949.
[73] *Flight*, 6 March 1953, p. 310.
[74] TNA, CO/937/193/1, Secretary of State for Colonies to Governor Singapore, 3 October 1950.

Asymmetric Air Agreements: Bilateral Air Route Negotiations with Britain, the United States, and Pakistan

The Chicago Convention fundamentally reconstituted the map of international air routes at almost the same time as India became independent. At least one historian has compared the first years after the Chicago convention to the 'scramble for Africa', as countries vied with each other for the most lucrative air routes.[75] The failure to establish an organization at the Chicago convention that allotted air routes and regulated quotas left negotiations on the five freedoms in the hands of individual states. The five freedoms, which continue into the present day, in order of numbering include: First the right of innocent passage over sovereign territory. Second the right to land for non-traffic purposes such as emergencies. Third the right to land passengers, mail, and freight in the airline's country of origin. Fourth the right to pick up passengers, mail, and freight to the airline's country of origin. A fifth freedom was the right to pick up passengers, mail, and freight between two countries. Under the bilateral negotiation system sovereign states could concede as many or as few of the five freedoms as they wished to foreign airlines. The first two freedoms were generally conceded by most states while the fifth freedom was rarely permitted, despite being widely advocated by the Americans, since it could potentially grant larger airlines an unfair advantage. A key reason for India's early entry into international aviation was the desire to leverage India's strategic position on the most direct route connecting Europe to East Asia in order to gain India the largest number of advantageous reciprocal air route agreements. Failure to enter into such agreements rapidly might have severely disadvantaged India in the long-term lending them a degree of urgency. Consequently, India engaged in negotiations with a wide number of states including the United Kingdom, the United States, Pakistan, France, and the Netherlands with important consequences for the territorialization of the new state's air space.

The first country to approach India for a bilateral air route agreement was the United States. As the premier civil aviation power after the war

---

[75] R.L. McCormack, 'Imperialism, Air Transport and Colonial Development: Kenya, 1920–46.' *The Journal of Commonwealth History,* 17, no. 3 (July 2008), pp. 374–395.

with an interest in establishing a round-the-world route, the United States, despatched a delegation to India to India on 4 October 1946 to negotiate an agreement as early as possible. Indeed, Pan-American airlines had already begun advertising flights to the USA in Calcutta in winter 1945, much to the annoyance of the DGCA.[76] India had to exercise care to avoid being overwhelmed by American airlines.[77] The format of bilateral negotiations that had emerged from the Anglo-American Bermuda agreement was unsuited for two states whose aviation assets were as asymmetrical as India and the United States. Whereas several American airlines including Pan-American, Transcontinental, and Western Airlines wished to acquire 'five freedoms' over India, India did not at the time even have a single airline that could fly to the United States. India, which at this time was formally under the Congress-Muslim League led Provisional government, would have to negotiate an agreement that would prevent American airlines from overrunning its air routes while reserving for itself the eventual right to designate an Indian airline to fly to the United States at some future date. While the Americans expected negotiations to last for one week they dragged on for six. The Indian delegation, led by DGCA Frederick Tymms, and the American delegation led by President Truman's personal representative, Brigadier-General George Brownell, worked hard to evolve a new framework that would protect Indian interests while remaining acceptable to the Americans. Though Indian officials were unable to convince the Americans that all of South Asia would function as part of India's domestic civil aviation sphere by reserving 'contiguous geographical area' traffic, it successfully limited the number of American airlines flying to India and ensured that in the future an Indian airline would be granted reciprocal rights in the United States. The earliest international air route agreement was thus signed on 14 November 1946 in New Delhi with George Merell, the U.S. Charge de Affairs and Brigadier General Brownell representing the United States of America, while Jawaharlal Nehru, India's external affairs member and Abdur Rab Nishtar, the member for communications represented

---

[76] Johnston, *To Organise the Air*, p. 122.
[77] Ibid., p 125. Much of the rest of this paragraph draws on Johnston's account of the negotiation which in turn draws on notes provided to him directly by DGCA Frederick Tymms while he was writing the latter's biography.

India.[78] While the precise details are difficult to establish, Tymms would inform his biographer that Nehru had closely followed the negotiations.[79] This is indeed likely to have been the case given the Nehru's deep interest in aviation. He had famously became, perhaps the first Indian politician to use aircraft for election campaigning and, as discussed previously, was a keen proponent of air power.[80]

The negotiation with the United States had been important for a number of reasons. The Indian government successfully staved off the threat of competition with American airlines and in doing so laid the foundation for Indian international aviation. This would set a precedent whereby it would strictly regulate the number and routes of foreign airlines flying to and over India while seeking reciprocal rights for its foreign airlines in the future. The Indian government would commonly permit one foreign airline to fly through India on a maximum of three routes with permission to carry fifth freedom traffic. This was the pattern for agreements signed with France and Netherlands in June and July of 1947 respectively.[81] KLM in the Dutch case and Air France in the French case would thus be designated to fly through India by their governments, effectively granting them a national monopoly. Even these relatively restrictive agreements were seen by many Indians inside and outside India's government, as being too liberal. J.R.D. Tata for instance argued that providing fifth freedom rights to foreign carriers would endanger the AII's traffic. Consequently, the Indian government would take the decision to denounce the agreement with the Netherlands and the United States, signing a new Air Services agreement with the latter in 1956.[82] India would also take a stronger stance against the United Kingdom in negotiations in 1951.[83]

---

[78] BL, IOR/V/27/770/5, Agreement between the Government of India and the Government of the United States of America relating to Air Services, (New Delhi, 1946).

[79] Johnston, *To Organise the Air,*, p. 124.

[80] For an evocative essay on India as seen from the air by Nehru see: Gopal and Iyengar eds, *Essential Writings of Jawaharlal Nehru*, p. 635.

[81] BL, IOR/V/27/770/6, Agreements relating to Air Services between the Government of India and the Government of the Netherlands, Government of France.

[82] Air Transport Agreement between the Government of India and the Government of the United States of America, 3 February 1956. Accessed 15 August 2020. https://mea.gov.in/bilateral-documents.htm?dtl/5186/Agreement+regarding+Air+Transport;

[83] TNA, CO 937/193/2, Note of a meeting held to discuss a briefing on for the Bilateral negotiations to be held in Delhi, 22 December 1950.

By far the most important state with which India had to undertake air route negotiations with was the United Kingdom. The UK not only sat at the end of India's most important air route but the British Empire continued to border India in the period under discussion. In 1947 the British Empire still included Singapore and Malaya on India's Eastern flank and large parts of the Middle East and East Africa to its West. Though the United Kingdom and India needed access to each other's territories negotiations between the two had broken down in 1949. Ironically the United Kingdom found itself advocating a Bermuda type agreement with India that would secure its significant fifth freedom rights despite its own reluctance to accede to such an agreement with America, while India called for a policy of pre-determination that would heavily regulate British air traffic not unlike Britain's vis-à-vis the United States. Having signed agreements granting fifth freedom rights to American and Dutch companies, albeit permitting only a single airline from each country to traverse its air space, the Indian government changed its stance in 1948 taking what the British termed 'an intensely nationalistic attitude' that considered these agreements to have been too liberal. When a British delegation led by L.J. Dunnett had attempted to negotiate a Bermuda type agreement with India in 1949, it was confronted with Indian demands that would effectively place quotas on fifth freedom traffic to India. A stalemate in negotiations had led L.J. Dunnett into an exchange of notes with the Indian High Commissioner to the United Kingdom, Krishna Menon, whereby the two countries agreed to continue pre-existing arrangements for a year. For the HMG's new Ministry of Civil Aviation, the Indian position appeared exceptionally stubborn. British officials felt that it was unreasonable for India to deny traffic to British airlines when most passengers flying on AII's London-Calcutta route were British, since few Indians could afford to make international flights due to the country's shortages of foreign exchange.[84]

A British delegation led by George Cribbett, of the Ministry of Civil Aviation, finally visited India in January 1951 to negotiate an agreement. They hoped to wean India away from pre-determined quotas and convince it to grant the United Kingdom a Bermuda type agreement that would permit BOAC access through India. During negotiations that took

[84] Ibid.

place in New Delhi over the course of fourteen days, the two countries were able to come to an agreement. While New Delhi did not concede full fifth freedom rights to the British explicitly, London made a number of important gains. BOAC could fly one service a week to Bombay, India's most important air hub. It could also retain previous services along with eight route transits across Indian territory. Fifth freedom limitations would apply but British airlines could carry 20 per cent of their total capacity provided this was under 40 per cent of the total. This would mean that BOAC could carry very large amounts of fifth freedom traffic. In return India insisted on a system of annual reviews whereby representatives of the two states would meet to discuss any perceived unfair actions by the airlines of the other. BOAC would not be permitted to increase its passenger capacity by more than 10 per cent without permission at the review. Further airlines in which Britain had an interest besides BOAC such as Quantas and Cathay Pacific would be severely restricted in India.[85] The agreement was beneficial to both states since it protected the Indian passenger market and also granted the United Kingdom a means to connect the Empire. The tough nature of the negotiations is revealing of the extent to which independent India had moved to establish a distinct aviation policy in the aftermath of independence. It also showed the extent to which bilateral negotiations privileged the interests of stronger aviation states. The best a poorer state like India could hope to do was to protect its airlines from being overwhelmed while placing restrictions on the airlines of richer states. The negotiations also demonstrated that independent India did in fact take 'an intensely nationalistic' position and regarded earlier restrictive agreements as being inadequate to protect India's sovereignty over its air space, and consequently sought even greater regulation.[86]

The Indian government found the asymmetry that it suffered from in terms of international aviation with Western states reversed when it came to negotiations with Pakistan. Pakistan's state airline, Oriental Airways remained small. The Vultee Convair long-range aircraft that it had ordered in 1947 to help connect East and West Pakistan had been severely delayed.[87] New Delhi hoped to secure significant concessions from Karachi

---

[85] Ibid.
[86] Ibid.
[87] BL, IOR L/E/8/6561, Extract from review of period from November 1948.

in light of its larger civil aviation sector and its need to connect India with the United Kingdom by air. Indeed Indian negotiators would briefly attempt to make the argument that Indian flights to Pakistan were not in fact international by arguing that Indian airlines ought to have the right to transport goods and passengers through Pakistan.[88] As seen above, the Indian DGCA had attempted unsuccessfully to protect Indian dominance of South Asia by seeking safeguards that would have considered the carriage of passengers and freight aboard Indian international flights to Pakistan as cabotage (transfer within domestic boundaries), during air route negotiations with the United States. Pakistan, like India, would stubbornly protect its sovereignty in the face of foreign aviation and come to a deal with India in 1948 that was not dissimilar from that later arrived at between the UK and India.

Civil aviation between India and Pakistan had continued without an agreement between the two through 1947 despite the fact that the two states were embroiled in a conflict in Kashmir.[89] Only in January 1948 did the two states sign a provisional air transport agreement that formalized existing arrangements pending the signing of a more permanent bilateral agreement later in the year.[90] When delegations representing the two countries met in Karachi in April 1948 negotiations were initially cordial. The Pakistan government was unwilling to concede Indian requests for reciprocal cabotage that would have seen Indian and Pakistani airlines flying through each other's territory effectively treated as domestic flights. Pakistan representatives however appeared to be willing to grant India the 15 air routes it requested through East and West Pakistan including three to the Middle East and one to the United Kingdom.[91] The two states were also able to agree on mechanisms to regulate airlines. Negotiations however proved inconclusive due to disagreements on Indian air routes to Afghanistan.

The Indian government had requested the right to operate airlines between Delhi and Kabul via Peshawar but was denied the route by Pakistan. India was engaged in a conflict at the time with tribesmen

[88] BL, IOR L/E/8/6561, Extract from Opdom No 26, UKHC India, 26 March to 2 April 1948.
[89] See Chapter III.
[90] BL, IOR L/E/8/6561, Civil Aviation in India, Extract from 'Commerce' 10 January 1948.
[91] BL, IOR L/E/8/6561, Extract from Opdom 28, United Kingdom High Commission in Pakistan, 1-7 April 1948.

backed by Pakistan in Kashmir at the time and the Pakistan delegation argued that Indian aircraft overflying tribal areas were vulnerable. As a Pakistani note would later state, 'The tribesmen are all armed and there is reason to believe that they take delight in (sic) having snap shots at the passing aircraft.'[92] Moreover, Pakistani government officials could claim to be upholding the old 'prohibited areas' legislation dating back two decades. It is likely however that Pakistan was more concerned with preventing closer links between India and Afghanistan, both of whom it had troubled relations with as it permitted Iranian aircraft to fly over the prohibited area.[93] Indian aircraft were forced to fly to Zahidan in Iran and thence to Kabul, an extra distance of a thousand kilometres, since they were prevented from using Karachi airport. The matter would eventually be resolved by the Provisional International Civil Aviation Organisation but it served to delay the signing of an air service agreement between India and Pakistan until India decided to temporarily drop the demand for an air route to Afghanistan.[94]

Sri Prakasa, the Indian High Commissioner to Pakistan and Sardar Abdur Rab Nishtar, Pakistan's Minister for Communications, signed a bilateral agreement on civil aviation on 23 June 1948. The agreement gave Pakistan the right to fly the route from Karachi-Bombay-Colombo and Karachi-Calcutta-Rangoon. India received the right to fly three routes to the Middle East via Karachi in the West and the Calcutta to China route via Chittagong in the East. India would operate ten routes in total while Pakistan could operate nine. Much like India in its later negotiations with the United Kingdom, Pakistan won the principle of 'equal rights' for airlines of both countries to operate reciprocal routes and also for both countries to consult on practices considered to be unfair that the other country's airline was engaged in. Much like the United Kingdom, however, India could afford to concede principles of regulation given that the size of its air fleet dwarfed Pakistan's, ensuring that Indian airlines could dominate routes both sides had equal rights to fly. As G.D. Anderson the

---

[92] *Flight*, 4 July 1952.
[93] *Flight*, 4 July 1952.
[94] For absence of a route to Kabul see: BL, IOR L/E/8/6561, Agreement between the Government of India and the Government of Pakistan relating to air services, Annex, 23 June 1948.

United Kingdom High Commissioner to India noted, 'India's present superiority in aircraft, facilities and organisation will mean that, for many years yet, she will not be giving much away.'[95]

Indian air route negotiations are revealing the nature of both the new Indian state and the post-war international order of which it now found itself a constituent. Air route negotiations showed India both the possibilities and limits of a world order that recognized sovereignty at the national level. In a global order that recognized all nation-states to be nominally equal, India could claim formal equality with both the United States and the United Kingdom. Aviation had failed to integrate states, as internationalists had hoped, but it had in a sense made neighbours out of previously distant countries. A world in which nation-states held absolute sovereignty over air space was one in which multiple agreements were necessary to set up air routes. However, it was also a world in which formal equality often gave way to the realities of unequal power. While the principle of reciprocity and therefore equality in air route allocation could be won by a newly independent state like India, it was difficult to reconcile this with material inferiority. In negotiations with the United Kingdom and the United States the best India could hope for was to protect its infant international airlines. The situation was reversed conspicuously in negotiations with Pakistan where India enjoyed substantial material superiority. If the new international system provided states with formal equality abroad then it also recognized and even encouraged state centralization at home. Sovereign states after all base their international legitimacy on the claim that they are the sole rightful representatives of entire 'domestic communities'.[96] The Indian airline scene would soon be transformed by the centralizing impulses of the Government of India which took the form of the nationalization of airline companies in 1953.

---

[95] BL, IOR L/E/8/6561, UKHC to B.D. Tims, Commonwealth Relations Office (CRO), 28 July 1948.

[96] I refer here to Cynthia Weber's concept of the 'alibi of the domestic community' whereby the state is said to represent a domestic community but on closer inspection it become unclear who exactly is part of this domestic community. Cynthia Weber, *Simulating Sovereignty Intervention, the State and Symbolic Exchange* (Cambridge: CUP, 1995), p. 27.

Nationalization of Civil Aviation

The Road to Nationalization 1944–1952

The nationalization of aviation in 1953 can justifiably be considered to mark the beginning of a new era in the history of aviation in India. The absorption of Indian aviation companies by the government of independent India marked the near total monopolization of Indian aviation by the state. With the exception of a few privately owned independent operators, private aircraft and some of the training aircraft at flying clubs aviation in India, all Indian aircraft would belong to the government for the next four decades until the liberalization of the aviation sector in 1991.[97] The reasons for the government takeover of aviation have been widely discussed and written about almost from the moment that it became clear that the state meant to implement nationalization.[98] This is partly due to the controversy generated by the decision, partly due to subsequent issues with the state corporations which ran Indian aviation, and partially because of the government's own opaque reasoning for the decision. While the discussion that follows will highlight some of the reasons why nationalization happened, it will seek to root nationalization in its wider historical context and to outline the ways in which nationalization was implemented. In doing so I will argue that nationalization was a multi-faceted event with diverse outcomes for different firms depending on their conditions at the time of nationalization.

Though nationalization finally occurred in 1953 it had long been under discussion by both the colonial and the independent governments of India. In a letter to J.R.D. Tata, as early as October 1944, the legislator F.E. James had mentioned that there 'was strong opinion in the highest quarters' of the government 'in favour of the state operating civil aviation, both internal and external'.[99] The Harewood Overseas Air Terminal Committee's 1945 report had needed to caution the colonial government against the extension of government control over civil aviation.[100] The Second World War had seen modest yet unprecedented state intervention

---

[97] *Indian Skyways*, 'Independents are essential to National Air Power', December 1955.
[98] See for instance: *Indian Skyways*, 'Our Nationalised Corporations', August 1955.
[99] TCA, T-53-DES-AVI-T9-4, F.E. James to JRD Tata, 11 October 1944.
[100] *Centenary of Civil Aviation in India*, p. 19.

in civil aviation and this had had the effect of prompting government officials to consider nationalization. DGCA Frederick Tymms who had been
given special responsibility for post-war planning however decided, after
two years of closely studying the Indian civil aviation sector, that nationalization was undesirable since the country was 'too large to be serviced
by a single operator, whether it be the State or private enterprise'.[101]
Tymms eponymous plan for post-war civil aviation therefore called for
the formation of an Air Transport Licensing Board which would limit the
number of operators to ensure private airline profitability with a degree
of government regulation. The Tymms plan was a victim of the dysfunction that characterized the politics of partition. In the lead up to Indian
independence, Abdur Rab Nishtar, the Muslim League member for communications of the interim government embarked on a liberal policy of
airline license distribution bringing a large number of companies into existence. After partition India found itself with 23 companies operating
only 22 routes between them.[102] This severely damaged the profitability
of the Indian airline sector and would eventually help justify nationalization. For the moment however despite the ongoing reversal of the Tymms
plan the interim government decided to forgo nationalization.

   This was not easy given the prevailing political sentiment of the time
which favoured the nationalization of all industries. Nationalization
was seen as a natural outcome of Indian independence and had been enshrined as an important objective of nationalist politics. The Congress
party, for instance, had pledged in its election manifesto of 1946 to bring
all industry under state control and it was not uncommon for Indian
politicians at the time to call for the nationalization of everything from
transportation to gold to land.[103] Much of the ardour for nationalization
sprang from the very vagueness of the term. Confronted by enthusiastic
calls for the nationalization of aviation on 16 November 1946, the communications member Abdur Rab Nishtar revealingly expressed his support for the principle of nationalization but pointed out that his fellow
legislators were simply not clear about what they meant by it. Did nationalization mean strict state control or did it mean state control along with

---

[101] *Times of India*, 8 May 1947.
[102] BL, IOR/L/E/8/6561, Progress of Civil Aviation in India, 7 June 1948.
[103] Congress Election Manifesto, *Our Industrial Policy* (New Delhi: Congress Parliamentary
Board, 1951), p. 3; 'Stable Conditions for Nationalisation', *Times of India*, 9 November 1946.

state investment? Did it mean a completely state-owned service or did it mean private domestic airlines and state-owned external services?[104] A couple of days before Vallabhbhai Patel, the Home Member had had to stanch demands that airlines be nationalized by pointing out that the interim government had not had the time to consider the nationalization of aviation.[105] Future events driven partly by the failure of the Tymms plan would however strengthen calls for nationalization.

The losses caused to the aircraft sector by the abandonment of the Tymms plan were exacerbated by the Partition of the subcontinent which resulted in the loss of the critical Karachi route. The refugee evacuation operations and the Kashmir operations offered Indian airline companies some respite but this was short-lived as losses began to mount in 1948. J.R.D. Tata, who had always been one of the Tymms plan's most ardent advocates, argued that one way in which the Government of India might have chosen to end the civil aviation sector's crisis might have been to permit 'the process of contraction' to take its course until only those companies survived that could make a profit.[106] Tata's sanguine view of the affair no doubt sprang from the fact that he ran one of the most well-established airlines which in turn was part of one of India's largest business empires. He was also annoyed that his rivals the Birlas, had made inroads into aviation, a field he considered to be something of a personal fiefdom, with the establishment of Bharat Airways.[107]

The imperatives that led the Government to, in 1949, grant ten-year licenses to the new airline operators who had thus far been running on provisional licenses are unclear. Tata claimed that government was unwilling to face the political costs of the airline company failure while at least one scholar has suggested that the move was prompted by Nehru-led government's socialistic views.[108] It is possible to argue that the decision might well have been driven by extra-business concerns. The large

---

[104] 'Nationalisation Salutary in Principle', *Times of India*, 18 November 1946.
[105] 'Stable Conditions for Nationalisation', *Times of India*, 9 November 1946; Lala, *Beyond the Last Blue Mountain*, p. 133.
[106] Tata, 'The Story of Air Transport', p. 9.
[107] Mirceau Raianau, *Tata: The Global Business that built Indian Capitalism* (Cambridge, Harvard University Press: 2021). I would like to thank Dr Raianau here for sharing a section of his book on the Tatas before it was published.
[108] Tata, 'The Story of Air Transport', p. 9; Nayar, *The State and International Aviation in India*, p. 56.

pool of aeroplanes that the airline companies represented had served the Government of India during the partition crisis, the Kashmir conflict and the Bengal crisis. Independent India's government might well have been reluctant to liquidate these companies through the withholding of ten-year licenses. Whatever the case, the effect of the grant of ten-year licenses effectively implicated the independent Indian government in the previous decision made by Abdur Rab Nishtar abandoning the Tymms plan.

The government cast about for means to address the deteriorating condition of the civil aviation sector. By mid-1948 Ambica Airlines and Jupiter airlines were bankrupt.[109] Small rises in fares were permitted, customs duties on aviation fuel were reduced, and aircraft were permitted to carry greater loads. When these proved to have a limited impact, the Ministry of Communications decided in October 1948 that the best way to aid aviation was to charter airlines for the carriage of mail. At a meeting on 12 January 1949 however airline operators who had sent in bids for the charter scheme were told that plans for the scheme had been dropped by the government. Instead, the government envisioned a night air mail scheme and invited bids from companies to operate on the Bombay to New Delhi route.[110] Three days later airline companies were informed that the Ministry of Communications planned to expand the Night air mail scheme to include the two new routes of Bombay-Nagpur-Calcutta and Delhi-Nagpur-Madras. Shockingly, this news was accompanied by the announcement that the two new routes had already been awarded by the ministry to Indian Overseas Airlines (IOA) Limited. Despite protests from other operators about the 'irregularity in the procedure adopted for granting a license to IOA' without seeking tenders, the night air mail scheme commenced on 31 January.[111]

The decision to grant IOA routes on the night air mail most likely sprang from the fact that the company was willing to operate on terms no other company would since it was in the process of going bankrupt.[112] By granting IOA the night air mail route licenses, the government simultaneously kept costs within what it considered reasonable limits and also simultaneously ensured that it had greater control of the scheme. This

[109] Lala, *Beyond the Last Blue Mountain*, p. 135.
[110] TCA, T53-DES-AVI-T9-5-PG-76, Night Air Mail.
[111] TCA, T53-DES-AVI-T9-5-PG-76, Night Air Mail.
[112] Tata, 'The Story of Air Transport', p. 10.

reflected independent Indian government's contradictory imperatives to simultaneously seek to aid the airline sector, which was facing heavy losses, and to curb what it saw as capitalistic excess. A strong element of anti-capitalism characterized the discourse of the Congress party before and after independence.[113] The government was keen to prevent taxpayer rupees from subsidising private enterprise while at the same time recognizing the need to keep civil aviation functional in the national interest. This would become a key source of contention between communications minister Rafi Ahmed Kidwai and J.R.D. Tata.

Another scheme conceived of by Rafi Ahmed Kidwai was the carriage of all mail by air using the night air mail scheme. Under the All-Up Night Air Mail Scheme, which was built on routes first used by the night mail scheme, Indian airline companies would fly aircraft from the four metropolises of Calcutta, Madras, Delhi, and Bombay to converge at Nagpur where the planes would exchange mail before either flying on to another city or flying back from their point of entry. According to Kidwai the scheme would serve two purposes. By aligning all posts from the metropolises it would ensure that letters posted in the evening reached their destination by the next morning. It would also attract more traffic to the airlines which were suffering from an excess of capacity.[114] The scheme was in certain ways not unlike the All-Up Empire Air Mail scheme which had also been an attempt by the state, in that instance the British government, to prop up failing air services. Like the All-Up Empire Air Mail Scheme the All-Up Night Mail Scheme was doomed to failure.

IOA which had been flying the Night Air Mail, commenced the All-Up Night Air Mail on 1 April 1949. By 14 May IOA, which had been facing bankruptcy, dropped out of the scheme as the company went into liquidation.[115] Indian National Airways and Deccan Airways, in which the Indian government had taken over the Hyderabad government's majority shares, stepped in to take over IOA's routes on a temporary basis pending

---

[113] The party also had a number of members friendly to capital the foremost of whom was Deputy Prime Minister Vallabhbhai Patel. Nevertheless, anti-capitalism was a highly popular idea at the time of independence. For a nuanced study of the relations between the Congress party and private enterprise. Maria Misra, *Business, Race and Politics in British India 1850–1960* (Oxford: OUP, 1999), p. 185; Also see: Aditya Mukherjee, *Imperialism, Nationalism and the Making of the Indian Capitalist Class 1920–47* (London: Sage, 2002).

[114] TCA, T53-DES-AVI-T9-5-PG-61, Rafi Ahmed Kidwai to J.R.D. Tata, 29 September 1949.

[115] TCA, T53-DES-AVI-T9-5-PG-76, Night Air Mail.

agreement between the communications ministry and airline companies. Subsequent attempts at negotiating the takeover of the All-Up Night air mail scheme by airline companies were the cause of disagreement between the government and airline operators. Much of this was due to the arbitrary behaviour of the communications ministry.

Even as IOA was showing signs of failing, communications minister Rafi Ahmed Kidwai summoned Air India's Delhi representative, Sir Gurunath Venkatesh Bewoor, and proposed that the airline take over the service. A former elite civil servant, Bewoor had served on the Viceroy's Executive Council and had run India's Posts and Air Department as Secretary during the war before joining service with the Tatas.[116] When Bewoor asked for time for Air India to respond to the minister's proposal, he was told that the decision would have to be taken immediately. Negotiations broke down when Bewoor insisted that he could not do this since the company's board was located in Bombay. Similar negotiations between the government and other operators including Air Services of India, Indian National Airways, and Deccan Airways also collapsed over the summer of 1949.[117]

An acrimonious exchange of letters between J.R.D. Tata and Rafi Ahmed Kidwai followed. Tata had always been at the forefront of opposition to the Night Mail scheme since he felt that Indian aviation was simply not prepared to safely fly night mail in 1949. From the economic perspective too, Tata felt that the scheme had not been well thought out by government. Tata excoriated Kidwai's suggestion that a Dakota carrying mail at 50 per cent capacity could hope to make a profit, since even a Dakota fully loaded with mail was likely to make a loss. Further, the entire night scheme failed to meet its stated purpose which was to subsidise the civil aviation sector, since it diverted the mails that were being carried by day to night services. Tata would argue that this purpose would have been better achieved by simply transferring several day services into night services.[118] Kidwai in turn felt that Sir Gurunath Bewoor had been most unhelpful in the matter of organizing an alternative to IOA's All-Up Night Mail Service. Bewoor had earlier criticized T.P. Bhalla the DGCA and a

---

[116] He had also represented India at the ICAO.
[117] TCA, T53-DES-AVI-T9-5-PG-09 Air India File F 35, Extract from note prepared by Sir G.V.B. Bewoor.
[118] TCA, T53-DES-AVI-T9-5-PG-62, J.R.D. Tata to Rafi Ahmed Kidwai, 30 September 1949.

key supporter of Kidwai for claiming that the All-Up Air Mail Scheme paid the companies 'something like 65 lakhs a year' whereas according to him Air India made one and a half lakhs a month.[119] Further, Kidwai accused Bewoor of organizing a 'Combine' of the operating companies to resist government's attempts to lowering down the charges.[120] Attempts to reconcile the commercial interests of airline companies with state support in the period after independence were clearly not successful. The Tata-Kidwai exchange, the Bewoor-Kidwai meeting, and the decision to hand IOA the Night mail license hint at a state that regarded airline operators as adversaries and prized government control.

As conditions in the airline industry worsened rather than improved, due to the All-Up Night Air Mail scheme, the government appointed an enquiry committee in February 1950 to look into ways to salvage an industry that was increasingly becoming a national embarrassment. The Rajadhyakhsha Air Transport Inquiry Committee (ATIC), named after the retired chief justice who headed it, blamed the deterioration of the Indian civil aviation sector on the licensing of too many companies.[121] It called for the rationalization of the airline sector through the merging of smaller companies and the non-renewal of licenses for those companies which had no hope of attaining profitability.[122] As I have argued before and as several contemporary observers pointed out, the ATIC effectively upheld the post-war Tymms plan, which had been abandoned by both the interim and independent governments of India. The report also considered nationalization at length before arguing against it. The ATIC held that there was no correlation between nationalization and improved airline performance and that nationalization ought to be postponed for at least five years. If nationalization was eventually embarked upon, then airlines ought to be placed under a statutory corporation with extremely limited government intervention. While private airlines ought to be carefully regulated through the Air Transport Licensing Board, they should also receive subsidies until they were able to attain profitability, something the report acknowledged was likely to take years given the state of

---

[119] TCA, T53-DES-AVI-A2-2, All Up Mail scheme.

[120] TCA, T53-DES-AVI-T9-5-PG-61, Rafi Ahmed Kidwai to J.R.D. Tata, 29 September 1949.

[121] NMML, G. Rajadhyaksha et al, Report of the Air Transport Enquiry Committee 1950, (New Delhi, 1950), p. 13.

[122] NMML, Rajadhyaksha et al, pp. 15–17.

the Indian airline sector.[123] The ATIC's recommendations that the airline industry be subsidised and that state control be limited was not calculated to receive the support of the government. Less than two years later the Government of India began the formal process of nationalization.

Nationalization and Its Consequences

The question of why the Indian government nationalized airlines is one of the most fraught in the history of aviation in independent India. Indeed, focus on the motivations behind nationalization has served to detract from the other aspects of nationalization. Part of the reason for this excessive speculation is the politically charged nature of the decision which touched on the question of the relationship between the state and private enterprise. The nationalization of aviation has rarely been examined as historically contingent, but has rather become a talking point in the broader discussions of the merits of nationalization versus privatization.[124] Nevertheless it is worthwhile dwelling briefly on the rationale for nationalization. Explaining the decision to nationalize in Parliament on 20 April 1953, the day of the debate on the issue, India's third communications minister Jagjivan Ram outlined four major imperatives driving nationalization. Firstly, the state could rationalize the assets of the different airlines under the umbrella of a single domestic state-run airline. Secondly, state control would permit better use of air assets for defence. Thirdly, air transport was a national asset which ought to be developed by the state free of the imperative of profit that governed private industries. Fourthly, the rising costs of aviation meant that only the state had resources adequate to keep Indian aviation's technological edge.[125]

J.R.D. Tata subsequently argued that the government had found it politically expedient to implement nationalization.[126] Certainly there was an appetite for nationalized aviation in political circles, though as I have

---

[123] Ibid., p. 27.

[124] Present day excoriations of nationalization as an unmitigated failure born of governmental overreach ironically echo past criticisms of private enterprise as an anachronism. See for instance Nawab, *Development of Indian Air Transport*.

[125] V. B. Singh, *Economic History of India, 1857-1956* (Bombay; London: Allied Publishers, 1965), p. 365.

[126] Tata, 'The Story of Air Transport', p. 13.

pointed out this dated to the period before independence. Panduranga Rao has shown for instance how the First Five Year Plan suggested that the airline sector ought to be pruned through nationalization in the interests of economy.[127] Baldev Nayar meanwhile has argued that the socialist predisposition of the government meant that nationalization had always been a certainty and that its implementation was inevitable.[128] Nayar states that the death of Vallabhbhai Patel, who had resisted earlier attempts to nationalize aviation, cleared the path for a decision that he attributes ultimately to Nehru. This is probably true, though it is also fair to point out that Patel was successfully able in large measure to oppose nationalization because it had yet to take concrete shape in 1946.

The nationalization decision was most likely motivated by several factors including the ones above. Much has also been made of the perceived abandonment of the ATIC report's recommendations. Other factors that have often been marginalized in the debate are worth highlighting however. While the ATIC report validated the Tymms plan it also did not necessarily condemn all of independent India's aviation policy decisions. The report's recommendation for the establishment of trunk routes connecting Hyderabad, Delhi, Bombay, and Calcutta was remarkably similar to the Night Air Mail Scheme.[129] Moreover, while the committee's call for nationalization with a statutory corporation was not heeded by the government, the suggestion for the establishment of a state-run corporation which evolved to include two corporations was eventually adopted. Arguably the most neglected of the government's reasons for nationalizing aviation however is Jagjivan Ram's claim that state-run corporations would be better able to respond to national emergencies, especially those pertaining to defence. The government's decision making after independence was opaque. The government did not, for instance, explain why it had not implemented the Rajaadhyaksha report. Yet given the historical context in which Jagjivan Ram was tasked with implementing nationalization it is not difficult to see why defence factored in as a key reason for nationalization. I have argued elsewhere that the lines between civil and military aviation in a poor state with limited aviation resources were

---

[127]   Rao and Rao, *Indian Airlines*, p. 82.
[128]   Nayar, *The State and International Aviation in India*, p. 56.
[129]   NMML, G. Rajadhyaksha et al, *Report of the Air Transport Enquiry Committee 1950* (New Delhi, 1950), p. 14.

blurred. Civil aircraft had over the first five years of Indian independence alone played a key role in the evacuation of refugees from West Pakistan in 1947 and East Pakistan in 1950 as well as been critical to the ferrying of troops to Kashmir.[130] When Pakistani authorities had cut the rail link connecting Calcutta with Guahati via East Bengal in late 1949 airline companies served as a sky bridge shipping 750,0000 pounds of essential goods per day until the establishment of new land links.[131] Indian airline companies had also played a critical role in the military-led flood relief operations in Assam in 1951. The First Five Year Plan which had taken forward the recommendations pertaining to nationalization of the ATIC, had explicitly pointed to the role of civil aircraft 'in the evacuation after partition and in West Bengal and Assam in 1949-1950'.[132] Significantly it also stated that, 'the defence aspect of civil aviation should not be lost sight of'.[133] More than one parliamentarian would rise during the Lok Sabha debate on nationalization to claim that state control of aviation was necessary for national defence. As Dr S.N. Sinha noted, 'We can remember the days of partition, the Kashmir conflict, also the Assam earthquake and many other emergencies. On those occasions civil aviation rose to the occasion.'[134] Total control of aviation would significantly increase the state's ability to project power.

The debate on nationalization in parliament on 20 April 1953 was remarkable for the lack of debate on whether aviation ought to be nationalized. Instead Jagjivan Ram was assailed from multiple directions for the perceived pro-capitalist bias of the nationalization bill. Communist members of the house, representing the main opposition party in independent India, expressed their anger at what they considered to be a bill that was not true nationalization.[135] Bhupesh Gupta, a Communist Member of Parliament, said that the bill did not represent 'genuine nationalization' since 'the multimillionaires who normally opposed the move, had welcomed it'. Communists also demanded that the state ought not to

[130] See for instance: Kumar, *An Incredible War.*
[131] Mustafa Anwar, *Civil Aviation in India* (Calcutta: Thacker, Spink and Co, 1954), p. 94.
[132] 'First Five Year Plan, Government of India'. Accessed August 31, 2020. https://niti.gov.in/planningcommission.gov.in/docs/plans/planrel/fiveyr/index5.html
[133] Ibid.
[134] Air Corporations Bill' 20 April 1953, *Parliament of India Digital Library,* https://eparlib.nic.in/bitstream/123456789/55889/1/lsd_01_03_20-04-1953.pdf, Accessed 9 July 2021.
[135] *House of the People, Parliamentary Debates: Official Report* (New Delhi, 1953), pp. 4635–36

compensate airline companies since their property was being expropriated for the national good.[136] Even Congress members were outraged by the shape of nationalization, in large part because it left J.R.D. Tata in charge of India's international aviation.[137] This was because nationalization had over the five years from Indian independence evolved from a 'salutary principle' to a concrete act; the Air Corporations Act 1953.

The principle of nationalization as I have shown was popular with both the colonial and independent governments of India. Much of this popularity stemmed from the ambiguity of what nationalization would entail. When the decision to nationalize was taken in early 1952, sometime after the First Five Year Plan, the final form that nationalization would take was the object of intense discussion. A report of the British civil aviation adviser noted as late as January 1953, 'The most striking feature here is firm determination of the government to nationalise and its complete weakness in settling the methods of nationalisation.'[138] Initially the government intended to follow the advice of the Planning Commission and set up a single state airline that would run both internal and external air routes. However, J.R.D. Tata was able to have a strong say on the matter as the Nehru-led government hoped to retain him as the Chairman of the Corporation despite his strong resistance to nationalization. Consequently, Tata insisted that he could only serve as Chairman if two corporations were established, one for foreign and the other for domestic flights. He would then serve as the Chairman of the foreign corporation which would effectively mean that he would continue to serve as the head of AII, since it was the largest external service.[139] The implementation of nationalization, a policy with strong anti-capitalist undertones, was thus significantly influenced by the scion of one of India's largest business families.

The Air Corporations Act 1953 brought into existence two corporations. AII would consist of the previously established company of the same name and Bharat Airways' Far Eastern service. It would, as its name indicated, serve as India's international flag carrier. India's domestic needs would be served by Indian Airlines Corporation (IAC) which

---

[136] 'Expansion and Development of Civil Aviation', *Times of India*, 21, April 1953.
[137] *Times of India*, 19 May 1953.
[138] DO 35/ 4919, Confidential report, January 1953.
[139] Ibid.

would absorb eight domestic airlines; Deccan Airways, Airways India, Bharat Airways, Himalayan Aviation, Kalinga Airlines, Indian National Airways, Air Services India, and Air India. With 99 aircraft it was one of the largest domestic airlines in Asia. Government would eventually pay out 6.2 crores in compensation to shareholders.[140] Jagjivan Ram had hoped to pass the nationalization bill in time for the Corporations to be inaugurated on 1 April 1953.[141] Parliamentary delays however meant that the Corporations were only inaugurated on 1 August 1953.[142] At a large ceremony attended by the minister of communications and a large number of members of Parliament, Prime Minister Jawaharlal Nehru was to press an electronic switch that would unveil a curtain on a former Indian National Airways Dakota aeroplane. Behind the curtain were the words 'Indian Airlines'. When Nehru pressed the button however there was no parting of the curtains. It took some time for the realization that the button was not in fact connected with electricity. With this mistake rectified Nehru officially completed the ceremony that would make aviation into a state monopoly for the next four decades.[143]

Nationalization had different consequences for India's airlines and their employees. The question of compensation had been a vexatious one from the time the government had seriously begun considering it. Airline companies, led by J.R.D. Tata, attempted to resist nationalization, but when it became clear that this would not be possible began to look into the best deal that they could extract from the government.[144] They chiefly sought the costs of their equipment at international market rates and compensation for business lost. However, the government countered that their equipment could not be sold abroad due to government restrictions and that it would have few buyers domestically. Indian airline companies were offered the cost price of their equipment minus 18 per cent a year in depreciation.[145] There is some evidence to show that larger

[140] Singh ed, *Economic History of India, 1857–1956*, p. 364.

[141] This would have brought the corporations into existence on the twentieth anniversary of the raising of the first squadron of the Indian Air Force, though there is no reason to believe that this was the intention behind the date.

[142] DO 35/ 4919, Confidential report, August 1953.

[143] Ibid.

[144] For a detailed discussion of Tata's evolving stance on aviation see: Lala, *Beyond the Last Blue Mountain*, Chapter VIII.

[145] DO 35/ 4919, Confidential report, January 1953

companies were better able to confront nationalization. The most famous example was AII which retained its name, its chairman, its personnel, its equipment, and even its mascot; the iconic Maharaja. Others however also might have had opportunities to adapt to nationalization. Deccan Airways had functioned as a semi-nationalized company, ever since the Government of India had taken over the controlling stake that the independent Hyderabad government had exercised in the company.[146] For the pilots of Indian National Airways the prospect of better pay and benefits as a consequence of becoming government employees after nationalization was appealing.[147] Smaller companies however received aviation with less enthusiasm. The compensation which government was offering airlines would cause substantial losses for smaller operators like Himalayan aviation whose total capital amounted to only ten lakh rupees.[148] With depreciation rates for compensation fixed at 18 per cent the company's shareholders would be unable to recoup even their initial investments. Consequently, while larger companies attempted to maintain their air fleets in an attempt to get the largest possible compensation, smaller operators adopted a policy resembling scorched earth, whereby equipment maintenance was discontinued so that government would inherit barely functional aircraft after nationalization.[149] Even when companies did receive adequate compensation, the results were likely to be mixed. Air India for instance received 284 lakh rupees in bonds from the government after a long negotiation in October 1954. This included government compensation for losses between January and August when the uncertainty caused by nationalization drove stock prices down. Despite granting compensation however the government withheld the payment of salaries for the period when Air India staff had been on leave.[150] The process of distributing government compensation to shareholders would then drag on well beyond 1955.[151]

Nationalization's varied results for the two air corporations were widely recognized even at the time.[152] AII substantially retained its identity and

[146] Reddy, *Aviation in the Hyderabad Dominions*, p. 157.
[147] DO 35/4919, Confidential report, August 1953.
[148] TCA, T53-DES-AVI-T9-5-PG-91, Extract from meeting of the ATLB, 3 January 1950.
[149] DO 35/4919, Confidential report, August 1953.
[150] TCA, JRDT AVI A2 4-TA AI 29, Extract from minutes of the agents meeting, 15 December 1954.
[151] TCA, T53-DES-AVI-A2-2-PG-15, Air India Limited to Shareholders, 6 May 1955.
[152] *Indian Skyways*, 'Our Nationalised Corporations', August 1955.

structure and after nationalization continued to remain one of the leading Asian airlines.[153] Indeed J.R.D. Tata was able to use the airline's monopoly on external services and his own close links to the government to win concessions at the cost of Indian Air Lines Corporation. Santa Cruz airport, for instance, was reserved exclusively for AII aircraft despite its obvious importance for the domestic airline.[154] AII would remain internationally competitive for the next two decades partly because of the state support that J.R.D. Tata could expect to enjoy. IAC in contrast would go on to make losses for several years and become something of an example of government mismanagement.[155] This was in large part due to the twin problems of integration and management. Whereas AII consisted overwhelmingly of the personnel and equipment of the pre-nationalization corporation of the same name, IAC had to integrate nine different airlines with their varied equipment into one corporation. This merger, difficult as it was, might well have been achieved since early nationalization plans after all called for the merging of all of India's airline companies. However, matters were complicated by poor state management. The First Five Year Plan had called for nationalization to occur but for the state to limit its involvement in any corporation.[156] This principle was duly abandoned by a government for which the very reason for nationalization was the imposition of closer state control. As a result of this the IAC would go on to become a byword for crippling bureaucratic mismanagement. The losses incurred by IAC have since been the subject of much of the analysis of nationalization, to the detriment of historicising the process.

Nationalization was meant to serve as a means to standardize the chaotic organization of Indian civil aviation which involved a number of competing airlines operating different equipment. Instead, it served to sweep away a number of smaller companies, many of which were likely to have been liquidated in a few years because they could not afford to upgrade to newer, larger, and costlier aircraft. A focus on the consequences and causes of nationalization however fails to situate it in its historically

---

[153] D. Shaftel, 'Karachi to Bombay to Calcutta', *Air and Space Magazine*, November 2011. http://www.airspacemag.com/history-of-flight/karachi-to-bombay-to-calcutta-77003851/ accessed 5/03/2017.

[154] *Indian Skyways*, 'Indian Airline Corporation's finances', August 1955.

[155] *Indian Skyways*, 'Be fair to the "IAC"', October 1955.

[156] 'First Five Year Plan, Government of India'. Accessed August 31, 2020. https://niti.gov.in/planningcommission.gov.in/docs/plans/planrel/fiveyr/index5.html.

contingent context. Nationalization was popular with the colonial government, the composite Muslim League-Congress interim government, and the independent Congress-led government in ways that few policies have been. Indeed, it is not an exaggeration to state that nationalization was internationally popular, the United Kingdom to which India looked for guidance on aviation matter had continued to maintain nationalized airlines in the period after the Second World War.[157] Indian airline companies were nationalized for a variety of reasons not the least of which was their vast defence potential. Narratives of nationalization have thus far tended to focus on how the failures of Indian aviation led to its takeover by the state. It is possible however to make the opposite argument as well. Indian airline companies might well have been victims of their success in serving the state in emergencies. As I have argued through much of this book, the services of Indian airline companies in multiple crises from partition to the 1950 Bengal evacuations helped defend the interests of the state. If aircraft had not been available during partition, in the Kashmir operations, and the 1950 Bengal crisis the political and humanitarian cost would have been immense. The possibility of totally controlling extremely valuable assets for state security was very attractive to the Government of India and ought to be taken seriously in writing on the subject.

Conclusion

The half decade after Indian independence was formative for both Indian aviation and the state. For Indian aviation the period was one of contradiction. After the war the civil aviation sector had boomed, yet by 1950, it was in a state of severe decline. It was simultaneously more internationalized than ever and subject to nationalization. Much of this contradiction is explained by the expansion of the independent state in its quest for sovereignty both domestically and abroad. In 1948 India was a state that had just emerged from a war with Pakistan and the partition of the subcontinent. By 1953 the Government of India had effectively imposed its control over private enterprise, in the field of aviation, and was well on its way

---

[157] See for instance: R. Higham, *Speedbird* (London: I.B. Tauris, 1974).

to completing the Indianization of the IAF. Three moments in the history of aviation enable us to trace the transformation of India from newly independent dominion to increasingly confident republic; the 1950 Bengal crisis, the establishment of Air India in 1948, and the nationalization of airlines in 1953.

Taken together the three moments reveal that independent India exercised sovereignty on three interconnected levels. Internationally, India emphasized its status as an independent nation-state in a world order that solely recognized nation-states. In doing so India was not distinct from other members of the new post-war international order. Indeed, it is possible to make a case for the fact that Indian sovereignty at this level, at least within the field of aviation, sprang from the actions of other states, such as Canada, which had sought to assert the freedom of the nation-state at the cost of the old imperial order. Regionally, India defined itself in opposition to Pakistan with which it was drawn reluctantly into an arms race. Domestically, the independent Indian state sought increased control over aviation technology. The importance of the aeroplane in serving the state through multiple crises and its potential for projecting state power, among other things, set the Indian government down a path that would culminate in the nationalization of private airline companies. This inaugurated a new era for Indian aviation; four decades of state control.

Conclusion

The nationalization of airline companies in 1953 represented the final cul-
mination of the Indian state's engagement with aviation in the years after
independence. With aviation firmly under its control the Indian government committed itself to expensive expansion plans that would have
been inconceivable even a decade before. The Indian Air Force began an
ambitious programme of modernization in 1957. In the next few years,
it would more than double in size, growing from 15 to 33 squadrons. Its
piston-powered fighter planes would be replaced by jet fighters.[1] Indian
civil aviation too entered the jet age in 1960, with the induction of the
Boeing 707 jetliners into the Air India fleet, which were paid for by loans
raised from the World Bank, guaranteed by the Government of India.[2]

The story of India and the aeroplane from the late 1950s to the present
is necessarily a complex one characterized by both stunning successes and
appalling failures. Today the Indian Air Force is one of the largest air forces
in the world and is in the midst of inducting some of the world's most advanced, and expensive, aircraft into its fleet. The civil aviation sector has also
grown substantially and flies more passengers than ever before. Despite this
Indian aviation also forces significant challenges. Seven decades after independence, India has had mixed results at best with indigenizing aircraft
production.[3] Jawaharlal Nehru's fears that India would be forced to remain
dependent on arms imports from abroad continues to remain relevant.
India's flag carrier, Air India, has suffered heavy losses in the decades after air
transport liberalization in 1994. It's once a stellar reputation for promptness
and profitability has been tarnished by years of mismanagement. Though

---

[1] Singh, *History of Indian Aviation*, pp. 116–117.
[2] Ibid., p. 63.
[3] For a brief look at India's attempts to produce modern aircraft see: Edgerton, *Shock of the Old*, p. 126.

The Aeroplane and the Making of Modern India. Aashique Ahmed Iqbal, Oxford University Press.
© Oxford University Press 2023. DOI: 10.1093/oso/9780192864208.003.0007

many Indians have optimistically greeted the acquisition of the airline by the Tata group in 2021 as a 'return' to the conglomerate that was responsible for its establishment in 1932, the challenges that the airline faces are substantial.[4] Other private airline companies have often fared badly. In the words of one observer, 'airline after airline kept nosediving.'[5] Indeed the sorry state of private airline companies in the first two decades of the 21st century recalls the difficult period that preceded nationalization when many airlines went bankrupt and others sought subsidies from the government to continue operating.

The history of aviation in India after 1953 raises many important questions. How should India's attempts to produce military aircraft be assessed? How have attitudes towards national flag carriers changed in the age of neoliberalism? What does the emergence of new technologies like unmanned aerial vehicles portend for the projection of state power in India? The paucity of work on the era means that these pressing questions are yet to be answered by historians though there is little doubt increasing interest in India's technological history will fuel exciting research in the years to come.[6]

A key aim of the present work has been to place India's experience with aviation in a wider collage of the experiences of poor countries with high technology in the interests of making the history of technology more inclusive. Histories of aviation have thus far mainly told the story of a handful of countries that possess the majority of the world's aeroplanes. Yet the majority of the world's states, like India, have had to make do with a handful of aircraft. This book has tried to take seriously David Edgerton's argument that in order to be considered truly global,

---

[4] Aashique Iqbal, 'Plane Tales: Air India's Return to the Tatas', 27 October 2021, *The India Forum*, Accessed 11 May 2022. https://www.theindiaforum.in/article/plane-tales-air-india-s-return-tatas.

[5] Shelley Viswajeet, *The Indigo Story: Inside the Upstart that redefined Indian Aviation* (New Delhi: Rupa books, 2018), p. 49.

[6] A few notable works on aviation in the years after nationalization include: Nayar, *The State and International Aviation in India*; Rao, *Indian Airlines*; Nawab, *Economic Development of Indian Air Transport*; P.V.S. Jagan Mohan and Samir Chopra, *Eagles over Bangladesh: The Indian Air Force in the 1971 Liberation War* (New Delhi: Harper Collins, 2013); P.V.S. Jagan Mohan and Samir Chopra *The India-Pakistan Air War of 1965* (New Delhi: Manohar, 2005); K.S. Nair, *Ganesha's Flyboys: The Indian Air Force in Congo 1960–62* (New Delhi: Anveshan Enterprises, 2012); Bharat Kumar, *Unknown and Unsung: The Indian Air Force in the Sino-Indian War of 1962* (New Delhi: Knowledge World Publishers, 2012); Bharat Kumar, *The Duels of the Himalayan Eagle: The First Indo-Pak Air War* (New Delhi: Natraj Publishers, 2015). For an insider view of Air India see: Jitender Bhargava, *The Descent of Air India* (New Delhi: Self-Published, 2016).

histories of technology must take the experiences of poor countries into account.[7] The Indian state's experience with aviation is strikingly similar to the story of aviation in other post-colonial societies. Indians were hardly the only people to struggle to fashion a new modernity around aircraft. Egyptians during the interwar years sought closer association with and access to aviation. Indeed, the word 'Indianization', which was at the centre of debates to grant Indians an air force, might well have come from the word 'Egyptianization'.[8] As in India, the British focused only on the development of the Imperial Air Route from London to Sydney in Egypt. The Egyptian government would only come to control aviation after the outbreak of the Second World War when it nationalized the sole air carrier in the country, renaming it *Misr lil-Tayaran*.[9] Egypt too tried to indigenize the production of military aircraft.[10] Like its Indian counterpart the Egyptian Air Force continues to be heavily reliant on imports. In Peru, as Willie Hiatt has shown, nationalists were enthusiastic about the possibilities the aeroplane offered for airlifting 'a backward country into the modern age'.[11] To this end the Peruvian state spent prodigious sums purchasing aircraft from the United States and Europe, often with mixed results. Attempts were also made to associate the aeroplane with newly fashioned, regional, and national identities.[12] Like India, Peru's flag carrier Aeroperu suffered the ravages of neoliberalism and was eventually shut down after racking up over 174 million dollars in debts.[13] Despite being located on three different continents India, Egypt, and Peru have had remarkably similar historical trajectories in the field of aviation. The experiences of all three countries have much more in common with each other than they do with those of the advanced Western states that have been the subjects of most of the writing on aviation. They are also much more representative of the relationships most states had with aviation in the 20th century. The parallels in the three country's histories of aviation

---

[7] David Edgerton, *Shock of the Old* (London: Profile books, 2019 (2006)), p. 212.
[8] Aparajith Ramnath has argued the term 'Indianization' might have been modeled on the term 'Egyptianization' though the meaning of Egpytianization was quite different in the 19th century. Ramnath, *Birth of an Indian Profession*, p. 28.
[9] Capua, 'Common Skies, Divided Horizons', p. 932.
[10] Edgerton, *Shock of the Old*, p. 125.
[11] Willie. *The Rarified Air of the Modern*, Kindle.
[12] Ibid.
[13] Ibid.

also point to the obsession with becoming modern that characterized decolonizing states. To be modern was to be a legitimate member of the world order of nation-states that became dominant, especially after the Second World War. To not to be modern on the other hand meant being subjected to degrading violence by modern powers.

In India, as in other decolonizing societies, modernity was seen not merely as a desirable aspiration but as a condition for survival. Colonized Indians, in the years after the Great War, saw the aeroplane not only as a necessary means of defending the subcontinent in the modern era but also as the ultimate guarantee of independence. Without its own air power, India would find itself left behind technologically and remain dependent on its British colonizers for air defence. On the other hand, if Indians mastered aviation, then they would have the substance of sovereignty regardless of whether they remained within the British Empire or not. This view was deepened by the Second World War which saw the colonial state reluctantly hand control of military aviation to Indians. It was then further entrenched by the crises surrounding Partition, the war in Kashmir, the integration of the princely states, and the 1950 Bengal confrontation. Limited civil aviation resources meant that the Indian leadership had to carefully prioritize the use of aircraft. It also meant that the lines between civil and military aviation were frequently blurred with civil aircraft being frequently called on to defend the interests of the Indian state while military aircraft served in a number of civil emergencies. Control of high technologies like aviation was highly crucial in regaining the state's monopoly on violence after independence. The small but highly crucial role played by both civil and military aviation in defending India in the years immediately after independence played a role in convincing Indian policymakers across the political spectrum to make aviation a state monopoly in 1953. No more lines would separate aviation from the state.

By associating sovereignty with violence, and violence with the aeroplane, Indian nationalists ensured that aviation and the Indian state would be enmeshed well before independence was a reality. Aviation was envisioned as a technology that would produce sovereignty by projecting the centralized state over vast regions and diverse peoples. Aircraft territorialized the skies, imposed order on rioting populaces, and literally shaped the boundaries of modern India and Pakistan. They served also to craft, protect, and crush diverse notions of sovereignty.

The story that the book you hold in your hands has tried to tell is the story of how colonial subjects tried to make aeroplanes Indian. It is also the story of how the aeroplane made Indians of colonial subjects.

Glossary

Ansar Auxiliary Pakistan force

Azad Hind Fauj Indian National Army

Azad Independent

Crores Ten million

Dewan Prime Minister

Durbar Royal Court

Lakhs One hundred thousand

Maharaja Great king

Nawab Mughal era title for governor

Nizam Hereditary ruler of Hyderabad

Quran Sacred book of Islam

Raja King

Razakar Volunteer Hyderabad militia

Bibliography

Primary Sources

Archival and Manuscript Sources

Karnataka State Archives, Bangalore
Industries and Commerce files (1940–2).
General and Revenue Secretariat files.

Cambridge University Library, Cambridge
GBR/00115/RCMS 20-Frederick Tymms Collection on Civil Aviation.

Churchill Archives Centre, Churchill College, Cambridge
GBR/0014/ELMT-Papers of Air Marshal Thomas Elmhirst.

Andhra Pradesh State Archives, Hyderabad
1942 Hyderabad Directory.
H.E.H. The Nizams State Railway Annual report of the General Manager Financial year 1938–9.
Niz/ADM-Hyderabad State Administrative reports (1948–50).

Private collection of Mrs. P.A. Anuradha Reddy, Hyderabad
Includes a collection of images gathered by Mrs. Reddy over two decades.
Indian Aviation magazine, 1948.

Mehrangarh Museum Archives, Jodhpur
Mahakma Khas Aviation Files
Household Records

The National Archives, London
AIR-Air ministry files (1939–46).
AVIA-Ministry of Aviation (1939–46).
BT 217-Air Ministry and Successors, Civil Aviation Files (1945–7).
CO 937-Colonial and Commonwealth Office, Communications Department (1951).
DO 35-Dominions and Commonwealth Office, Original Correspondence (1950).
FO 371-Foreign Office, Political Departments, General Correspondence from 1906–66 (1950).
DO 133-Commonwealth Relations officers and successors: High Commission and Consular Papers, India (1948).
DO 134-Commonwealth Relations officers and successors: High Commission and Consular Papers, Pakistan (1947–8).

DO 142-Commonwealth Relations Office, India: Registered files (1947–8).
PREM 8-Prime Minister's Office, Correspondence and papers (1945–51).
T-Treasury Supply Branch Series (1938–9).

National Army Museum, London
7901-8-6-1-Papers of General Sir Roy Bucher.

Royal Air Force Museum, London
X003-Reports on 1946 RAF and RIAF strikes.

British Library, London
IOR/L/MIL-Records of the Military Department, India Office records (1940).
IOR/L/WS-War Staff series, India Office records (1939–46).
IOR Neg 15538-67-Papers of Earl Mountbatten of Burma as Viceroy 1947 and
    Governor General 1947–48 of India.
IOR/L/E/8-Economic Record Department 1786-1950, Departmental papers:
    Annual Files (1930–50).
IOR/V/27/770-India, Communications Department, Aviation files (1946-7).
MSS Eur D/670-Papers of George Cunningham, Governor of the NWFP.

Tata Central Archives, Pune
T53-DES-AVI-T9-4-Mainly documents pertaining to Post-War civil aviation.
T53-DES-AVI-T9-5-Letters from 1948–1950.
T53-DES-AVI-A3-BO-1-Minutes of the meetings of the board of directors of Air
    India International.
T53-DES-AVI-A2-2-Mainly letters, lists and a brief history of the company
    until 1946.
JRDT AVI A2 4-TA AI 29-Compensation for Nationalisation file.

Interservices History Division, Ministry of Defence, Government of India,
New Delhi
Operations Records books for RIAF Squadrons No. 1, No. 3, No. 7, No. 8, and No.
    10 (1942-6).
MoD (I), 601/14185/H-R. Singh, Draft History of the Military Evacuation
    Organisation (unpublished).
MoD (I), 601/14476/H-*Partition Proceedings,* vol. V.
MoD (I) 601/14292/H-601/14566/H-Ministry of Defence files (1947–9).
MoD(I), 601/14513/H-Expansion of Air Force and Air Force matters.
MoD(I), 601/14362/H-History of the Indian Air Force 1932–56.

Private collection of Mr. J.R. Nanda, New Delhi
Harjinder Singh papers.
Includes a collection of images and articles gathered by the former chairman of Avi-
    Oil India.

Nehru Memorial Museum and Library, New Delhi
Mirza Ismail papers.
Mokshagundam Visvesvaraya papers.
Walchand Hirachand papers.

National Archives of India, New Delhi
F & P- Foreign and Political Series (1931–46).
Vallabhai Patel papers

Balliol College Archives, Oxford
Dep Monckton Trustees-Sir Walter Monckton Papers.

Printed Sources

British Library, London
A. Skeen et al, *Report of the Indian Sandhurst Committee* (London, 1927).
Millions on the Move (New Delhi, 1948).

Royal Air Force Museum, London
RIAF journals 1945–6.

Nehru Memorial Museum and Library, New Delhi
Air Force Instructions, 1934–44.
G. Rajadhyaksha et al., *Report of the Air Transport Enquiry Committee 1950* (New Delhi, 1950).
Indian Aircraft Manual (New Delhi, 1934).
Pakistan Times 1947–9.
White Paper on Jammu and Kashmir (New Delhi, 1948).
White Paper on Hyderabad (New Delhi, 1948).

Central Secretariat Library, New Delhi
Council of State Debates (1921–46).
Legislative Assembly Debates (1919–46).
Legislative Department Proceedings (1911–20).

United Services Institute of India, New Delhi
United Services Institute Journals (1919–46)

Bodleian Library, Oxford
The Aeroplane (1946–7).

Brayne, Frank Lugard. *Village Uplift in India.* Gurgaon: Rural Community Council, 1928.
Brayne, Frank Lugard *Socrates in an Indian Village.* New Delhi: OUP India Branch, 1937.
Das, Durga. *Sardar Vallabhai Patel's Correspondence 1945-1950.* Ahmedabad: Navjivan Publication House, 1974.
Congress Election Manifesto. *Our Industrial Policy.* New Delhi: Congress Parliamentary Board, 1951.
Fraser, Hastings. *Our Faithful Ally, the Nizam of Hyderabad, a Historical Sketch.* London: unknown publisher, 1865.
Gopal, Sarvepalli et al. Selected Works of Jawaharlal Nehru. New Delhi: Orient Longman, 1972.

Hamid, Shahid. *Disastrous Twilight: A Personal Record of the Partition of India*. New Delhi: Leo Cooper, 1993.

Moon, Penderel eds. *Transfer of Power*. New Delhi: Stationery Office, 1970–83, IX–XII.

Nanda, Bal Ram eds. *Selected Works of Ballabh Pant*. New Delhi: OUP, 1993.

Nehru, Jawaharlal, Sarvepalli Gopal, and Uma Iyengar. *The Essential Writings of Jawaharlal Nehru*. New Delhi: Oxford University Press, 2003.

Parthasarathi, Gopalasami. eds. *Letters to the Chief Ministers 1947–64*. Oxford: OUP,1985.

Parliamentary Reports, House of the People: Official Reports. New Delhi: Parliament Secretariat, 1948–54.

Patel, Manibahen Patel ed. *Sardar's Letters: Mostly Unknown*. Ahmedabad: Vallabhai Patel Smarak Bhavan, 1978.

Sachar, Rajendra. et al. *Social, Economic and Educational Status of the Muslim Community in India: A Report*. New Delhi, Prime Ministers High Level committee, 2006.

Tata, Jehangir, Ratanjee Dadabhoy. 'The story of Air Transport', *The Journal of the Royal Aeronautical Society* 65 (1965): 1–25.

Audio Visual Material

Nehru Memorial Museum and Library and Museum, New Delhi
Manimugdha Sharma photograph taken at Nehru Memorial Museum and Library, 2015.

National Film Archive of India, Pune
Aiming High (1942).
Behind the Wings (1943).
Cavalry of the Clouds (1941).

Miscellaneous

Choudhary, Ratnadeep, 'Biju Patnaik: The Two Time Odisha Chief Minister who Was a RAF Pilot in World War 2', *The Print*, 5th March 2019 https://theprint.in/thepr int-profile/biju-patnaik-the-two-time-odisha-chief-minister-who-was-raf-pilot-in-world-war-2/201326/, Accessed 9 July 2021.

Flight Magazine (1910-53). Accessed April 16, 2017. https://www.flightglobal.com/pdfarchive.

Parliamentary Digital Library (1920–54). Accessed July 9, 2021. https://eparlib.nic.in/

Proquest. *Times of India* (1946-8), Accessed April 7, 2017. http://ezproxyprd.bodle ian.ox.ac.uk:2059/publication/54644?OpenUrlRefId=info:xri/sid:primo.

Secondary Sources

Books and Articles

The Constitution of India. New Delhi: Government of India, 1996.

Centenary of Civil Aviation in India. New Delhi: Ministry of Civil Aviation, Government of India, 2011.

Abraham, Itty. *The Making of the Indian Atomic Bomb: Science, Secrecy and the Postcolonial State.* Postcolonial Encounters. London: Zed Books, 1998.

Ahmad, Syed Mohammad. *A Lucky Pilot: Memoirs of Wing Commander Lanky Ahmad.* Lahore: Ferozsons, 1997.

Ahmed, Sara. *The Cultural Politics of Emotion.* Edinburgh: Edinburgh University Press, 2004.

Ali, Faizan, and Bidita Lal Dey. *Is Pakistan International Airlines Up to the Mark?.* Bradford: VDM Verlag, 2011.

Arnold, David. *Science, Technology and Medicine in Colonial India.* Cambridge: CUP, 2000.

Arnold, David. *Everyday Technology: Machines and the Making of India's Modernity.* Chicago: University of Chicago Press, 2013.

Bailes, Kendall E. 'Technology and Legitimacy: Soviet Aviation and Stalinism in the 1930s'. *Technology and Culture* 17, no. 1 (January 1976): 55–81.

Bangash, Yaqoob Khan. *A Princely Affair: The Accession and Integration of the Princely States of Pakistan, 1947–1955.* Karachi: OUP, 2015.

Bandopadhyay, Sekhara. *From Plassey to Partition.* New Delhi: Orient Longman, 2004.

Bannerjee, Debdas. *Colonialism in Action.* Hyderabad: Orient Longman, 1999.

Barkawi, Tarak. *Soldiers of Empire: Indian and British Armies in World War II.* Cambridge: CUP, 2017.

Barrier, Norman Gerald. *Banned: Controversial Literature and Political Control in British India, 1907–1947.* University of Missouri Studies (1926); v.61. Columbia: University of Missouri Press, 1976.

Baumler, Alan. 'Aviation and Asian Modernity 1900–1950.' In *Oxford Research Encyclopaedia of Asian History,* 2017, Accessed 5 May 2022. https://oxfordre.com/asianhistory/view/10.1093/acrefore/9780190277727.001.0001/acrefore-9780190277727-e-177.

Bawa, Vasant Kumar. *The Nizam between Mughals and British: Hyderabad under Salar Jung I.* New Delhi: S. Chand, 1996.

Bawa, Vasant Kumar. *The Last Nizam: The Life and the Times of Mir Osman Ali Khan,* New Delhi: Penguin Books, 1992.

Bawa, Vasant Kumar. 'Salar Jung and the Nizam's State Railway 1860–1883', *Indian Economic and Social History Review* 2, no. 4 (1965): 307–340.

Bayly, Christopher Alan, and Tim. Harper. *Forgotten Armies.* London: Penguin Books, 2005.

Benichou, Lucien. *From Autocracy to Integration.* Chennai: Orient Longman, 2000.

Beverly, Eric Lewis. *Hyderabad, British India and the World.* Cambridge: CUP, 2015.

Bhagwan, Manu Belur. *Sovereign Spheres: Princes, Education, and Empire in Colonia India.* Delhi; Oxford: OUP, 2003.

Bhargava, Jitender. *The Descent of Air India*. Revised Edition, New Delhi: Self-published, 2016.

Bhatt, Saligram. *The New Aviation Policy of India*. New Delhi: Lancers Books, 1997.

Bhattacharjea, Ajit. *Sheikh Abdullah*. New Delhi: Roli Books, 2008.

Bhattacharya, Sanjoy. *Propaganda and Information in Eastern India, 1939–45*. Richmond, Surrey: Curzon, 2001.

Bialer, Uri. *The Shadow of the Bomber*. London: Royal Historical Society, 1980.

Biersteker, Thomas J., and Cynthia Weber. *State Sovereignty as Social Construct*. Cambridge Studies in International Relations; 46. Cambridge: Cambridge University Press, 1996.

Birdwood, Chistopher B. *Two Nations and Kashmir*. London: Robert Hale, 1956.

Black, Jeremy. *Rethinking Military History*. London: Routledge, 2004.

Bloeria, Sudhir S. *The Battles of Zojila*. New Delhi: Har-Anand Publications, 1997.

Bohn, Willard. 'The Poetics of Flight: Futurist "Aeropoesia".' *MLN* 121, no. 1 (2006): 207–24.

Bothwell, Robert, and Jack Lawrence Granatstein. 'Canada and Wartime Negotiations over Civil Aviation: The Functional Principle in Operation'. *International History Review* 2, no. 4 (1980): 585–681.

Brown, Jeffrey. *Indian Air Mail Postage Rates until 1956*. London: The India Study Circle for Philately, 2000.

Brown, Judith. *Nehru*. Profiles in Power. London, England: Harlow: Longman, 1999.

Butalia, Urvashi. *The Other Side of Silence: Voices from the Partition of India*. New Delhi: Penguin Books, 1998.

Call, Stephen. *Selling Air Power: Military Aviation and American Popular Culture after World War II*. 1st ed. Williams-Ford Texas A&M University Military History Series; No. 124. College Station, Texas A & M Press, 2009.

Carozza, Anthony. *William D. Pawley*. Washington: Potomac Books, 2012.

Carter, Lionel. *Chronicles of British Business in Asia, 1850–1960*. New Delhi: Manohar Publishers, 2002.

Chakrabarty, Dipesh. *Provincialising Europe*. Princeton: Princeton University Press, 2000.

Chakrabarty, Prafulla K. *The Marginal Men*. Calcutta: Naya Udyog, 1999.

Chandra, Bipan. *India's Struggle for Independence 1857–1947*. New Delhi; Harmondsworth: Penguin Books, 1989.

Chapman, John Ivelaw. *High Endeavour: The Life of Air Chief Marshal Sir Ronald Ivelaw-Chapman, GCB, KBE, DFC, AFC*. London: Leo Cooper, 1993.

Chaturvedi, Mohan Swaroop. *History of the Indian Air Force*. New Delhi: Vikas Publishing House, 1978.

Chatterjee, Joya. *Bengal Divided: Hindu Communalism and Partition*. Cambridge: CUP, 1994.

Chatterjee, Partha. *The Nation and Its Fragments*. Princeton: Princeton University Press, 1993.

Chatterjee, Partha. 'Sovereign Violence and the Domain of the Political.' In *Sovereign Bodies*, edited by Thomas Blom Hansen, 82–102. Princeton: Princeton University Press, 2005.

Chattopadhyay, Raghabendra. 'Liaquat Ali Khan's Budget of 1947–48: The Tryst with Destiny.' *Social Scientist* 16, no. 6/7 (1988): 77–89.

Chaudhury, Zafar A. *Mosaic of Memory*. Lahore: self-published, 1985.

Cheema, Parvaiz. *Pakistan's Defence Policy 1947–58*. Basingstoke: Macmillan, 1990.

Chhina, Rana Tej Pratap Singh. *The Eagle Strikes: The Royal Indian Air Force 1932–50*. New Delhi: Ambi Knowledge Resources, 2006.

Chhina, Rana Tej Pratap Singh. *Air Marshal Subroto Mukherjee*. Secunderabad. Indian Air Force Warriors Study Cell, 2002.

Childs, David. *Britain since 1945: A Political History*. 5th ed. London; New York: Routledge, 2001.

Chopra, Surendra. *U.N. Mediation in Kashmir: A Study in Power Politics*. Kurukshetra: Vishal Publications, 1971.

Cohen, Benjamin. *Kingship and Colonialism in India's Deccan 1850–1948*. Basingstoke: Palgrave Macmillan, 2007.

Cohen, Maurice. *Thunder over Kashmir*. Bombay: Orient Longmans, 1955.

Congress Presidential Addresses. Madras: G.A. Natesan, 1934.

Collins, Larry, and Dominique Lapierre. *Freedom at Midnight*. London: Granada, 1982.

Copland, Ian. *The Princes of India in the Endgame of Empire*. Cambridge: CUP, 1997.

Copland, Ian. *The British Raj and the Indian Princes*. Bombay: Orient Longman, 1982.

Copland, Ian. 'The Abdullah Factor: Kashmiri Muslims and the Crisis of 1947.' In *The Political Inheritance of Pakistan*, edited by D.A. Low, 218–54. Basingstoke: Macmillan Academic and Professional, 1991.

Corn, Joseph J. *The Winged Gospel: America's Romance with Aviation*, edited by John Hopkins Paperbacks. Baltimore, Md.; London: Johns Hopkins University Press, 2002.

Das, Suranjan. *Kashmir and Sindh: Nation-building, Ethnicity and Regional Politics in South Asia*. Kolkata: K.P Bagchi and Co, 2001.

Dasgupta, Chandrashekhar. *War and Diplomacy in Kashmir 1947–48*. New Delhi: Sage, 2002.

Deshpande, Anirudh. *British Military Policy in India 1900–1945: Colonial Constraints and Declining Power*. New Delhi: Manohar, 2005.

Deshpande, Anirudh. *Hope and Despair: Mutiny, Rebellion and Death in India, 1946*. New Delhi: Primus Books, 2016.

Di-Capua, Yoav. 'Common Skies Divided Horizons: Aviation, Class and Modernity in Early Twentieth Century Egypt.' *Journal of Social History* 41, no. 4 (2008): 917–42.

Devji, Faisal. *Muslim Zion: Pakistan as a Political Idea*. London: Hurst, 2013.

Devreux, D.R. 'British Planning for Post-war Civil Aviation 1942–45.' *Twentieth Century British History* 2, no. 1 (1991): 26–46.

Dhulipala, Venkat. *Creating a New Medina: State Power, Islam, and the Quest for Pakistan in Late Colonial North India*. Cambridge: CUP, 2016.

Dirks, Nicholas. *The Hollow Crown*. Ann Arbor: University of Michigan Press, 1993.

Doe, Helen. *Fighter Pilot*. Stroud, Gloucestershire: Amberley Publishing, 2015.

Duncan, David. *Mutiny in the RAF*. London: Socialist History Society, 1998.

Edgerton, David. *The Shock of the Old: Technology and Global History since 1900*. London: Profile Books, 2019 (2006).

Edgerton, David. *England and the Aeroplane: Militarism, Modernity and Machines*. London: Penguin, 2013.

Edwards, Mike. *Spitfire Singh*. New Delhi: Bloomsbury Publishing, 2016.

Ellinwood, DeWitt C., and Satyendra Dev Pradhan. *India and World War I*. New Delhi: Manohar, 1978.

Ewer, Peter. 'A Gentlemen's Club in the Clouds: Re-assessing the Empire Air Mail Scheme 1933–1939.' *Journal of Transport History* 28, no. 1 (March 2007): 75–92.

Ferris, John R. 'The Air Force Brats' View of History: Recent Writing and the Royal Air Force, 1918–1960.' *The International History Review* 20, no. 1 (1998): 118–43.

Fricker, John. *Battle for Pakistan: The Air War of 1965*. London: I. Allan, 1979.

Fuller, Christopher John, and Véronique Benei. *The Everyday State and Society in Modern India*. London: Hurst, 2001.

Gaekwad, Fatesinhrao. *Sayajirao of Baroda: The Prince and the Man*. Bombay: Popular Prakashan, 1989.

Ganachari, Aravind. 'First World War: Purchasing Indian Loyalties: Imperial Policy of Recruitment and 'Rewards.' *Economic and Political Weekly* 40, no. 8 (2005): 779–88.

Ganguly, Sumit. *The Origins of War in South Asia: Indo-Pakistani Conflicts since 1947*. 2nd ed. Boulder, Colorado; Oxford: Westview, 1994.

Gibbs, Gerald. *Survivor's Story*. London: Hutchinson, 1956.

Gopal, Sarvepalli. *Jawaharlal Nehru: A Biography*. London: Jonathan Cape, 1975.

Gould, William. *Hindu Nationalism and the Language of Politics in Late Colonial India*. Cambridge Studies in Indian History and Society; 11. Cambridge: Cambridge University Press, 2004.

Gowda, Made. *Modern Mysore State, 1881–1902: A Study of the Elite, Polity, and Society*. Other Publications, 117. Mysore: Prasaranga, University of Mysore, 1997.

Gowda, Chandan. 'Empire and Developmentalism in Colonial India.' In *Sociology & Empire: The Imperial Entanglements of a Discipline*, edited by George Steinmetz, 340–65. Durham, N.C., 2013.

Grieveson, Lee, and Colin MacCabe. *Film and the End of Empire. Cultural Histories of Cinema*. London: Palgrave MacMillan on Behalf of the British Film Institute, 2011.

Guha, Ramachandra. *India after Gandhi: The History of the World's Largest Democracy*. London: Macmillan, 2007.

Gulati, M.N. *Military Plight of Pakistan: Indo-Pak War, 1947–48*. New Delhi: Manas Publications, 2000.

Gupta, Amit Kumar. *Myth and Reality: The Struggle for Freedom in India, 1945–47*. New Delhi: Manohar, 1987.

Gupta, Partha Sarathi, and Anirudh Deshpande. *The British Raj and Its Indian Armed Forces, 1857–1939*. New Delhi; Oxford: Oxford University Press, 2002.

Gupta, S.C., and Bisheshwar Prasad. *History of the Indian Air Force, 1933–45*. Official History of the Indian Armed Forces in the Second World War, 1939–45. Delhi: Combined Inter-services Historical Section, India & Pakistan: Distributors: Orient Longmans, 1961.

Haines, Daniel. *Building the Empire, Building the Nation: Development, Legitimacy and Hydro-politics in Sind, 1919–1969*. Karachi: OUP, 2013.

Haines, Daniel. *Rivers Divided: Indus Basin Waters in the Making of India and Pakistan*. Gurgaon: Viking, 2017.

Halley, James *The Squadrons of the Royal Air Force & Commonwealth 1918–1988*. Rev. ed. Tonbridge: Air-Britain (Historians), 1988.

Herdeck, Margaret, and Gita Piramal. *India's Industrialists*. Washington, D.C: Three Continents Press, 1985.

Heiferman, Ronald. *Flying Tigers: Chennault in China.* Ballantine's Illustrated History of World War II. Weapons Book. Pan Books: London, 1972.

Higham, Robin. *Speedbird: The Complete History of BOAC.* London, I.B. Tauris 2013.

Hiatt, Willie. *The Rarified Air of the Modern: Airplanes and Technological Modernity in the Andes.* New York, 2016.

Hooja, Rima. *A History of Rajasthan.* New Delhi: Rupa & Co, 2006.

Huntington, Samuel. *The Soldier and the State: The Theory and Politics of Civil-military Relations.* Cambridge, Mass: Belknap Press of Harvard University Press, 1957.

Hussain, Syed Shabbir, and M. Tariq. Qureshi. *History of the Pakistan Air Force, 1947–1982.* Masroor: PAF Press, 1982.

Hurd, John, and Ian Kerr. *India's Railway History: A Research Handbook..* Leiden: Brill, 2012.

Ikegame, Aya. *Princely India Re-imagined: A Historical Anthropology of Mysore from 1799 to the Present.* Routledge/Edinburgh South Asian Studies Series. London: Routledge, 2013.

Ismail, Mirza Muhammad. *My Public Life: Recollections and Reflections of Sir Mirza Ismail.* London: George Allen & Unwin, 1954.

Jaffrelot, Christophe. *The Hindu Nationalist Movement and Indian Politics, 1925 to the 1990s: Strategies of Identity-building, Implantation and Mobilisation (with Special Reference to Central India).* London: Hurst, 1996.

Jain, Rajendra Kumar. *US-South Asian Relations, 1947–1982.* New Delhi: Radiant, 1983.

Jalal, Ayesha. *The Sole Spokesman: Jinnah, the Muslim League, and the Demand for Pakistan.* Cambridge: Cambridge University Press, 1985.

Jalal, Ayesha. *The State of Martial Rule: The Origins of Pakistan's Political Economy of Defence.* Cambridge South Asian Studies; 46. Cambridge, 1990.

John, J.P., and B.S.K. Kumar. *Wing Commander K.K. Majumdar DFC BAR.* Secunderabad: Indian Air Force Warrior Study Cell, 2003.

Johnston, Ernest. *To Organise the Air: The Evolution of Civil Aviation and the Role of Sir Frederick Tymms, the Flying Civil Servant.* Cranfield: Cranfield University Press, 1995.

Jeffrey, Robin. *People, Princes, and Paramount Power: Society and Politics in the Indian Princely States.* Delhi: Oxford University Press, 1978.

Kamtekar, Indivar. 'The Shiver of 1942.' *Studies in History* 18, no. 1 (February 2002): 81–102.

Kant, Vedica. *'If I Die Here, Who Will Remember Me?': India and the First World War.* New Delhi, India, 2014.

Karnad, Raghu. *Farthest Field: An Indian Story of the Second World War.* Noida: Harper Collins, 2015.

Kerr, Ian. *Railways in Modern India.* Oxford in India Readings. Themes in Indian History. Delhi; Oxford: Oxford University Press, 2001.

Kerr, Ian. *Building the Railways of the Raj, 1850–1900.* Delhi: Oxford University Press, 1995.

Kerr, Ian. *Engines of Change: The Railroads That Made India.* Moving through History. Westport, Conn.: Praeger, 2007.

Khan, Mohammad Asghar. *My Political Struggle.* Oxford: Oxford University Press, 2008.

Khan, Yasmin. *The Great Partition: The Making of India and Pakistan*. New Haven; London: Yale University Press, 2007.

Khan, Yasmin. *The Raj at War: A People's History of India's Second World War*. Gurgaon, Penguin Random House, 2015.

Khandekar, Prashant Purushottam. *Air Commodore Mehar Singh*. Secunderabad, Indian Air Force Air Warrior Study Cell, 2006.

Khandekar, Prashant Purushottam, ed. *Dragons Forever: History of No. 6 Squadron*. Secunderabad, Indian Air Force Air Warrior Study Cell, 2006.

Kheechee, Sahdev Singh. *Economic Reforms of Maharaja Umaid Singh's Reign*. 1st ed. Jodhpur: Maharaja Mana Singh Pustak Prakash Research Centre, 2004.

Khosla, Gopal Das D. *Stern Reckoning: A Survey of the Events Leading up to and following the Partition of India*. New Delhi: OUP, 1952.

Khosla, G.S. *A History of Indian Railways*. 1st ed. New Delhi: Ministry of Railways (Railway Board), Government of India, 1988.

Kooka, Sorab Kaikhashroo. *Foolishly Yours*. Bombay, 1965.

Krasner, Stephen D. *Sovereignty: Organized Hypocrisy*. Princeton, N.J.; Chichester: Princeton University Press, 1999.

Kumar, Bharat. *An Incredible War: Indian Air Force in Kashmir War, 1947–48*. 2nd ed. New Delhi: Knowledge World in Association with Centre for Air Power Studies (2007) 2014.

Kumar, Bharat. *Unknown and Unsung: The Indian Air Force in the Sino-Indian War of 1962*, New Delhi: Knowledge World Publishers, 2012.

Kumar, Bharat. *The Duels of the Himalayan Eagle: The First Indo-Pak Air War*, New Delhi: Natraj Publishers, 2015.

Kumar, Deepak. *Science and the Raj: A Study of British India*. 2nd ed. New Delhi; Oxford: Oxford University Press, 2006.

Lala, Russi M. *Beyond the Last Blue Mountain: A Life of J.R.D. Tata*. New Delhi: Viking, 1992.

Lala, Russi M. *The Joy of Achievement: Conversations with J.R.D. Tata*. New Delhi: Viking, 1995.

Lala, Russi M. *A Touch of Greatness: Encounters with the Eminent*. New Delhi; New York, NY: Viking, 2001.

Lal, Pratap C. *My Years with the IAF*. New Delhi: Lancer, 1986.

Lamb, Alastair. *Kashmir: A Disputed Legacy, 1846–1990*. Karachi: Oxford University Press, 1992.

Lamb, Alastair. 'Pakistani Kashmir since the 1965 War.' *Journal of The Royal Central Asian Society* 54, no. 2 (1967): 151–55.

Lamb, Alastair. *Incomplete Partition: The Genesis of the Kashmir Dispute*. Hertingfordbury: Roxford Books, 1997.

Leonard, Karen Isaksen. *Hyderabad and Hyderabadis*. New Delhi, 2014.

Lieven, Anatol. *Pakistan: A Hard Country*. London: Penguin, 2012.

Lindqvist, Sven, and Linda Haverty Rugg. *A History of Bombing*. London: Granta, 2001.

Loveday, Jack. *RAF & Raj: An Aircraftman's Life 1944–1948*. Norwich: J. Loveday, 2002.

MacLeod, Roy Malcolm, and Deepak Kumar. *Technology and the Raj: Western Technology and Technical Transfers to India 1700–1947*. New Delhi; London: Sage, 1995.

Madsen, Chris. 'The Long Goodbye: British Agency in the Creation of Navies for India and Pakistan.' *The Journal of Commonwealth and Imperial History* 43, no. 3 (December, 2014): 463–488.

Madsen, Chris. 'The Royal Indian Navy Mutiny, 1946.' in *Naval Mutinies of the Twentieth Century: An International Perspective*, edited by Christopher M. Bell, and Bruce A. Elleman, 212–31. Cass Series—Naval Policy and History, 19. London: Frank Cass, 2003.

Manor, James. *Political Change in an Indian State: Mysore, 1917–1955*. Australian National University Monographs on South Asia (New Delhi, India); 2. New Delhi: Manohar, 1977.

Marston, Daniel, and Chandar S. Sundaram. *A Military History of India and South Asia: From the East India Company to the Nuclear Era*, Westport: Indiana University Press, 2007.

Marston, Daniel. *The Indian Army and the End of the Raj*. Cambridge Studies in Indian History and Society; 23. Cambridge: Cambridge University Press, 2016.

Mazumdar, Arijit. '"Deregulation of the Airline Industry in India": Issues, Causes and Rationale.' *The Indian Journal of Political Science* 70, no. 2 (2009): 451–69.

Mbembe, Achille. *On the Postcolony*. Studies on the History of Society and Culture; 41. Berkeley: University of California Press, 2001.

McCarthy, Michael. 'Historic Aircraft Wrecks as Archaeological Sites.' *Bulletin of the Australasian Institute for Maritime Archaeology* no. 28 (2004): 81–90.

McCormack, Robert L. 'Imperialism, Air Transport and Colonial Development: Kenya, 1920–46.' *The Journal of Commonwealth History* 17, no. 3 (July 2008): 374–395.

McGarr, Paul M. *The Cold War in South Asia: Britain, the United States and the Indian Subcontinent, 1945–1965*. Cambridge Core. Cambridge, 2013.

McLeod, John. *Sovereignty, Power, Control: Politics in the States of Western India, 1916–1947*. Brill's Indological Library; v. 15. Leiden; Boston: Brill, 1999.

Mehra, Om Prakash. *Memories: Sweet and Sour*. New Delhi: Knowledge World Publishers, 2010.

Menon, Vappalla Panguni. *Integration of the Indian States*. Hyderabad: Orient Longman, 1985.

Metcalf, Thomas R. *Ideologies of the Raj*. Cambridge University Press, 1995.

Meyer, John M. 'The Royal Indian Naval Mutiny of 1946: Nationalist Competition and Civil Military Relations in India.' *The Journal of Commonwealth and Imperial History* 45, no. 1 (December 2016): 46–69.

Mikesh, Robert C. *Broken Wings of the Samurai: The Destruction of the Japanese Airforce*. Shrewsbury: Airlife, 1993.

Misra, Maria. *Business, Race, and Politics in British India, C.1850–1960*. Oxford Historical Monographs. Oxford: OUP, 1999.

Mohan, P.V.S. Jagan, and Samir Chopra. *Eagles over Bangladesh: The Indian Air Force in the 1971 Liberation War*. New Delhi: Harper Collins, 2013.

Mohan, P.V.S. Jagan, and Samir Chopra. *The India-Pakistan Air War of 1965*. New Delhi: Manohar, 2005.

Mukherjee, Aditya. *Imperialism, Nationalism and the Making of the Indian Capitalist Class 1920–47*. London: Sage Publications, 2002.

Mukherjee, Hena. *The Early History of the East Indian Railway, 1845–1879.* Calcutta: Firma KLM, 1994.

Nair, Janaki. *Mysore Modern: Rethinking the Region under Princely Rule.* Minneapolis: University of Minnesota Press, 2011.

Nair, K. Sree. *The Forgotten Few: The Indian Air Force in World War II.* New Delhi: Harper Collins, 2019.

Nair, K. Sree. *Ganesha's Flyboys: The Indian Air Force in Congo 1960–62,* New Delhi: Anveshan Enterprises, 2012.

Nawab, A.W. *Economic Development of Indian Air Transport.* Delhi: National Pub. House, 1967.

Nawaz, Shuja. *Crossed Swords: Pakistan, Its Army, and the Wars Within.* Oxford Pakistan Paperbacks. Karachi: Oxford University Press, 2008.

Nayar, Baldev Raj. *The State and International Aviation in India: Performance and Policy on the Eve of Aviation Globalization.* New Delhi: Manohar Publishers & Distributors, 1994.

Nayar, Baldev Raj. *The Myth of the Shrinking State: Globalization and the State in India.* Delhi; Oxford: Oxford University Press, 2009.

Noorani, Abdul Ghafur. *The Kashmir Dispute, 1947–2012.* Karachi: OUP, 2014.

Noorani, Abdul Ghafur. *The Destruction of Hyderabad.* London: Hurst and Co., 2014.

Olsen, John A. *Global Air Power.* Washington: Potomac Books, 2011.

Omissi, David E. *Air Power and Colonial Control: The Royal Air Force, 1919–1939.* Studies in Imperialism (Manchester, England). Manchester: Manchester University Press, 1990.

Omissi, David E. *The Sepoy and the Raj: The Indian Army, 1860–1940.* Studies in Military and Strategic History. Basingstoke: Macmillan in Association with King's College, London, 1994.

Pal, R.K. *Sentinels of the Sky: Glimpses of the Indian Air Force.* New Delhi: Ritana, 1999.

Pandey, Gyanendra. 'Can a Muslim Be an Indian?' *Comparative Studies in Society and History* 41, no. 4 (1999): 608–29.

Panduranga Rao, D., and J.V. Rāmārāvu. *Indian Airlines: A Study of Its Performance.* New Delhi: Inter-India Publications, 1997.

Patel, H.M., and Sucheta Mahajan. *Rites of Passage: A Civil Servant Remembers.* New Delhi: Rupa & Co, 2005.

Phalkey, Jahnavi. *Atomic State: Big Science in Twentieth-century India.* Indian Century Series. Ranikhet: Permanent Black, 2013.

Philips, Cyril Henry. *The Partition of India, 1947: The Twenty-fourth Montague Burton Lecture on International Relations.* Montague Burton Lecture on International Relations; Leeds: Leeds University Press, 1967.

Piramal, Gita. *Business Legends.* New Delhi: Viking, 1998.

Pirie, Gordon. *Air Empire: British Imperial Civil Aviation, 1919–39* (Manchester: Manchester University Press, 2009).

Plating, John D. *The Hump: America's Strategy for Keeping China in World War II.* 1st ed. Williams-Ford Texas A&M University Military History Series; No. 134. College Station: Texas A&M University Press, 2011. Proquest Ebook Central. ISBN 10: 1603442375, ISBN 13: 978-1603442374.

Potter, David C. 'Manpower Shortage and the End of Colonialism: The Case of the Indian Civil Service.' *Modern Asian Studies* 7, no. 1 (1973): 47–73.

Potter, David C. *India's Political Administrators: From ICS to IAS.* 1st Indian Ed., Rev. and Updated ed. Oxford India Paperbacks. Delhi: Oxford University Press, 1996.

Prakash, Gyan. *Another Reason: Science and the Imagination of Modern India.* New Delhi: Oxford University Press, 2000.

Prasad, Bisheshwar, Prasad, Sri Nandan, and Desika Char, S.V. *Expansion of the Armed Forces and Defence Organisation, 1939–45.* Official History of the Indian Armed Forces in the Second World War, 1939–45. Calcutta: Combined Inter-Services Historical Section (India & Pakistan), 1956.

Prasad, Sri Nandan, and Dharm Pal. *History of Operations in Jammu & Kashmir, 1947–48.* Armed Forces of the Indian Union. New Delhi: History Division, Ministry of Defence, Govt. of India: Distributed by Controller of Publications, Govt. of India, 1987.

Prasad, Sri Nandan, and Dharm Pal. *Operation Polo.* New Delhi: Manager of Publications (1972) 2005.

Purushotham, Sunil. 'Internal Violence: The "Police Action" in Hyderabad.' *Comparative Studies in Society and History* 57, no. 2 (2015): 435–466.

Purushotham, Sunil. 'Destroying Hyderabad and Making the Nation.' *Economic and Political Weekly,* 49, no. 22 (2014): 29–33.

Raghavan, Pallavi. *Animosity at Bay: An Alternative History of the India-Pakistan Relationship, 1947–1952.* Oxford University Press, 2020.

Raghavan, Srinath. *War and Peace in Modern India.* Ranikhet: Permanent Black, 2010.

Raghavan, Srinath. *India's War: The Making of Modern South Asia, 1939–1945.* London: Allen Lane, 2016.

Raianu, Mircea. *Tata: The Global Corporation That Built Indian Capitalism.* Cambridge: Harvard University Press, 2021.

Rai, Mridu. *Hindu Rulers, Muslim Subjects: Islam, Rights, and the History of Kashmir.* London: Hurst & Co, 2004.

Ramusack, Barbara N. *The Indian Princes and Their States.* New Cambridge History of India; III, 6. Cambridge: Cambridge University Press, 2004.

Ramnath, Aparajith. *The Birth of an Indian Profession: Engineers, Industry, and the State, 1900–47.* First ed. New Delhi, India, 2017.

Reddy, Anuradha P. *Aviation in the Hyderabad Dominions.* Secunderabad: Avi-Oil, 2001.

Reeves, Nicholas. 'Film Propaganda and Its Audience: The Example of Britain's Official Films during the First World War.' *Journal of Contemporary History* 18, no. 3 (1983): 463–94.

Rice, Rondall R. *The Politics of Air Power: From Confrontation to Cooperation in Army Aviation Civil-military Relations.* Lincoln: University of Nebraska Press, 2004.

Richards, Clive. 'The Origins of Military Aviation in India and the Creation of the Indian Air Force 1910-1932: Part Two.' *Air Power Review* 11, no. 1 (Spring, 2008): 20–50.

Richards, Clive. 'First into Indian Skies: The Indian Army, Military Aviation and the Creation of the Indian Air Force 1910–32.' *in The British Indian Army,* edited by Robert Johnson. Newcastle: Cambridge Scholars Publishing, 2014.

Riza, Shaukat. *The Pakistan Army, 1947–1949.* 1st Indian ed. Dehra Dun: Natraj, 1977.

Rodriguez, Gabriel. Mocho. 'Focus: Aviation Overview.' *International Union Rights* 20, no. 1 (2013): 3–5.

Roy, Kaushik. *War and Society in Colonial India, 1807–1945.* Oxford in India Readings. Themes in Indian History. New Delhi; Oxford: Oxford University Press, 2006.

Roy, Kaushik. *India and World War II: War, Armed Forces, and Society, 1939–45.* First ed. New Delhi, 2016.

Roy, Kaushik. *Brown Warriors of the Raj: Recruitment and the Mechanics of Command in the Sepoy Army, 1859–1913.* New Delhi: Manohar Publishers & Distributors, 2008.

Roy, Kaushik. *The Army in British India: From Colonial Warfare to Total War, 1857–1947.* London: Bloomsbury, 2013.

Roy, Haimanti. *Partitioned Lives: Migrants, Refugees, Citizens in India and Pakistan, 1947–65.* Oxford University Press, 2013.

Russell, Graham. *For King and Another Country: An Amazing Life Story of an Indian World War Two RAF Fighter Pilot: The Recollections of Squadron Leader Mahinder S. Pujji.* Ilfracombe: Arthur H. Stockwell, 2010.

Russell, Wilfrid W. *Forgotten Skies: The Story of the Air Forces in India and Burma.* London; New York: Hutchinson, 1946.

Sahani, Bhishma. *Tamas.* New Delhi: Penguin Books India, 2001.

Saigal, A.L. *Birth of an Air Force.* New Delhi: South Asia books, 1977.

Salt, Alexander Edward Wrottesley. *Imperial Air Routes.* London: J. Murray, 1930.

Sampath, Vikram. *Splendours of Royal Mysore: The Untold Story of the Wodeyars.* New Delhi: Rupa & Co, 2008.

Sampson, Anthony. *Empires of the Sky: The Politics, Contests and Cartels of World Airlines.* London: Hodder and Stoughton, 1984.

Sapru, Somnath, *Combat Lore.* New Delhi: Knowledge World, 2014.

Sardesai, B.D. *Walchand Diamond Jubilee Commemoration Volume.* Bombay: Walchand Diamond Jubilee Celebration Committee, 1942.

Sarkar, Sumit. *Modern India: 1885–1947.* Delhi: Macmillan, 1983.

Satia, Priya. *Spies in Arabia: The Great War and the Cultural Foundations of Britain's Covert Empire in the Middle East.* New York; Oxford: Oxford University Press, 2008.

Satia, Priya. 'The Defence of Inhumanity: Air Control and the British Idea of Arabia.' *The American Historical Review* 111, no. 1 (2006): 16–51.

Schofield, Victoria. *Wavell: Soldier & Statesman.* London: John Murray, 2006.

Schofield, Victoria. *Kashmir in Conflict: India, Pakistan and the Unending War.* New ed. London: I. B. Tauris, 2003.

Scott, James C. *Seeing like a State: How Certain Schemes to Improve the Human Condition Have Failed.* Yale Agrarian Studies. New Haven, Yale University Press, 1998.

Sen, Lionel Protip. *Slender Was the Thread: Kashmir Confrontation, 1947–48.* Bombay: Orient Longmans, 1969.

Seth, Vijay. *The Flying Machines.* New Delhi: Seth Communications, 2000.

Sharma, S.N. *History of Greater Indian Peninsular Railways.* Bombay: Chief Public Relations Officer, 1990.

Siddiqa-Agha, Ayesha. *Military Inc.: Inside Pakistan's Military Economy.* London: Pluto, 2007.

Sinha, Jagdish N. *Science, War and Imperialism: India in the Second World War.* Social Sciences in Asia; v. 18. Leiden: Brill, 2008.

Singh, Anita Inder. *The Limits of British Influence: South Asia and the Anglo-American Relationship, 1947–56*. London: New York: Pinter; St. Martin's Press, 1993.

Singh, Dhananajaya. *The House of Marwar*. New Delhi: Lotus Collection, Roli Books, 1994.

Singh, Gajendra. *The Testimonies of Indian Soldiers and the Two World Wars: Between Self and Sepoy*. London: Bloomsbury Academic, 2014.

Singh, Jasjit. *Defence from the Skies*. New Delhi: KW Publishers, 2007.

Singh, Jasjit. *The Icon: Marshal of the Indian Air Force Arjan Singh, DFC: An Authorised Biography*. New Delhi: KW Publishers, 2009.

Singh, Pushpindar. *Aircraft of the Indian Air Force, 1933–73*. New Delhi: English Book Store, 1974.

Singh, Pushpindar. *Himalayan Eagles: History of the Indian Air Force*. New Delhi: Society for Aerospace Studies, 2007.

Singh, Pushpindar. *History of Aviation in India: Spanning the Century of Flight*. New Delhi: Society for Aerospace Studies, 2003.

Singh, Rajendra, and Bisheshwar Prasad. *Post-war Occupation Forces: Japan & Southeast Asia*. Official History of the Indian Armed Forces in the Second World War, 1939–45. Campaigns in the Eastern Theatre. New Delhi: Combined Inter-services Historical Section (India & Pakistan), 1958.

Singh, Satyindra. *Under Two Ensigns: The Indian Navy, 1945–1950*. New Delhi: Oxford & IBH Pub., 1986.

Singh, V.B., eds. *Economic History of India, 1857–1956*. Bombay; London: Allied Publishers, 1965.

Slayton, Robert A. *Master of the Air: William Tunner and the Success of Military Airlift*. Tuscaloosa: University of Alabama Press, 2010. Proquest Ebook Central. eISBN: 978-0-8173-8354-1.

Slim, William Joseph. *Defeat into Victory*. Unabridged ed. London: Cassell, 1971.

Snedden, Christopher. *The Untold Story of the People of Azad Kashmir*. London: Hurst, 2012.

Snedden, Christopher. 'What Happened to Muslims of Jammu? Local Identity, "the Massacre" of 1947 and the Roots of the "Kashmir Problem".' *South Asia: Journal of South Asian Studies* 24, no. 2 (2001): 111–34.

Sochor, Eugene. *The Politics of International Aviation*. Basingstoke: Macmillan, 1991.

Spector, Ronald. 'The Royal Indian Navy Strike of 1946: A Study of Cohesion and Disintegration in Colonial Armed Forces.' *Armed Forces and Society* 7, no. 2 (January 1981): 271–284.

Spence, Daniel Owen. *Colonial Naval Culture and British Imperialism, 1922–67*. Studies in Imperialism. Manchester: Manchester University Press, 2015.

Spence, Daniel Owen. 'Beyond Talwar: A Cultural Reappraisal of the 1946 Royal Indian Navy Mutiny', *The Journal of Commonwealth and Imperial History* 43, no. 3 (2015): 489–508.

Srinivasan, Roopa, Manish Tiwari, and Sandeep Silas. *Our Indian Railway: Themes in India's Railway History*. 1st ed. New Delhi: Foundation Books, 2006.

Strang, David. 'Contested Sovereignty: The Social Construction of Colonial Imperialism.' In *State Sovereignty as Social Construct*, edited by Thomas J. Biersteker, and Cynthia Weber. Cambridge Studies in International Relations; v. 46. Cambridge: Cambridge University Press, 1996.

Sukumar, Arun Mohan. *Midnight's Machines: A Political History of Technology in India*. Gurgaon, Haryana, India, 2019.

Subramaniam, Arjun. *India's Wars: A Military History, 1947–1971*. First Naval Institute Press ed. Annapolis, Maryland, 2017.

Sukhwant Singh. *India's Wars since Independence*. New Delhi: Vikas Pub. House, 1980.

Sundaram, V. *An Airman's Saga*. Mumbai: Bharatiya Vidya Bhavan, 1998.

Talbot, Ian. *The Independence of India and Pakistan: New Approaches and Reflections*. Karachi: OUP, 2013.

Talbot, Ian, and Gurharpal Singh. *The Partition of India*. New Approaches to Asian History. Cambridge: Cambridge University Press, 2009.

Toland, John. *The Flying Tigers*. Landmark Books, 105. New York: Random House, 1963.

Upadhyaya, Nirmala M. *The Administration of Jodhpur State, 1800–1947 A.D.* 1st ed. Jodhpur: International Publishers, 1973.

Vacher, Peter. *History of the Jodhpur Flying Club*. Ontario: Griffin Media, 2008.

Van Creveld, Martin. *The Age of Airpower*. New York: Public Affairs, 2012.

Vidal, Gore. *Armageddon? Essays 1983–1987*. London: Deutsch, 1987.

Viswajeet, Shelley. *The Indigo Story: Inside the Upstart that Redefined Indian Aviation*. New Delhi: Rupa Publications, 2018.

Wainwright, Mary. 'Keeping the peace in India 1946–47: The Role of Lt. General Tuker in Eastern Command.' In *Partition of India: Policy and Perspectives 1935–47*, edited by Cyril Henry Philips. London: Allen and Unwin, 1970.

Weber, Cynthia. 'Reconsidering Statehood: Examining the Sovereignty/Intervention Boundary.' *Review of International Studies* 18, no. 3 (1992): 199–216.

Weber, Cynthia. *Simulating Sovereignty: Intervention, the State and Symbolic Exchange*. Cambridge Studies in International Relations; v. 37. Cambridge: Cambridge University Press, 1995.

Whitehead, Andrew. *A Mission in Kashmir*. New Delhi: Penguin, 2007.

Wilkinson, Steven. *Army and Nation: The Military and Indian Democracy since Independence*. Cambridge, Massachusetts: Harvard University Press, 2015.

Wolpert, Stanley A. *Shameful Flight: The Last Years of the British Empire in India*. Ebook Central. Oxford; New York: Oxford University Press, 2006.

Young, Edward. Aerial Nationalism. United States: Smithsonian, 1995.

Zachariah, Benjamin. *Nehru*. Routledge Historical Biographies. London: Routledge, 2004.

Zachariah, Benjamin. *Developing India: An Intellectual and Social History 1930–50*. Oxford India Paperbacks. New Delhi: Oxford University Press, 2012.

Zaidi, S.W. '"Wings for Peace" versus Airopia: Contested Visions of Post-War European Aviation in World War II Britain.' In *Linking Networks: The Formation of Common Standards and Visions for Infrastructure Development*, edited by Martin Schiefelbusch and Hans Liudger. Transport and Society. Farnham, Surrey: Ashgate, 2014: 151–168.

Zaidi, Waqar. 'Pakistani Civil Aviation and US Aid to Pakistan, 1950 to 1961.' *History of Global Arms Transfer* 8 (2019): 83–97.

Zamindar, Vazira Fazila-Yacoobali. *The Long Partition and the Making of Modern South Asia: Refugees, Boundaries, Histories*. Cultures of History. New York; Chichester: Columbia University Press, 2007.

Zutshi, Chitralekha. *Languages of Belonging: Islam, Regional Identity, and the Making of Kashmir*. London: Hurst & Co, 2004.

Unpublished PhD theses

Fountain, Julie A. 'Modern Jobs for Modern Women, Female Military Service in Britain 1945–62.' PhD thesis, University of Illinois at Chicago, 2015.

Singh, Sharmila. 'Partition of the Indian Armed Forces between India and Pakistan.' PhD thesis, Jawaharlal Nehru University, 1994.

Witmer, Michael. 'The 1947–48 India Hyderabad Conflict.' PhD thesis, Temple University, 1995.

Websites

Aashique Iqbal, 'Plane Tales: Air India's Return to the Tatas.' 27 October 2021, *The India Forum*, Accessed 11 May 2022. https://www.theindiaforum.in/article/plane-tales-air-india-s-return-tatas.

Alikhan, Anwar. 'The Real Zubeida.' *Rediff.com Movies*, January 17, 2001. Accessed July 7, 2016. http://www.rediff.com/movies/2001/jan/17zub.htm.

Bharat Rakshak. 'Make India Strong (poster).' 31 January 2010. Accessed July 17, 2015. http://www.bharat-rakshak.com/IAF/Galleries/History/WW2/Ads/IAFPos ter.jpg.html.

Bharat Rakshak. 'Protectors Today, Pioneers Tomorrow.' 13 February 2010. Accessed July 17, 2015. http://www.bharat-rakshak.com/IAF/Galleries/History/WW2/Ads/.

Bharat Rakshak. 'Indian Air Force Databases.' Accessed August 28, 2020. http://www.bharat-rakshak.com/IAF/Database/

Bharat Rakshak. K. Sree Kumar, 'No. 6 Squadron.' 16 July 2019. Accessed August 29, 2020. http://www.bharat-rakshak.com/IAF/units/squadrons/6-6-squadron.html#gsc.tab=0.

First Five Year Plan, Government of India. 1951 Accessed August 31, 2020. https://niti.gov.in/planningcommission.gov.in/docs/plans/planrel/fiveyr/index5.html.

Harding, Norman. 'Odd Events: In 1945–6 and Now.' *Staying Red* (blog). Accessed April 17, 2017. https://stayingred.files.wordpress.com/2012/03/odd-events-lab our-1945-63.pdf.

India Today. 'Derek O'Brien on Minorities of India and Pakistan.' 11 August 2012. Accessed April 20, 2015. http://indiatoday.intoday.in/story/derek-obrien-minorit ies-of-india-and-pakistan/1/212816.html.

Kurian, George. Verghese. 'Partition Troubles.' Bharat Rakshak. 27 March 2015, Accessed August 29, 2020. http://www.bharat-rakshak.com/IAF/history/1950s/1208-kuriyan.html#gsc.tab=0.

Pakistan Defence. 'From Orient to PIA (Pakistan International Airlines).' 27 January 2013, Accessed April 19, 2015. http://defence.pk/threads/frm-orient-to-pia.232677/.

Pillariseti, Jagan. 'No. 2 Squadron.' *Bharat Rakshak.* June 14, 2017. Accessed August 29, 2020. http://www.bharat-rakshak.com/IAF/units/squadrons/2-history/2-squadron-winged-arrows.html#gsc.tab=0.

Singh, Pushpindar. 'Squadron No 1 IAF squadron.' June 14 2017. Accessed December 12, 2016.http://www.bharat-rakshak.com/IAF/units/squadrons/1-squadron-tigers.html.

Richards, Denis. 'Courtney, Sir Christopher Lloyd.' September 23 2004, *Oxford Dictionary of National Biography.* Accessed July 5, 2016. http://www.oxforddnb.com/view/article/30975.

Sahni, Bhism. 'Tamas.' (Jai Ratan translation). 1981. Accessed August 30, 2020. https://archive.org/stream/Tamas-English-BhishamSahni/tamas-english_djvu.txt.

Shaftel, David. 'Karachi to Bombay to Calcutta.' *Air and Space Magazine*, November 2011. Accessed March 5, 2017. http://www.airspacemag.com/history-of-flight/karachi-to-bombay-to-calcutta-77003851/.

Singh, Polly. 'India's Gift Squadrons: A Look at RAF Squadrons Gifted by Indian People.' *Bharat Rakshak.* Last updated June 12, 2017. Accessed June 19, 2015.http://www.bharat-rakshak.com/IAF/history/ww2/1203-gift-squadrons.html.

Venkataramakrishnan, Rohan. 'The Berlin Airlift During WWII was Remarkable but the Largest Civilian Airlift was by India.' July 2, 2014. Accessed March 16, 2017. http://scroll.in/article/668866/the-berlin-airlift-during-ww-ii-was-remarkable-but-the-largest-civilian-airlift-was-by-india.

Index

Ingram Content Group UK Ltd.
Milton Keynes UK
UKHW022043250523
422366UK00005B/53